A MUTED FURY

A MUTED FURY

POPULISTS, PROGRESSIVES, AND LABOR UNIONS CONFRONT THE COURTS, 1890–1937

William G. Ross

PRINCETON UNIVERSITY PRESS

PRINCETON, NEW JERSEY

COPYRIGHT © 1994 BY PRINCETON UNIVERSITY PRESS
PUBLISHED BY PRINCETON UNIVERSITY PRESS, 41 WILLIAM STREET,
PRINCETON, NEW JERSEY 08540
IN THE UNITED KINGDOM: PRINCETON UNIVERSITY PRESS, CHICHESTER,
WEST SUSSEX

LIBRARY OF CONGRESS CATALOGING-IN-PUBLICATION DATA

ROSS, WILLIAM G., 1954–
A MUTED FURY : POPULISTS, PROGRESSIVES, AND LABOR UNIONS CONFRONT
THE COURTS, 1890–1937 / WILLIAM G. ROSS.
P. CM.
INCLUDES INDEX.
ISBN 0-691-03264-5
1. JUDICIAL REVIEW—UNITED STATES—HISTORY. 2. JUDICIAL POWER—
UNITED STATES—HISTORY. 3. TRADE-UNIONS—LAW AND LEGISLATION—
UNITED STATES—HISTORY. I. TITLE.
KF4575.R67 1994
347.73′12—DC20
[347.30712] 93-13698
CIP

THIS BOOK HAS BEEN COMPOSED IN LINOTRON BASKERVILLE

PRINCETON UNIVERSITY PRESS BOOKS ARE PRINTED ON ACID-FREE PAPER AND
MEET THE GUIDELINES FOR PERMANENCE AND DURABILITY OF THE COMMITTEE
ON PRODUCTION GUIDELINES FOR BOOK LONGEVITY OF THE COUNCIL ON
LIBRARY RESOURCES

PRINTED IN THE UNITED STATES OF AMERICA

1 3 5 7 9 10 8 6 4 2

To My Mother and My Father

CONTENTS

ACKNOWLEDGMENTS

MANY persons made unique contributions to this book. It is a pleasure to acknowledge them. Two were indispensable. Dean Parham H. Williams, Jr., of the Cumberland School of Law of Samford University provided generous financial assistance in the form of summer research stipends and travel allowances. His many words of encouragement also were greatly appreciated. My friend and colleague Professor David J. Langum drew upon his experience as the author of award winning books of legal history in offering wise advice about this book's research, writing, editing, and production. His comments on an early draft were particularly helpful.

The book also greatly benefited from the comments of Professor Thomas A. Green of the University of Michigan, who read an early draft, and Professors Maxwell H. Bloomfield of the Catholic University of America and Victoria Hattam of Yale, who read a later draft. Max also critiqued a summary of this book that I delivered as a paper at the 1991 meeting of the American Society for Legal History, and his comments and kind words on that occasion were much appreciated. Advice and encouragement also were provided by Jonathan Lurie of Rutgers, Kermit L. Hall of the University of Tulsa, William E. Nelson of New York University, James W. Ely, Jr., of Vanderbilt, William Lasser of Clemson, Louis Fisher of the Library of Congress, my colleagues Howard F. Walthall and Thomas C. Berg, and my former colleagues W. Hubert Plummer, and Anthony B. Ching.

Several student research assistants at Cumberland helped with this book. I would particularly like to thank Ronald Keith Thompson, who worked on this project for more than a year during its early stages, and Christopher Lee George, Mary Margaret Bailey, Lyle D. Griffin, and Jane Hauth, who helped with the examination of citations.

Professor Laurel Rebecca Clapp and Edward L. Craig, Jr., of Cumberland's Cordell Hull Law Library were always resourceful and prompt in obtaining books on interlibrary loan. Also noteworthy were the services of the librarians at the various archives that I visited, particularly the dedicated professionals at the Manuscript Division of the Library of Congress.

Special thanks is due to Lauren Osborne and Alessandra Bocco of Princeton University Press; and Robert Burdette, who copyedited the manuscript.

W.G.R.
Birmingham, Alabama

A MUTED FURY

INTRODUCTION

T HE PROPER SCOPE of judicial power in America is a source of perennial controversy. During every period of the Republic's history, critics of the courts have assailed the judiciary with invective and have proposed measures to curtail the institutional prerogatives of the courts.[1] Many periods of acute conflict have received careful scholarly attention. Indeed, the Jeffersonian antagonism toward the Marshall Court, the firestorm over the *Dred Scott* decision, the controversies of the Reconstruction era, Franklin Roosevelt's Court-packing plan, and the bitter reactions to the Warren Court's activism have become staples of the lore of American legal history.

One period of fierce controversy, however, has received less attention than it deserves. Between 1890 and 1937, populists, progressives, and labor leaders subjected both state and federal courts to vigorous and persistent criticism and proposed numerous plans to abridge judicial power. The conflict between Franklin D. Roosevelt and the Supreme Court that reached its denouement in 1937 was merely the culmination of a struggle that had raged with varying degrees of intensity for a half century. Decades before the New Dealers denounced the Supreme Court's "nine old men," Chief Justice Walter Clark of North Carolina, the tireless scourge of the federal judiciary, had railed against the "five elderly lawyers" who composed the Supreme Court's conservative majority.[2] Clark and countless other antagonists of the courts between 1890 and 1937 alleged that a "judicial oligarchy" had usurped the powers of Congress and thwarted the will of the people by interfering with the activities of labor unions and nullifying legislation that was designed to ameliorate the more baneful effects of the Industrial Revolution.

This book traces and analyzes the grievances of these critics of the judiciary and their myriad proposals for judicial reform. Prolific and often shrill in their denunciations of the judiciary and their demands

[1] See, e.g., William Lasser, *The Limits of Judicial Power: The Supreme Court in American Politics* (Chapel Hill: University of North Carolina Press, 1988); Gary L. McDowell, *Curbing the Courts: The Constitution and the Limits of Judicial Power* (Baton Rouge: Louisiana State University Press, 1988); Gerald Gunther, "Congressional Power to Curtail Federal Court Jurisdiction: An Opinionated Guide to the Ongoing Debate," *Stanford Law Review* 36 (April 1984): 895–922; Stuart S. Nagel, "Court—Curbing Periods in American History," *Vanderbilt Law Review* 18 (June 1965): 925–944.

[2] Walter Clark, "Some Defects in the Constitution of the United States," *American Law Register* 45 (May 1906): 281.

for curtailment of judicial power, the antagonists of the courts were anything but mute. It is the thesis of this book, however, that the intense fury of populists, progressives, and labor unions was nonetheless muted by many factors and circumstances that were both internal and external to their reform movements. These included a pervasive and profound public respect for the judiciary as a guardian of personal liberties and property rights; institutional obstacles that impeded the viability of legislation to curtail judicial power; divisions and disputes among critics of the judiciary that precluded agreement on any plan of action; organized campaigns by the elite bar in opposition to plans to curb judicial power; the prevailing conservatism of Congress, presidents, and much of the electorate; the availability and success of moderate alternatives to radical judicial reform; the recognition by critics of the judiciary that a strong judiciary could serve as an ally of social and economic reform; and the flexibility of judges in adapting their jurisprudence to the changing needs of society.

Some of these circumstances were fortuitous. Others were natural and perhaps inevitable consequences of the American political culture. The survival of a strong judiciary, however, was not inevitable. Even though proponents of radical judicial reform faced formidable obstacles, they might have succeeded in imposing significant curbs on judicial power if these various circumstances had not converged. Moreover, although all attempts to curtail judicial power failed and the courts emerged from five decades of attacks with their powers unimpaired and in some respects enhanced, the antagonists of the judiciary nonetheless succeeded in mitigating judicial resistance toward reform legislation and hostility toward organized labor. Even though judicial antagonism toward reform measures and organized labor continued to vex progressives and labor unions until 1937, the ostensibly hyperbolic rhetoric and quixotic proposals of the critics of the courts had a significant impact upon judicial behavior.

The muted fury of the critics of the courts between 1890 and 1937 illustrates a pervasive ambivalence about judicial power that has made the courts both vulnerable and resistant to popular pressures. Americans revere and revile their courts. This ambivalence has exposed the courts to intense criticism during every period of American history, yet it has ensured the courts a central role in the American political system. A study of the controversy over judicial power from 1890 to 1937 is therefore relevant to an understanding of the subtle and delicate balances of power among the three branches of government and between public opinion and the judiciary in both earlier and later periods, including the present.

Ambivalence about the judiciary is the inevitable product of the paradox of judicial power in America, for it reflects the inherent tensions of a political system that enshrines both democracy and legalism. Although courts have created and sustained a legal system that has preserved the democratic character of the American polity, the courts are the least democratic of American political institutions. Both in theory and in practice, the judiciary is less responsive to the immediate will of the people than are the executive and legislative branches of the government. For nearly two centuries, however, Americans have expected their courts to respond to profound public needs by providing solutions to problems with which the executive and legislative branches of government have been unable or unwilling to cope. Americans expect the judiciary to fill a political vacuum by providing cohesion for a pluralistic society and acting as the ultimate guardians of the public interest. In serving this role, the judiciary is expected to interpret the Constitution, statutes, and common law of the land in a way that transcends overt politics and the more transient winds of popular opinion.

The popular perception that courts are above politics enhances public respect for the judiciary. But although the judiciary may eschew raw partisanship, the judiciary can never be apolitical. Even though the political dimension of judicial decision making is often not visible, political choices and assumptions are a necessary ingredient of judicial decisions, just as fire is part of iron. Although the courts are bound to honor the language of constitutions, statutes, and the common law, interpretations of those laws vary widely according to the social, economic, and political predilections of judges. The political character of adjudication is particularly evident in the U.S. Supreme Court, where constitutional interpretation virtually necessitates the making of political choices. Although a scrupulous justice may attempt to interpret the Constitution in a manner consistent with its literal text or the original intent of the Framers, neither text nor original intent will offer satisfactory answers to questions that neither the document nor its authors anticipated. Even when the courts attempt to interpret the law in a manner consistent with the values and traditions of the nation, common values and traditions may be difficult to discern in a highly heterogenous community. Judges thus will inevitably offend significant elements of public opinion, particularly when they exercise their so-called countermajoritarian function by protecting the rights of minorities. Moreover, the very nature of the judicial process, which permits courts to render decisions only in cases arising out of actual controversies, ensures that the courts must favor certain parties at the expense of others. The proper scope of judicial power will therefore remain the source of perennial tension.

The controversy over the scope of judicial power has ancient roots.

The development of predictable rules for the governance of human conduct has helped to rescue humankind from the tyranny of despots, who naturally have been loath to surrender arbitrary power to the rule of law. The reverence for the judiciary that is so deeply ingrained in American culture may be traced to England, where the development of the English common law and judicial independence during the Middle Ages helped to reduce royal absolutism. The growing rigidity of the common law during the late medieval period, however, demonstrated that a legal system that did not respond to changing social exigencies could be as unjust as any monarch. Although the Crown's introduction of courts of equity helped to restore justice and balance to the English legal system, the growth of royal absolutism during the sixteenth and early seventeenth centuries provoked a constitutional crisis that led to civil war. Opponents of the new royal prerogatives appealed to traditional liberties accorded by the common law. The most forceful exponent of the common law, Edward Coke, insisted that both Crown and Parliament were bound by the common law and that it was the duty of the judges to interpret that law. Although Coke's ideas were never wholly accepted in England, they presaged the triumph of judicial independence later in the seventeenth century and exercised a powerful influence in the American colonies.

Having left England to obtain greater religious and economic freedom, the American colonists embraced Coke's faith in the supremacy of the common law and the primacy of personal liberties. The colonists appealed to the common law in their revolt against British rule, and the Declaration of Independence is replete with references to the illegal acts of the Crown. Following the Revolution, the founders of the new Republic hoped that a rule of law would mitigate the need for a strong central government. Fearing mobocracy as much as autocracy, the social and economic elites expected state judges to check the passions of an unbridled democracy and restrain nascent despotism. Economic and social problems during the early years of independence, however, revealed the need for a more powerful central government.

The Constitution adopted in 1787 reflected the Framers' desire to reconcile the public good with private rights. The separation of powers in the government was designed to decrease this tension by creating loci of power that would be strong enough to protect both public and private interests but not so strong as to interfere arbitrarily with those interests. In contrast to the Articles of Confederation, the Constitution created a federal judiciary that was designed to be a coordinate of the executive and legislative branches. In addition to checking the power of the executive and legislative branches, the federal judiciary was intended to help maintain a proper equilibrium between state and federal power. In particular, the creation of a Supreme Court was necessary to give force to the supremacy clause of Article VI of the Constitution, which provides that the Constitution shall be the supreme law of the land.

Even though the Framers of the Constitution believed that the federal judiciary was integral to federalism and the separation of powers, they did little to define the scope of federal judicial power. Although the Framers were highly cognizant of the conflicts between the Crown and the courts of England, judicial power does not appear to have been an important issue at the Constitutional Convention or the state ratifying conventions.[3] The power of what James Madison described as "the least dangerous branch" of government was understandably less controversial than were the powers of the executive and legislative branches. Although most Framers believed that the creation of a supreme court was essential for ensuring an effective federal system, the creation of lower federal courts was more controversial, particularly in the ratifying conventions.[4] Although some of the anti-federalists also decried the Constitution's provision for life tenure of federal judges,[5] Alexander Hamilton argued in *The Federalist* that security of tenure would not produce judicial despotism since the judiciary would have "no influence over either the sword or the purse."[6]

Even though the Framers may have envisioned a significant role for the federal judiciary, it is most unlikely that they perceived that federal courts would become so powerful or would exercise so profound an influence upon the nation's destiny. The linchpin of federal judicial power has been judicial review of the constitutionality of state and federal legislation. The power of judicial review was a distinctly American innovation, and the United States has remained the nation in which this power is most potent. The question of whether the federal courts would have the power to review the constitutionality of state and federal legislation was not widely discussed during the convention or the ratification period. Although the issue of whether the Framers envisioned judicial review has engendered fierce debates among scholars, there is substantial evidence that the opinion of the Framers on judicial

[3] Jack M. Sosin, *The Aristocracy of the Long Robe: The Origins of Judicial Review in America* (Westport, Conn.: Greenwood Press, 1989), pp. 251–69.

[4] Paul M. Bator, Paul J. Mishkin, David L. Shapiro, and Herbert Wechsler, eds., *Hart and Wechsler's The Federal Courts and the Federal System*, 2d ed. (Mineola, N.Y.: Foundation Press, 1973), pp. 11–12.

[5] Merrill Jensen, ed., *The Documentary History of the Ratification of the Constitution*, vol. 3 (Madison: State Historical Society of Wisconsin, 1978), p. 440.

[6] Alexander Hamilton, *The Federalist No. 78*, ed. Roy P. Fairfield (Baltimore: Johns Hopkins University Press, 1981), pp. 227–28.

review ranged widely from acceptance to opposition. Many probably lacked any clearly defined opinion.[7]

After the adoption of the Constitution, judicial review developed incrementally. During the 1790s, several state courts and lower federal courts began to review the constitutionality of state legislation.[8] The early examples of judicial review of federal legislation in decisions preceding *Marbury v. Madison*[9] do not appear to have created much controversy. Even *Marbury*, which firmly established the right of the Supreme Court to review acts of Congress, seems not to have generated major outcry. Far more controversial were early Supreme Court decisions that asserted federal power at the expense of the states. The first major decision of the Supreme Court, *Chisholm v. Georgia* in 1793,[10] which permitted citizens to maintain federal lawsuits against states in which they did not reside, provoked an uproar that led to the nullification of the decision in the Eleventh Amendment. The later series of decisions in which the Supreme Court firmly established its right to review the constitutionality of state legislation and state judicial decisions[11] precipitated fierce criticism of the Court by Jeffersonians who believed that the federal government was improperly infringing on the rights of the states and the liberties of the people. Many of these decisions were particularly controversial since they promoted the economic interests of finance capitalists who were anathema to the agrarian and working-class Jeffersonians.

Although Jefferson, Jackson, and their followers frequently complained that the federal courts were usurping state power and poisoning democracy, federal judicial power and the judiciary's solicitude for the rights of private property continued to grow throughout the antebellum period. The emergence of a Democratic majority on the federal bench during the Jacksonian era did not diminish the role of the federal courts. Even when the courts invoked theories of states' rights and economic egalitarianism, they did so in ways that enhanced the power of the federal courts as the ultimate arbiters of the Constitution. By the time sectional divisions became acute during the 1850s, public respect

---

[7] Raoul Berger, *Congress v. The Supreme Court* (Cambridge, Mass.: Harvard University Press, 1969), pp. 47–119.

[8] Alfred H. Kelly and Winfred A. Harbison, *The American Constitution: Its Origins and Development*, 5th ed. (New York: W. W. Norton, 1976), pp. 178–82.

[9] 5 U.S. (1 Cranch) 137 (1803).

[10] 2 U.S. (2 Dall.) 419 (1793).

[11] *United States v. Peters*, 9 U.S. (5 Cranch) 115 (1809); *Fletcher v. Peck*, 10 U.S. (6 Cranch) 87 (1810); *Martin v. Hunter's Lessee*, 14 U.S. (1 Wheat.) 304 (1816); *Sturges v. Crowinshield*, 17 U.S. (4 Wheat.) 122 (1819); *McCulloch v. Maryland*, 17 U.S. (4 Wheat.) 316 (1819); *Dartmouth College v. Woodward*, 17 U.S. (4 Wheat.) 518 (1819); *Cohens v. Virginia*, 19 U.S. (6 Wheat.) 264 (1821).

for the Supreme Court was so great that Americans looked to the Court for solutions to the great controversy over slavery.

The Court's failure to provide a satisfactory solution in its notorious *Dred Scott* decision diminished the prestige of the Court and helped to provoke the Civil War. The victory of the Union in the war ensured that the federal courts would continue to have a profound impact upon the development of both state and federal law. Although the prestige of the federal courts remained at a low ebb during Reconstruction, the courts steadily regained their power and influence. Writing in 1891 at the outset of the storm of controversy that is the subject of this book, James Bryce aptly observed that "the credit and dignity of the Supreme court stand very high" even though many judicial decisions had inspired intense opposition.[12]

But although Bryce and other commentators for more than a century have marveled at the power and prestige of this uniquely American institution, the Court is not the sole source of constitutional law. Although the Court may be the ultimate arbiter of the Constitution, the Court both influences and is influenced by the other two branches of government and the people in what Alexander M. Bickel and Louis Fisher have aptly described as a continuing dialogue.[13] Despite perennial tensions arising from the exercise of judicial power, this dialogue generally has ensured that judicial decisions and public opinion have remained relatively harmonious. The Constitution, however, offers a number of safety valves to ensure that the people can curb the powers of courts if the judiciary becomes too far estranged from public opinion. The temptation to propose such measures is great since the balance of powers between the branches of government that is so subtly woven into the Constitution provides Congress with a broad array of means for curbing judicial power.

The most fundamental power of Congress over the courts is its power to prescribe jurisdiction. The Constitution mandates only a minimal role for the federal courts, leaving Congress the discretion to confer or curtail broader powers. Article III of the Constitution requires the existence of only one federal court, the Supreme Court, and vests a very limited original jurisdiction in that Court. Although Article III provides that federal judicial power shall extend to a broad class of cases, including all cases arising under the Constitution, Article III permits Congress to make exceptions and regulations concerning the Court's jurisdiction. Congress also has discretion over the size of the

---

[12] James Bryce, *The American Commonwealth*, 2d ed., vol. 1 (London, 1891), p. 264.

[13] Alexander M. Bickel, *The Least Dangerous Branch: The Supreme Court at the Bar of Politics* (Indianapolis: Bobbs-Merrill, 1962), p. 240; Louis Fisher, *Constitutional Dialogues* (Princeton, N.J.: Princeton University Press, 1988).

Supreme Court, since the Constitution does not prescribe the number of justices.

Although the literal language of the Constitution would seem to permit Congress to abolish the appellate jurisdiction of the Supreme Court and dissolve the lower federal courts that have been created by statute since the adoption of the Constitution, many constitutional scholars believe that such legislation would be constitutionally dubious. In particular, there is widespread agreement that the power to curtail the jurisdiction of the lower federal courts must not be exercised in a manner that would interfere with the Constitution's supremacy clause, destroy the courts' fundamental role, or deprive any person of life, liberty, or property without due process of law.[14]

Yet even if there are limits to congressional power to abrogate the jurisdiction of the federal courts, Congress might be able to prune federal jurisdiction over limited classes of cases without provoking a constitutional crisis.[15] Moreover, the constitutional amendment process is always available to circumscribe federal jurisdiction, even beyond the minimal confines prescribed by the Constitution. In addition to limitations on federal jurisdiction, there are numerous other means by which Congress can curtail or regulate the federal courts. The constitutional amendment process may be used to supersede Supreme Court decisions, and the amendment process could also be used to override any judicial decision. Several of the seventeen constitutional amendments enacted since the promulgation of the first ten amendments have overturned Supreme Court decisions.

Moreover, an amendment could alter procedures for the selection and tenure of judges. Although the Constitution provides that federal judges shall be selected by the president with the advice and consent of the Senate and that they shall serve "during good Behaviour," the constitutional amendment process could be used to provide for judicial election or limitation of tenure. Impeachment is also a potential weapon against recalcitrant judges, although overt political use of the

[14] Louis Fisher, *American Constitutional Law* (New York: McGraw-Hill, 1990), p. 1325; Lasser, "The Limits of Judicial Power," pp. 236–39; Gunther, "Congressional Power," pp. 895–922; Henry M. Hart, Jr., "The Power of Congress to Limit the Jurisdiction of Federal Courts: An Exercise in Dialectic," *Harvard Law Review* 66 (1953): 1362–1402; Martin H. Redish, "Congressional Power to Regulate Supreme Court Appellate Jurisdiction Under the Exceptions Clause: An Internal and External Examination," *Villanova Law Review* 27 (May 1982): 900–928; Leonard G. Ratner, "Majoritarian Constraints on Judicial Review: Congressional Control of Supreme Court Jurisdiction," ibid., pp. 929–58; Barry Friedman, "A Different Dialogue: The Supreme Court, Congress and Federal Jurisdiction," *Northwestern University Law Review* 85 (Fall 1990): 1–61.

[15] Gunther, "Congressional Power to Curtail," pp. 914–15; McDowell, *Curbing the Courts*, pp. 123–30.

remedy of impeachment has lain dormant since 1805 when the Jeffersonians failed to unseat the ultra-Federalist justice Samuel Chase. Congress also has the power to alter the number of federal judges and may freeze—but not diminish—their salaries. Finally, Congress may enact legislation that has the effect of ameliorating, modifying, or overturning Supreme Court decisions. Altogether, Congress has enacted more than 120 such statutes during the past two centuries.[16]

Critics of the federal courts have attempted to use every constitutional means—some of highly questionable constitutionality—to curtail the power of the courts. Foes of the Supreme Court's growing power during the era of the Marshall Court proposed a multitude of measures to restrict federal judicial power, including a constitutional amendment to divest the Supreme Court of the power to review state court decisions and statutes to restrict the Court's jurisdiction to the minimum level prescribed by the Constitution.[17] During the years immediately preceding the Civil War, abolitionists proposed similar measures.[18] Following the war, radical Republicans proposed legislation to restrict the Court's power of judicial review,[19] and a statute that limited the Court's habeas corpus power was upheld by the Court in *Ex parte McCardle*.[20] The hostility of the Court to the legislation of the New Deal during the 1930s inspired Franklin Roosevelt's Court-packing plan, and the controversial decisions of the Warren Court on desegregation, criminal procedure, school prayer, and reapportionment provoked a multitude of proposals for curbing the Court's jurisdiction or overriding its decisions.[21]

During recent years, when rancor against the Court has subsided and shifted to a different point on the political spectrum, there has been less discussion about making fundamental alterations to the power of the federal courts. Critics of the courts have tended to accept the reality of judicial power and to work within the system by influencing the nomination and confirmation processes. Bills to elect federal judges and to limit their tenure, however, have regularly continued to be introduced in Congress. And members of Congress have continued

[16] Richard A. Paschal, "The Continuing Colloquy: Congress and the Finality of the Supreme Court," *Journal of Law and Politics* 8 (Fall 1991): 217–25.

[17] Maurice S. Culp, "A Survey of the Proposals to Limit or Deny the Power of Judicial Review by the Supreme Court of the United States," *Indiana Law Journal* 4 (March 1929): 386, 388–89, 392–95; ibid. (April 1929): 474–77, 480–84.

[18] Charles Warren, *The Supreme Court in United States History*, rev. ed., vol. 2 (Boston: Little, Brown, 1926), pp. 333–36.

[19] Ibid., pp. 455–97.

[20] 74 U.S. (7 Wall.) 506 (1869).

[21] See Lasser, "Limits of Judicial Power," pp. 151–85; C. Herman Pritchett, *Congress versus the Supreme Court: 1957–1960* (Minneapolis: University of Minnesota Press, 1961).

to propose legislation that would overturn or modify Supreme Court decisions. Between 1985 and 1990, for example, some 166 bills in Congress were directed against 114 Supreme Court decisions.[22] Critics of the Supreme Court's decisions that the First Amendment protects flag desecration,[23] for example, proposed various statutes and constitutional amendments to overcome the effects of those decisions.[24] Although most bills to circumvent Supreme Court decisions never receive serious consideration, between 1985 and 1990 Congress did enact sixteen measures that were designed to alter the effects of Court decisions.[25] Congress has also regularly overturned or modified the Court's statutory interpretation decisions.[26]

During the period that is the subject of this book, antagonists of the courts threatened the judiciary with all of the court-curbing measures that the Constitution affords as well as others that were constitutionally dubious. The preferred methods of curtailment, however, differed widely among the critics of the courts and frequently shifted along with the circumstances that had inspired calls for judicial reform.

The criticisms of the courts from 1890 to 1937 were as diffuse as the many persons and organizations that protested judicial decisions and challenged judicial power. The immediate cause of populist antagonism toward the courts was judicial solicitude for the rights of the railroads and other corporations that allegedly exploited the farmers and workers who formed the core of the populist constituency. The populist hostility toward the judiciary had deeper roots, however, since it reflected populism's antielitism and its faith in direct democracy. The widespread hostility toward the federal courts among southern populists also reflected an abiding antagonism toward federal authority.

The various elements of the labor movement likewise assailed the courts for many different reasons, although the preeminence of the American Federation of Labor permits greater generalization about the views of organized labor. Like populist critics of the courts, organized labor was animated in part by hostility toward individual judicial decisions. Unlike populism, however, the principal labor unions lacked any inherent hostility toward the judiciary and were willing to support a powerful judiciary to the extent that the courts would provide a legal

[22] Paschal, "Continuing Colloquy," pp. 199–200, 211–16.

[23] *Texas v. Johnson*, 491 U.S. 397 (1989); *United States v. Eichman*, 496 U.S. 310 (1990).

[24] Mark E. Hermann, "Looking Down from the Hill: Factors Determining the Success of Congressional Efforts to Reverse Supreme Court Interpretations of the Constitution," *William and Mary Law Review* 33 (Winter 1992): 586–606.

[25] Paschal, "Continuing Colloquy," pp. 203, 224–25.

[26] William N. Eskridge, Jr., "Overriding Supreme Court Statutory Interpretation Decisions," *Yale Law Journal* 101 (November 1991): 331–53.

foundation for trade unionism. Trying to minimize partisan entanglements and emphasizing a "pure and simple unionism" that eschewed support for a broad social welfare program, the AFL narrowly focused its criticisms on decisions that directly affected the organizational rights of organized labor and the limited social reforms that received the AFL's support.

In particular, the AFL waged a campaign against injunctions that restricted union activities.[27] Although the widespread use of injunctions in labor disputes was based upon traditional principles of equity,[28] the courts during the late nineteenth and early twentieth centuries expanded the scope of equitable doctrines to protect employers from the activities of labor unions.[29] Accordingly, the strategy and

[27] William E. Forbath, "The Shaping of the American Labor Movement," *Harvard Law Review* 102 (April 1989): 1146, 1148–49, 1203, 1208, 1235; Christopher Tomlins, *The State and the Unions: Labor Relations, Law, and the Organized Labor Movement in America, 1880–1960* (New York: Cambridge University Press, 1985), p. 57; Philip Taft, *The A.F. of L. in the Time of Gompers* (New York: Harper, 1957), pp. 142–48; William M. Dick, *Labor and Socialism in America: The Gompers Era* (Port Washington, N.Y.: Kennikat Press, 1972), pp. 115–16. A revised and expanded version of Professor Forbath's article was published as *Law and the Shaping of the American Labor Movement* (Cambridge, Mass.: Harvard University Press, 1991).

[28] Sylvester Petro, "Injunctions and Labor Disputes: 1880–1932, Part I: What the Courts Actually Did—and Why," *Wake Forest Law Review* 14 (June 1978): 378.

[29] In issuing injunctions to protect property, for example, courts expanded the definition of *property* to include the intangible interests of employers in conducting a profit-making business (Forbath, "Shaping of American Labor Movement," pp. 1169–70). Judicial reliance upon injunctions grew as strikes became increasingly national in their scope since orchestrated national action against a single employer offended traditional legal doctrines of individualism. Judges also resented labor unions as rival lawmakers ibid., pp. 1152–53, 1155). During the late nineteenth century, the judiciary also increasingly favored injunctions because legislation had restricted the judiciary's use of the common law of conspiracy to curtail union activities. As Professor Hattam has pointed out, "now the courts could recognize the newly won right of workers to collective action while still preserving some form of judicial regulation of industrial relations. The injunction provided the courts with a more finely tuned mechanism for regulating labor unions than the conspiracy doctrine had. Rather than being forced to choose between conviction or acquittal, as was the case with conspiracy, the injunction permitted the courts to acknowledge workers' industrial rights and yet continue to regulate labor activity in many industrial disputes." Victoria Hattam, "Economic Visions and Political Strategies: American Labor and the State, 1865–1896," *Studies in American Political Development* 4 (1990): 117–18. Moreover, as Haggai Hurvitz has explained, the use of injunctions enabled courts to restrict union activities by transforming employers' economic interests into protectable property rights to which workers' civil liberties were subordinated. By recognizing workers' theoretical right to act concertedly, the courts ostensibly treated workers and businesses alike and thereby avoided equal protection objections. "Decisions to curb union pressures or legislative acts could now be presented not as discrimination against organized labor, but as protection against attacks on property rights," Hag-

ideology of the American labor movement remained at odds with a legal culture that gave corporations the expansive rights of individuals while imposing significant restrictions on the scope of trade union activity.[30] As the AFL's general counsel declared in 1924, "To the courts the Constitution is a peg on which to hang predilections in politics and sociology and call them law."[31]

The attitudes of progressives toward the courts, the principal subject of this book, were more complex and reflected divisions and contradictions within the progressive movement. The diverse strands of social reformers, intellectuals, small businesspeople, agrarian radicals, middle-class professionals, and liberal industrialists who composed the progressive movement had many reasons for criticizing the courts, and they differed widely on the remedies they proposed. The observation of various historians that progressivism was a kaleidoscope of shifting alliances[32] is demonstrated in the attitudes of progressives toward the courts.

Although progressivism has meant many different things to different historians,[33] there is general agreement with Robert H. Wiebe's thesis that progressivism was an attempt to ameliorate the social, economic, and political dislocations created by the rapid industrialization of the United States during the decades following the Civil War.[34] In particular, progressives sought to restore harmony to a society that seemed increasingly divided and to assert control over the social and economic forces that had transformed American life and often seemed to threaten the democratic experiment.

Although progressives purported to attempt to purify American democracy from the plutocratic elements that had corrupted it, progressivism was not inherently populistic or hostile toward business interests. Even though the progressive movement had a mass base and

---

gai Hurvitz, "American Labor Law and the Doctrine of Entrepreneurial Property Rights: Boycotts, Courts, and the Juridical Reorientation of 1886–1895," *Industrial Relations Law Journal* (1986): 356–61.

[30] Tomlins, *State and Unions*, pp. 58–59.

[31] Jackson Harvey Ralston, "Shall We Curb the Supreme Court? I—Labor and Law," *The Forum*, May 1924, p. 564.

[32] John D. Buenker, "Essay," in Buenker, Burnham, and Crunden, *Progressivism* (Cambridge, Mass.: Schenkman, 1977), p. 47; John Whiteclay Chambers II, *The Tyranny of Change: America in the Progressive Era, 1900–1917* (New York: St. Martin's Press, 1980), pp. 110, 137.

[33] See David M. Kennedy, "Overview: The Progressive Era," *The Historian* 37 (May 1975): 453–68.

[34] Robert H. Wiebe, *The Search For Order, 1877–1920* (New York: Hill and Wang, 1967).

national appeal,[35] it was not dominated by the common people. "Few reform movements," George E. Mowry observed, "have had the support of more wealthy men."[36] While Richard Hofstadter may have exaggerated the degree to which progressivism represented a reaction of the old social elites to reassert their control, he aptly pointed out that the progressive appeal was directed at people who felt that they had something to lose.[37]

Similarly, although some historians may have overemphasized the degree to which the progressive movement was influenced by business interests that sought to stabilize capitalism, it is clear that many businesspeople had good reasons for favoring reform and regulation and that progressivism was strongly influenced by its business elements.[38] Although some progressives were socialists, most progressives never fundamentally opposed capitalism or corporatism. They sought to tame the economic system rather than reject it. The progressives sought to preserve the benefits of the large-scale capitalism while retaining the scheme of individualistic values that this organization was destroying.[39] Even the humanitarian reforms that were among the most enduring legacies of progressivism were motivated in large measure by a conservative desire to decrease the growing class tension that seemed to threaten social upheaval.[40]

Although judicial hostility toward reform legislation inspired much progressive animus toward the courts and provided the primary mo-

[35] Arthur S. Link and Richard L. McCormick, *Progressivism* (Arlington Heights, Ill.: Harlan Davidson, 1983), p. 8.

[36] George E. Mowry, *Theodore Roosevelt and the Progressive Movement* (Madison: University of Wisconsin Press, 1947), p. 10.

[37] Richard Hofstadter, *The Age of Reform: From Bryan to F.D.R.* (New York: Alfred A. Knopf, 1955), pp. 135–38; 165.

[38] Gabriel Kolko, *The Triumph of Conservatism: A Reinterpretation of American History, 1900–1916* (Cambridge, Mass.: Harvard University Press, 1962); Gabriel Kolko, *Railroads and Regulation, 1877–1916* (Princeton, N.J.: Princeton University Press, 1965); James Weinstein, *The Corporate Ideal in the Liberal State, 1900–1918* (Boston: Beacon Press, 1968); Robert H. Wiebe, *Businessmen and Reform: A Study of the Progressive Movement* (Cambridge, Mass.: Harvard University Press, 1962); Samuel P. Hays, *The Response to Industrialism 1885–1914* (Chicago: University of Chicago Press, 1957); George E. Mowry, *The Era of Theodore Roosevelt, 1900–1912* (New York: Harper and Brothers, 1958); Otis L. Graham, Jr., *The Great Campaigns: Reform and War in America, 1900–1918* (Englewood Cliffs, N.J.: Prentice-Hall, 1971); Roy Lubove, *The Progressives and the Slums, Tenement House Reform in New York City, 1890–1917* (Pittsburgh: University of Pittsburgh Press, 1962); Chambers, *Tyranny of Change*.

[39] Hofstadter, *Age of Reform*, p. 215.

[40] Don S. Kirschner, "The Ambiguous Legacy-Social Justice and Social Control in the Progressive Era," *Historical Reflections* 2 (Summer 1975): 69–88; Link and McCormick, *Progressivism*, pp. 69–70, 117–18; Chambers, *Tyranny of Change*, pp. 133–36.

tivation for progressive proposals to alter the judicial system, progressives were profoundly ambivalent about the effectiveness of legislation as an instrument of reform.[41] Despite their initial predilection for individual action and personal regeneration, progressives increasingly came to believe that reform could best be achieved through more organized efforts. After recognizing the need for collective action, progressives at first preferred to achieve their goals through private and voluntary organizations.[42]

The magnitude of the problems facing society and the limitations of voluntary action eventually convinced some progressives, including the economist Richard T. Ely and later the publicist Herbert Croly, the sociologist Edward A. Ross, and the journalist Walter Lippmann, that reform must be directed by the state. Faith in the state was particularly pronounced among those reformers who believed that scientific methods could bring greater rationality and order to society. Although the progressive faith in science and the progressive cult of efficiency reflected the influence of Darwinistic concepts of social evolution, progressives rejected the fatalistic determinism of Spencerian Darwinism and subscribed to a dynamic philosophy that acknowledged that human effort could create a better world. Influenced by pragmatists such as John Dewey and Ross, many progressives ultimately adopted a utilitarian and instrumentalist philosophy that advocated collective action to improve society.[43]

Many reformers, however, remained profoundly suspicious of the state, fearing that big business would dominate big government—a fear that subsequent history proved far from unfounded. Although the interventionist views of Croly and other progressives found expression in Theodore Roosevelt's "New Nationalism" and were accepted by a large segment of the progressive movement, many other progressives favored the more Jeffersonian views embodied in Woodrow Wilson's "New Freedom" program. The more moralistic elements of the progressive movement remained particularly suspicious of the state, be-

[41] See, e.g., John C. Burnham "Essay," in Buenker, Burnham, and Crunden, *Progressivism*, pp. 14–16.

[42] See Jonathan Lurie, *The Chicago Board of Trade, 1859–1905: The Dynamics of Self-Regulation* (Urbana: University of Illinois Press, 1979), pp. 200–205; Chambers, *Tyranny of Change*, p. 120; Link and McCormick, *Progressivism*, p. 71; Burnham, "Essay," in Buenker et al., *Progressivism*, pp. 12, 21; James T. Kloppenberg, *Uncertain Victory: Social Democracy and Progressivism in European and American Thought, 1870–1920* (New York: Oxford University Press, 1986), p. 358.

[43] Chambers, *Tyranny of Change*, pp. 99–102. See Richard Hofstadter, *Social Darwinism in American Thought* (Boston: Beacon Press, 1955), pp. 123–42; Walter Lippmann, *Drift and Mastery* (New York: Mitchell Kennerley, 1914).

lieving that social regeneration must come from the conscience of individuals.[44]

The ambivalence of progressives about the need for legislation to achieve reform helped to mute their fury against courts that nullified reform legislation. Moreover, the progressive fury against the courts was muted by a deeply ingrained respect for the judiciary and the recognition that courts could serve as allies of the progressive movement. Although progressives often derogated the courts for catering to the plutocratic interests that the progressives so detested or failing to act in the broad public interest that progressives professed to support, few progressives were willing seriously to challenge the fundamental powers of an institution that had traditionally been a staunch defender of the rights of private property and that was more immune than the other two branches of government to the caprice and corruption of the masses. Mowry observed that the typical California progressive politician saw himself as a sort of Platonic guardian of the public interest.[45] Certainly the courts, with their centralized and cerebral decision-making process and their relative immunity from popular clamor, were peculiarly well suited to acting the part of Platonic guardian.

The divisions within the progressive movement and the tensions between the different constituencies and goals of the labor and progressive movements hindered the critics of the judiciary from agreeing upon specific programs for reform. But although critics of the courts varied widely in their strategies and proposals for reform, the essential complaints of progressives and trade unionists against the judiciary remained remarkably uniform and consistent from 1890 to 1937. These recurring complaints were comprehensively summarized by the progressive Republican senator Robert M. La Follette of Wisconsin in March 1912:

> The judiciary has grown to be the most powerful institution in our government. It, more than any other, may advance or retard human progress. Evidence abounds that, as constituted to-day, the courts pervert justice almost as often as they administer it. Precedent and procedure have combined to make one law for the rich and another for the poor. The regard of the courts for fossilized precedent, their absorption in technicalities, their detachment from the vital, living facts of the present day, their constant thinking on the side of the rich and powerful and privileged classes have brought our courts into conflict with the democratic spirit and

[44] See David B. Danbom, *"The World of Hope": Progressives and the Struggle for an Ethical Public Life* (Philadelphia: Temple University Press, 1987).

[45] George E. Mowry, *The California Progressives* (Chicago: Quadrangle, 1963), p. 101

purposes of this generation. Moreover, by usurping the power to declare statutes unconstitutional and by presuming to read their own views into statutes without regard to the plain intention of the legislators, they have become in reality the supreme law-making and law-giving institution of our government. They have taken to themselves a power it was never intended they should exercise; a power greater than that entrusted to the courts of any other enlightened nation. And because this tremendous power has been so generally exercised on the side of the wealthy and powerful few, the courts have become at last the strongest bulwark of special privilege. They have come to constitute what may indeed be termed a "judicial oligarchy."[46]

Criticism of the courts by the progressives was inevitable, for it was part of a broader questioning of public institutions that characterized the Progressive Era.[47] It also reflected the rejection by progressive intellectuals of what Duncan Kennedy has called "classical legal thought," the nineteenth-century jurisprudence that attempted to insulate the law from politics by constructing modes of categorical doctrines. By insisting that social, political, and economic factors profoundly influenced judicial decision-making, the so-called sociological jurisprudence of the Progressive Era presaged the legal realism movement of the 1930s and the critical legal studies movement that emerged during the 1980s. Morton J. Horwitz contends that "for many purposes, it is best to see Legal Realism as simply a continuation of the reformist agenda of early-twentieth-century Progressivism."[48]

Criticism of the judiciary was particularly intense during the early twentieth century because the courts thwarted so many of the reforms for which the progressives and their ilk had crusaded. The judicial attitude toward reform legislation, however, was anything but uniform or monolithic. The traditional view, originally fostered by the progressives, that the courts of the progressive era were recalcitrant defenders of a rigid doctrine of laissez-faire, has given way to an increasing recognition that the courts were remarkably amenable to progressive reforms. In addition to making many modifications to common law that had the effect of subordinating property rights and liberty of contract to broader communal rights, the courts upheld far more progressive

[46] Robert M. La Follette, Introduction to Gilbert E. Roe, *Our Judicial Oligarchy* (New York: B. W. Huebsch, 1912), pp. vi–vii.

[47] As Roscoe Pound observed in 1912, "A generation ago we were sure of our political institutions. Now criticism has become the fashionable note"; Ralph W. Breckinridge, "The Constitution, the Court and the People," *Yale Law Journal* 22 (January 1913): 185 (quoting Pound's address before the Missouri State Bar Association, St. Louis, October 1912.)

[48] Morton J. Horwitz, *The Transformation of American Law 1870–1960: The Crisis of Legal Orthodoxy* (New York: Oxford University Press, 1992), pp. 169–71, 273.

measures than they struck down. As early as 1913, Charles Warren argued that his examination of the Supreme Court's decisions of the past quarter century had demonstrated that the Supreme Court had been "steady and consistent in upholding all State legislation of a progressive type."[49]

Although Warren was not an unbiased observer, many scholars today agree that the courts of the Progressive Era were not the citadels of reaction that many progressives portrayed in their polemics against the courts.[50] Melvin I. Urofsky has gone so far as to argue that the Supreme Court during the early years of the twentieth century was "as progressive as most reformers could desire."[51] Urofsky also contends that the state courts did not seriously thwart the progressive agenda.[52]

Although Loren P. Beth has warned against excessive revisionism, he has acknowledged that the Supreme Court's "fumbling and vacillating response" to progressive reform ultimately "was astonishingly but accidentally successful in allowing both for increasing governmental regulation of the worst aspects of the Industrial Revolution and for the maintenance of the system (sometimes loosely called 'free enterprise') which was creating the revolution." The Court's pragmatism was quite consistent with the ad hoc and nonideological character of the case system used by American courts.[53]

Judicial suspicion of governmental economic regulation was natural, for the concept of limited government is at the core of the Constitution. During the nineteenth century, courts had developed an elaborate structure of both private and public law to protect individual rights.[54] Historians have differed about whether the judiciary's protection of individualism was a cloak for protection of powerful commercial interests or expressed a more principled commitment to liberty for all Americans.[55] Although the motives of the judiciary are likely to

[49] Charles Warren, "The Progressiveness of the United States Supreme Court," *Columbia Law Review* 13 (April 1913): 294, 295. See also Charles Warren, "A Bulwark to the State Police Power—the United States Supreme Court," *Columbia Law Review* 13 (December 1913): 667–95.

[50] For a thorough reassessment, see John Semonche, *Charting the Future: The Supreme Court Responds to a Changing Society, 1890–1920* (Westport, Conn.: Greenwood Press, 1978).

[51] Melvin I. Urofsky, "Myth and Reality: The Supreme Court and Protective Legislation in the Progressive Era," *Yearbook 1983 Supreme Court Historical Society*, p. 55.

[52] Melvin I. Urofsky, "State Courts and Protective Legislation during the Progressive Era: A Reevaluation," *Journal of American History* 72 (June 1985): 63–92.

[53] Loren P. Beth, *The Development of the American Constitution, 1877–1917* (New York: Harper and Row, 1971), p. 141.

[54] Lawrence M. Friedman, *A History of American Law* (New York: Simon and Schuster, 1980).

[55] See Michael Les Benedict, "Laissez Faire and Liberty: A Re-Evaluation of the

remain controversial, the primacy of individualism in nineteenth-century American legal thought is beyond question, even though this strong judicial bias in favor of private rights was tempered by the recognition for limited state regulation in the public interest.[56] As Aviam Soifer has pointed out, Supreme Court justices who scrutinized paternalistic legislation "tapped into a fundamental American theme when they set out to choose who was a permissible subject for protection and what legislative initiatives were acceptable."[57] Moreover, Urofsky has observed that "even if all judges had been prescient, it is unlikely they would have rushed to approve a wide spectrum of innovative laws, many of which ran counter to long established common law principles, until the courts could develop measures by which to evaluate them."[58]

The courts' rather checkered responses to reform thus expressed the inherent conservatism of the judicial process rather than simple political reaction. As William M. Wiecek has observed, "Caution and hesitancy, rather than incoherence or contradiction, characterized the Supreme Court's reaction to the appearance of the bureaucratic administrative state."[59] Although the pro-business biases of many judges certainly colored many judicial decisions, many decisions that progressives abhorred reflected judicial adherence to precedent rather than judicial activism on behalf of big business.

Although the doctrine of the police power provided a basis for legislative activism, the scope of the police power remained a source of controversy throughout the Progressive Era.[60] Even though the courts

---

Meaning and Origins of Laissez-Faire Constitutionalism," *Law and History Review* 3 (Fall 1985): 297–98, 311, 327–31; Owen M. Fiss, *The Oliver Wendell Holmes Devise History of the Supreme Court of the United States*, vol. 8, *Troubled Beginnings of the Modern State, 1888–1910* (New York: Macmillan) (galleys), pp. 12–21, 389–94. Professor Fiss has stated that it is plausible that "the failure of the Fuller Court [1888–1910] lay not in the Court's understanding of its place in the American political system but in its attachment to a conception of liberty that consisted almost entirely of a demand for limited government." *Ibid.* p. 19.

[56] Harry N. Scheiber, "Regulation, Property Rights, and Definition of 'The Market': Law and the American Economy," *Journal of Economic History* 41 (March 1981): 106; Benedict, *ibid.*

[57] Aviam Soifer, "The Paradox of Paternalism and Laissez-Faire Constitutionalism: United States Supreme Court, 1888–1921," *Law and History Review* 5 (Spring 1987): 278. Similarly, Professor Fiss has argued that Supreme Court justices "cabined the legislative power by a set of rules that bore a striking similarity to those that constituted the common law-Judge created, these rules emerged on a case-by-case basis over time and were founded on principle." Fiss, *Troubled Beginnings*, pp. 105–6 (galleys).

[58] Urofsky, "Myth and Reality," p. 59.

[59] William M. Wiecek, *Liberty under Law: The Supreme Court in American Life* (Baltimore: Johns Hopkins University Press, 1988), p. 129.

[60] Urofsky, "Myth and Reality," pp. 59–60.

of the Progressive Era generally responded favorably to the exigencies of reform, it is not surprising that progressives viewed the courts with deep suspicion. Even when judges permitted progressive legislation to stand, the courts implicitly or explicitly avowed a belief that the judiciary had the duty to undertake a very careful scrutiny of any regulatory legislation.[61] As Wiebe aptly declared, "Rather than wedding the judiciary to a particular ideology, judges had set themselves apart as social guardians. Yeasayers as much as naysayers, they would determine which political policies to stop and which to let pass as their sense of society's safety changed."[62] Similarly, Beth has observed that "what was important was that no law of any great significance could be enacted by Congress without having to run the gauntlet of judicial review."[63] And Lawrence M. Friedman has argued that state courts exercised judicial review in a random and irresponsible manner.[64]

Faced constantly with the specter of judicial nullification of reform legislation, the progressives were naturally relentless in their warnings against the perils of judicial hostility toward reform. Progressive antagonism toward the courts was periodically reinforced by state and federal decisions that nullified reform legislation. Even though such decisions were the exception rather than the norm, they were common enough to provide persistent reminders of the judiciary's ability to thwart reform and to reinforce fears that an increased judicial activism might jeopardize the success of the entire reform movement. As Harvard law professor Felix Frankfurter pointed out in 1924, a "numerical tally of the cases does not tell the tale," since not all laws were of the same importance and a decision involving only one state law often decided the body of laws in other states.[65]

Decisions such as the Court's nullification of federal child-labor statutes[66] created widespread despair in progressive and union circles, and decisions such as the Court's invalidation of a Kansas statute prohibiting "yellow dog" contracts[67] had the effect of nullifying or preven-

[61] Paul Kens, "The Source of a Myth: Police Powers of the States and Laissez Faire Constitutionalism, 1900–1937," *American Journal of Legal History* 35 (January 1991): 94–97.

[62] Wiebe, *Search for Order,*, p. 107.

[63] Beth, *Development of American Constitution*, p. 45.

[64] Friedman, *History of American Law*, p. 317.

[65] Editorial, "The Red Terror of Judicial Reform," *New Republic*, October 1, 1924, p. 112; repr. Philip B. Kurland, ed., *Felix Frankfurter on the Supreme Court: Extrajudicial Essays on the Court and the Constitution* (Cambridge, Mass.: Harvard University Press, 1970), p. 164.

[66] *Hammer v. Dagenhart*, 247 U.S. 251 (1918); *Bailey v. Drexel Furniture Co.*, 259 U.S. 20 (1922).

[67] *Coppage v. Kansas*, 236 U.S. 1 (1915).

ting the enactment of similar legislation in other states. Progressive hostility toward the courts also festered because many progressives could not perceive why the courts should nullify *any* legislation that did not blatantly exceed the state's police power. While decisions such as *Lochner v. New York* in 1905[68] created only limited and temporary setbacks for advocates of reform legislation, they became symbols of judicial intransigence and provided lightning rods for progressive criticism of the courts.

Agitation against the courts, both state and federal, occurred in several cycles. The first began during the 1890s when the state and federal courts began to nullify redistributive economic legislation. A second and sharper period of criticism started after *Lochner* when progressives began to express frustration over judicial decisions that invoked substantive due process, conservative concepts of interstate commerce, and other doctrines to strike down social welfare measures, and organized labor began to lose patience with the judiciary's use of the injunction in labor disputes. Criticism of the courts gathered momentum along with the progressive movement itself and reached a crescendo between 1910 and 1912. The principal remedies proposed as correctives to judicial abuse of power during this period were the recall of judges and the so-called recall of judicial decisions. These measures were characteristic of progressive thinking at the time since they proposed to increase popular participation in government. Most of the reform proposals were directed against the state judiciary since the state courts during the period were perceived to be more conservative than the federal courts.

Agitation against the courts subsided between 1913 and 1918 when both federal and state courts seemed more amenable to social and labor legislation. Between 1918 and 1924, however, the renewed conservatism of the Supreme Court and many lower federal courts precipitated a third wave of progressive and trade unionist criticism of the courts and engendered a raft of proposals to abrogate the power of judicial review. The Court issue was particularly prominent between 1922 and 1924, and it emerged as a significant, albeit somewhat specious issue in the 1924 presidential campaign. In contrast to the earlier proposals, the reforms suggested during the 1920s were primarily directed at the federal courts and generally would have transferred power from the courts to the legislature rather than to the people.

In analyzing these proposals to curtail judicial power, it is important to remember the warning of various historians that the rhetoric of the

[68] 198 U.S. 45 (1905).

progressives should not be confused with their actual goals.[69] While some progressives and labor leaders favored curtailment of judicial power as a matter of principle, many of the critics of the courts were motivated primarily by a pragmatic desire to prevent judicial annulment of progressive legislation, and their advocacy of various quixotic proposals to curtail judicial power often was intended merely to dramatize their grievances and remind the courts that an angry public possessed the means of curbing judicial power if the courts continued to thwart the popular will as expressed in the statutes enacted by Congress and the state legislatures.

This book will explain the ways in which these and other characteristics, contradictions and tensions within populism, progressivism, and the labor movement interacted with judicial attitudes and various external political factors to create, sustain, and ultimately mute the widespread fury against the judiciary between 1890 and 1937. The history of the attacks on the courts during the period helps to explain why attempts to curtail judicial power during every period of American history have failed, yet why those attempts have influenced judicial decision making and have had a salubrious impact upon the vitality of American democracy.

[69] Link and McCormick, *Progressivism*, p. 10; Samuel P. Hays, "The Politics of Reform in Municipal Government in the Progressive Era," *Pacific Northwest Quarterly* 55 (October 1964): 167–68.

ONE

THE SEEDS OF DISCORD

> Twenty-five to fifty years ago there were time-honored
> phrases which were applied by lawyers with more or less
> popular approval to the American judiciary. The courts
> were the "Palladium of our liberties," the "Guardians of
> the Ark of the Covenant." To-day the public attitude has
> largely changed. These phrases are no longer current.
> The people are dissatisfied with the guardians, and in
> some quarters there is dissatisfaction with the ark itself.
> (*George W. Alger*, Atlantic Monthly, *March 1913*)[1]

I N NOVEMBER 1911, as the progressive movement was reaching
its crest, Senator Henry Cabot Lodge of Massachusetts expressed
regret that reverence for the Constitution and the Founding Fathers had diminished during the quarter century since the Republic
had celebrated the centennials of the Constitution's adoption and ratification: "Instead of the universal chorus of praise and gratitude to the
framers of the Constitution the air is now rent with harsh voices of
criticism and attack." Although Lodge averred that the vast mass of
Americans continued to respect their Constitution, he observed with
sadness that "every one who is in distress, or in debt, or discontented,
now assails the Constitution merely because such is the present
passion."[2]

Lodge's observations were widely shared by many Americans who
for the past several years had discerned growing criticism of the courts
and the Constitution. Late in 1907, the *New York Times* lamented that

---

[1] George W. Alger, "The Courts and Legislative Freedom," *Atlantic Monthly*, March
1913, p. 345.

[2] Henry Cabot Lodge, "The Constitution and Its Makers," in Henry Cabot Lodge,
Democracy of the Constitution (1915; repr. Freeport, N.Y.: Books for Libraries, Inc., 1966),
p. 35 (speech delivered before the Literary and Historical Association of North Carolina
at Raleigh, November 28, 1911, published in *North American Review*, July 1912, pp. 20–51
and in S. Doc. 122, 62nd Cong., 2d sess. [1911]). Michael Kammen has pointed out that
Lodge's recollection of the nation's mood at the time of the centennial may have been
distorted by a "haze of nostalgia" since, as vice-president of the Centennial Commission
in 1887, he should have "been aware of the agonies that group went through to achieve
any sort of respectable festivity." Michael Kammen, *A Machine That Would Go of Itself: The
Constitution in American Culture* (New York: Knopf, 1986), p. 154.

the.courts had "fallen upon evil days," suffering the slings of critics as diverse as labor organizations and business magnates who disagreed with judicial decisions that contravened their interests.[3] In 1908, the president of the American Bar Association told the association's annual meeting that public respect for the judiciary had declined markedly in recent years and that critics of the judiciary had assailed the very foundations of the judicial system.[4] Early in 1911, Justice Horace Lurton detected a "restless tugging against the bonds of the law and the yoke of the Constitution" and warned against a growing "tendency to applaud the doing of things which we wish done, regardless of whether lawful or unlawful."[5]

Progressives fully agreed with such conservatives as Lodge and Lurton that public respect for the courts had diminished. Writing in 1913, the noted political scientist W. F. Dodd observed that popular attitudes toward the courts had markedly changed in recent years and that the "judicial functions, which until recently were regarded with a reverence approaching awe, are being subjected to sharp analysis and criticism."[6] Jane Addams suggested in 1908 that "perhaps the one symptom among working men which most definitely indicates a class feeling is a growing distrust of the integrity of the courts, the belief that the present judge has been a corporation attorney, that his sympathies and experience and his whole view of life is on the corporation side."[7] Likewise, the New York attorney William L. Ransom stated in 1912 that the intensity of the current controversy over judicial power was rivaled only by the controversies over the Marshall Court's decisions and the *Dred Scott* decision. Ransom believed, however, that the current period of criticism had engendered "less of hate and impatience, and far more of good humor and self-restraint" than the earlier periods of criticism.[8]

Lodge, however, was less sanguine. He believed that such criticism was "quite new in our history" because it questioned the very essence of the Constitution, in contrast to earlier periods when the people had expressed reverence for the Constitution even though they may have taken issue with the way judges interpreted it. Lodge observed that "even the Abolitionists, when they denounced the Constitution . . .

[3] "The Courts and the People," *New York Times*, December 2, 1907, p. 8.

[4] "Defends the Judiciary," *New York Times*, August 26, 1908, p. 6.

[5] Horace H. Lurton, "A Government of Law or a Government of Men?" *North American Review*, January 1911, p. 9.

[6] W. F. Dodd, "Social Legislation and the Courts," *Political Science Quarterly* 28 (March 1913): 1.

[7] Jane Addams, "Class Conflict in America," *American Journal of Sociology* 13 (May 1908): 772.

[8] William L. Ransom, *Majority Rule and the Judiciary* (New York: Charles Scribner's Sons, 1912), pp. 27, 30, 33.

did not deny its success in other directions, and their hostility to the Constitution was one of the most deadly weapons used against them."[9]

Although both conservatives and progressives correctly perceived that public criticism of the courts increased markedly after about 1906, the roots of public discontent with the courts stretched back two decades. Even though public criticism of the judiciary reached new levels of intensity during the height of the Progressive Era, the widespread judicial animus against social reform had already begun to attract a notable degree of hostility during the waning years of the nineteenth century.

The seeds of progressive discontent with the courts were sown in 1873 when the four dissenters in the *Slaughterhouse Cases* argued that Louisiana's regulation of slaughterhouses contravened the Fourteenth Amendment by violating the economic rights of New Orleans abattoirs who were adversely affected by the legislation.[10] Although the dissenters accepted the well-established doctrine that the state may exercise its "police power" to protect the welfare and safety of its citizens, the dissent argued that the scope of the due process clause of the Fourteenth Amendment significantly circumscribed the scope of the police power. According to the dissenters, "due process" not only embraced the procedural protections in judicial proceedings that traditionally had defined due process but also placed limitations on the content and substance of legislation. While state and federal courts in earlier decisions had recognized that due process might limit legislative power over the use of private property,[11] the seminal dissents of Justices Stephen J. Field and Joseph P. Bradley in the *Slaughterhouse Cases* articulated a clearer and broader scope for the doctrine that Bradley called "substantive due process."

The extent to which courts could place substantive limitations upon legislation became increasingly important during the years after 1873 when growing agricultural and industrial unrest led to the enactment of numerous laws to regulate economic activities. After a series of decisions in which the Supreme Court gradually recognized the merits of substantive due process,[12] in 1890 the Court held that a Minnesota

[9] Lodge, "Constitution and Its Makers," p. 36. Similarly, the *New York Times* contended in 1907 that recent criticism of the courts was more unrestrained and more bitter than were previous criticisms ("Courts and People").

[10] *Slaughterhouse Cases*, 83 U.S. (16 Wall.) 36, 83–130 (1873).

[11] See *Wynehamer v. New York*, 13 N.Y. 378 (1856); *Dred Scott v. Sandford*, 60 U.S. (19 How.) 393 (1857); *Hepburn v. Griswold*, 75 U.S. (8 Wall.) 603 (1870).

[12] Although the Court during this period upheld regulatory legislation, the Court became increasingly assertive in its reminders that it could review the reasonableness of statutes that regulated economic activity. See *Munn v. Illinois*, 94 U.S. 113 (1877); *Railroad Commission Cases*, 116 U.S. 307 (1886); *Mugler v. Kansas*, 123 U.S. 623 (1887). The Court

rail-rate statute violated the Fourteenth Amendment because the statute failed to provide for judicial review. The reasonableness of the rates set by the commission, the Court declared, was "eminently a question for judicial investigation."[13] Even though the Court during the next few years upheld regulatory legislation enacted by New York, North Dakota, and Texas, the Court's opinions in those cases confirmed that the Court would continue to act as the arbiter of whether state legislation constituted a reasonable exercise of the police power.[14] The Court's transformation of the Constitution from "a charter of powers . . . into a bill of limitations" enhanced the prominence and power of the Court.[15] This inevitably embroiled the Court in greater controversy and made it a target of criticism among reformers.

At the same time that the Supreme Court was developing its doctrine of substantive due process, state courts were forging similar theories to scrutinize the constitutionality of state regulations of private enterprise. Like the federal courts, the state courts often did not defer to the wisdom of the legislatures. In a landmark decision in 1885, for example, the New York Court of Appeals unanimously struck down a statute that had attempted to protect the health of low paid workers by prohibiting the manufacture of cigars in tenement houses.[16] Disagreeing with the conclusions of a legislative committee that had studied conditions in the sweatshops, the court concluded that the law bore no relation to health or safety and arbitrarily interfered with property rights.

During the next several years, as the growth of agrarian discontent frightened conservatives, judicial hostility toward labor and reform legislation grew more intense.[17] Between 1880 and 1900, state courts invalidated approximately five dozen labor laws, including measures

---

took another long stride toward protection of wealth when it ruled in 1886 that corporations were "persons" within the meaning of the Fourteenth Amendment. *Santa Clara County v. Southern Pacific Railroad*, 118 U.S. 394, 396 (1886).

[13] *Chicago, Milwaukee, and St. Paul Railway Co. v. Minnesota*, 134 U.S. 418, 458 (1890).

[14] *Budd v. New York*, 143 U.S. 517 (1892); *Brass v. North Dakota*, 153 U.S. 391 (1894); *Reagan v. Farmers Loan and Trust Co.*, 154 U.S. 362 (1894).

[15] Loren P. Beth, *The Development of the American Constitution, 1877–1917* (New York: Harper and Row, 1971), pp. 42–43.

[16] *In the Matter of Jacobs*, 98 N.Y. 98 (1885).

[17] Arnold M. Paul, *Conservative Crisis and the Rule of Law: Attitudes of Bar and Bench, 1887–1895* (1960; repr. Gloucester, Mass.: Peter Smith, 1976), p. 45. Similarly, Professor Fiss contends that the fear that "America was at the edge of revolution" explains "much of the Supreme Court's work of the early 1890s." Owen M. Fiss, *Oliver Wendell Holmes Devise History of the Supreme Court of the United States, vol. 8, Troubled Beginnings of the Modern State, 1888–1910* (New York: Macmillan) (galleys), p. 53. Unlike Paul, who argued that the Court rationalized its class interests, Fiss contends more persuasively that the Court was attempting to "explicate and protect" a dubious constitutional theory of individual liberty. *Ibid.*, p. 19.

that prohibited discrimination against union members, forbade payment of wages in script, required regular payment of wages, regulated hours, and limited the use of the power of contempt to punish violations of injunctions. During the same period, state courts upheld only about two dozen such laws.[18]

Judicial attempts to constrict the scope of the police power attracted widespread disapproval among lawyers, who retained a resilient tradition of egalitarianism and antimonopolism.[19] The nascent populist movement also questioned judicial power. In his 1892 manifesto, *A Call to Action*, James B. Weaver devoted a long chapter to criticism of the Supreme Court's solicitude toward corporate interests and its alleged arrogation of the power of judicial review. In language that progressives would echo, Weaver warned that the elevation of judicial power over legislative power "dethrones the people who should be Sovereign and enthrones an oligarchy." Like earlier and later antagonists of the federal judiciary, Weaver called for "new safeguards" to restore the Court's "sense of accountability to the people." In particular, Weaver favored abrogation of judicial review "or at least . . . some modification of present judicial pretensions," and he opposed the appointment of judges and lifetime judicial tenure. However, Weaver did not advocate any specific plan to curb judicial power, and he seemed to retain hope that judicial restraint would restore public confidence in the Supreme Court, which he regarded as "the hope and refuge of the people."[20] The platform on which Weaver ran as the presidential candidate of the newly formed People's party in 1892 did not contain any plank that criticized the judiciary or called for any abrogation of judicial power.[21]

Criticism of the courts flourished briefly during the unhappy years of the second Cleveland administration when a number of judicial decisions roiled public waters troubled by an economic depression and widespread labor unrest. By early 1895, one observer of judicial issues warned that "the federal judiciary is in great danger from itself" and that Congress might abolish the lower federal courts if the courts were not shorn of their arbitrary power.[22] Several Supreme Court decisions

[18] William E. Forbath, "The Shaping of the American Labor Movement," *Harvard Law Review* 102 (April 1989): 1237–43.

[19] Paul, *Conservative Crisis*, pp. 4, 61–81, 221–37.

[20] James B. Weaver, *A Call to Action* (Des Moines: Des Moines Printing Co., 1892), pp. 67–135; 74–75; 86.

[21] Donald Bruce Johnson, ed., *National Party Platforms*, vol. 1, *1840–1956* (Champaign: University of Illinois Press, 1978), pp. 89–91. The preamble to the platform contended, however, that the corruption that was alleged to dominate Congress and the legislatures "touches even the ermine of the bench"; ibid., p. 89.

[22] Henry Wollman, "The Danger of the Federal Judiciary," *North American Review*, March 1895, p. 377.

in 1895 were the subject of particular controversy since the Court in each of those cases expounded an interpretation of the Constitution favoring the plutocracy that had flourished during the three decades since the end of the Civil War.

In the first case, the Court appeared to emasculate the Sherman Antitrust Act, holding that the defendants had not violated the anti-trust laws even though they controlled more than 90 percent of the manufacture of refined sugar in the United States. Acknowledging that the defendants had combined to monopolize the manufacture of sugar, the Court contended that the antitrust laws did not apply to manufacturing activities because the Constitution gave Congress only the power to regulate interstate commerce.[23] In two decisions in April and May 1895, the Court overturned a century of precedent to invalidate a federal income tax that farm and labor interests had vigorously championed.[24]

One week after its second decision invalidating the income tax, the Court dealt another defeat to labor when it upheld a prison sentence against Eugene V. Debs, the socialist leader of the American Railway Union who had been convicted of violating a federal injunction against disorder during a strike.[25] The Court ruled that the federal courts had broad powers under the supremacy and commerce clauses to issue injunctions to prevent obstructions to interstate commerce or transportation of the mails. The Court's narrow definition of governmental powers in the *Sugar Trust* and *Income Tax* decisions contrasted sharply with its expansive definition of governmental powers in *Debs*. That contrast seemed to underscore the Court's tendency to use the law as a shield for business and a sword against labor.

Although reaction against the decision in *Debs* was primarily confined to the ranks of trade unionists, the Court's decisions in the *Sugar Trust Case* and the *Income Tax Cases* dismayed a broad cross section of public opinion. The tone for the criticism of the *Sugar Trust Case* was set by the vehement dissent of Justice John Marshall Harlan, who declared that the Court's decision abandoned the public to "the mercy of combinations." Harlan protested that "the general government is not placed by the Constitution in such a condition of helplessness that it must fold its arms and remain inactive while capital combines . . . to destroy competition."[26]

Harlan's opinion was widely echoed by critics of the decision who

[23] *United States v. E.C. Knight Co.*, 156 U.S. 1 (1895).
[24] *Pollock v. Farmer's Loan and Trust Co.*, 157 U.S. 429 (1895); *Pollock v. Farmers Loan and Trust Co.*, 158 U.S. 601 (1895).
[25] *In re Debs*, 158 U.S. 564 (1895).
[26] 156 U.S. at 43 (Harlan dissenting).

alleged that it emasculated governmental attempts to protect the public from predatory business practices. Ardemus Stewart of the *American Law Register* declared that "if this decision stands . . . then this government is a failure, and the sooner the social and political revolution which many far-sighted men can see already darkening the horizon overtakes us, the better."[27] Seymour D. Thompson, editor of the *American Law Review*, denounced the decision as "the most deplorable one that has been rendered in favor of incorporated power and greed, and against popular right, since the Dartmouth College case."[28] The *Income Tax* decision was likewise widely execrated, with Justices Harlan and Henry B. Brown firing the first volleys in their dissents. Harlan denounced the ruling as a "judicial revolution," and Brown warned that the decision might be "the first step toward the submergence of the liberties of the people in a sordid despotism of wealth."[29] *The American Law Review* declared that the justices lacked any "adequate idea of the dividing line between judicial and legislative power."[30]

Even though this triad of decisions dismayed populists, trade unionists, and other proponents of social changes, they triggered fewer protests and proposals for fundamental changes in the federal judiciary than the unpopular decisions of the 1910s and the 1920s. The American Federation of Labor, for example, reacted with an equanimity that sharply contrasted with its vitriolic denunciation of pro-business decisions during the 1910s and 1920s. A columnist in the *American Federationist* characterized the Supreme Court's decisions in the *Income Tax Cases* as "cowardly," an adjective that pales beside the invective with which trade unionists skewered later decisions of the Court.[31] The AFL accepted even the *Debs* decision with relative calm.[32]

The remedies that organized labor proposed for responding to these decisions were likewise temperate. The AFL responded to *Debs* and other injunction cases by proposing legislation to impose limitations on the power of federal courts to impose punishment for contempt of court. Although the *American Federationist* alleged that the courts were "addicted to the usurpation of legislative functions," it advocated no

---

[27] Ardemus Stewart, ed., "Progress of the Law," *American Law Register* 43 (February 1895): 90. See also Ardemus Stewart, "The Irresponsibility of the Judiciary," ibid., June 1895, pp. 383–88.

[28] *American Law Review* 29 (March–April 1895): 306. In *Dartmouth College v. Woodward*, 4 Wheaton 518 (1819), the Supreme Court had provided the constitutional foundations for judicial protection of corporations by holding that a corporate charter was a contract that a state legislature could not arbitrarily alter.

[29] *Pollock*, 158 U.S. 665 (Harlan dissenting), 695 (Brown dissenting).

[30] *American Law Review* 29 (March–April 1895): 428.

[31] S. B. Hoefgen, "Income Tax Decision," *American Federationist*, June 1895, p. 58.

[32] Editorial, "The Debs Case," *American Federationist*, June 1895, p. 68.

general abrogation of jurisdiction.[33] One trade unionist proposed in 1895 that the ballot box was the remedy for antilabor decisions. Observing that judges primarily associated with a class of persons who opposed the income tax or a more equitable distribution of the products of labor, he explained that the people must attempt to elect a president who would select judges "who will be swayed by the many rather than by the few with whom they have personal intercourse."[34]

The moderation of the responses of organized labor to hostile judicial decisions demonstrated in part the numerical and financial weakness of organized labor and the parlous social and legal status of trade unions. The AFL's caution also reflected its transformation from a class-based union that advocated broad social reforms to a more narrow craft union that eschewed politics and attempted to work within the capitalist system as an independent power that did not need to rely upon indulgence from the state.

Although many historians have traditionally attributed this "pure and simple" trade unionism to an inherent conservatism that distinguished the AFL from the more radical and class-conscious unions of Europe, William E. Forbath has argued persuasively that the AFL's retreat from politics was deeply influenced by judicial hostility toward labor. In the face of so many broken strikes and so much nullified legislation, the AFL concluded that "what worked was not radical reforms or inclusive unions but minimalist politics, craft unionism, and restrained but staunch strike policies."[35] Labor's voluntarism, Forbath contends, was "a constrained but canny response to the inescapable power of the courts and common law over labor's fortunes."[36] The AFL also feared that political activism would permit politicians to exploit the unions.[37] Moreover, it feared that advocacy of measures that transcended the immediate needs of the unions would vitiate the union movement, which needed to conserve its limited resources.[38]

[33] Editorial, "Crimes Against Judges," *American Federationist*, December 1895, p. 171. The bill sponsored by the AFL would have deprived the federal courts when sitting as courts of equity to punish for contempt when the contempt charged was the violation of an order or decree of the court or when the contempt charged made the offender the principal in or accessory to a crime.

[34] Hoefgen, "Income Tax Decision."

[35] Forbath, "Shaping of American Labor," pp. 1133–49, 1177–79; William E. Forbath, "Courts, Constitutions and Labor Policies in England and America: A Study of the Constructive Power of Law," *Law and Social Inquiry* 16 (Winter 1991): 1–34.

[36] Forbath, "Shaping of American Labor," p. 1208.

[37] William M. Dick, *Labor and Socialism in America: The Gompers Era* (Port Washington, N.Y.: Kennikat Press, 1972), p. 35.

[38] Samuel P. Hays, *The Response to Industrialism, 1885–1914* (Chicago: University of Chicago Press, 1957), p. 66.

Motivated by a desire to achieve respectability, Samuel Gompers and other union leaders also sought to dissociate themselves from any taint of lawlessness.[39] In an era when prevalent business and political opinion denied the legitimacy of union representation and the violence of many labor protests had created widespread distrust of union aims, it did not behoove responsible union leaders to advocate fundamental abrogations of judicial power. The AFL was influenced by Marxism to the extent that it believed that labor and capital were engaged in a class struggle, but its national leadership and most of its constituent organizations rejected socialism and became so suspicious of statism that the AFL disfavored even much meliorative social legislation. For many years during the early twentieth century, for example, Gompers opposed federal wages-and-hours legislation and social insurance measures.[40] Gompers worried that such measures would increase judicial power over labor.[41] Since the AFL generally did not advocate reform legislation, it had no reason to seek curtailment of the power of judicial review. The AFL asked only that the courts remove impediments to union organization.

During the 1890s and early 1900s, the judiciary seemed to be removing those impediments. Labor's belief that the courts were gradually developing a more tolerant attitude toward unionization was reflected in the reluctance of labor leaders to advocate fundamental judicial reforms, including abrogation of the power of judicial review. In particular, judicial refusal to invoke conspiracy laws against unions represented a major advance for the unions. One trade unionist, for example, observed that even in the *Debs* decision the Court "went out of its way to declare most earnestly that the right of labor to strike in a body is not challenged by the courts, however great may be the injury to the employer thus crippled."[42]

Labor's sanguine attitude toward the courts, however, was tempered by the growing tendency of the courts to use the injunction to interfere with strikes. The courts enjoined approximately 10 percent of sympathy strikes during the 1880s and 15 percent during the 1890s.[43] Gompers, who denounced the growing use of injunctions as "simply

[39] Daniel Bell, "The Great Totem," in Gerald Emanuel Stearn, ed., *Gompers* (Englewood Cliffs, N.J.: Prentice-Hall, 1971), p. 157.

[40] Bernard Mandel, *Samuel Gompers* (Yellow Springs, Ohio: Antioch Press, 1963), pp. 177–79; Philip Taft, *The A.F. of L. in the Time of Gompers* (New York: Octagon, 1970), pp. 146–48; Chambers, *Tyranny of Change*, p. 63.

[41] Bell, "Great Totem," p. 154.

[42] Victor Yarros, "Labor's Rights in the Courts," *American Federationist*, November 1896, p. 181.

[43] Forbath, "Shaping of American Labor," p. 1249.

outrageous" and "a gross perversion" of judicial power, argued that the use of injunctions was worse than the old conspiracy laws since conspiracy cases were heard by a jury. Yet even Gompers proposed a moderate remedy—the right to a jury trial in contempt cases.[44]

Moderation characterized virtually all the AFL's discussions of judicial power during the 1890s. Although the *American Federationist* urged "the smashing of some rotten constitutional planks" that had led to annulment of pro-labor legislation, this seemed to envision constitutional amendments rather than any curb on judicial power.[45] Labor's proposals for remedies at the state level likewise did not strike at fundamental aspects of judicial power. An editorial in the *American Federationist* in 1894, for example, proposed the adoption of the initiative and referendum in state government.[46]

Populists tended to be somewhat more vociferous than organized labor in their denunciation of the courts. Like Weaver, many populists questioned the power of the federal courts to review the constitutionality of legislation. During 1895 and 1896, for example, Governor Sylvester Pennoyer of Oregon published articles in which he challenged the power of the courts to review the constitutionality of legislation.[47] Pennoyer accused the Court of having "usurped the legislative prerogative of declaring what the laws shall not be" and alleged that "our constitutional government has been supplanted by a judicial oligarchy." Pennoyer urged Congress to impeach and remove from office the justices who voted against the constitutionality of the income tax and to instruct the president to enforce the collection of the tax.[48]

Although Pennoyer's hostility toward the Court may have been inspired in part by his pique over having lost a case before that tribunal,[49] other populists advocated measures to curtail judicial power. For example, former congressman James M. Ashley called for a constitutional amendment to permit Congress to reenact federal statutes that the Supreme Court had nullified.[50] A more widely favored remedy was the

[44] "Government by Injunction," *American Federationist*, June 1897, p. 82 (repr. from *Washington Post*).

[45] Editorial, "Constitutional Farce," *American Federationist*, July 1895, p. 90.

[46] Editorial, "Direct Legislation," *American Federationist*, June 1894, p. 77.

[47] Sylvester Pennoyer, "The Income Tax Decision and the Power of the Supreme Court to Nullify Acts of Congress," *American Law Review* 29 (July–August 1895): 550–58; "The Power of the Supreme Court to Declare an Act of Congress Unconstitutional: The Case of Marbury v. Madison," *American Law Review* 30 (March–April 1896): 188–202.

[48] Pennoyer, "Income Tax Decision," p. 558.

[49] Wendy Collins Perdue, "Sin, Scandal, and Substantive Due Process: Personal Jurisdiction and *Pennoyer* Reconsidered," *Washington Law Review* 62 (July 1987): 488–89.

[50] James M. Ashley, "Should the Supreme Court be Reorganized?" *The Arena*, October

election of federal judges. Walter Clark, an associate justice of the North Carolina Supreme Court who had strong ties to the People's party, was one of the most prominent and outspoken advocates of the election of federal judges. Disparaging the federal bench as the "stronghold of the money power," Clark declared in 1896 that the Court's decisions on injunctions and the federal income tax had "rudely broken public confidence in the federal judiciary and necessitate its reconstitution on modern lines," with the election of judges for limited terms. Clark proposed that the chief justice should be elected in the same manner as the president and that the Union should be divided into election districts for the selection of associate justices.[51]

Clark, who served as an associate justice on the North Carolina Supreme Court from 1889 until 1903 and as chief justice from 1903 until his death in 1924, remained a vocal critic of the courts throughout his life. Although Clark was not the most scholarly or politically powerful antagonist of the federal courts during the first quarter of the twentieth century, he was surely the most persistent and prolific. In innumerable speeches and articles, Clark called for various reforms to make the courts more responsive to the popular will. In 1898 and again in 1903 he published articles in the *American Law Review*, the leading law periodical of the day, in which he reiterated his proposal for election of federal judges and called for a constitutional convention.[52] As we shall see in chapters 7 and 9, Clark later became a leading advocate of the curtailment of judicial review. His position as chief judicial officer of a relatively large state made his pronouncements especially resonant. Clark was the only prominent judge of his period who had the temerity to publicly attack the conservatism of his judicial brethren, denigrate the Constitution, and question the doctrine of judicial review.

Clark's antagonism toward the courts, especially the federal courts, reflected his background. As a scion of wealthy planters and a proud veteran of the Confederate army, Clark never wavered in his dedication to states' rights, and he feared that industrialism would corrupt the South. Although he advocated the economic development of the South, Clark sought to spare his state from the worst abuses of modern capitalism. Adhering to a highly egalitarian political philosophy, Clark believed in activist government to remedy social ills and promote the

---

1895, pp. 221–22. Ashley also contended that the Court should not have the power to nullify federal statutes by a bare majority.

[51] Walter Clark, "If Silver Wins: II. Inevitable Constitutional Changes," *North American Review*, October 1896, pp. 464–65.

[52] Walter Clark, "The Revision of the Constitution of the United States," *American Law Review* 32 (January–February 1898): 1–13; Walter Clark, "Law and Human Progress," *American Law Review* 37 (July–August 1903): 512, 517–19.

public welfare. Throughout his public career, he was a sharp critic of the business interests that held sway in North Carolina. Although the tobacco and railroad interests actively opposed Clark's bids for the chief justiceship, he was regularly reelected by large margins.[53]

Although most populists shared a distrust of the federal judiciary, not all were as fierce as Clark in their denunciations of the courts. The widely circulated journal published by Tom Watson, for example, generally ignored the courts.[54] Although populist members of Congress introduced various bills to curb judicial power,[55] the only anticourt measure that received serious attention during this period was a proposal for the election of federal judges.[56]

Like organized labor, the populists may have muted their antagonism toward the courts because they recognized that the judiciary could serve as an ally of their movement. As Norman Pollack has pointed out, the populists deeply respected the Supreme Court's "potentiality as the bulwark of popular rights." For example, Weaver believed that the courts provided a source of peaceful settlement of social conflict.[57]

A growing antagonism toward the judiciary was reflected in the 1896 presidential campaign in which the Supreme Court's labor and income tax decisions emerged as election issues. Since many populists believed that those decisions sharpened the "crown of thorns" that William Jennings Bryan alleged that plutocrats were trying to "press down upon the brow of labor," the free-silver crusaders did not spare the

[53] See Aubrey Lee Brooks, *Walter Clark: Fighting Judge* (Chapel Hill: University of North Carolina Press, 1944).

[54] See *People's Party Paper*, 1891–1898.

[55] A bill introduced by Senator Wilkinson Call, a Florida Democrat, sought "to prevent the oppressive exercise of judicial power in the Courts of the United States"; S. 1729, 54th Cong., 1st sess., 1895. Senator William A. Peffer, a Kansas Populist, introduced a bill to protect the rights of defendants in injunction cases; S. 237, ibid. and Representative Charles J. Boatner, a Louisiana Democrat, sponsored legislation to limit judicial power to punish for contempt of court; H.R. 311, ibid. Another measure would have prevented the Court from nullifying any federal statute without the concurrence of all of the justices. Maurice A. Culp, "A Survey of the Proposals to Limit or Deny the Power of Judicial Review by the Supreme Court of the United States," *Indiana Law Journal* 4 (March 1929): 396.

[56] Culp, "Survey of Proposals," p. 396.

[57] Norman Pollack, *The Just Polity: Populism, Law and Human Welfare* (Urbana: University of Illinois Press, 1987), p. 64. Moreover, populists generally were not greatly dismayed by the Court's narrow construction of the Sherman Act in Knight. Although opposition to monopoly was a central component of the progressive movement in its efforts to restore social harmony and individualism, Owen M. Fiss has pointed out that "populists had little interest in the Sherman Act" because populists, unlike progressives, did not seek to "restore the competitive ethic." Fiss, *Troubled Beginnings*, p. 111 (galleys).

Court from criticism. The Democratic platform expressed objection "to government by injunction as a new and highly dangerous form of oppression by which Federal Judges . . . become at once legislators, judges and executioners," and the platform supported pending federal legislation to provide for trial by jury in certain cases of contempt. The Democratic platform also blamed the national deficit on the Court's decisions in the *Income Tax Cases,* which the platform derided for overruling nearly a century of its own precedents. Rather than calling for an amendment to overturn the decision, the platform declared that it was the duty of Congress to use whatever constitutional power remained to it "or which may come from its reversal by the court as it may hereinafter be constituted" to ensure an equitable allocation of taxation. Similarly, the People's party platform declared that the *Income Tax* decision was "a misinterpretation of the Constitution and an invasion of the rightful powers of Congress over the subject of taxation."[58]

As the indefatigable Bryan campaigned through the nation, he frequently implied that the Court's decisions had tightened the yoke of oppression from which he promised to free the people. In contrast to Theodore Roosevelt in 1912 and Robert La Follette in 1924, however, the Great Commoner proposed no institutional changes and generally eschewed the acerbic rhetoric with which later reformers would assail the courts. Bryan believed that criticism of the courts would bolster Republican warnings that he was a revolutionary, and he apparently made a conscious effort to demonstrate that he did not challenge judicial authority. In the legendary "Cross of Gold" speech that clinched his nomination, for example, Bryan denied that populists had criticized the Court. Rebuking conservatives who "criticize us for our criticism of the Supreme Court," Bryan protested that populists had merely called attention to the Court's inconsistency and had defended the justice of an income tax.[59] Similarly, Bryan declared in his acceptance speech that "we expressly recognize the binding force of that decision so long as it stands as a part of the law of the land" and that the Democratic platform contained "no suggestion of an attempt to dispute the authority of the Supreme Court."[60]

Bryan's apparent belief that any general attacks on the judiciary would backfire suggests that public discontent with the courts was lim-

---

[58] Johnson, *National Party Platforms,* vol. 1, pp. 98, 99, 105. Although the People's party nominated William Jennings Bryan for president, Bryan did not accept that party's platform.

[59] Arthur Schlesinger, Jr., ed., *History of American Presidential Elections,* vol. 2, *1789–1968* (New York: Chelsea House, 1971), p. 1847.

[60] Ibid., p. 1853.

ited to disagreement with the outcome of specific decisions and did not involve any general hostility toward the courts. Although Bryan's circumspection may have also reflected his own distaste for fundamental changes in the judicial system, Bryan's outspoken criticism of the courts in later decades suggests that his reticence during the 1896 campaign was dictated more by politics than by principle. In 1902, for example, Bryan privately expressed support for the election of federal judges but explained, "I have not thought it wise to crowd too many reforms at once, and at this time when we are likely to have a struggle to hold the ground we have already taken, it would . . . be inopportune to push this question upon which the people have not had time to think."[61]

Even though Bryan and most of his supporters were circumspect in their remarks about the judiciary, the Republicans throughout the 1896 election campaign attempted to exploit Democratic criticism of the courts. In his letter accepting the nomination, for example, William McKinley vowed that his party would vanquish "the sudden, dangerous and revolutionary assault upon law and order."[62] McKinley's ominous warnings were expressed with greater bluntness by many of his supporters.[63]

Meanwhile, the platform of a hastily organized group of anti-Bryan Democrats, the National Democratic party, vowed support for the independence and authority of the Supreme Court and condemned "all efforts to degrade that tribunal or impair the confidence and respect which it has deservedly held."[64]

[61] William Jennings Bryan to Walter Clark, April 7, 1902, *The Papers of Walter Clark*, vol. 2, ed. Aubrey Lee Brooks and Hugh Talmage Leflar (Chapel Hill: University of North Carolina Press, 1950), p. 9.

[62] "Mr. McKinley Accepts," *New York Times*, August 27, 1896, p. 1.

[63] Former president Benjamin Harrison told a mass rally at Carnegie Hall that no issue was more important than the Democratic proposal for "prostituting the power and duty of the national courts and national Executive." Harrison declared that the tariff and bimetallism issues would "be of little moment if our constitutional government is overthrown." He interpreted the Democratic platform to call for the packing of the Supreme Court whenever the Court's interpretation of a law displeased Congress. "Gen. Harrison Heard," *New York Times*, August 28, 1896, p. 1. Archbishop John Ireland of St. Paul, Minnesota, accused the Democrats of attempting to strip the courts of their power and warned that this reckless scheme might light up in the country the lurid fires of a 'commune'" (*Current Opinion*, October 22, 1896, p. 517). The industrialist Chauncey M. DePew alleged that Bryan proposed to "abolish the Supreme Court and make it the creature of the party caucus whenever a new congress comes in." DePew, *Speeches and Addresses of Chauncey M. DePew* (New York, 1898), p. 62. For a detailed discussion of editorial and other public reaction to the Democratic platform, see Alan F. Westin, "The Supreme Court, the Populist Movement and the Campaign of 1896," *Journal of Politics* 15 (1953): 30–39.

[64] Johnson, *National Party Platforms*, vol. 1, p. 103.

As part of the campaign of distortion that the Republicans waged against Bryan, some Republicans alleged that the Democratic platform advocated the abolition of judicial review. An article in the *North American Review*, for example, alleged that the Democratic platform vowed to reduce the Court "to a mere creature of legislative will and subject it to the dangerous influence of party expediency or caprice" because Democrats recognized that the Court would annul any free-silver legislation. Distorting the careful language of the platform, which specifically stated that Congress would remain within the bounds laid down by the Court, the article condemned the platform for favoring "doctrines which are utterly repugnant to the principles of constitutional government," promoting "a dangerous innovation" and "a revolutionary spirit," and striking "at the very root of our system of government."[65]

Shortly after the election, Lodge argued that the platform embodied a demand "for making the courts a mere mouthpiece of the victorious political party."[66] Similarly, Andrew Carnegie contended that the Democratic platform's criticisms of the Supreme Court, together with its denunciation of injunctions and its class consciousness, were even more dangerous than its free-silver proposal. Carnegie contended that "the country could undergo the loss and misery certain to flow from a dangerous experiment with money, but the triumph of these revolutionary issues would have been fatal to its life as a nation founded upon law."[67]

The judicial issue no doubt cost Bryan some votes, although most voters who were frightened by Republican characterizations of the Democratic party's court planks were probably also so frightened of Bryan's inflationary schemes that they would still not have voted for him.[68] An article in the *Yale Review* following the election concluded that Bryan's defeat was "undoubtedly due in part" to the Democratic platform's "attack upon the Supreme Court."[69]

[65] George A. Benham, "Notes and Comments: The Supreme Court of the United States," *North American Review*, October 1896, pp. 506–7.

[66] Henry Cabot Lodge, "The Meaning of the Votes," *North American Review*, January 1897, pp. 2–3.

[67] Andrew Carnegie, "Mr. Bryan the Conjurer," *North American Review*, January 1897, pp. 106–7.

[68] Alan Westin has pointed out that press comment after the election demonstrates that the judicial issue was a significant component in the election. Many newspapers interpreted the outcome as representing popular support for maintaining the power of the courts. Westin, "Campaign of 1896," p. 38.

[69] The article argued that many voters who supported the free-silver plank and "were ready to fall in line with Bryan and his followers, drew back when they realized that the programme included an assault upon the 'bulwark of the Constitution' or an attempt to still its 'living voice.'" Thomas Thacher, "Limits of Constitutional Law," *Yale Review* 6 (May 1897): 7.

Yet while Republican misrepresentations of the Democratic platform may have cost the Democrats some votes, the Democrats might have gained votes if their criticism of specific unpopular decisions had been more forceful. One assessment of the election has suggested that Bryan "grossly underplayed two planks of wide appeal to Eastern workers and union members—government by injunction and the income tax." Bryan's decision to make free silver the paramount issue of the campaign pleased Republican managers, who may have recognized that the injunction and income tax issues might have had wider appeal.[70] Although any criticism of the courts would have provoked more apocalyptic forecasts from the Republicans, Bryan might have minimized the impact of such warnings by confining his criticism to a few narrow issues and emphasizing his fidelity to judicial review and other constitutional principles. The virulent Republican response to the benign criticism of the courts in the Democratic platform, however, appears to have persuaded Bryan that any additional criticism would be too dangerous. Bryan's failure to say more about the courts during the campaign must ultimately be attributed to his fixation with the silver issue.

The return of prosperity and the diminution of class tensions that followed the 1896 election reduced criticism of the judiciary. During the final years of the old century and the first years of the new century, the courts continued to chart a highly uneven course in their review of regulatory legislation and their attitudes toward organized labor. On the whole, however, proponents of social and economic reform had reason to discern a positive trend in judicial decisions. Starting in 1899, the Supreme Court diminished the impact of the *Sugar Trust* decision by ruling that manufacturers had violated the antitrust laws when their activities had a demonstrable impact on interstate commerce.[71] In a subsequent antitrust case decided in 1905, the Court held that a meat-packer's activities fell within the regulation of the antitrust laws because the defendant's stockyards were part of interstate commerce.[72] During the following year, the Court further extended the scope of the antitrust laws by accepting the argument that the merger of two large railroads was unlawful.[73]

At the same time that the Court was adjudicating the first antitrust cases, however, the Court was perfecting the doctrine of substantive due process. In 1897, a quarter century after the dissenters in the

[70] Louis W. Koenig, *Bryan: A Political Biography of William Jennings Bryan* (New York: G. P. Putnam, 1971), p. 225.

[71] *Addyston Pipe & Steel Co. v. United States*, 175 U.S. 211 (1899).

[72] *Swift & Co. v. United States*, 196 U.S. 375 (1905).

[73] *Northern Securities Co. v. United States*, 193 U.S. 197 (1904).

Slaughterhouse Cases had begun the transformation of the Fourteenth Amendment by arguing that the due process clause imposes limits on governmental regulation of business, the Court in *Allgeyer v. Louisiana* finally gave formal recognition to that doctrine. The Court explained that liberty included more than freedom from physical restraint of the person; it also embraced "the right of the citizen to be free in the enjoyment of all of his faculties," to select his occupation and his place of work, and to enter into any contracts that might be "proper, necessary and essential" for the advancement of his calling.[74]

Although substantive due process provided courts with a weapon against liberal legislation, the Court's benign use of this doctrine in the first years following *Allgeyer* did not provide the moribund populist movement and the nascent progressive movement with much cause for criticism. In 1898, for example, the Court in *Holden v. Hardy* upheld a Utah law that established an eight-hour limit on the daily hours of miners.[75] The decision was significant not only because it liberally interpreted the scope of the police power but also because it recognized that employees and employers did not have equal bargaining power.[76] The *American Federationist* hailed the decision as "a land mark in our economic and judicial history" and declared that the decision was "of the greatest importance to organized labor in this country."[77] Five years later, the Court upheld a Kansas statute that established the same limitation on the hours of persons employed on public works projects.[78]

The decline in visible public dissatisfaction with the courts further suggests that popular discontent with the judiciary was largely directed against individual decisions and usually did not involve hostility against judges as a class or the doctrine of judicial review. Writing in the *Yale Review* in 1896, a Boston attorney of reformist impulses contended that judicial decisions annulling popular state legislation, like executive vetoes, "are by no means unpopular with the masses of the people. The American public understands its constitution, and admires courage; and when a court annuls a measure as unconstitutional, its rejection is frequently taken as final. In some cases, new bills are framed to meet

[74] *Allgeyer v. Louisiana*, 165 U.S. 578 (1897). The Court struck down a Louisiana statute that had prohibited companies that were not licensed to do business in that state from selling insurance for any property located within the state.

[75] *Holden v. Hardy*, 169 U.S. 366 (1898). By upholding special protection of workers in a highly hazardous occupation, the decision was consistent with the traditional doctrine that the police power could be exercised to protect public health, safety, welfare, or morals. See Fiss, *Troubled Beginnings*, pp. 172–74 (galleys).

[76] Melvin I. Urofsky, "Myth and Reality: The Supreme Court and Protective Legislation in the Progressive Era," *Yearbook 1983, Supreme Court Historical Society*, pp. 61–62.

[77] *American Federationist*, April 1898, pp. 23, 25.

[78] *Atkin v. Kansas*, 191 U.S. 207 (1903).

the court's objections, but always good naturedly, by the agitators for new legislation."[79] Similarly, an editorial in the *American Federationist* in March 1901 declared that "in the last three or four years there has manifested itself in our courts a remarkable tendency toward the application of modern, enlightened principles to controversies between labor and capital." Although the editorial acknowledged that labor still had far to go in overcoming judicial hostility, it expressed guarded optimism about the ability of the judiciary to respond to changing conditions and averred that extreme decisions "serve organized labor's purpose by discrediting the old doctrines and commending the new ones to fair-minded judges and legislators."[80]

Although these articles correctly perceived that public respect for the judiciary remained solid and that agitation for fundamental institutional changes was not yet likely to attract a favorable reception, they may have underestimated the depth of popular frustration over judicial nullification of legislation. A more realistic estimation of the popular mood at the end of the century was perhaps provided by the president of the Georgia Bar Association, who declared in 1898 that "there are unmistakable signs of profound public dissatisfaction at the more recent attitude of the Federal judiciary toward some of the most burning questions of the hour." Although he acknowledged that Americans "are prone to acquiesce in the decisions of their courts," he warned that they would continue to respect the judiciary only "so long as these courts obey the law and give effect to the rights of the weak as well as the strong."[81]

The increasing zeal with which conservative judges used the injunction to restrict the activities of labor unions remained a particular source of discontent that tested even the patience of the long-suffering leaders of the AFL. Although many labor leaders rejoiced over decisions, such as *Holden v. Hardy*, that evinced a judicial willingness to tolerate legislative regulations that favored labor, they perceived that the expanded use of the injunction threatened the very foundations of the labor movement. Deploring the trend toward "government by injunction," a writer in the *American Federationist* in February 1899 declared that a "few years ago labor had reason to congratulate itself upon having vindicated its rights as against judicial quibbling and con-

[79] F. J. Stimson, "Recent Economic and Social Legislation in the United States," *Yale Review* 5 (November 1896): 254.

[80] "Conflicting Decisions on Labor's Rights," *American Federationist*, March 1901, p. 80, 81.

[81] John W. Akin, "Aggressions of the Federal Courts," *American Law Review* 32 (September–October 1898): 696.

servatism. . . . Today . . . the old prejudices are being revived and once more we hear that unions are trusts and conspiracies."[82] Several more years of "government by injunction" led the attorney and social activist Louis F. Post to declare in the *American Federationist* in October 1902 that "the spirit of liberty can not exist in the same country and at the same time with star chamber courts."[83] A few months later, Gompers declared that this "judicial usurpation and tyranny" threatened to "destroy the American Republic."[84]

Although proponents of social reform continued to grumble about the judiciary during the decade from 1897 to 1906, criticism was muted and received little national attention. Aside from the perennial introduction of futile bills for the election of a federal judiciary, the issue faded from politics. Issues concerning the courts were absent from the national elections in 1900 and 1904. In neither year did the Democratic party's platform presume to criticize any decision of the Supreme Court. Although the 1900 platform made a ritual denunciation of government by injunction and the 1904 platform called for reform of injunction procedures, neither otherwise referred to judicial issues. Even the platforms of the Socialist parties in 1900 and 1904 failed to denounce the courts or demand judicial reform.[85] In 1904, the Democrats went so far as to nominate for president a conservative judge, Alton B. Parker of the New York Court of Appeals.

In 1905, however, the Court revived the worst suspicions of its critics when it handed down its most notorious substantive due process decision, *Lochner v. New York.* The Court held that a New York statute that limited hours of labor in a bakeshop to ten hours a day or sixty hours a week violated the liberty of contract guaranteed by the Fourteenth Amendment.[86] Although *Lochner* has come to epitomize judicial solicitude for business during the early twentieth century, the statute had been upheld by three courts in New York that had reviewed the legislation, and the Supreme Court was sharply divided in a 5–4 vote. Moreover, the decision was soon followed by several other cases in which the Supreme Court upheld limitations on the hours of employees. In one

---

[82] Victor Yarros, "Labor and 'Government by Injunction,'" *American Federationist,* February 1899, p. 233.

[83] Post stated that "orderly liberty demands that the nature of lawlessness shall be defined, not by judges, but by legislatures; and that the facts in particular cases shall be determined, not by judges, but by juries." Louis F. Post, "The Abuse of Injunctions," *American Federationist,* October 1902, p. 685.

[84] Samuel Gompers, "New Judicial Usurpation Through Injunctions," *American Federationist,* May 1903, p. 364.

[85] Johnson, *National Party Platforms,* vol. 1, pp. 115, 127–29, 132, 140–43.

[86] *Lochner v. New York,* 198 U.S. 45 (1905).

case, the Court without opinion upheld a Missouri statute limiting mine workers to eight hours of labor per day.[87] In 1907, the Court upheld a federal eight-hour day for government employees,[88] and in *Muller v. Oregon* in 1908 the Court unanimously upheld an Oregon statute that prohibited the employment of women in heavy industries and laundries for more than ten hours per day. The Court distinguished *Lochner* on the ground that women needed special protection.[89]

Although the *Lochner* decision did not therefore represent an unequivocal legal triumph for untrammeled capitalism, the decision nevertheless demonstrated again that the fate of progressive legislation was at the mercy of a conservative judiciary that was not loath to read its own economic and social predilections into the Constitution. The judicial attitudes that found expression in *Lochner* were bound to vex progressives and make them fear for the prospects of future legislation.[90] The timing of *Lochner* also had an ominous irony. The Court handed down its decision in April 1905, barely a month after the second inauguration of Theodore Roosevelt, who had won a landslide victory in 1904 as a champion of progressive measures.

Criticism of *Lochner* began on the Court itself when Justice Holmes filed his celebrated dissent declaring that "the 14th Amendment does not enact Mr. Herbert Spencer's Social Statics,"[91] and Justice Harlan argued that the Court should have deferred to the New York legislature's determination that the statute was needed to guard the health of the state's bakers.[92] Although the Court's *Lochner* decision involved state rather than federal legislation, it seemed an ominous portent for the fate of federal legislation as well as state legislation. In addition to providing a painful reminder of the Court's conservatism, the decision encouraged state courts to take a more restrictive view of social legislation, and it seemed likely to discourage reform initiatives in the state legislatures.

Although the immediate reaction to *Lochner* was muted,[93] a new

[87] *Cantwell v. Missouri*, 199 U.S. 602 (1905). See *State v. Cantwell*, 179 Mo. 245, 78 S.W. 569 (1904), for details of the statute in question.

[88] *Ellis v. United States*, 206 U.S. 246 (1907).

[89] 208 U.S. 412, 419–23 (1908).

[90] Paul Kens, *Judicial Power and Reform Politics: The Anatomy of* Lochner v. New York (Lawrence: University Press of Kansas, 1990), pp. 136–37.

[91] *Lochner*, 198 U.S. 75 (Holmes dissenting.) Professor Fiss has argued that *Lochner* "was not a brief on behalf of a particular economic policy, but rather reflected a particular conception of state authority" that had roots that were "far more extensive" than Holmes's reference to Spencer implied. Fiss, *Troubled Beginnings*, pp. 157–58 (galleys). See generally, *ibid.* chapter 6.

[92] Ibid., pp. 65–74 (Harlan dissenting in opinion in which White and Day concurred).

[93] Although *Lochner* received widespread criticism in the press, particularly labor

surge of public criticism of the judiciary was discernible within a year of the decision as the progressive movement continued to gather momentum. The Court in the years immediately following *Lochner* handed down a number of decisions in which the Court invoked questionable constitutional principles to strike down state and federal regulatory legislation. In 1908, the Court struck down two significant federal labor statutes. In the *First Employers' Liability Cases*, the Court invalidated a 1906 statute that had made railroads and other common carriers liable for work-related injuries to employees. In a 5–4 decision, the Court held that the statute was overly broad because it applied to employees who were not engaged in interstate commerce.[94] Three weeks later, the Court in *Adair v. United States* voided a statute that prohibited employers engaged in interstate commerce from requiring employees to agree to refrain from membership in labor unions.[95] In a third case decided in 1908, the Court again antagonized organized labor by ruling in *Loewe v. Lawlor* that a secondary boycott by a labor union violated the antitrust laws.

The Court's unanimous decision in this case seemed to underscore once again the Court's antilabor bias since the workers were engaged in manufacturing, which the Court had placed beyond the scope of the antitrust laws in the *Sugar Trust Case* when it suited the interests of business. The Court in *Loewe* compounded labor's antagonism by imposing treble damages on the union, even though courts had rarely expected businesses to pay the treble damages permitted by the antitrust laws.[96]

Labor's hostility toward the courts was also intensified by the protracted litigation involving the Buck's Stove & Range Company. In 1908, Gompers and two other AFL leaders were sentenced to prison for defying a federal court decree enjoining the *American Federationist* to refrain from urging its readers to boycott that company. The judge's venomous remarks in pronouncing the sentence, which drove Gompers to tears, helped to confirm labor's fears of judicial tyranny.[97] The ultimate decisions of the Supreme Court, which held that the

---

journals, the editorials avoided the apocalyptic tone that characterized the reactions to many later decisions of the Supreme Court. "Labor Press On The Ten-Hour Law," *Literary Digest,* May 6, 1905, p. 654. A number of publications hailed the decision as a vindication of personal liberty. "Supreme Court On the Ten-Hour Law," *Literary Digest,* April 29, 1905, pp. 613–14; "The Ten-Hour Day Unconstitutional," *World's Work,* June 1905, p. 6233.

[94] *First Employers' Liability Cases,* 207 U.S. 463, 501, 504 (1908).

[95] *Adair v. United States,* 208 U.S. 161, 180 (1908).

[96] *Loewe v. Lawlor,* 208 U.S. 274 (1908).

[97] Mandel, *Samuel Gompers,* pp. 263–83; Philip Taft, *The A.F. of L. in the Time of Gompers* (New York: Harper, 1957), pp. 268–71.

issues involved in the injunction proceeding were moot and overturned the convictions of the AFL leaders on technicalities,[98] did little
to assuage labor's worries.[99]

These and other federal and state decisions significantly crippled
the agendas of organized labor and progressives and offended political
liberals of almost every stripe. The judiciary's nullification of reform
measures and its predilection for the use of temporary injunctions
without notice in labor disputes led President Roosevelt to denounce
conservative jurists in his 1908 message to Congress.[100] The decisions
were particularly ominous because they restricted federal power at the
very time when progressives were pressing demands for more federal
legislation.[101] Although the Supreme Court upheld far more state and
federal legislation than it struck down, there were, as Melvin I. Urofsky
acknowledges, "enough decisions of the Court opposed to reform demands to give some credence to the critical chorus."[102] While the willingness of the Court to uphold so much reform legislation helped to
mute that chorus, the Court's critical review of even those statutes that
it sustained reminded progressives that all reforms had to run the
gauntlet of judicial review.

Few decisions, however, helped to crystallize criticism of the Court
more than the Court's 1911 opinions in *Standard Oil Co. of New Jersey v.
United States*[103] and *United States v. American Tobacco Co.*,[104] which allegedly emasculated the Sherman Act and provided examples of many
of the judicial abuses of which the critics of the judiciary had com-

[98] *Buck's Stove & Range Co. v. American Federation of Labor, et al.*, 219 U.S. 581 (1911);
Gompers v. Buck's Stove & Range Co., 221 U.S. 418 (1911); *Gompers v. United States*, 233 U.S.
604 (1914).

[99] Samuel Gompers, *Seventy Years of Life and Labor: An Autobiography* (1925; repr.
Ithaca, N.Y.: ILR Press, 1984), p. 171.

[100] Fred L. Israel, ed., *The State of the Union Messages of the Presidents 1790–1966*, vol. 3,
1905–1966 (New York: Chelsea House), pp. 2307–16. Roosevelt contended that a minority of judges had jeopardized public confidence in the judiciary by refusing "to put a stop
to the wrongdoing of very rich men under modern industrial conditions" and denying
"relief to men of small means or wageworkers who are crushed down by these modern
industrial conditions." He argued that "what would have been an infringement upon
liberty half a century ago may be the necessary safeguard of liberty to-day" (ibid., p.
2309). According to Roosevelt, "The talk about preserving to the misery-hunted beings
who make contracts for . . . service their 'liberty' to make them, is either to speak in a
spirit of heartless irony or else to show an utter lack of knowledge of the conditions of life
among the great masses of our fellow-countrymen, a lack which unfits a judge to do good
service just as it would unfit any executive or legislative officer" (ibid., p. 2310).

[101] John E. Semonche, *Charting the Future: The Supreme Court Responds to a Changing
Society, 1890–1920* (Westport, Conn.: Greenwood Press, 1978), pp. 217–18.

[102] Urofsky, "Myth and Reality," p. 69.

[103] 221 U.S. 1 (1911).

[104] 221 U.S. 106 (1911).

plained. Although the Court in *Standard Oil* had denied an appeal from a lower court decision that had ordered the gigantic Standard Oil Company to dissolve into its components parts, the language of the decision seemed to many progressives to plant the seeds for a more lax judicial scrutiny of trusts. The Court ruled that the Sherman Act's prohibition against restraint of trade extended only to "undue restraints" and must be interpreted in accordance with "the standard of reason."[105]

The outcry over the Court's decision was initiated and significantly abetted by the acrimonious dissent of Justice Harlan. The seventy-eight-year-old justice excoriated his brethren in an oral dissent delivered from the bench, and he later published a more careful but no less impassioned dissenting opinion. In both dissents, Harlan arraigned the Court for indulging in "judicial legislation."[106] According to Harlan, such judicial activism endangered the "safety and integrity" of the courts and was the "most alarming tendency" of the age. Harlan complained from the bench that business interests that had failed to work their will on the legislature sought refuge in the courts, trying to persuade the courts to "construe the Constitution or the statutes . . . to mean what they want it to mean."[107] In his written dissent, Harlan averred that courts should refrain from examining "the wisdom or policy of an act of Congress."[108] Harlan's dissent riled President Taft, who complained that it was "intended to furnish La Follette and his crowd as much pablum as possible."[109]

Public debate about the *Standard Oil* decision had barely begun when the Court's decision in *American Tobacco Co.* confirmed progressives' fears about the ominously fecund implications of the "rule of reason." In its decision, the Court refused to order the complete dissolution of the American Tobacco Company's trust, although the Court required the company to reorganize. Chief Justice Edward D. White explained that it could not give the Sherman Act "a narrow, unreasoning and unheard of construction."[110] Once again Harlan delivered a tart oral dissent[111] followed with a written opinion reiterating his charge that the Court had invaded the exclusive prov-

---

[105] *Standard Oil Co. of New Jersey*, 221 U.S. 59–60.

[106] *Standard Oil*, 221 U.S. 102–6 (Harlan concurring in part and dissenting in part); *American Tobacco*, 221 U.S. 192–93 (Harlan concurring in part and dissenting in part).

[107] "Justice Harlan's Dissenting Opinion," *New York Times*, May 17, 1911, p. 6.

[108] *Standard Oil*, 221 U.S. 104.

[109] William Howard Taft to Helen H. Taft, May 16, 1911, *Taft Papers*, Series 3, reel 125, Manuscript Division, Library of Congress.

[110] *United States v. American Tobacco Co.*, 221 U.S. 106 (1911).

[111] "Justice Harlan Caustic," *New York Times*, May 30, 1911, p. 6.

ince of Congress by undertaking to qualify the statute in a manner that contravened its plain language and obvious meaning.[112]

Progressives particularly complained because as Harlan had pointed out in both his dissents, the Court had specifically rejected a rule of reason in at least two earlier decisions.[113] Although both of White's opinions had insisted that the rule of reason had guided the Court in its earlier decisions, even if the Court had not specifically embraced the doctrine,[114] this did not dispel progressive criticism. Many progressives agreed with Harlan that White's reading of the rule of reason into the earlier decisions was as surprising as if he had averred "that black was white or white was black."[115] To the critics of the judiciary, the Court's refusal to abide by its own precedent provided another example of the arbitrary and well-nigh lawless process by which the courts adjudicated cases.

Like the U.S. Supreme Court, the state courts during this period carefully scrutinized state legislation, striking down some progressive measures and upholding many others. The scrutiny of various measures differed widely among the states, resulting in disparities. For example, Illinois in 1895 and New York in 1907 held that state laws that limited the working hours of women were void because they denied women equal protection with men under the law.[116] In other states, however, courts upheld such statutes.[117] Illinois in 1910 and New York in 1915 finally upheld laws regulating womens' working hours after advocates of those laws persuaded the state courts, as they had persuaded the Supreme Court in *Muller*, that the health of women needed special protection.[118]

One of the most notorious state decisions was rendered in 1911, when the New York Court of Appeals in *Ives v. South Buffalo Railway Co.* branded the New York workers' compensation law "plainly revolution-

---

[112] *American Tobacco Co.*, 221 U.S. 189–93 (Harlan concurring in part and dissenting in part).

[113] *Standard Oil*, 221 U.S. 89–101; *American Tobacco*, 221 U.S. 191–92 (citing *United States v. Trans-Missouri Freight Ass'n*, 166 U.S. 290 [1897], *United States v. Joint Traffic Ass'n*, 171 U.S. 505 [1898].

[114] *Standard Oil*, 221 U.S. 66–67; *American Tobacco*, 221 U.S. 178–80.

[115] *American Tobacco*, 221 U.S. 191 (Harlan concurring in part and dissenting in part).

[116] *Ritchie v. People*, 155 Ill. 98, 40 N.E. 454 (1895); *People v. Williams*, 189 N.Y. 131, 81 N.E. 778 (1907).

[117] See, e. g., *Muller v. State*, 48 Ore. 252, 85 P. 855 (1906), *aff'd.*, 208 U.S. 412 (1908). For a general discussion of state court decisions during this period, see Melvin I. Urofsky, "State Courts and Protective Legislation during the Progressive Era: A Reevaluation," *Journal of American History* 72 (June 1985): 63–91.

[118] *W.C. Ritchie & Co. v. Wayman*, 244 Ill. 509, 91 N.E. 695 (1910); *People v. Charles Schweinler Press*, 214 N.Y. 395, 405–6, 108 N.E. 639, 640–41 (1915).

ary" and nullified it under the due process clauses of the state constitution and the Fourteenth Amendment.[119] Only one day after the court's decision was announced, 146 women, mostly Jewish and Italian immigrants, died in a fire at the Triangle Shirtwaist Company factory in Manhattan when they were unable to flee through doors their employer had locked for fear that they would steal bits of fabric. By calling attention to the need for legislation to protect workers, this tragedy intensified outrage over the *Ives* decision. The fire also underscored the argument of proponents of workers' compensation statutes that workers' injuries were usually not caused by their own negligence.[120]

Writing in 1913, Professor W. F. Dodd concluded that state courts were more hostile toward social legislation than the Supreme Court. "Except for the rather unfortunate lapse in the New York bakeshop case, the Supreme Court . . . has in the main taken a liberal attitude toward legislation aimed to meet new social and industrial needs," Dodd declared. "Yet there remains the fact that perhaps the greater number of our state courts are illiberal and, under our present constitutional and judicial organization, are able to block needed social and industrial legislation."[121] Despite the conservatism of most state courts, however, the trend of their decisions favored progressive legislation.[122] As we shall see, the growing disparity between the relative progressivism of the state courts and the growing conservatism of the Supreme Court during the later 1910s shifted criticism from the state to the federal courts.

Although the renewed criticism of the courts after 1906 was inspired by the same issues that had motivated the controversy over the courts during the 1890s, the criticism of the Progressive Era was quantitatively and qualitatively different from the criticism of the 1890s. Quantitatively, the magnitude of criticism from 1906 to 1913 was far greater than it had been during the 1890s. The progressive critique of the courts was qualitatively different because it spawned a profusion of proposals for specific reforms.

Although a few critics of the courts such as Walter Clark had advocated specific proposals for reform during the 1890s, critics of that decade were largely content to urge judicial restraint and hope for the appointment of judges who would exercise such restraint. As Alan Westin has observed in discussing the historiography of judicial review, "while their tone was bitter and their own intentions were radical, the commentators between 1895 and 1900 were rather traditional in their

119 201 N.Y. 271, 94 N.E. 431 (1911).
120 "Can a Free People Be Free?" *The Outlook*, April 29, 1911, p. 955.
121 W. F. Dodd, "Social Legislation," p. 5.
122 See Urofsky, "State Courts," pp. 63–81.

arguments. The Founding Fathers were still revered and only their particular intent as to judicial review was disputed. For truly radical examinations of the issue, men with far less pietistic a view of the Fathers and less of a States Rights blinder would have to take up the dispute."[123] Like earlier critics of the courts, many progressives questioned the doctrine of judicial review and called for judicial restraint. But during the early years of the century, they also advocated many other measures, including the recall of judges, popular referenda on judicial decisions, the appointment of more liberal judges to the bench, the education of judges about modern social and industrial conditions, and the reform of judicial procedures. These proposals and others would inspire widespread debate and generate extensive controversy.

[123] Alan F. Westin, "Charles Beard and American Debate Over Judicial Review, 1790–1961," Introduction to Charles A. Beard, *The Supreme Court and the Constitution* (Englewood Cliffs, N. J.: Prentice-Hall, 1962), p. 22.

TWO

CHALLENGES TO CONSTITUTIONAL

ORTHODOXY

> To advance the view that Congress may pass what law it
> will and that the . . . Judiciary . . . must lend its aid to the
> usurpation . . . is to be so radical that a listener fairly
> catches his breath, no matter who is the spokesman.
> (*William M. Meigs, 1906*)[1]

T HE RISING TIDE of criticism of the judiciary that followed
Lochner was accompanied by increasingly radical demands for
the curtailment of judicial power, including the abrogation of
judicial review. By challenging one of the principal foundations of the
American constitutional system, opponents of judicial review manifested the intensity of their frustration with judicial hostility toward
reform legislation and organized labor and demonstrated their impatience with all constitutional orthodoxies, including the Constitution
itself. Although demands for abrogation of judicial review would recur
throughout the period studied by this book, the early proposals that
are the subject of this chapter are worthy of special attention because
they laid the political and intellectual foundations for similar proposals
in later years.

The resentments against the Supreme Court that had smoldered
beneath the surface of public discourse for more than a decade finally
burst into the public forum during the spring of 1906. In a widely
quoted speech at the University of Pennsylvania Law School on April
27, 1906, Walter Clark denounced the Supreme Court for its alleged
usurpation of the power to review state and federal legislation. Recit-
ing arguments that would become a familiar litany among progressive
opponents of judicial review, Clark argued that the text of the Constitution failed to provide any express or implied authority for that
power, that the Framers of the Constitution did not anticipate judicial
review, and that judicial review did not exist in any other country. Clark
also contended that the Constitution itself was a "reactionary" and

---

[1] William M. Meigs, "Some Recent Attacks on the American Doctrine of Judicial
Power," *American Law Review* 40 (September–October 1906): 641–42.

antidemocratic document that was intended "to suppress, or at least disregard, the wishes and the consent of the governed. It was admirably adapted for what has come to pass—the absolute domination of the government by the 'business interests.'" Anticipating the thesis that Columbia professor Charles A. Beard would present several years later in his *Economic Interpretation of the Constitution of the United States*, Clark suggested that the principal goal of the Framers was to protect private property.[2]

One month after Clark spoke in Philadelphia, another prominent attorney, William Trickett, the dean of the Dickinson School of Law in Carlisle, Pennsylvania, also alleged that the Supreme Court had usurped the power of judicial review. Writing in the *American Law Review*, Trickett contended that most of the Founding Fathers had intended that Congress should be the ultimate arbiter of the constitutionality of its own legislation, although he conceded that some members of the constitutional convention had anticipated judicial review.[3] During the following year, Professor J. Allen Smith of the University of Washington published a widely circulated book in which he denounced the power of judicial review as a "dangerous innovation" that enabled the courts to protect powerful business interests in contravention of the popular will.[4] In 1912, the socialist journalist Gustavus Myers reiterated this theme in more scathing terms in a treatise on the history of the Supreme Court that made the Court seem more like a conspiracy than a judicial tribunal.[5]

The most prolific academic critic of judicial review during the Progressive Era was Louis B. Boudin, who argued in 1911 that attempts to establish judicial review prior to the constitutional convention were "isolated and timid" and that there was "absolutely no evidence" that the Framers had intended to vest the Supreme Court with the power of judicial review. Boudin also denied that the text of the Constitution provided any support for judicial review. He further contended that *Marbury v. Madison* did not firmly establish the power of judicial review and that the scope of judicial review had grown ever wider. Uncompromising in his opposition to judicial review, Boudin argued that "the power itself spells despotism" since the judiciary was not responsible to

[2] Walter Clark, "Some Defects in the Constitution of the United States," *American Law Register* 54 (May 1906): 263, 265, 278, 270–71, 273, 277–82.

[3] William Trickett, "The Great Usurpation," *American Law Review* 40 (May–June 1906): 356.

[4] J. Allen Smith, *The Spirit of American Government* (New York: Macmillan, 1907), pp. 103, 65–124.

[5] Gustavus Myers, *History of the Supreme Court of the United States* (Chicago: Charles H. Kerr, 1912).

the people.[6] Boudin's attacks on judicial review continued for another two decades and culminated in 1932 in the publication of his magnum opus, the two-volume *Government by Judiciary*.[7]

The views of Clark, Trickett, Smith, Myers, and Boudin were not novel. Since the time of Jefferson, critics of the federal courts had decried judicial review. As we have seen, James B. Weaver and Sylvester Pennoyer had denounced judicial review as recently as the 1890s.[8] The attacks on judicial review that began in 1906, however, received more serious attention than the criticisms of the previous decade since they were propounded by persons who commanded widespread respect and came at a time when the role of the judiciary was beginning to undergo intense scrutiny.[9] The view that the Court had usurped the power of judicial review, however, flew in the face of a growing scholarly consensus that the text and historical origins of the Constitution supported the exercise of judicial review and that judicial review was a valid constitutional power, albeit one that demanded great circumspection in its exercise.[10] As Weaver had admitted in 1892, the Court's power of judicial review "seems to be no longer questioned."[11]

The issue of judicial review had received serious scholarly attention

[6] Louis B. Boudin, "Government by Judiciary," *Political Science Quarterly* 26 (June 1911): 238, 244, 248, 264.

[7] Louis B. Boudin, *Government by Judiciary* (New York: William Godwin, 1932).

[8] James B. Weaver, *A Call to Action* (Des Moines: Iowa Printing, 1892), pp. 74–75; Sylvester Pennoyer, "The Income Tax Decision and the Power of the Supreme Court to Nullify Acts of Congress," *American Law Review* 29 (July–August 1895): 550–58. In more measured teams, one commentator in 1900 had called for a reconsideration of judicial review. Henry Flanders, "Has the Supreme Court of the United States the Constitutional Power to Declare Void an Act of Congress?" *American Law Register* 39 (July 1900): 385–90.

[9] Writing in 1908, a Nebraska attorney contrasted the serious debate inspired by Clark and Trickett with the proposal of Pennoyer, which had "caused a ripple of amused comment as an ebullition of personal eccentricity." William G. Hastings, "Is It Usurpation to Hold as Void Unconstitutional Laws?" *Green Bag*, September 1908, p. 453.

[10] See, for example, Richard C. Dale, "The Obligation of the Legislature as Well as of the Judiciary to Respect Constitutional Limitations," *American Law Register* 39 (August 1900): 441–67); Richard C. Dale, "Implied Limitations upon the Exercise of the Legislative Power," *American Law Register* 40 (October 1901): 580–604. Like other proponents of judicial review, Dale warned that the judiciary should not rule upon the wisdom or expediency of legislation. Although defenders of judicial review would continue to urge judicial restraint, the subsequent controversy over judicial review demonstrated a wide latitude of opinion about the proper scope of judicial deference to legislative bodies. For a useful discussion of the historical evolution of the controversy over judicial review, see Alan F. Westin, "Charles Beard and American Debate over Judicial Review, 1790–1961," Introduction to Charles Beard, *The Supreme Court and the Constitution* (Englewood Cliffs, N.J.: Prentice-Hall, 1962)

[11] Weaver, *Call to Action*, p. 74.

since the 1880s when the historian George Bancroft and William M. Meigs, a Philadelphia attorney, had published seminal studies of the historical origins of the doctrine of judicial review. Meigs and Bancroft concluded that significant precedents for judicial review predated the Constitutional Convention. They argued, however, that the Supreme Court's decisions concerning the constitutionality of actions by other federal departments were binding only on the parties to the immediate case. Bancroft and Meigs contended that although Congress and the president should accord deference to the Court's interpretation, they would need not abide by it unless they found it persuasive.[12] Similarly, James B. Thayer of the Harvard Law School stated in 1893 that the Framers had recognized the power but warned that they had envisioned a high degree of judicial restraint. Thayer pointed out that precedents for judicial review predated the Constitution but that such precedents were not conclusive.[13]

Brinton Coxe presented a stronger and highly polemical argument in favor of the historical validity of judicial review in a book published in 1893. Coxe tried to demonstrate that various European governments over a long period had countenanced a remarkably large number of judicial restraints on legislative action and that the Framers were well aware of those precedents.[14] Meanwhile, legal historians attempted to demonstrate that significant precedents for judicial review existed during the colonial period.[15] Coxe's study convinced Meigs that his 1885 study had overemphasized the novelty of judicial review.[16]

Even some scholars who conceded that the Framers did not necessarily envision judicial review defended the legitimacy of judicial review. Although Professor Edward S. Corwin of Princeton concluded that the debates on the adoption and ratification of the Constitution "reveal a diversity of opinion," he argued that the Constitution itself embodied the doctrine of judicial review because the doctrine was inherent in the Framers' belief in the need for an institutional check

[12] George Bancroft, *History of the Formation of the Constitution of the United States of America,* vol. 2 (1882; repr. Littleton, Colo.: Fred B. Rothman, 1983), pp. 198–206; William M. Meigs, "The Relation of the Judiciary to the Constitution," *American Law Review* 19 March–April (1885): 175.

[13] James B. Thayer, "The Origin and Scope of the American Doctrine of Constitutional Law," *Harvard Law Review* 7 (October 25, 1893): 129–56.

[14] Brinton Coxe, *An Essay on Judicial Power and Unconstitutional Legislation, Being a Commmentary on Parts of the Constitution of the United States* (1893; repr. New York: Da Capo Press, 1970).

[15] Austin Scott, "*Holmes v. Walton,* The New Jersey Precedent," *American Historical Review* 4 (1899): 456; Andrew M. Davis, "The Case of Frost v. Leighton," *American Historical Review* 2 (1897): 229.

[16] Meigs, "Some Recent Attacks," p. 664.

against legislative tyranny.[17] Professor Charles G. Haines and Andrew C. McLaughlin conducted researches that amplified Corwin's thesis that judicial review was a natural outgrowth of the ideas that provided the impetus for the Constitution.[18]

Perhaps the most celebrated contribution to the debate was made in 1912 by Beard, whose research inadvertently led him to conclude that the Framers intended to permit the Court to review the constitutionality of legislative acts.[19] As a progressive who was troubled by judicial hostility toward social reform, Beard originally had intended to prove that the Marshall Court had arbitrarily assumed a power that the Framers had not intended the Court to have.[20] Beard reached the opposite conclusion, however, after his research identified twenty-five members of the convention who seemed to have favored judicial review. Although Beard did not presume to present a comprehensive analysis of the ratifying conventions, he pointed out that the available evidence suggested that at least some of the conventions must have been aware that the Constitution contemplated judicial review. Like Corwin, Beard contended that the political philosophy that provided the basis for the Constitution suggested that the Framers favored judicial review. According to Beard, the advocates of the usurpation theory had the burden of proving "that the American federal system was not designed primarily to commit the established rights of property to the guardianship of a judiciary removed from direct contact with popular electorates."[21]

Although Beard later contended that his work had exorcised the "ghost of usurpation,"[22] critics of the Court continued to challenge the validity of judicial review. Even scholars who did not specifically oppose judicial review challenged Beard's thesis. Corwin, for example, contended that Beard's data were inconclusive.[23] Similarly, Horace A. Davis's research led him to conclude in 1913 that "there was in the convention itself great difference of opinion as to the best pol-

---

[17] Edward S. Corwin, "The Supreme Court and Unconstitutional Acts of Congress," *Michigan Law Review* 4 (June 1906): 616, 620.

[18] Charles G. Haines, *The American Doctrine of Judicial Supremacy* (1914; repr. New York: Da Capo Press, 1973), pp. 88–147; Andrew C. McLaughlin, *The Courts, the Constitution and Parties: Studies in Constitutional History and Politics* (1912; repr. New York: Da Capo Press, 1972), pp. 16–19.

[19] Charles A. Beard, *The Supreme Court and the Constitution*, (New York: Macmillan, 1912); Beard, "The Supreme Court: Usurper or Grantee?" *Political Science Quarterly* 27 (March 1912): 34.

[20] Westin, "Charles Beard," p. 25.

[21] Beard, "Usurper or Grantee?" p. 31.

[22] Charles A. Beard, "Introduction to the 1938 Edition," *The Supreme Court and the Constitution* (1962 Prentice-Hall ed.) p. 36.

[23] Corwin, "Unconstitutional Acts of Congress," pp. 618–22.

icy to be adopted" and that "the question was intentionally left open."[24]

Attempts by critics of judicial review to legitimate their position by proving that the power of judicial review lacked proper historical and constitutional antecedents were superfluous insofar as judicial review was an established part of the American constitutional system. Opposition to judicial review, moreover, ultimately rested not upon historical analysis or textual exigesis but rather upon a pragmatic hostility against the judiciary's interference with social reform and, to a lesser degree, a philosophical belief that judicial review as currently exercised was inconsistent with the essential character of American government.

Historical arguments were important, however, insofar as they reminded both the public and the courts that judicial review was not an original or inevitable feature of the nation's government. Writing in 1912 to Mayor William J. Gaynor of New York City, an outspoken critic of the courts, Boudin asserted that the inquiry into origins of judicial review had "more than academic interest." Boudin believed that public recognition of "the myth of the 'ordained' character of this power" would make Americans more indignant toward excesses in the exercise of judicial review. Similarly, Americans would be less tolerant of wide-ranging judicial review if they became aware "that even those who favored it in its inception never dreamed of the lengths to which it would be carried."[25]

Even a restrained exercise of judicial review troubled many progressives, who feared that any form of judicial review afforded the courts an opportunity to strike down arbitrarily legislation of which they personally disapproved. Even if judges purported to base their decisions upon appropriate legal grounds, the mere potential for judicial arrogation of legislative powers threatened the stability of the Republic. As James Manahan told the Minnesota Bar Association in 1911, there was nothing to prevent the Court from usurping legislative functions and contravening the clear will of Congress, even though the actual question of whether or not the Court in such cases as the *Sugar Trust Case* had wielded such power was debatable.[26]

Opponents of judicial review, as well as critics of the courts who did not oppose judicial review, also contended that the power to review the constitutionality of statutes inevitably gave the courts the discretion to

[24] Horace A. Davis, "Annulment of Legislation by the Supreme Court," *American Political Science Review* 7 (November 1913): 544.

[25] Louis B. Boudin to William J. Gaynor, May 27, 1912, *Papers of William J. Gaynor*, Box 86, Municipal Archives, New York City.

[26] James Manahan, "The Recall of Judges," S. Doc. 941, 62nd Cong., 2d sess., 1912, p. 9 (address before the Minnesota State Bar Association at Duluth, July 19, 1911).

read their social, political, and economic predilections into the Constitution they were purporting to interpret. Since the judges often looked askance at progressive legislation, progressives complained that judicial review was reactionary in practice if not in theory.

Conservatives denied that the courts made law. Columbia University president Nicholas Murray Butler, one of the most tenacious defenders of the courts during the 1910s and 1920s, stated in 1912 that "a judge declares law, but does not make it." Butler explained that "in declaring the law he is executing the people's highest and most mature will. . . . He is not imposing anything upon the people save what they have imposed upon themselves as the necessary and well-justified restraints upon appetite and passion."[27] Similarly, Justice Horace H. Lurton declared, "There is nothing in the past history of either the National or State judiciary which gives sanction to any . . . abuse of power or supports an expectation that the function of interpreting will be tortured into an exercise of legislative power." Lurton insisted that the rules for judicial interpretation of a statute were the same as those for construing a contract. In either situation, the rules of construction were "plain and simple of application."[28]

Taking issue with Lurton, Boudin argued that "there are now no such 'plain and simple' rules of interpretation as Judge Lurton claims; on the contrary, there are now practically no rules at all." Boudin argued that "each law is declared 'constitutional' or 'unconstitutional' according to the opinion the judges entertain as to its wisdom." As evidence of the political character of judicial decisions, Boudin pointed to the sharp division of opinions in Supreme Court cases and the inconsistency among the Court's decisions. Boudin declared that Lurton's denial that the Court exercised a legislative function "seems like adding insult to injury."[29]

In addition to these central criticisms of judicial review, opponents also argued that the doctrine led to various baneful collateral consequences. Clark, for example, complained in 1907 that the doctrine detracted from the stability and predictability of the law since it led to judicial inconsistencies, as when the Supreme Court had reversed itself on the legal tender and income tax issues.[30] Harrison S. Smalley, another opponent of judicial review, argued in 1911 that judicial review contravened the progressive ideal of efficiency because the resolution

---

[27] "Cheer as Butler Hits at Roosevelt," *New York Times*, April 10, 1912, p. 3.

[28] Horace H. Lurton, "A Government of Law or a Government of Men?" *North American Review*, January 1911, p. 24.

[29] Boudin, "Government by Judiciary," pp. 267–70.

[30] Walter Clark, "Constitutional Changes Demanded to Bulwark Democratic Government," *Arena*, February 1907, p. 150.

of questions concerning the constitutionality of statutes required so much time and expense. He pointed out that prolonged uncertainty concerning the construction of a statute that involved industrial issues could depress the economy. Smalley also contended that judicial review detracted from judicial dignity since it embroiled judges in the "turmoil of present-day industrial and political struggles."[31] Critics of judicial review, including such progressives as Roscoe Pound who did not favor abandonment of the doctrine, also warned that judicial review encouraged legislative carelessness since lazy legislators who drafted ambiguous statutes could rely on the courts to supply a more precise definition. Similarly, the doctrine bred legislative irresponsibility since craven legislators could depend upon the courts to provide a conservative interpretation of ambiguous terms.[32]

Although proponents of judicial review acknowledged that this power could be abused in the hands of some judges, they insisted that abrogation of judicial review would engender even more serious abuses of power by Congress or the president. Presaging arguments that conservatives would emphasize for decades, Meigs warned in 1906 that "if liberty were not most seriously infringed, property would certainly be a plaything."[33]

Despite the profusion of complaints about judicial review, few critics of the courts prior to 1918 advocated any practical measure for the actual curtailment of the power. This reluctance is partially attributable to a pragmatic recognition that a movement to abolish judicial review would be quixotic. Even so ferocious a critic of the courts as Walter Clark acknowledged in his 1906 Pennsylvania speech that "it may be that this power in the courts, however illegally grasped originally, has been too long acquiesced in to be now questioned." In that speech, Clark had reiterated his proposal for election of federal judges for limited terms. Clark further proposed "the speedy repeal of the Fourteenth Amendment or a recasting of its language" to prevent another decision like *Lochner*. He also called for a national constitutional convention.[34]

Even prior to 1918, however, progressives had proposed a number of plans that would have curtailed the power of the courts to review the

[31] Harrison S. Smalley, "Nullifying the Law by Judicial Interpretation," *Atlantic Monthly*, April 1911, p. 455.

[32] Roscoe Pound, "Courts and Legislation," *American Political Science Review* 7 (August 1913): 378–79; Smalley, ibid., p. 455, 461.

[33] Meigs, "Some Recent Attacks," p. 645.

[34] Clark, "Defects in the Constitution," pp. 277–82. Clark had called for a constitutional convention as early as the 1890s; see Walter Clark, "The Revision of the Constitution of the United States," 32 *American Law Review* (January–February 1898): 1–13.

constitutionality of legislation. Trickett, for example, proposed in 1907 that the Supreme Court should be forbidden to strike down an act of Congress unless all members of the court agreed that the statute was unconstitutional.[35] Late in 1907, the AFL adopted a resolution demanding that the lower state and federal courts be stripped of the power to annul state and federal statutes and that the power of judicial review be vested exclusively in the state supreme courts and the U.S. Supreme Court. The AFL also proposed a requirement of unanimity in any judicial decision that invalidated a state or federal statute.[36]

A number of court-curbing bills were introduced in Congress even prior to 1918. In 1912, for example, Republican representative Fred S. Jackson of Kansas sponsored legislation to permit automatic consideration of a constitutional amendment to override any Supreme Court decision that invalidated a federal law.[37] Between 1907 and 1909, Democratic representatives David A. De Armond of Missouri and William B. Wilson of Pennsylvania sponsored four bills to deny the lower federal courts to declare any act of Congress unconstitutional.[38] Three of those bills also proposed to deprive the lower federal courts of the power to invalidate state legislation.[39] Another measure, sponsored by Democratic representative William Walton Kitchin of North Carolina in 1907, would have restricted the power of the inferior federal courts to invalidate state legislation but would not have impaired the power of those courts to review federal legislation.[40] In 1912 and again in 1914, congressional resolutions were introduced to permit immediate consideration by the state legislatures of amendments to override any federal judicial decision that invalidated an act of Congress.[41]

[35] Trickett declared that "propriety and respect for the judgement of a coordinate branch of the Government imperatively require that the small court which condemns the legislation of a numerous Congress, supported by a numerous people, should be unanimous." William Trickett, "Judicial Nullification of Acts of Congress," *North American Review*, August 16, 1907, p. 848.

[36] "The Right to Declare Laws Unconstitutional," *American Federationist*, January 1908, p. 28.

[37] H.R. J. Res. 351, 62d Cong., 2d sess., 1912.

[38] H.R. 4324, 61st Cong., 1st sess., 1909 (sponsored by Rep. De Armond of Missouri); H.R. 10479, 60th Cong., 1st sess., 1907 (sponsored by De Armond); H.R. 3926, 60th Cong., 1st sess., 1907 (sponsored by De Armond); H.R. 4917, 60th Cong., 1st sess., 1907 (sponsored by Rep. Wilson, Pennsylvania).

[39] H.R. 4917; H.R. 10479; H.R. 4324. One bill provided that the inferior federal courts would not be permitted to invalidate a state statute unless that state's law permitted its inferior courts to pass upon constitutional questions in the absence of a decision of the state's highest court (H.R. 4324).

[40] H.R. 4872, 60th Cong., 1st sess., 1907.

[41] H.R. J. Res. 351, 62nd Cong., 2d sess., 1912; S.J. Res. 142, 62nd Cong., 3rd sess., 1912; H.R. J. Res. 221, 63rd Cong., 2d sess., 1914.

The bills to deprive the lower federal courts of the power to pass upon the constitutionality of federal legislation reflected a profound distrust of the corporate biases of the federal courts. However, the measures recognized the need for the Supreme Court to retain its position as the ultimate arbiter of the law. The desire to retain judicial review while narrowing the jurisdiction of the lower federal courts was also embodied in legislation that would have narrowed the circumstances under which corporations could take refuge in the federal courts. Corporations then as now often preferred to litigate actions in federal courts rather than state courts. By forcing an opponent to appear in a federal court far removed from the opponent's home, corporations could eliminate the threat of local prejudice and force the opponent to undergo the additional expense of litigating in a distant location. Accordingly, corporations often sued in federal court if they were plaintiffs or sought to remove actions to federal court if they were defendants.

Three measures sponsored by Democratic representative Gordon James Russell of Texas between 1904 and 1907 would have deprived corporations of this right. Russell's bills called for a constitutional amendment to deprive the federal courts of jurisdiction over actions between citizens of different states unless such citizens were natural persons.[42] Democratic senator Lee Slater Overman of North Carolina introduced similar legislation in 1910, as did Democratic representative John Edward Raker of California on several occasions between 1911 and 1917.[43]

Like so much of the judicial reform legislation supported by progressives and trade unionists, none of the bills to curtail the power of judicial review ever received serious attention in the judiciary committees. Unlike measures to curtail judicial power that were advocated after the First World War, none of these proposals inspired widespread public discussion. Although the failure of the anticourt measures demonstrated the strength of powerful interests that supported economic due process, the bills to abridge judicial review were also doomed because even many critics of the judiciary's economic activism regarded judicial review as an essential component of the American system of government. The failure of the movement to abrogate judicial review suggests that respect for judicial review remained widespread

[42] H.R. J. Res. 92, 58th Cong., 2d sess., 1904; H.R. J. Res. 250, 59th Cong., 2d sess., 1907; H.J. Res. 17, 60th Cong., 1st sess., 1907.

[43] S.J. Res. 68, 61st Cong., 1st sess., 1910; H.J. Res. 44, 45, 62nd Cong., 1st sess., 1911; H.R. J. Res. 38, 63rd Cong., 1st sess., 1913; H.J. Res. 16, 17, 64th Cong., 1st sess., 1915; H.R. J. Res. 17, 18, 65th Cong., 1st sess., 1917.

throughout the Progressive Era, despite the profusion of protests over how the judges exercised that power.

Since the courts obviously would not initiate abrogation of judicial review and were unlikely to countenance legislation that abridged or abolished the power, only two options for the abrogation of judicial review were remotely feasible. The first was to deprive the federal courts of judicial review in an ad hoc manner, as the Reconstruction Congress had done when it had deprived the Court of jurisdiction in all cases arising under the Habeas Corpus Act of 1867. Although the Court's decision in *McCardle* supported the validity of such legislation,[44] the creative and assertive justices who now sat on the Court might find a way to avoid the embarrassing precedent that their more timorous predecessors had established.

The constitutional amendment process provided another option for abrogation of judicial review. Although an amendment was a conclusive remedy that was immune to judicial challenge, the viability of the amendment option was limited. Since the cumbersome amendment process presented formidable challenges even for such popular measures as the prohibition of child labor, opponents of judicial review recognized that they could not hope to muster the necessary support for such an amendment.

The essential conservatism of the progressive movement also inhibited support for curtailment of judicial review. Ever since the days of the Marshall Court, judicial review had protected private property. Even though progressives may have been outraged that the courts had often carried their solicitude for private property to an extreme and were protecting plutocracy rather than capitalism, it is unlikely that many progressives were willing to advocate a reform that would imperil economic and political stability by upsetting the delicate divisions of governmental powers.

In addition to economic considerations, there were cultural reasons why progressives generally did not press for abolition of judicial review. Dominated by middle-class old-stock Protestants, the progressive movement was deeply infused with a respect for fundamental American values, which prominently included a deep respect for law, the courts, and the Constitution. As Richard Hofstadter pointed out, the Anglo Saxon tradition that dominated the progressive movement emphasized governance by legal rules. Accordingly, progressives tended to believe that "if the laws are the right laws, and if they can be enforced by the right men . . . everything would be better."[45]

[44] *Ex parte McCardle*, 74 U.S. (7 Wall.) 506 (1869).
[45] Hofstadter, *The Age of Reform: From Bryan to F.D.R.* (New York: Alfred A. Knopf,

Faced with the alternative of transferring judicial powers to the legislative or executive branches of government, many progressives must have recognized that the judiciary, despite all its flaws, was the best agency to serve as the ultimate arbiter of the Constitution. Even though many progressives mourned the annulment of hard-fought legislative victories for social and regulatory measures, few progressives were willing to make Congress the judge of its own constitutional powers. Fearful of the growing power of the masses and the influence of political machines, the progressives were loath to replace the "judicial oligarchy" with a legislative oligarchy that was likely to be even more self-interested and irrational than the courts. Progressive reluctance to expand congressional power also reflected progressive ambivalence about the efficacy of legislation. Even those progressives who recognized the need for legislation retained some ambivalence about legislative remedies and remained deeply suspicious of legislative power. Although progressives increasingly relied upon legislation to accomplish their goals, many progressives continued to prefer voluntary action.

Similarly, only a few progressives were willing to transfer judicial power to the executive branch. One of the few proponents of executive review of legislation was Professor Gardiner of Columbia, who argued in 1905 that the executive has the constitutional right to do any official act that it believes to be within its functions, restrained only by impeachment.[46] Executive discretion to interpret the Constitution was also advocated by Smalley, who proposed the creation of a permanent commission on statutory construction to review statutes that pertained to political, social, or economic subjects. As an alternative to the commission, Smalley proposed that Congress might confer on the heads of administrative agencies the power and duty to interpret all statutes that pertained to their departments.[47]

Reverence for the law and acceptance of judicial review was particularly ingrained in the progressive movement because so many progressives were lawyers. Even the most progressive lawyers were generally committed to the concepts of judicial supremacy that had been forged during the 1890s and perfected during the early 1900s. They

[46] Meigs, "Some Recent Attacks," p. 642 (citing paper delivered by Gardiner to Pennsylvania State Bar Association).

[47] Smalley, "Nullifying the Law," pp. 462–63. Smalley's naive proposal was characteristically progressive since as it sought to depoliticize the process of decision making by assigning power to an institution that presumably would act in the broad public interest, assisted by experts. Smalley made a facile and unworkable distinction between "social" legislation and "legal" legislation, failed to recognize that the potential for politicization of constitutional issues was no less in an executive agency than in a court, and did not explain why people appointed to a commission would turn out to be less hostile toward business than those appointed by the same executive to a court.

recognized that attenuation of judicial review would erode the stability and predictability of the law by exposing critical decision-making functions to the uncertainties of the political processes that progressives perceived to have been corrupted by immigrants who were believed to value personal relations over the rule of law.[48] By resolving disputes in a manner that helped to avert the chaos that progressives so feared, judicial review also provided a means of maintaining and restoring the order that progressives craved.

Although progressives were disappointed that the courts often failed to take a broad view of the public interest, most were not naive enough to suppose that any other agency of government was likely to have broader vision. While the concentration of power in the courts was superficially inconsistent with the progressives' opposition to centralization of political and economic power, progressives generally conceded the need for various modes of centralization in a complex society[49] and were seldom loath to advocate concentration of power when it suited their needs. The progressives' increasing acceptance of the need to use government to achieve reform and their attempts to use the state as a counterbalance to the business autocracy that threatened the individual freedom they cherished tended to mitigate progressive hostility toward judicial power. Although progressives may have often disagreed with the way that power was exercised, they recognized that judicial power could help to maintain democracy.

Therefore, the courts in many ways were well adapted to serve progressive ends and were potential allies of the reform movement. If, as Otis L. Graham, Jr., has contended, the progressives sought "to vest control in safe hands, and fewer hands,"[50] the judges had the best hands. The complexity of the law helped to ensure that judges would generally be better educated than legislators or executives and that they therefore might have a broader and more scientific understanding of the public interest. The relative insulation of the judiciary from political pressure also seemed to ensure that judges would be more immune from the caprices of the masses and the pressures of the plutocrats. Vexed by the increasing complexity of society and their loss of control over economic and political forces, progressives may have perceived that the judiciary was more susceptible to progressive influ-

[48] Barbara C. Steidle, "Conservative Progressives: A Study of the Attitudes and Role of Bar and Bench, 1905–1912," Ph.D. diss., Rutgers University, 1969, p. 181.

[49] Otis L. Graham, Jr., *The Great Campaigns: Reform and War in America, 1900–1928* (Englewood Cliffs, N.J.: Prentice-Hall, 1971), pp. 33–34; John Whiteclay Chambers II, *The Tyranny of Change: America in the Progressive Era, 1900–1917* (New York: St. Martin's Press, 1980), pp. 108–9, 137.

[50] Graham, *ibid.*, p. 132.

ences than most other agencies of government. In contrast to the impracticability of abolishing judicial review, it was feasible for progressives to influence judicial selection and judicial thinking.

The essential conservatism of much of the progressive movement in matters relating to the judiciary was also reflected in progressive criticisms of the Constitution. Like Clark, many progressives blamed the Constitution for permitting the alleged development and maintenance of an irresponsible oligarchy of businessmen and politicians. Disparagement of the Constitution became intellectually fashionable in 1913 when Beard's *An Economic Interpretation of the Constitution of the United States* purported to demonstrate that the establishment of a strong central government was heavily influenced by the Framers' desire to protect their economic interests. As Hofstadter observed, this book confronted "a nation of Constitution-worshippers . . . with a scholarly muck-raking of the Founding Fathers and the Constitution itself."[51] Criticism of the Constitution and refusal to accept it as dogma reflected the progressives' pragmatism and empiricism. Herbert Croly, for example, denigrated the Constitution's pretensions to immutability and called for an experimental political program guided only by faith in democracy.[52]

But although many progressives refused to revere the Constitution, few dared to urge its abandonment. Like the muckrakers who exposed corruption in business and local government, few of the progressives who so gleefully stripped the Framers of their haloes sought any radical transformation of American society or government. Calls by Clark and some other critics of the courts for a constitutional convention[53] generated little support among progressives.

The dearth of any widespread support for a constitutional convention is particularly notable since progressives succeeded in bringing about the convocation of a number of state constitutional conventions.[54] The contrast between progressive enthusiasm for state conventions and progressive indifference toward a federal convention may be explained partly by the contrast between the narrowness of many state constitutions and the flexibility of the federal constitution. It may also be explained partly by the fear of northern progressives that a constitutional convention might enable southerners to secure the victory for states' rights that they had failed to win during the Civil War.

[51] Hofstadter, *Age of Reform*, p. 199.

[52] Herbert Croly, *Progressive Democracy* (New York: Macmillan, 1914).

[53] See, e.g., Yandell Henderson, "The Progressive Movement and Constitutional Reform," *Yale Review* 23 (October 1913): 90.

[54] See, e.g., Hoyt Landon Warner, *Progressivism in Ohio, 1897–1917* (Columbus: Ohio State University Press, 1964), pp. 312–53.

But the movement for a constitutional convention failed to generate more widespread interest among progressives primarily because progressives recognized that the existing constitutional structure could accommodate reform. Although radical reformers like the Socialist congressman Victor L. Berger of Wisconsin expressed doubt that meaningful reform could be achieved under the Constitution, the mainstream of the progressive movement retained faith in the resiliency of the nation's charter. Denouncing both the Left and the Right for their cramped interpretation of the Constitution, The Outlook observed in 1911 that the Constitution "is not a set of cast-iron rules. It is a statesman's definition of great principles laid down in general terms for the very purpose of enabling the Nation to enter . . . on paths before untrod."[55]

Although criticism of the Constitution, like opposition to judicial review, was generally confined to academic debates and political polemics, it did not lack practical significance. Just as the academic controversy over the historical origins of judicial review underscored abuses in the exercise of that power, Beard's research and other constitutional iconoclasm demonstrated the need for constitutional changes that would serve the exigencies of reform. Robert M. Crunden has observed that "since real, self-interested human beings had written the document, the implication was clearly that equally real, modern progressives could change it. Times, interests, and power shifts had created a new situation which demanded a revised Constitution."[56] The progressive concept of revision, however, was limited to measures that fell far short of the adoption of a new constitution. Criticism of the Constitution was directed more at the way the courts interpreted the Constitution than the Constitution itself.

Rather than propose any fundamental change that would upset the distribution of powers among the branches of government, progressives preferred to urge that the courts exercise greater restraint in reviewing the constitutionality of legislation. Far from seeking to abrogate judicial review, progressive lawyers tended to urge the courts to exercise greater moderation so that popular discontent would not lead to curtailment of judicial power.[57] The progressive belief in judicial restraint, which lay at the core of progressive criticism of the courts, also reflected the conservatism of the progressive movement. Seeking to preserve and indeed to reinvigorate private enterprise, progressives feared that judicial hostility toward moderate social reform played into

[55] "Extremes Meet," The Outlook, May 13, 1911, p. 54.
[56] Robert M. Crunden, Ministers of Reform: The Progressives' Achievement in American Civilization, 1889–1920, (New York: Basic Books, 1982), p. 79.
[57] Steidle, "Conservative Progressives," pp. 382–84.

the hands of socialists and revolutionaries. Writing in 1911, George W. Alger explained that progressives sought from the courts "a conservatism which is consistent with a not too remote possibility of progress, a conservatism free from all entanglements with either radicalism or reaction, a conservatism which harmonizes the past with the future by preserving the present from violent oscillations through contending forces."[58] In the same year Boudin observed that the epithet *revolutionary*, which Justice Lurton had applied to the demands of the progressives, "could be more fitly applied to the latest actions of our courts."[59]

Since the Fourteenth Amendment so frequently was the rope with which the courts strangled social legislation, critics of the courts had more reason to question economic due process than to challenge the far more fundamental doctrine of judicial review. Even those who acknowledged that the Constitution anticipated judicial review or otherwise favored its retention could agree that the courts overstepped the proper boundaries of review when judges read their own political beliefs into the vague language of provisions such as the Fourteenth Amendment. As Edward S. Corwin declared in 1912, "The modern concept of due process of law is not a legal concept at all; it comprises nothing more or less than a roving commission to judges to sink whatever legislative craft may appear to them to be, from the stand-point of vested interests, of a piratical tendency."[60]

Critics of the courts often expressed outrage over the curious process by which the Fourteenth Amendment was transformed from a shield for the freed bondsman into a sword for the free bond trader. Clark, for example, complained that while the Fourteenth Amendment was "adopted for the protection of the negro, it has become the asylum of the millionaire."[61] Nevertheless, critics of the courts undertook remarkably little historical analysis of the background of the Fourteenth Amendment to demonstrate that it was not intended to protect business from economic regulation. In contrast to the heated controversy over the origins of judicial review, the Progressive Era produced little discussion about the intent of the framers of the Fourteenth Amendment. Progressives who constructed elaborate arguments to demonstrate that judicial review was a usurpation devoted remarkably

[58] George W. Alger, "Criticizing the Courts," *Atlantic Monthly*, November 1911, p. 666.

[59] Boudin, "Government by Judiciary," p. 242.

[60] Edward S. Corwin, review of *Social Reform and the Constitution*, by Frank J. Goodnow, *American Political Science Review* 6 (May 1912): 271.

[61] Walter Clark, "'Aaron's Rod'; or, Government by Federal Judges," *Arena*, November 1907, p. 479. Similarly, another critic complained that the Fourteenth Amendment had become "the protector of all forms of commercial enterprises in all kinds of industrial pursuits" and no longer protected African Americans. Clifford Thorne, "Will the Supreme Court Become the Supreme Legislator of the United States?" *American Law Review* 43 (March–April 1909): 263.

little effort to showing that the Court had perverted the intention of the framers of the Fourteenth Amendment.

This may seem surprising, since progressives could make a far better argument that the framers of the Fourteenth Amendment had not foreseen economic due process than that the Framers of the Constitution had not foreseen judicial review. Perhaps they believed that such an examination of original intent was superfluous because the Framers so obviously had not intended such a result. As Gilbert Roe wrote in 1912, "Every one knows that the sole intent and purpose of the people in adding this amendment to the Constitution, was to protect the then recently emancipated negroes in their rights of citizenship." Roe, a prominent New York attorney who was a close adviser to La Follette, complained that the courts "have made this amendment include all manner of trusts and corporations, and of contracts and practices, none of which were even in the thought of the people when they adopted the amendment." Observing that "this amendment has become a shield to protect corporations and combinations of wealth from the legislation aimed at them by an indignant public, and also a sword by which statute after statute has been cut down," Roe declared that the people would not have permitted the ratification of the Fourteenth Amendment "had they even suspected the use that would be made of it."[62]

Corwin was one of the few scholars who wrote seriously about the transformation of the Fourteenth Amendment. In one of a series of pioneering articles in the *Michigan Law Review* in 1909, Corwin explained how the Supreme Court during the late nineteenth century had begun "a reinterpretation of the Fourteenth Amendment in the light of the principles of Lockian individualism and of Spencerian *Laissez Faire*" that led the Court to assert a broader power over state laws than it formerly had exercised. Corwin, however, took for granted that the framers of the amendment had intended to protect African Americans rather than property or corporations. Although Corwin concluded that this result was "not entirely devoid of irony," he emphasized that it was not devoid of historical justification since the Court prior to the enactment of the Fourteenth Amendment had established the Constitution as the bulwark of property rights.[63]

---

[62] Gilbert E. Roe, *Our Judicial Oligarchy* (New York: B. W. Huebsch, 1912), pp. 36–38. Although Roe and other progressives correctly pointed out that the principal purpose of the Fourteenth Amendment was to protect the emancipated blacks, many historians now believe that at least some of the framers of the Fourteenth Amendment anticipated that the clause would apply to corporations. See, e.g., Henry J. Abraham, *Freedom and the Court*, 4th ed. (New York: Oxford University Press, 1982), p. 38 n. 11.

[63] Edward S. Corwin, "The Supreme Court and the Fourteenth Amendment," *Michigan Law Review* 7 (June 1909): 643, 646, 672.

Even though the Court's critics complained that the Court had distorted the meaning of the Fourteenth Amendment, few critics lamented the Court's reluctance to use the Fourteenth Amendment as a means of protecting the civil liberties of African Americans. The attitudes of critics of the Court toward African-American liberties ranged from outright hostility among the populists to indifference—sometimes benign and sometimes malign—among most elements of the labor and progressive movements.[64] Indeed, some of the most vehement critics of the Supreme Court praised the Court for ignoring injustices against African Americans. For example, Democratic senator Robert L. Owen of Oklahoma declared in 1917 that the Court's decision in the *Civil Rights Cases* (1883)[65] to nullify the public accommodations section of the Civil Rights Act of 1875 was virtually the only judicial invalidation of federal legislation of which he fully approved.[66]

Defenders of the Court in turn sometimes used the Court's decision in the *Civil Rights Cases* as an argument in favor of judicial review. In denouncing Owen's advocacy of the abolition of judicial review, for example, a prominent Oklahoma City attorney lauded the Supreme Court for having "saved our children from the humiliation and disgrace of having to elbow with those who were our slaves."[67] Since few critics of the Court worried about African-American rights, it is not surprising that many of them advocated abolition of the Fourteenth Amendment. Since the Court rarely invoked the Fourteenth Amendment to protect African Americans, even opponents of the Court who believed that the law should protect civil liberties could have perceived little harm in the abolition of the Fourteenth Amendment.

Although Clark, Gilbert E. Roe, William L. Ransom, Felix Frankfurter, and other progressives favored abolition of the Fourteenth Amendment, they must have recognized that under present conditions, there was no more possibility that Congress would strike down the Fourteenth Amendment than that Congress would vote for the abolition of judicial review. Many other progressives who opposed economic due process nevertheless favored retention of the Fourteenth Amendment. Although racial equality was not a matter of pressing concern to most progressives, some may have favored reten-

[64] See generally, Graham, *Great Campaigns*, pp. 145, 150.

[65] 109 U.S. 3 (1883).

[66] Robert L. Owen, "Withdrawing Power from Federal Courts to Declare Acts of Congress Void," 64th Cong., 2d sess., S. Doc. 737, 1917, p. 23 (address delivered. at Oklahoma City, January 27, 1917).

[67] C. B. Stuart, "Power of the Supreme Court to Declare Acts of Congress Unconstitutional," 64th Cong., 2d sess., S. Doc. 708, 1917, pp. 10–11 (address delivered at Oklahoma City, January 23, 1917).

tion of the Fourteenth Amendment because they recognized that it continued to afford some protection to African Americans and that someday the Supreme Court might breathe life into the amendment in civil rights cases. Moreover, the right to remain free from deprivation of life, liberty, or property without due process of law was so fundamental to American concepts of freedom that progressives might not have wished to have deleted those cherished words from the Fourteenth Amendment, even though due process would remain in the Fifth Amendment as a restraint against federal action.

Even though the Supreme Court had not yet used the Fourteenth Amendment to incorporate the guarantees of the Bill of Rights into state law, progressives might have recognized that the Fourteenth Amendment, at least potentially, could help to protect personal rights outside the context of race. At the very least, the abolition of due process would restrict the circumstances under which the federal courts could review the constitutionality of state legislation, and many progressives of the nationalist stripe favored a broad scope of federal review. The recognition of the importance of due process as a check against the arbitrariness of the states led some progressives to argue that due process should be abolished only at the state level. Professor Dodd, for example, suggested that state court abuse of due process and inconsistencies between federal and state interpretations of due process could be reduced if the states eliminated the due process and equal protection clauses from their constitutions.[68]

Even though critics of the Court recognized that the explicit abolition of judicial review or abrogation of the Fourteenth Amendment was quixotic, some of them contended that Congress could avoid the full consequences of judicial nullification of legislation by reenacting certain measures that the Court had invalidated. Prior to 1906, Congress had only rarely enacted legislation to overcome the effects of Supreme Court decisions,[69] and the constitutionality of this circumvention of the Court remained unclear. The availability of this remedy, however, provided an attractive alternative to the abrogation of judicial review and was used several times during the Progressive Era.

Congressional attitudes toward this expedient were illustrated during the debate on the income tax amendment in 1909. Several members of Congress argued that reenactment of the invalidated legislation was more practicable than a constitutional amendment. Proponents of reenactment were divided between those who favored outright defi-

[68] W. F. Dodd, "The Recall and the Political Responsibility of Judges," *Michigan Law Review* 10 (December 1911): 79, 90–91.

[69] Richard A. Paschal, "The Continuing Colloquy: Congress and the Finality of the Supreme Court," *Journal of Law and Politics* 8 (Fall 1991): 217 (appendix A).

ance of the Court's 1895 decisions and those who believed that the Court might uphold the new statute. The latter pointed out that the Court had decided the principal case by a 5–4 vote and that three of the five justices who had voted to invalidate the statute were no longer members of the Court. Moreover, the unpopularity of the Court's decisions and the change in political climate during the intervening fourteen years might make the Court more hospitable to a new statute.[70] Democratic representative David A. De Armond of Missouri explained that Congress had the duty to enact any legislation that it believed to be constititional "and leave to the Supreme Court the responsibility of determining the constitutionality when presented."[71] Even so orthodox a constitutionalist as President Taft acknowledged that Congress could properly enact a statute that invited the Court to reconsider its earlier decision. Taft, however, concluded that a constitutional amendment was preferable.[72]

Proponents of reenactment argued that congressional acquiescence to an erroneous decision would erode popular confidence in government. "No earthly tribunal has ever yet reached a position so exalted as to be beyond the reach of the shafts of honest and legitimate criticism when in error," declared Democratic Representative Cordell Hull of Tennessee. Hull warned that the public would show little patience with members who would maintain "that a Supreme Court decision, however erroneous, is sacred and must be acquiesced in and accepted by all the sufferers of its injustice without even respectfully asking its authors to correct their own wrong."[73]

Reenactment of the statute without regard to the probable outcome of another Supreme Court decision was distinguishable in theory from outright abolition of judicial review. Critics of the Court argued that the *Pollack* decisions were not entitled to deference because the decision was wrongly decided as a matter of law. To those who argued that disregard of judicial decisions was lawless, the Court's critics pointed

[70] See 44 *Congressional Record*, 61st Cong., 2d sess., July 12, 1909, p. 4398 (remarks of Rep. James); ibid. p. 4409 (remarks of Rep. Bartlett, Georgia); ibid. p. 4412 (remarks of Rep. Henry, Texas). As Rep. Henry observed, "The court did not hesistate to overturn the established law of a hundred years, and why should we halt in asking them to reconsider, in the interests of more than eighty millions of people, their judgment so universally condemned by the American bar and citizenship?" (ibid., p. 4413).

[71] Ibid., p. 4419.

[72] In a message to Congress, Taft explained that "for the Congress to assume that the court will reverse itself, and to enact legislation on such an assumption, will not strengthen popular confidence in the stability of judicial construction of the Constitution." *Message from the President of the United States*, 61st Cong., 1st sess., S. Doc. 98, 1909, p. 2.

[73] 44 *Congressional Record*, 61st Cong., 1st sess., July 12, 1909, pp. 4402, 4403.

out that the Court itself in *Pollack* had disregarded nearly a century of its own precedent. Democratic senator Anselm J. McLaurin of Mississippi, for example, declared that he did not believe that Congress "should be called upon to zigzag around the inconsistent rulings" of the Court, and he averred that there were "just as good lawyers" in Congress as on the Supreme Court.[74] In response to those who contended that a constitutional amendment would be a more appropriate manner of circumventing the Court's decision on the income tax, Democratic senator Joseph W. Bailey of Texas pointed out that the amendment process was so cumbersome that it was virtually impracticable.[75]

Despite misgivings over the constitutionality of congressional enactment of statutes that seemed to contravene Supreme Court decisions, between 1906 and 1914 Congress enacted several important statutes designed to overcome the effects of decisions by the Court. For example, the Hepburn Act of 1906 and the Mann Elkins Act of 1910 both strengthened the powers of the Interstate Commerce Commission in response to Supreme Court decisions that had limited the power of the ICC. The Federal Employers' Liability Act of 1908, which applied only to railroad workers who were engaged in interstate commerce, was intended to overcome a decision that had struck down a previous statute because it was not limited to workers in interstate commerce. And the broad pro-labor language of the Clayton Act of 1914 arguably limited the Supreme Court's application of the Sherman Antitrust Act to secondary boycotts in *Loewe v. Lawlor*. Although the Court ultimately limited the scope of the Clayton Act's protections against boycotts, it upheld the Hepburn Act, the Mann-Elkins Act, the second Employers' Liability Act, and several other statutes that circumvented previous decisions of the Court.

The availability of a legislative remedy for Court decisions helped to diminish support for more radical measures. Like other reform proposals, the demand for abrogation of judicial review was frustrated by the abiding public respect for the judiciary, the failure of proponents to unite behind any specific measure, and the formidable institutional obstacles that any proposal for a radical abrogation of judicial power would have faced. Like other reform measures, however, the bills to curb the power of judicial review provided a reminder that an angry public had the power to strip the courts of fundamental jurisdiction. But while proposals for limiting judicial review served as a useful vehicle of protest, most progressives and trade unionists prior to the 1920s preferred to devote their energies to more practical proposals for judicial reform.

---

[74] Ibid., July 3, 1909, p. 4067.
[75] 44 *Congressional Record*, 61st Cong., 1st sess. July 5, 1909, p. 4116.

THREE

MELIORATIVE MEASURES

The legal profession is pushing certain reforms and
innovations which repel the charge that it is
unduly conservative.
(The Green Bag, *April 1912*)[1]

DESPITE THE GROWING dissatisfaction with the courts and
the recrudescence of attacks on judicial review from 1906 to
1912, many critics of the courts continued to prefer to circumvent judicial obstruction of social legislation without challenging judicial power. Accordingly, many advocated procedural reforms that
would not alter any institutional aspect of the courts or curtail any
fundamental element of their jurisdiction. While this failure to advocate fundamental constitutional changes reflected in part a pragmatic
recognition that such efforts would fail, it also suggests again that most
critics of the judiciary opposed the way judicial power was exercised
rather than the power itself. The movement for many moderate reforms received the support of conservatives, particularly in the organized bar. By propounding popular reforms, the bar demonstrated an
adeptness at muting hostility toward the judiciary that it also displayed
in its opposition to radical reform.

The moderation of critics of the judiciary was particularly evident in
the labor movement. Prior to 1918, organized labor preferred to
achieve its objectives through incremental legislation that would
strengthen labor without significantly clipping the wings of the courts.
The AFL's 1907 resolution to restrict the power of judicial review was
an exception to the AFL's prevailing moderation and pragmatism, and
its advocacy of that measure was short-lived and muted. By contrast,
the AFL agitated persistently for legislation to restrict the power of the
courts to issue injunctions. To ensure the enactment of such legislation,
labor also sought to elect sympathetic state and federal legislators.
Moreover, labor sought to change the character of the judiciary by
attempting to elect state judges who would be favorable toward labor
and a president who would nominate more liberal federal judges.

With the start of the new century, the AFL stepped up its campaign

[1] *Green Bag*, April 1912, p. 221.

for pro-labor legislation at the state and federal levels.[2] Although numerous states enacted legislation to protect unions from injunctions and the common law of conspiracy, federal and state courts invalidated these statutes or vitiated them by narrow construction.[3] Beginning in 1907, the AFL sponsored legislation to restrict the scope of the equity jurisdiction of the federal courts by excluding employment relations and the conduct of businesses from the definition of protectable property.[4] Although labor had little role in the 1904 presidential campaign, the AFL campaigned vigorously for the election of members of Congress who favored pro-labor legislation.[5] Setbacks suffered by labor during 1905, including the *Lochner* decision, forced the AFL to retreat from its oft-stated position that it could achieve its goals through economic power alone.

Meanwhile, political successes of trade unionists in Britain encouraged greater political participation by American labor. The election of fifty Labour members to the British Parliament early in 1906 demonstrated that labor could be a strong independent political force. And the Liberal government's enactment of legislation to repudiate the notorious *Taff Vale* decision, which had subjected trade unions to liability for conspiracy, provided a reminder of the usefulness of legislation as a remedy for judicial abuses.[6] In March 1906, the AFL promulgated a "Bill of Grievances" that called for various reforms, including limitations upon the power of courts to issue injunctions.[7] When Roosevelt and Congress largely rebuffed labor's demands, the AFL escalated its political activities. In 1906 the AFL conducted a vigorous campaign to publicize the labor records of elected state judges and candidates for Congress.

Gompers's faith in the ability of the legislature to effect reforms that would not strip the judiciary of any significant power was illustrated in 1908 when the Supreme Court tightened the Sherman Act's grip on labor in *Loewe v. Lawlor*. Although Gompers deplored the decision as

---

[2] William E. Forbath, "The Shaping of the American Labor Movement," *Harvard Law Review* 102 (April 1989): 1220; Felix Frankfurter and Nathan Greene, *The Labor Injunction* (Gloucester, Mass.: Peter Smith, 1963; repr. 1930 MacMillan ed.), pp. 139–41.

[3] Forbath, "Shaping of American Labor," pp. 1220–22.

[4] Christopher L. Tomlins, *The State and Unions: Labor Relations, Law, and the Organized Labor Movement in America, 1880–1960* (New York: Cambridge University Press, 1985) p. 64; Forbath, "Shaping of Labor Movement," p. 1224.

[5] Philip S. Foner, *History of the Labor Movement in the United States*, vol. 3, *The Policies and Practices of the American Federation of Labor, 1900–1909* (New York: International, 1964), pp. 301–4.

[6] Ibid., pp. 312–13.

[7] "Labor's Bill of Grievances," *American Federationist*, May 1906, pp. 293–96; Foner, *History*, pp. 314–19.

the worst "invasion of the rights and liberties of our people" in the nation's history, his public criticism of the Court was circumspect. Gompers criticized the justices for arrogating legislative powers and failing to keep abreast of recent industrial developments but affirmed that each justice had "honestly and conscientiously" rendered his opinion. "We do not agree with those who charge the court with being influenced by sinister motives, or under the domination of corporate influence," he declared. For relief, Gompers urged union members to look to Congress. He expressed faith that "Congress will appreciate the injustice which has been done directly to the workers and hence indirectly to all the people" and that "the present Congress will take prompt action to so amend or modify the Sherman law."[8] At Gompers's behest, the AFL Executive Council drafted a "Protest to Congress" calling for amendment of the Sherman Act, and union members deluged members of Congress with resolutions and letters demanding such an amendment.[9] Meanwhile, Gompers admonished AFL members to obey the Court's decision.[10]

Gompers urged the ever-increasing ranks of AFL members to work at the state level for the defeat of "injunction judges." Gompers explained that the way to secure pro-labor legislation was "to defeat every bigoted, ignorant, or class-serving judge, and every legislator who would not oppose judicial tyranny and judicial insolence."[11]

The AFL became active during the 1908 presidential campaign after the Republican party failed to support anti-injunction legislation. Although Roosevelt complained about the misuse of injunctions in his 1905, 1906, and 1907 messages to Congress and urged a moderate reform in a special message in January 1908,[12] the GOP convention adopted a more tepid position. The platform opposed the issuance of injunctions without notice, but only where no irreparable injury would

[8] Samuel Gompers, Editorial, "Labor Organizations Must Not Be Outlawed—The Supreme Court's Decision in the Hatters' Case," *American Federationist*, March 1908, p. 180, 181, 184, 185, 190; Gompers, "To Organized Labor and Friends," ibid., p. 193.

[9] Foner, *History*, pp. 344–46; "Labor's Protest to Congress," *American Federationist*, April 1908, pp. 261–69.

[10] Gompers, "To Organized Labor," p. 193.

[11] Samuel Gompers, Editorial, "The Injunction in Labor Disputes Must Go!" *American Federationist*, April 1906, p. 228. Gompers declared that "judicial candidates everywhere must be made to understand that the working masses mean to assert and defend their rights as citizens and free men—the right to trial by jury, the right to free speech and free association within the law, the right of moral suasion, the right to induce men to join unions, the right to use the streets and highways peaceably and in an orderly manner."

[12] Fred L. Israel, ed., *The State of the Union Messages of the Presidents, 1790–1966*, vol. 3, *1905–1966* (New York: Chelsea House, 1966), pp. 2154, 2197–98, 2256; 42 *Congressional Record* 60th Cong., 1st sess., January 31, 1908, pp. 1347–48.

result from the failure to restrain union activity.[13] Believing that the exception swallowed the rule, the AFL was bitterly disappointed by the platform. The Republican Gompers, who had pleaded with GOP leaders to adopt an anti-injunction plank, stated that the proposal for procedural change would actually strengthen the power of the courts to issue injunctions because it would provide a new statutory authority for injunctions in labor cases. Gompers denounced the platform's pledge of fidelity to judicial integrity as "a gratuitous, indefensible and covert insult, not only to . . . labor but to the courts themselves" because it suggested that "the integrity and legal authority of the courts have been questioned."[14] The AFL was also displeased by the nomination of Taft, whose record during his eight years as a federal district court judge the AFL denounced as antilabor.[15]

The AFL was well satisfied with the Democratic platform, which called for signficant procedural reforms relating to the issuance of injunctions. Affirming its respect for the courts, the Democratic platform declared that "we resent the attempt of the Republican party to raise a false issue respecting the judiciary. It is an unjust reflection upon a great body of our citizens to assume that they lack respect for the courts." The Democratic platform also expressed support for an eight-hour day for government employees, the enactment of a general federal employers' liability act, and the creation of a department of labor.[16]

In a circular issued three weeks before the election, Gompers declared that abuse of judicial power was the paramount issue of the campaign, alleging that trusts and corporations were attempting to transform judges into "irresponsible despots" who would do the bidding of giant business interests. Stating that this "revolution has already progressed very far," Gompers contended that the courts had deprived the workers of their rights as citizens by forbidding the exercise of freedoms of speech, press, assembly, and petition when the courts determined that the exercise of those rights might injure business corporations. Declaring that despotic power under a judicial gown "is as dangerous as despotic power under the crown," Gompers decried the Republican platform's temperate injunction plank and denounced Taft as "the originator and specific champion" of "government by in-

[13] Donald Bruce Johnson, ed., *National Party Platforms*, vol. 1, *1840–1956* (Urbana: University of Illinois Press, 1978), p. 160.

[14] Samuel Gompers, Editorial, "Both Parties Have Spoken—Choose Between Them," *American Federationist*, August 1908, p. 598.

[15] "Candidate Taft, Take Notice!," *American Federationist*, November 1908, pp. 960–65.

[16] Johnson, *National Party Platforms*, pp. 147–48.

junction." In contrast, Gompers contended, the Democratic Party and its candidate, William Jennings Bryan, "stand for government by law vested in the people."[17]

Despite his many public criticisms of the courts, Roosevelt professed to be outraged by the AFL's statements concerning the judiciary during the campaign. In his final annual message, delivered in December 1908, Roosevelt denounced the AFL's "violent and sweeping attack upon the entire judiciary."[18] Gompers's reply was swift and bitter. Accusing Roosevelt of a willful distortion of the truth, Gompers denied that any representative of labor had "made any attack upon any individual judge or the judiciary as such."[19] Despite his attack on the AFL, Roosevelt in his final message to Congress reiterated his proposals for procedural reforms to restrict the issuance of injunctions without notice and to expedite hearings.[20]

In his inaugural address on March 4, 1909, Taft defended the use of injunctions, warning that the deprivation of judicial power to issue injunctions in labor disputes would encourage lawlessness. Taft, however, expressed support for legislation to limit the "inconsiderate exercise" of the temporary restraining order without notice.[21] In his first message to Congress in December 1909, Taft proposed legislation to forbid any injunction or temporary restraining order without previous notice and a reasonable opportunity for the parties to be heard, unless the court from evidence should make a written finding that the delay necessary for such notice and hearing would result in irreparable injury.[22] Gompers contended that nothing in Taft's proposal would "materially alter existing conditions" since it would not limit the jurisdiction of the courts. Gompers noted that the injunction in one particularly notorious case complied with the procedural formalities embodied in the administration's bill. Gompers declared that "popular government, democratic institutions, can not exist together with the unlimited discretionary power of either a king or a judge."[23]

[17] "Official Circular," signed by Samuel Gompers and dated October 12, 1908, *American Federationist*, November 1908, pp. 955–57.

[18] Israel, *State of the Union Messages*, p. 2307.

[19] "Gompers Assails Roosevelt," *New York Times*, December 23, 1908, p. 2.

[20] Israel, *State of the Union Messages*, p. 2311.

[21] *The Chief Executive: Inaugural Addresses of the Presidents of the United States from George Washington to Lyndon B. Johnson* (New York: Crown, 1965), pp. 218–19.

[22] Israel, pp. 2360–61. Taft's proposal also provided that every injunction or temporary restraining order issued without notice would expire no later than one week after its issuance (ibid., p. 2361). Taft's proposal was embodied in a bill that was introduced in Congress in 1910 (H.R. 21334, 61st Cong., 2d sess., 1910).

[23] "A Protest Against Legalizing the Injunction Abuse" (providing text of letter from Samuel Gompers to Reuben O. Moon), March 2, 1910, *American Federationist*, April 1910, pp. 318–20.

The AFL favored a stronger bill introduced by a Pennsylvania representative in 1910.[24] In his second annual message to Congress in 1910, Taft charged that the AFL measure would "sap the foundations of judicial power, and legalize that cruel social instrument, the secondary boycott."[25] In disputing Taft's contention, Gompers declared that the bill would "instill greater respect for and confidence in the judiciary and thereby strengthen the lawful powers vested in it."[26] Although opposition by both the AFL and conservatives succeeded in defeating the administration's bill, the AFL's bill also failed. Labor had to wait until the enactment of the Clayton Act in 1914 before it obtained a statute that limited the injunction power.

Since judicial use of the injunction was the principal source of labor's antagonism toward the courts, the AFL's efforts to curb the power to issue injunctions and its frequent defiance of court orders may seem like exceptions swallowing the rule that the AFL was generally deferential toward judicial power. The AFL's toleration of judicial review and its attempts to bend the law to its own purposes, however, suggest that the AFL recognized that courts could develop legal doctrines that would help to protect trade unionism from the shifting tides of political fortune. As William E. Forbath has argued, "The courts' very sway made common law and constitutional discourse beckon as the surest framework within which to contend for legitimacy and relief. Thus, labor leaders at all levels began to speak and think more and more in the language of the law."[27] Appropriating for labor's purposes the legal theories of individualism upon which employers had based their opposition to unionism, organized labor continued to attempt to achieve a legal parity with capital that would enable labor and capital to enter into mutually beneficial commercial arrangements, with a minimum of state intervention.[28]

Like the AFL, many prominent progressives eschewed radical plans for abrogation of judicial power and preferred to work for more modest measures. In particular, many progressive critics of the courts argued that procedural reforms would help to make the courts more

[24] This bill provided that no restraining order could be granted in any labor dispute "unless necessary to prevent irreparable injury to property or property right," which would have to be described with particularity in the application for the injunction. The bill excluded from the definition of "property" or "property right" any right to continue the relationship of employer or employee or to carry on a business. The bill also excluded union activities from the scope of the conspiracy and antitrust laws (H.R. 25188, 61st Cong., 1st sess., 1910).

[25] Israel, *State of the Union Messages*, pp. 2401–2.

[26] Editorial, "The President's Habit of mind on Injunctions," *American Federationist*, January 1911, p. 33.

[27] Forbath, "Shaping of American Labor," p. 1116.

[28] See Tomlins, *State and Unions*, p. 77.

effective allies of the reform movement. Progressives especially sought remedies for the delays and expense that retarded justice. The need to scrape away a multitude of procedural encrustations was so obvious that even the staunchest defenders of the courts did not deny the need for change or flinch from proposing reforms. Indeed, conservatives took the lead in the procedural reform movement. The need for procedural reform was one of the few judicial issues about which progressives, the labor movement, and conservatives tended to agree, even though they did not always share the same vision of the precise forms the changes should take.

Since the weeds of procedural anachronism will choke the fruits of any legal garden that is not regularly pruned, procedural reform is a continous process, and Americans of every era have complained about the unnecessary expense and delay in the legal system. Demand for procedural reform was particularly insistent during the Progressive Era, however. The widespread frustration with judicial antagonism toward progressive measures exacerbated popular vexation over the inefficiencies and inequities of the judicial process. Exasperation with the more antiquated or abusive features of the judicial system in turn helped to build support for proposals to curb judicial power. It is not entirely coincidental that movements for procedural reform were most active from 1906 to 1925, the very period when criticism of the courts was widespread and calls for abridgement of judicial powers were vociferous.

Roscoe Pound sounded the keynote for procedural reform in his celebrated speech before the American Bar Association in 1906 in which he attributed much of the popular dissatisfaction with justice to the contentious character of procedural rules and the antiquated organization of the courts. In appealing for reform, Pound argued that much procedure was based upon the "sporting theory of justice," which made lawsuits a contest between parties rather than a search for truth and justice. "The idea that procedure must of necessity be wholly contentious disfigures our judicial administration at every point," Pound declared.[29]

A number of other legal scholars and progressives concurred in Pound's belief that the public perception of law as a game had severely eroded respect for the courts and the legal process.[30] Other leading public figures identified other shortcomings in the legal system that

---

[29] Roscoe Pound, "The Causes of Popular Dissatisfaction with the Administration of Justice," address delivered at the Annual Convention of the American Bar Association in 1906 (American Judicature Society repr., 1980), p. 12.

[30] See, e.g., George W. Alger, "Swift and Cheap Justice, IV. The Sporting Theory of Justice," *The World's Work*, January 1914, p. 338.

eroded public confidence in the courts. In a paper delivered to the Massachusetts Bar Association in 1912, for example, Harvard president emeritus Charles W. Eliot pointed to many practical problems, including jury selection procedures, the contentiousness of attorneys, the abuse of expert testimony, the use of torture in extracting confessions, the multiplicity of appeals and retrials, the delay of decisions, and the narrowness of legal education.[31]

In formulating means of improving judicial procedure, progressives characteristically urged the adoption of "scientific" methods. Progressives believed that the concept and practice of efficiency served the public interest and would be an antidote to social disorder.[32] Indeed, the progressives tended to equate justice with the application of their scientific principles.[33]

It is somewhat ironic that progressive proposals for the reform of judicial procedure, like other progressive reforms,[34] were influenced by the model of the large-scale corporation. One of the most influential advocates of streamlining the courts along the lines of a business was George W. Alger, a New York attorney who had long crusaded for industrial and social reform. In a series of five widely read articles published in *The World's Work* during late 1913 and early 1914 under the title "Swift and Cheap Justice," Alger identified and analyzed a host of problems that beset the legal system and proposed various remedies.[35] Complaining about the lack of oversight of judges and the paucity of administrative organization and leadership, Alger declared that "there is no branch of our public business . . . which makes so little accounting of its services as the judiciary." To make the courts more responsible, Alger urged businesspeople to proffer advice to the courts concerning management techniques. And with a characteristically progressive faith in the usefulness of statistics, he endorsed the proposal of the New York Commission on the Law's Delay for the establishment of

[31] Charles W. Eliot, "The Popular Dissatisfaction with the Administration of Justice in the United States," *Green Bag*, February 1913, pp. 65–74 (repr. from *Springfield Republican*).

[32] Samuel P. Hays, *The Response to Industrialism 1885–1914* (Chicago: University of Chicago Press, 1957), pp. 88, 157.

[33] Arthur L. Link and Richard L. McCormick, *Progressivism* (Arlington Heights, Ill.: Harlan Davidson, 1983), p. 95.

[34] John Whiteclay Chambers II, *The Tyranny of Change: America in the Progressive Era, 1900–1917* (New York: St. Martin's Press, 1980), pp. 112–13; David B. Danbom, "*The World of Hope": Progressives and the Struggle for an Ethical Public Life* (Philadelphia: Temple University Press, 1987), p. 133.

[35] George W. Alger, "Swift and Cheap Justice," *World's Work*, October 1913, pp. 653–66; ibid., November 1913, pp. 53–62; ibid., December 1913, pp. 160–75; ibid., January 1914, pp. 338–46; ibid., February 1914, pp. 424–32.

a scientific system of compiling judicial statistics so that the public might be better informed about the condition of their courts.[36] Alger also urged that judges be given greater flexibility in establishing rules of procedure.[37]

Judicial reform was embraced with fervor by people who occupied the most powerful offices in the legal profession and the judiciary. Thomas W. Shelton, a vice president of the ABA, stated in 1917 that "leading American authorities, including President Wilson, ex-President Taft, the American Bar Association and forty-five State Bar Associations, are upon record that present juridical conditions do not justify popular faith in or respect for the courts, or their creators. All the national civic and industrial organizations have called for relief."[38] As chairman of the ABA's Committee on Uniform Court Procedure during the early 1920s, Shelton worked for standardization of procedure among the states.

The most prominent and persistent of the more conservative critics of the courts during the progressive period was William Howard Taft. As president and later as a Yale Law School professor, ABA president, and chief justice, Taft assailed the shortcomings of the judicial system with a vigor unsurpassed by any radical or progressive and worked sedulously for procedural reform. During the 1908 presidential campaign, Taft asserted his belief that "the greatest question now before the American public is the improvement of the administration of justice, civil and criminal, both in the matter of its prompt dispatch and the cheapening of its use." Taft proposed various remedies, including expanded use of arbitration, diminished reliance upon juries, and encouragement of swifter action by judges.[39]

As president, Taft honored his campaign promise to work for judicial reform. Although reform of judicial procedure is an unusual cause for a president to embrace, Taft was no usual president. Throughout his two decades in the executive branch, Taft yearned to return to the bench. Taft, whose ultimate aspiration was the chief justiceship rather than the presidency, viewed the law and the courts with reverence. As Taft explained in 1911 in a speech in Pocatello in which he roundly denounced the judicial recall, "I love judges and I love courts. They are my ideals on earth that typify what we shall meet afterward in Heaven under a just God."[40] Taft's intense interest in judicial affairs made him

[36] Ibid., October 1913, p. 655; ibid., November 1913, p. 54, 61.

[37] Ibid., pp. 54, 55–56, 59–60, 62.

[38] Thomas W. Shelton, " 'Justice Is the Greatest Interest of Mankind on Earth'—A Plea to the President and Congress," *Central Law Journal* 85 (December 1917): 421.

[39] "Taft Wants Quick and Cheap Justice," *New York Times*, August 2, 1908, p. 1; "Promoting Justice," ibid., August 8, 1908, p. 4.

[40] "Taft Again Defends the Supreme Court," *New York Times*, October 7, 1911, p. 6.

acutely aware of the shortcomings of the legal system. Although Taft believed that the reforms that he advocated would improve the legal system by making it more modern, efficient, and fair, he also recognized that reform was necessary if the broad judicial power in which he so strongly believed was to remain unimpaired.

After his inauguration, Taft declared that the poor man should "have as nearly as possible an opportunity of litigating as the rich man, and under present conditions, ashamed as we may be of it, this is not the fact." Taft proposed the creation of a congressional commission to recommend a system for "quick and cheap justice" in the federal courts that might also serve as a model for the states. Taft was even more critical of the criminal justice system, which he flayed as "a disgrace to our civilization." Echoing Pound's doubts about the sporting theory of justice, Taft declared that criminal trials were games "in which the criminal has the advantage, and if he wins he seems to have the sympathy of a sporting public." As a partial remedy, Taft proposed giving the judges greater power in the criminal trials by enabling judges to assist the jury in its consideration of facts and to exercise more control over the arguments advanced by lawyers.[41] In his first annual message to Congress, Taft expressed his belief that "much of the lawless violence and cruelty exhibited in lynchings is directly due to the uncertainties and injustice growing out of the delays in trials, judgments, and the executions thereof by our courts."[42]

The movement for judicial reform bore impressive results. The paper Pound delivered to the ABA in 1906 led to the ABA's recommendation of reforms that were widely adopted.[43] By 1911, the *Green Bag* reported that there were many signs of a tendency toward improvement of the administration of the courts.[44] Two years later, *The World's Work* observed that some judges seemed to "appreciate the need of change even more than the lawyers and laymen" and that their "utmost eagerness" for reform belied the mistaken popular belief that they exalted law over justice.[45]

The movement for procedural reform led to many lasting changes

[41] "Our Criminal Trials Disgrace, Says Taft," *New York Times*, September 17, 1909, p. 2.

[42] Israel, *State of the Union Messages*, p. 2359.

[43] Felix Frankfurter and James M. Landis, *The Business of the Supreme Court: A Study in the Federal Judicial System* (New York: Macmillan, 1928), p. 223.

[44] *The Green Bag*, December 1911, pp. 660–61. In an effort to reduce delays, a judge in Westchester County, New York, during the autumn of 1911 told lawyers that he would adjourn court for the term if they were not prepared to proceed with their cases. At the same time, a judge in Queens served notice that he would dismiss the cases of unprepared lawyers. Meanwhile, a St. Louis judge fined an attorney for blocking a damage suit by filing a trivial motion and leaving it unargued for months.

[45] "Court Reform Making Progress," *The World's Work*, March 1914, p. 492.

in the judicial system. Chicago and a number of other cities turned mazes of local courts into single, unified systems. Following the lead of Wisconsin in 1913, a number of states established judicial councils to act as clearinghouses for information and to make rational allocations of judicial resources. Similar reforms were enacted at the federal level by the Judiciary Act of 1922, which established a multitude of new judgeships, created a judicial council chaired by the chief justice, and provided for the assignment of judges to understaffed areas outside their home circuits or districts.[46] The direction provided by the council led during the 1920s to a number of significant reforms in procedure. Recognizing that the judiciary had often nullified reform legislation because it was badly drafted or in conflict with constitutional law, progressives in many states also established legislative reference libraries that were staffed with legislative experts who helped to draft state legislation and provided legislators with information they needed for the proper discharge of their duties.[47]

Although many of the proposals for alterations in the process of judicial review never came to pass, progressives succeeded in effecting one major change—a significant extension of the federal judiciary's power to review state decisions that upheld challenges to social legislation.[48] It is ironic that this measure, the most tangible progressive reform involving the judiciary, enhanced the power of the federal courts. As enacted by Congress in 1914, this law permitted appeals from state to federal courts on all questions arising under the Constitution and federal laws.

Until the enactment of this statute, the Supreme Court could exercise jurisdiction over appeals from state courts on constitutional questions only when the state court had denied a claim arising under the Constitution, a treaty, or a federal statute.[49] Accordingly, the federal courts had no power to review a state decision if the court had sustained a claim arising under federal law. The statute, which originated in the Judiciary Act of 1789, was intended to safeguard the powers of the United States and to protect the rights of individuals under federal law.[50] Although there was some agitation during the early years of the

[46] Frankfurter and Landis, *Business of the Courts*, pp. 223–54.

[47] Russel B. Nye, *Midwestern Progressive Politics: A Historical Study of Its Origins and Development* (East Lansing: Michigan State College Press, 1951), p. 219.

[48] For a general discussion of the events that led to this reform, see Frankfurter and Landis, *Business of the Court*, pp. 190–98.

[49] 36 Stat. 1156 (1911).

[50] Until the Civil War established the supremacy of federal law, the statute's principal critics were states' rights advocates who objected even to the limited jurisdiction the statute conferred on the federal courts. Although there was some agitation during the early years of the Republic for removal of the limitation, it generally seemed innocuous.

Republic for removal of the limitation,[51] it seemed generally innocuous. In enacting the statute, Congress had apparently presumed that there was no purpose served by allowing the Supreme Court to review a state court's vindication of a federal constitutional claim since the federal court could only be expected to affirm the state court decision.[52]

By the early 1900s, however, when state courts frequently invoked the Fourteenth Amendment in striking down progressive state legislation, this provision became a serious impediment to the progressive movement. Since many of the state courts were more hostile toward social legislation than the federal courts, progressives had reason to believe that the Supreme Court might overrule the state decisions if only the Supreme Court was allowed to review those decisions. Noting that conditions had changed since the adoption of the Judiciary Act, Professor W. F. Dodd of the University of Illinois observed in 1911 that "the states and their citizens really need the protection of the United States Supreme Court against the strict and often illiberal decisions of their own courts on federal questions." Dodd contended that "individual rights involving a federal question are not properly safeguarded, because the party who sets up the federal question has a right of appeal if the decision goes against him, while the party against whom the federal question is raised has no such right, although his interests may be equally affected."[53]

Progressives were particularly vexed by state interpretations of due process that contravened the Supreme Court's interpretation of due process in cases that involved virtually identical issues. For example, courts in Missouri (1904) and Texas (1907) held that the federal and state constitutions did not permit the state to forbid payment of wages in store orders not redeemable in cash,[54] even though the Supreme Court in 1901 had upheld a federal law substantially identical to the Texas and Missouri statutes.[55] In a number of other cases, state courts interpreted state "due process" provisions in a manner inconsistent with the Supreme Court's interpretation of the federal due process

---

Charles Warren, "Legislative and Judicial Attacks on the Supreme Court of the United States—A History of the Twenty-Fifth Section of the Judiciary Act," *American Law Review* 47 (January–February 1913): 1–34; ibid., March–April 1913, pp. 161–89.

[51] Ibid., pp. 2–3.

[52] Walter James Shepard, "Appeal and the Referendum," *The Nation*, April 4, 1912, p. 335.

[53] W. F. Dodd, "The United States Supreme Court as the Final Interpreter of the Federal Constitution," *Illinois Law Review* 6 (December 1911): 293, 299.

[54] *State v. Missouri Tie and Timber Co.*, 181 Mo. 536, 80 S.W. 933 (1904); *Jordan v. State*, 51 Tex. Crim. App. 531, 103 S.W. 633 (1907). The Texas decision also was based on the federal constitution.

[55] *Knoxville Iron Co. v. Harbison*, 183 U.S. 13 (1901).

clauses.[56] Inconsistencies between state and federal laws also arose when the Court upheld social welfare legislation that resembled statutes that state courts had earlier struck down.[57]

As Professor Henry Schofield of Northwestern observed, state supreme courts had the de facto although not the de jure power to "shut their eyes to, refuse to follow, and go directly against, decisions of the federal Supreme Court expounding the constitution and laws of the United States," subject only to the limitation that they "confine their activity to pressing the screws of the limitations of the Constitution and laws of the United States down on to their respective states tighter than the Federal Supreme Court does."[58]

Progressives also complained that the limitation on jurisdiction created inconsistencies between the laws of the states.[59] Only a few months after the New York Court of Appeals struck down the Empire State's workers' compensation law in *Ives*, the supreme court in Washington State upheld a similar law.[60] The following year, New Jersey's supreme court upheld New Jersey's workers' compensation statute.[61] As the House Judiciary Committee report on the reform legislation observed, "The fourteenth amendment meant one thing on the east bank of the Hudson and the opposite on the west bank."[62] More than any other

[56] In 1899, for example, only one year after the Supreme Court had upheld Utah's eight-hour day for miners, the Colorado Supreme Court held that an eight-hour day for miners and smelters violated the state constitution (*Holden v. Hardy*, 169 U.S. 366 [1898]; *In re Morgan*, 26 Colo. 415, 58 P. 1071 [1899]. Likewise, the New York Court of Appeals in 1904 annulled as a violation of the state constitution a statute that regulated the hours and conditions of labor on state and municipal works, even though the Supreme Court in *Atkin v. Kansas* in 1903 had upheld such a law under the Fourteenth Amendment (*People ex rel. Cossey v. Grout*, 179 N.Y. 417, 72 N.E. 464 [1904]; *Atkin v. Kansas*, 191 U.S. 207 [1903]).

[57] For example, although the Utah Supreme Court in 1904 and the New York Court of Appeals had held in 1905 that statutes that restricted sales of merchandise in bulk violated both the state and federal constitutions, the Supreme Court in 1910 upheld a similar statute. *Block v. Schwartz*, 27 Utah 387, 76 P. 22 (1904); *Wright v. Hart*, 182 N.Y. 330, 74 N.E. 404 (1905); *Kidd, Dater and Price Co. v. Musselman Grocer Co.*, 217 U.S. 461 (1910). An amended bulk-sale law was upheld by the New York Appellate Division in 1908; *Sprintz v. Saxton*, 126 A. D. 421, 110 N.Y.S. 585 (1908).

[58] Henry Schofield, "Comment on Recent Cases: Unreviewable Wrong or Doubtful State Decisions of Questions of Federal Constitutional Law—Their Effect on Private Interests and on the Reserved Powers of the States," *Illinois Law Review* 3 (December 1908): 303.

[59] William L. Ransom, *Majority Rule and the Judiciary* (New York: Scribner, 1912), pp. 51–52.

[60] *State ex rel. Davis-Smith Co. v. Clausen*, 65 Wash. 156, 117 P. 1101 (1911).

[61] *Sexton v. Newark District Telegraph Co.*, 84 N.J. 85, 86 A. 451 (1913).

[62] House Report 1222, 63rd Cong., 3rd sess., 1914, p. 2. Similarly, the New York lawyer William L. Ransom declared in 1912, "It is hard to explain, even to the most

case, *Ives* called attention to the inability of the Supreme Court to review state decisions that had struck down progressive social legislation. As the House report on the reform legislation observed, "Lawyers, as a class, are conservative and slow to change existing laws. Reforms in the law grow out of some concrete experience that so forcibly presents the necessity of change as to arouse public interest. The decision in the Ives case in New York . . . served this purpose."[63]

Not everyone agreed that amendment of the statute would significantly protect progressive legislation. Since many state decisions striking down legislation were based solely upon state grounds or both state and federal constitutional grounds, some progressives feared that state courts would continue to strike down statutes on the basis of state constitutional provisions even if the Supreme Court overruled the state court's decision that the law violated the federal Constitution. Professor Dodd, however, pointed out that the amendment of the federal judicial code might provide an impetus for progressives to work for constitutional amendments in the states that would overrule decisions that were based upon constructions of the state constitution.[64] Prior to the amendment of the federal judicial code, progressives had less reason to work for the amendment of state constitutions because any subsequent nullification of a statute under the federal Constitution was not reviewable by the Supreme Court. For example, the amendment of the New York Constitution to overrule the *Ives* decision would not necessarily have accomplished any benefit since the court of appeals would have remained free to invalidate the new law under the federal Constitution.[65]

Skeptics about the benefits of amending the judicial code also questioned whether the Supreme Court would accord the Constitution a broader interpretation than the state courts. Karl T. Frederick warned in 1912 that the Supreme Court was "not apparently disposed to be so much more liberal in its interpretation of the scope of the police power, or of due process of law, as to make it a genuine haven of refuge for the more ardent advocates of so-called 'social justice.'" Pointing out that it was not many years since the Supreme Court decided *Lochner*, Freder-

---

intelligent of citizens, why beneficial legislation which the Supreme Court of the United States has held to be 'constitutional' when enacted by Oregon or Kansas, should be left nugatory in New York on the theory that it violates the very provision of the Federal and State constitution which the highest court of the land has specifically held it not to violate" (Ransom, *Majority Rule*, pp. 51–52).

[63] House Report 1222, p. 2.

[64] Dodd, "Final Interpreter," pp. 308–9; W. F. Dodd, "To Amend The Federal Judicial Code," *The Nation*, April 25, 1912, p. 409.

[65] Karl T. Frederick, "The Significance of the Recall of Judicial Decisions," *Atlantic Monthly*, July 1912, p. 51.

ick contended that "the margin of advantage is likely to prove so narrow as to make it improbable that there will be any very substantial increase in popular satisfaction."[66]

Although supporters of reforming the federal code acknowledged that the proposed revision was no panacea, they believed that review by the Court would have to be better than no review at all. Reform of the code received support even from quarters that did not look favorably upon most other proposals for judicial reforms. *The Nation*, for example, declared in 1913 that the existing law was "an anomaly" and "a real grievance" that had survived "out of sheer inertia."[67] The reform also received the support of the American Bar Association, which in 1911 drafted a bill to amend the judicial code to provide a right of appeal to the Supreme Court from state decisions in which the state supreme court had sustained a federal right.

The ABA bill was introduced in both houses of Congress late in 1911[68] and received the vigorous approval of Senator Elihu Root. The Senate in 1912 approved an amended version of the bill that would have permitted the Supreme Court to exercise discretion in hearing such appeals.[69] The House adjourned without acting on the amended version of the bill. Although several reform measures were introduced when Congress reconvened in 1913, the press of New Freedom legislation pushed the bills to a low priority on the congressional agenda, and the decrease in public outrage over the *Ives* decision made the reform seem less urgent. After prodding from the Wisconsin legislature and the ABA,[70] a measure that provided for discretionary appeals was finally enacted on December 23, 1914.[71] The measure received widespread and bipartisan approval.

Although attempts to reform judicial procedure may have helped to diminish some of the popular antipathy toward the courts, no clarity and efficiency in the judicial process could remove popular discontent over judicial review of legislation or the way courts chose to exercise

---

[66] Ibid., p. 52.

[67] "'Recall' of the Ives Decision," *The Nation*, December 4, 1913, p. 526.

[68] Frankfurter and Landis, *Business of the Court*, p. 196.

[69] According to Root, the Senate had substituted *certiorari* for the writ of error because it feared that an unlimited right of appeal "would load down the calendar of the Supreme Court of the United States with a vast multitude of cases in which an appeal was taken for purposes of delay." Root explained that the Senate believed that "in every case of public importance and concern involving a constitutional question the Supreme Court would exercise its jurisdiction." *Hearings Before the Committee on the Judiciary, House of Representatives, on Reforms in Judicial Procedure American Bar Association Bills, Serial 8—Part 2*, 63rd Cong., 2d sess., 1914, p. 32 (testimony of Senator Elihu Root).

[70] Frankfurter and Landis, *Business of the Court*, p. 197.

[71] 38 Stat. 790.

that power. The use of the business corporation as a model for reform in government failed to recognize that even the most efficient corporations were established for profit and power rather than the public good.[72] The emphasis on efficiency was therefore not necessarily compatible with the progressive quest for a state that governed in the best interests of the entire community. Many progressives perceived that procedural reform alone would not prevent the judiciary from continuing to arrogate the legislative power and thwart the popular will. For example, William L. Ransom contended in 1912 that proposals for simplification of procedure and the elimination of delay "offer substantially nothing for relief of the condition responsible for the present outcry."[73]

Similarly, Gilbert E. Roe argued that procedural reform failed to provide a remedy for judicial insensitivity toward social legislation. "The public complains less that decisions are a long time in coming than it does that they are wrong when they do come," Roe declared. Roe suggested that some critics of the courts believed that bar associations and judges were advocating remedies for delay, expense, and reversals for technical causes to divert public attention from the real abuses.[74] Even while many progressives and labor leaders supported procedural reform, they continued to advocate measures that would more directly affect the outcome of cases involving social and industrial issues. Beginning about 1908, they increasingly turned their attention to measures to influence the selection, removal, and thinking of state and federal judges.

[72] Danbom, "World of Hope", p. 133.

[73] Ransom, Majority Rule, pp. 40–41.

[74] Gilbert E. Roe, Our Judicial Oligarchy (New York: B. W. Huebsch, 1912), p. 189. Roe stated that he did not accuse the judges and bar associations of any ulterior motive.

FOUR

RECONSTRUCTING THE BENCH

If the people are to be trusted to select the Executive and
the Legislature they are also fit to select the judges.
(*Chief Justice Walter Clark of North Carolina, 1907, advocating
the election of federal judges*)[1]

It is in the Federal judge, shabby in the emoluments of his
place but strong in its security, that the Horation ideal can
be found of the just man who . . . disdains with
equanimity the frowns of a tyrant and the
clamors of a mob.
(*Frederick Bausman, Seattle attorney, opposing the election of
federal judges, 1903*)[2]

I N ADDITION TO advocating procedural reforms that did not
deprive the judiciary of any fundamental powers, progressives
also tried to transform the character of the bench by influencing
the selection of new judges and the judicial philosophy of incumbent
judges. Like the movement for procedural reform, attempts to influence the judicial selection process and judicial thought were more
serious and more successful than attempts to curb judicial power. Ultimately, however, the selection of some progressive judges and the in-
culcation of certain progressive ideas in conservative judges failed to
prevent judicial obstruction of progressive programs, just as procedural reforms had proved no panacea. And, like other attempts to
make the courts more responsive to progressive aspirations, the movement to influence the character of the bench was hindered by institutional obstacles that a deeply divided and often ambivalent progressive
movement was incapable of surmounting.

Although populists and progressives characteristically disagreed
over the means of selecting and influencing judges, they generally
agreed that too many judges were deeply biased in favor of corporations. As early as 1892, James B. Weaver had decried the influence of

[1] Walter Clark, "Is the Supreme Court Unconstitutional?" *Independent*, September 26,
1907, p. 726.
[2] Frederick Bausman, "Election of Federal Judges," *American Law Review* 37
(November–December 1903): 890.

corporations on the judiciary.[3] By the time the progressive movement reached its full tide two decades later, "muckraking" of the judiciary in the popular press had become common. One of the more notable examples was a series of five scathing articles in *Everybody's Magazine* in 1912, in which the lawyer and journalist C. P. Connolly alleged that the judiciary was corrupted by the influence of business interests.[4] Walter Clark spoke for virtually every critic of the courts when he observed in 1907 that judicial decisions were affected by the "natural and perhaps unconscious bias" of judges who had spent their lives at the bar in advocacy of corporate claims."[5]

Unlike Clark, however, most progressives prior to the 1920s preferred to alter the character of the bench rather than curtail judicial power. As public criticism of the judiciary grew more widespread, progressives and labor became increasingly aware of the vast influence of the Supreme Court over the fate of the measures for which they worked.[6] The increased awareness of the growing importance of the Court inevitably led to growing public interest in Court nominations and more concern over the judicial selection potentialities of presidential candidates. *The World's Work* stated in September 1910 that "the nation understands today, as it has not understood before, how completely the future lies in the hands of the Supreme Court."[7] By the early years of the century, progressives and labor leaders were increasingly active in efforts to ensure the appointment of liberal federal judges and the election of presidents who would nominate such judges.

During the early years of the progressive movement, Theodore Roosevelt's nominations to the Supreme Court aroused no opposition among trade unionists or progressives, for Roosevelt's nominees enjoyed benign reputations in labor and progressive circles. Indeed, Roosevelt deliberately sought to nominate persons who would uphold progressive legislation. Roosevelt's first nominee, Oliver Wendell Holmes, Jr., had established a reputation during his brief career as a legal scholar and his long tenure as a justice of the highest court of Massachusetts as a proponent of judicial deference to the legislature in eco-

[3] James B. Weaver, *A Call to Arms* (Des Moines: Des Moines Printing, 1892), pp. 81–82.
[4] C. P. Connolly, "Big Business and the Bench: How Courts Have Been Invaded and Judges Swayed by the Powers of Corruption," *Everybody's Magazine*, February 1912, pp. 147–60; "The Part the Railways Play in Corrupting Our Courts," ibid., March 1912, pp. 291–306; "Political Rings and Corporations join Forces to control Courts," ibid., April 1912, pp. 439–53; "Trust-Busting That Helps the Trusts," ibid., May 1912, pp. 659–72; "The Federal Courts—Last Refuge for the Interests," ibid., June 1912, pp. 827–41; "Now Let's Clean—Not Whitewash—the Courthouse," ibid., July 1912, pp. 116–28.
[5] Clark, "Is the Supreme Court Unconstitutional?" p. 726.
[6] *The World's Work*, June 1910, p. 12987.
[7] *The World's Work*, September 1910, p. 13347.

nomic matters. Holmes also propounded the philosophy, dear to progressive hearts, of adapting the law to fit the changing needs of society. Indeed, the most famous line of Holmes's 1881 masterpiece, *The Common Law*, anticipated progressive thought in its declaration that the "life of the law has not been logic: it has been experience."[8] Roosevelt's next appointee, William R. Day, had established a moderately liberal reputation during his years in Ohio politics and his service on the Sixth Circuit Court of Appeals. Roosevelt's third and final nominee, William Moody, had confirmed his credentials as a moderate progressive during his service as Roosevelt's attorney general.[9] All three of Roosevelt's appointees, notably Holmes, were generally deferential to progressive legislation during their time on the Supreme Court.

Judicial selection emerged as a significant issue during the 1908 presidential campaign since four of the justices were seventy or older. Accordingly, many voters were expected to consider what types of people Taft or Bryan would nominate to the Supreme Court. Predicting that at least four vacancies would occur during the next four years, *The World's Work* declared that "few more important questions than this will come up during the campaign."[10] Similarly, the *New York Times* stated in February that the likelihood that Roosevelt's successor would name four justices to the Court was attracting widespread attention among politicians.[11] A number of prominent New York Democrats were so worried that fears about Bryan's appointments would erode Democratic support among businesspeople that they urged Bryan to declare in public that he would nominate conservatives to the Court. Bryan flatly refused.[12]

---

[8] Oliver Wendell Holmes, Jr., *The Common Law* (Boston: Little, Brown, 1881), p. 1. As Professor Horwitz has pointed out, however, it was Holmes's 1897 lecture "The Path of the Law" that "pushed American legal thought into the twentieth century" by renouncing "the belief in a conception of legal thought independent of politics and separate from social reality," Morton J. Horwitz, *The Transformation of American Law 1870: 1960: The Crisis of Legal Orthodoxy* (New York: Oxford University Press, 1992), pp. 141–42.

[9] Henry J. Abraham, *Justices and Presidents: A Political History of the Supreme Court* (New York: Oxford University Press, 1974), pp. 151–54; James F. Watts, Jr., "William R. Day," "William Moody," in Leon Friedman and Fred L. Israel, eds., *The Justices of the Supreme Court 1789–1969: Their Lives and Major Opinions*, vol. 3 (New York: Chelsea House, 1969), pp. 1778–83, 1804–14.

[10] "The Presidency and the Supreme Court," *The World's Work*, May 1908, p. 10171; "The Supreme Court and the Next President," ibid., October 1908, p. 10740.

[11] "Campaign to Affect Court," *New York Times*, February 10, 1908, p. 1.

[12] Josephus Daniels, *Editor in Politics* (Chapel Hill: University of North Carolina Press, 1941), pp. 548–50. Bryan explained that such a statement would hurt his cause because it would suggest that his own supporters did not trust him and that he would discriminate against his more liberal supporters. Since Taft enjoyed strong support in the business

The judicial significance of the election was even greater than most voters could have supposed, for Taft had the opportunity to make six appointments during his one term. Taft's appointments encountered opposition among progressives and trade unionists, since his appointments reflected his conservative inclinations. Taft's first nominee, Horace H. Lurton, was unpopular with liberals and organized labor since Lurton's record on the Sixth Circuit suggested that he elevated corporate rights over individual rights.[13]

In addition to revealing a growing recognition of the importance of Supreme Court appointments, the attempts by progressives and trade unionists to influence judicial selection reflected an increasing fear that corporate interests unduly influenced the nomination process. This fear was fueled in part by Bryan's assertion in the wake of the *Standard Oil* decision that Taft and the Court had entered into a "gigantic conspiracy" by which the nation had been "turned over to the trusts." Bryan alleged that Taft's elevation of Justice Edward D. White to the chief justiceship in preference to the seventy-seven-year-old Justice John Marshall Harlan and nomination of Lurton, Willis Van Devanter, and Joseph R. Lamar were part of the conspiracy.[14]

The growing concern about the influence of business interests upon the federal judicial selection process was embodied in a bill that the House passed in February 1912 that would have required the president, prior to any nomination of a federal judge, to make public all endorsements made on behalf of any candidate. Although the House passed the measure by 148–82, the measure failed to attract support in the more conservative Senate. Critics of the bill pointed out that it would interfere with the president's right to receive confidential infor-

community, it is unlikely that anything that Bryan could have said would have won the votes or financial support of the business community, although it might have dampened enthusiasm for Taft.

[13] "The Latest Addition to the Supreme Court," *Current Literature*, March 1910, p. 272. Prior to the nomination, a number of union leaders wrote to Taft in an effort to dissuade him from selecting Lurton. The Order of Railway Conductors of America informed Taft that Lurton's record as a federal judge demonstrated that he would not approach cases involving the rights of railroad workers with an "open, unbiased consideration." The union also warned that nomination of Lurton "would militate strongly against that respectful acceptance of the decisions of that court that should be universal in the minds of all classes of citizens" (A. B. Garretson to William Howard Taft, December 9, 1909, National Archives (NA), General Records of the Department of Justice, Record Group 60, File 348, Box 2, Lurton folder). Similarly, the Brotherhood of Locomotive Firemen and Enginemen expressed the fear that "the same influence which apparently has controlled Judge Lurton's official acts in the past would control his actions in the future" (W. F. Carter to William Howard Taft, December 13, 1909, ibid).

[14] *Current Literature*, December 1911, pp. 591–92.

mation and that it would be ineffective because it did not provide for the publication of protests.[15]

Concerns about corporate influence upon the judicial selection process were intensified in February 1912 when Taft nominated Mahlon Pitney, a New Jersey judge, to succeed Harlan. Although Pitney's popularity with New Jersey progressives may have influenced Taft's decision, the nomination encountered opposition from organized labor and some progressives because Pitney had rendered many decisions unpopular with labor.[16] Although a number of senators opposed the nomination, progressives failed to unite in opposition to Pitney. Only four Republican senators voted in opposition to the confirmation, and the prominent progressive Republican senator William E. Borah of Idaho was one of Pitney's principal defenders.[17] Pitney's nomination was confirmed on March 13, 1912 by a 50–26 vote,[18] the narrowest margin for a Supreme Court nominee in a quarter century.

Wilson's election in 1912 cheered progressives and trade unionists, who hoped that the appointment of liberal judges would reduce their conflict with the federal judiciary. Wishing to hasten Wilson's opportunities to make appointments, Democratic senator Thomas P. Gore of Oklahoma, a former populist, went so far as to introduce a bill in 1913 that would have increased the membership of the Supreme Court from nine to eleven.[19] But while progressives could expect Wilson to make congenial appointments, progressives could not reasonably hope that Wilson's election would lead to a significant alteration of the character of the federal judiciary. Wilson could not be expected to make enough appointments in four years to transform the federal judiciary, and Wilson's prospects for serving eight years were not bright since he faced an uphill struggle for reelection in 1916 if the Republican party reunited.

[15] *Current Literature*, March 1912, p. 257.

[16] Michal R. Belknap, "Mr. Justice Pitney and Progressivism," *Seton Hall Law Review* 16 (1986): 400–405. For a detailed discussion of the circumstances surrounding Pitney's nomination and confirmation, see Alexander M. Bickel and Benno C. Schmidt, Jr., *The Oliver Wendell Holmes Devise History of the Supreme Court of the United States*, vol. 9, *The Judiciary and Responsible Government 1910–1921* (New York: Macmillan, 1984), pp. 324–25, 327–32.

[17] See "Pitney Opposition Wanes," *New York Times*, March 1, 1912, p. 1; "Halt Pitney's Confirmation," ibid., March 9, 1912, p. 1; "Fight Pitney Confirmation," ibid., March 12, 1912, p. 1; "Many Oppose Pitney," ibid., March 13, 1912, p. 7; Bickel and Schmidt, *The Judiciary and Responsible Government*, pp. 331–32.

[18] "Confirm Justice Pitney," *New York Times*, March 14, 1912, p. 8. See *Congressional Record*, 62nd Cong., 2d sess., March 14, 1912, p. 3259.

[19] S. 8116, 62nd Cong., 3d sess., 1913; "To Enlarge the Supreme Bench," *The World's Work*, March 1913, p. 500.

Although the next Republican president might be a progressive, the Republican Old Guard would surely influence the judicial appointments of even a liberal Republican. Likewise, Wilson's judicial selections would need to consider the wishes of the more conservative elements of the Democratic party. Although Wilson was relatively free to name progressives to the Supreme Court, the time-honored tradition of senatorial courtesy would moderate his appointments to the lower federal benches. Moreover, Wilson faced intense patronage pressure, since the Democrats had not controlled the White House for sixteen years. Many of the political functionaries who would clamor for recognition of long and unrewarded party service were expected to be unsympathetic to the progressive and labor causes.

Even though Taft's appointment of five new members had given the Supreme Court an unusually youthful and healthy complexion, Wilson was able to make three appointments to the Court since Lurton failed to live past seventy, Lamar died prematurely at fifty-eight, and Charles Evans Hughes, another Taft appointee, resigned to challenge Wilson for the presidency. When Lurton died during the summer of 1914, Wilson may have considered the possibility of filling the vacancy with the Court's most persistent critic, Walter Clark. Although leading North Carolina political figures urged Wilson to nominate Clark,[20] the appointment appears to have generated no organized support among prominent critics of the courts. Although a congressman who led a North Carolina delegation that had lobbied for Clark told him that Wilson had expressed admiration for his ability and was seriously considering the appointment,[21] Wilson may have concluded that the sixty-seven-year-old Clark was too old.[22]

In addition to his possible consideration of Clark, Wilson considered Louis D. Brandeis, but the development of vehement opposition chilled Wilson. Beleaguered by the recent death of his wife, the outbreak of war in Europe, the continuing revolution in Mexico, and senatorial opposition to two Federal Reserve nominees, Wilson had little energy to spare for any consideration of the Court nomination. Lacking the time or energy to study the merits of more exotic possibilities, Wilson reached into his cabinet to select a personal acquaintance, fellow southerner, and fellow University of Virginia Law School alumnus, Attorney General James C. McReynolds. McReynolds's ap-

[20] Aubrey Lee Brooks, *Walter Clark, Fighting Judge* (Chapel Hill: University of North Carolina Press, 1944), pp. 190–91; Platt D. Walker to Woodrow Wilson, July 20, 1914, in Aubrey Lee Brooks and Hugh Talmage Lefler, eds., *The Papers of Walter Clark*, vol. 2, *1920–1924* (Chapel Hill: University of North Carolina Press, 1950), pp. 253–54.

[21] Brook, *Walter Clark*, pp. 190–91.

[22] Ibid.; Brooks and Lefler, *Papers of Walter Clark*.

pointment demonstrated to progressives the dangers of hoping to alter the character of the courts by influencing the appointment process, since McReynolds's record on the Court confounded the expectations of Wilson and the progressives. Throughout his twenty-seven years on the bench, McReynolds was the most recalcitrant of conservatives.

Prior to Wilson's nominations of McReynolds in 1914 and Brandeis and John H. Clarke in 1916, trade unionists and progressives attempted to dissuade Wilson from nominating William Howard Taft to the Supreme Court. In a long letter to Wilson, Samuel Gompers contended that Taft's formalistic legal philosophy and his conservative political views deprived him of "heart understanding" of the needs and aspirations of the labor movement. Gompers alleged that the formalistic Taft saw "law as something detached from human frailties, based upon absolute concepts of pure justice," a philosophy that contravened the growing recognition "that greater justice can prevail only when the law and legal procedures are humanized."[23] A number of AFL affiliates formally opposed Taft's nomination,[24] as did the United Mine Workers Union, which declared that Taft's nomination "would be regarded as an unfriendly act toward the toiling masses of America" because Taft lacked an "understanding of the needs of the masses" and failed "to comprehend the humanizing influence of labor organizations."[25] Many progressives also tried to dissuade Wilson from appointing Taft. In 1914, for example, a Chicago attorney warned Wilson that Taft's appointment would be "a political calamity" that would

[23] Samuel Gompers to Woodrow Wilson, January 7, 1916, NA, General Records of the Department of Justice, Record Group 60, File 348, Box 5, Taft folder.

[24] For example, the Chattanooga Central Labor Union adopted a resolution opposing the appointment of Taft. In a letter to Wilson, the union argued that some of Taft's judicial decisions favored the privileged classes and were "painful examples of his disassociation with the constitutional and common ideals of our people." Similarly, a local of the Brotherhood Railway Carmen of America told Wilson that its members did not find Taft "a fair and impartial man towards the toiling masses." A Virginia local of the International Association of Machinists urged Wilson to appoint a man "whose entire past record has not been antagonistic to the aims of the entire contingent of working men." The president also received a protest from the Central Federated Union of Greater New York, which alleged that Taft had shown "especial antagonism to the organized labor movement." Matt Gerlach, Secretary, Chattanooga Central Labor Union, to Wilson, January 26, 1916; M. R. Turner, Recording Secretary, Lookout Lodge Number 211, Brotherhood Railway Carmen of America, St. Elmo, Tennessee, to Wilson, January 25, 1916; Legislative Committee, Melrose Lodge No. 560, International Association of Machinists, Roanoke, Viriginia, to Wilson, January 24, 1916; Ernest Boher, Corresponding Secretary of the Central Federated Union of New York and Vicinity to Wilson, January 22, 1916; NA, General Records of the Department of Justice, Taft folder.

[25] William Green to Woodrow Wilson, January 25, 1916; "Resolution" dated January 24, 1916, NA, General Records of the Department of Justice, Taft folder.

shake the faith of progressives in Wilson. Similarly, a Republican attorney advised Wilson in 1916 that Wilson could not make "a worse nor more reactionary nor more unpopular appointment."[26]

Since Wilson had no intention of appointing a former political antagonist whose views on key judicial questions were likely to differ from his, opposition to Taft appears to have been superfluous. Indeed it is unlikely that the intensely partisan Wilson would have placed any Republican on the Court. Progressive opposition to the prospect of a Taft appointment, however, illustrates the growing progressive recognition of the importance of attempting to influence judicial nominations. It is ironic, but characteristic, that progressives were divided when Wilson nominated the progressive activist Brandeis to the Court in 1916. Although La Follette and many other progressives hailed the nomination, William E. Borah and Albert B. Cummins of Iowa, both serving on the Senate Judiciary Committee, opposed the nomination, partly because they suspected that Brandeis, an easterner, was insufficiently hostile toward the powerful corporations whose regulation he urged.[27]

Not all progressives were convinced that alteration of the judicial selection and education processes would significantly change the character of the bench. Accordingly, many advocated the election of federal judges and the limitation of tenure. As early as 1890, Seymour D. Thompson, an elected Missouri judge and editor of the *American Law Review*, had predicted ruefully that unpopular Supreme Court deci-

[26] Frank D. Burgess to Woodrow Wilson, March 11, 1914, NA, General Records of the Department of Justice, Taft folder. Eugene Montgomery to Wilson, January 14, 1916, NA, General Records, Dept. Justice, Taft folder. Likewise, J. P. Edwards, a Louisville attorney, complained that Taft's every act as president "indicated his total lack of sympathy with the people of the Country and his predilection toward the great corporate interests." Edwards cautioned Wilson that even honest judges "are but human and their course and prejudices upon the Bench either consciously or unconsciously is sure to follow the path pursued by them in their work as lawyers before donning the ermine." A Boston attorney complained to Wilson that Taft had "boldly opposed most of the splendid progressive measures you have so ably championed." From South Carolina came a letter from an attorney who described Taft as "a personally attractive and cultured member of the great national gang of privilege and pillage." And an Ohio physician alleged that Taft had appointed reactionaries to the Supreme Court and that "to appoint the Prince of Reactionaries to that bench now would be little short of a catastrophe." J. P. Edwards to Wilson, January 24, 1916; B. O. Flower to Wilson, January 15, 1916; William F. Robertson to Wilson, January 22, 1916; J. F. Baldwin to Wilson, January 16, 1916; ibid.

[27] See Bickel and Schmidt, *The Judiciary and Responsible Government*, pp. 388–89; A. L. Todd, *Justice on Trial: The Case of Louis D. Brandeis* (New York: McGraw-Hill, 1964), pp. 195, 226, 244–46; *Views of the Minority*, U.S. Senate, 64th Cong., 1st sess., 1916, Ex. Rept. 2, pt. 2, in Roy M. Mersky and J. Myron Jacobstein, *The Supreme Court of the United States: Hearings and Reports on Successful and Unsuccessful Nominations of Supreme Court Justices by the Senate Judiciary Committee, 1916–1975, vol. 3* (Buffalo: William S. Hein, 1977), pp. 297–305.

sions would generate successful agitation for the election of federal judges.[28] Although Thompson correctly foresaw that the Court's decisions would continue to vex liberals, he and critics of the Court underestimated the resilience of the status quo. Although advocacy of the election of federal judges was the one remedy widely advocated during each of the successive waves of criticism of the courts, none of these proposals ever came close to enactment by Congress.

A bill to amend the Constitution to impose a ten-year limit upon the tenure of federal judges, including Supreme Court justices, was favorably reported by the House Judiciary Committee in 1894.[29] As discontent with the federal judiciary became more intense, later proposals tended to advocate the election of judges and limitation of their tenure. Proposals for the election of federal judges for limited terms were presented in various bills introduced in Congress during the late nineteenth and early twentieth centuries. Some measures were simply enabling laws that would have permitted Congress to prescribe elections and terms of office.[30] Others were more specific. A number proposed amendments that would have mandated popular election of judges and prescribed limited terms.[31]

[28] Editorial, "The Election of Federal Judges by a Popular Vote," *American Law Review* 24 (May–June 1890): 479–80. In a much quoted speech before the Illinois State Bar Association, Thompson stated that "if the proposition . . . to make the Federal judiciary elective instead of appointive, is once seriously discussed before the people, nothing can stay the growth of that sentiment, and it is almost certain that every session of the Federal Supreme Court will furnish material to stimulate its growth." "Elective and Appointive Judges," *American Law Review* 25 (March–April 1891): 288–89. Although Thompson conceded that elected judges were sometimes abler than appointive judges and that federal judges tended to render decisions "on the side of money and power," he preferred an appointive judiciary because he contended that appointive judges were more independent and less susceptible to corruption (ibid., pp. 289–91); "Elected Judges" (editorial), ibid., January–February 1891, pp. 128–29; "Elected Judges" (editorial), *American Law Review* 24 (September–October 1890): 807–8.

[29] H. Res. 109, 53rd Cong., 2d sess., 1894.

[30] In 1897, 1899, 1901, and 1903, for example, Samuel Bronson Cooper, a Democratic congressman from Texas, introduced a bill to amend the Constitution to permit Congress to determine the method of electing or appointing all federal judges for a tenure prescribed by Congress. H. Res. 107, 55th Cong., 2d sess., 1897; H. J. Res. 36, 56th Cong., 1st sess., 1899; H. J. Res. 77, 57th Cong., 1st sess., 1901; H. J. Res. 38, 58th Cong., 1st sess., 1903. A similar measure introduced by Representative William W. Kitchin of North Carolina, at Walter Clark's behest, at both congresses that sat during 1907 would have permitted Congress to provide for the popular election of district and circuit judges and to prescribe the length of their terms. H. J. Res. 248, 59th Cong., 2d sess., 1907; H. J. Res. 42, 60th Cong., 1st sess., 1907.

[31] Prompted by Clark, Senator Butler of North Carolina introduced a bill in 1899 for a constitutional amendment that would have required the election of all federal judges, including Supreme Court justices, for terms of eight years. Supreme Court justices would have numbered between nine and thirteen, as Congress provided, and would have

In 1907, for example, Clark proposed an amendment to make all federal judgeships elective for a term of six, eight, or ten years. Voters would elect district and circuit judges in their judicial districts and elect Supreme Court justices in nine national judicial divisions. The nine justices would select one of their own to serve as chief justice.[32] Between 1894 and 1924, more than three dozen congressional resolutions called for election of federal judges or limitations on their tenure.

One measure introduced in the House in 1910 by Gordon J. Russell, a Texas Democrat, called for the election of judges for terms of twelve years on the Supreme Court, eight years on the courts of appeals, and six years on the district courts.[33] A bill introduced by Senator Robert L. Owen in 1911 provided for the election of district and circuit court judges to four-year terms. Although Owen's bill did not provide for election of Supreme Court justices or the abolition of their lifetime tenure, it permitted Congress to recall Supreme Court justices as well as lower federal judges.[34] Whether the limitations on terms would apply to judges who were serving at the time of the enactment of the constitutional amendment was not addressed in most bills, although some would have applied retroactively.[35]

---

been elected from a circuit to which they would have been assigned. Butler's bill provided for the election of the chief justice by voters in all the states. Vacancies would be filled by presidential appointment until the next general election. S. R. 47, 55th Cong., 1st sess., 1899. Similarly, two bills introduced in 1907 by Democratic representative William B. Lamar of Florida called for an amendment under which all federal judges would serve for eight-year terms. Like Butler's bill, Lamar's provided for the election of Supreme Court justices from circuits to which they would be assigned. In accordance with Clark's proposal, justices would have selected a chief justice from their number. Circuit and district judges would likewise have been elected for their respective districts and circuits. H. J. Res. 226, 59th Cong., 2d sess., 1907; H. J. Res. 50, 60th Cong., 1st sess., 1907. Lamar's proposal was based upon a draft supplied by Walter Clark (W. B. Lamar to Walter Clark, January 18, 1907, in Brooks, *Papers of Walter Clark*, vol. 2, p. 86.

[32] Walter Clark, "'Aaron's Rod'; or, Government by Federal Judges," *Arena*, November 1907, p. 481. This proposal differed only slightly from Clark's 1896 proposal, discussed in chapter 1.

[33] H. J. Res. 80, 61st Cong., 2d sess., 1910.

[34] S. 3112, 62nd Cong., 1st sess., 1911.

[35] Four bills introduced by Representative Russell between 1904 and 1909, however, provided an affirmative answer to this question. Prescribing terms of twelve years for Supreme Court justices, eight years for circuit judges, and six years for district judges, Russell's bills provided that proposed terms would apply retroactively and that judges who had served longer than the prescribed terms would be forced to vacate their offices. Since Chief Justice Fuller and Justices Harlan, Brewer, Brown, and White had served more than a dozen years when Russell first introduced his bills, the amendment would have created five vacancies on the Supreme Court and created a sixth in the near future when Justice Peckham reached the end of his twelfth year on the Court. H. J. Res. 93, 58th Cong., 2d sess., 1904; H. J. Res. 249, 59th Cong., 2d sess., 1907; H. J. Res. 15, 60th Cong., 1st sess., 1907; H. J. Res. 80, 61st Cong., 2d sess., 1909. In contrast to Russell's

Advocates of an elective judiciary argued that the system of appointing judges ensured the perpetuation of corporate domination of the judiciary. Clark, the most indefatigable proponent of an elective judiciary, argued that the insulation of judges from popular selection and review had conferred arbitrary power upon the judges and that the corporations had seized control of the federal judiciary "simply by naming a majority of the judges." Writing in 1907, Clark observed that while Congress could curb judicial arbitrariness by restricting judicial power or abolishing judicial districts, a constitutional amendment to elect judges and abolish "the thoroughly undemocratic and dangerous life tenure" was "the only root and branch remedy."[36] Likewise, a leader of the boilermakers' union declared after the Court announced its decision in *Loewe v. Lawlor* that the judicial election was "the sure and the only cure" for judicial abuses, since the people were "so far removed" from the Court.[37]

Advocates of an elective judiciary also professed faith that the elected judges would loosen the grip of corporate interests over the judiciary. In recommending the proposed constitutional amendment for ten-year terms for federal judges, the House Committee on the Judiciary declared in 1894 that the measure would help to restore popular confidence in a judiciary that was "frequently suspected of having no sympathy" with the people and was seen as "exhibiting partiality toward corporations and personal favorites."[38] Similarly, Clark complained that appointive judges were drawn from the ranks of successful corporate practitioners who had absorbed the outlook of their clients.[39] The progressive social reformer Ernest H. Crosby argued in a 1906 article in the *American Federationist* that appointed judges were inevitably leaders of the bar who were "totally out of touch with true democracy" because their wealthy clients had hired them to fight their "battles against the people through thick and thin."

Crosby believed that it was impossible for appointed judges "to change the habits of thought of a lifetime, and they naturally continue to serve the money power which created them."[40] Clark contended that

---

rather draconian measure, a bill introduced by Senator Crawford in 1912 would have established ten-year terms for circuit and district judges but permitted Supreme Court justices to hold their offices during good behavior. S. J. Res. 109, 62nd Cong., 2d sess., 1912.

[36] Clark, "'Aaron's Rod,'" p. 481.

[37] "Supreme Court Decision in the Hatters' Case" (statement of William J. Gilthorpe), *American Federationist*, March 1908, p. 177.

[38] House Committee on the Judiciary, *Term of Office of Judges of U.S. Courts: Report to Accompany H.R. 109*, 53rd Cong., 2d sess., H. Rep. 466, 1894.

[39] Clark, "Supreme Court Unconstitutional?" p. 726.

[40] Ernest Crosby, "Jerome and the Judges," *American Federationist*, February 1906, p. 82.

most of the few federal judges who had not practiced corporate law owed their appointment to corporate influences. According to Clark, there was not one federal judge "whose appointment would have been confirmed by the plutocratic Senate, if confirmation had been opposed by the capitalistic combinations to whom a majority of the senators owe their seats."[41] Clark also believed that the conservatism of the Senate chilled the progressive impulses of district and circuit judges since they recognized that the "plutocratic majority in the Senate" would block their nomination to a higher court if they expressed "any judicial views not in accordance with the 'safe, sane and sound' predominance of wealth."[42]

The movement for an elective judiciary inspired spirited defenses of the status quo. Many opponents of an elective judiciary argued that the election of judges would politicize the judicial selection process and endanger the personal and economic liberties enjoyed by Americans. For example, a 1909 article in the *American Law Review* warned that "popular judges render popular decisions; popular decisions reflect transitory popular sentiment—the antithesis to law and justice"—and that the popular election of judges would lead to the abrogation of vested rights, competition, the right of contract, and the freedoms of speech and religion.[43] Since the record of elected state judges was not nearly so dismal, some opponents of an elected federal judiciary contended that the danger was judicial parochialism rather than lack of judicial independence. As James M. Gray, a prominent Brooklyn attorney, explained in 1908, "It is desirable that Federal officials should owe their selection as far as possible to the national authority—that they should have no divided allegiance, and derive no authority from any but a national source. As they cannot well be elected by the whole nation, appointment by the President is the only practicable method."[44]

Opponents of change also foresaw great evils in the limitation of the tenure of federal judges. For example, members of the House Committee on the Judiciary who opposed the 1894 bill for ten-year judicial terms warned in their minority report that the measure would threaten the liberties of persons and the security of property by undermining the stability of judicial precedent. They also warned that the "judges of the courts holding office for ten years would strive for popularity, and might improve their opportunity to make popular decisions with a view

---

[41] Clark, "'Aaron's Rod,'" p. 479.

[42] Clark, "Supreme Court Unconstitutional?" p. 726.

[43] Hal Greer, "Elective Judiciary and Democracy," *American Law Review* 43 (July–August 1909): 525.

[44] James M. Gray, "How to Bring Federal Courts Closer to the Common People," *American Law Review* 42 (July–August 1908): 502.

of becoming candidates for office." The minority report and Gray also warned that eligibility for reappointment would undermine judicial independence by making the judges too dependent on the president.[45]

Opponents of change also contended that the election of judges for limited terms would tend to decrease the average length of judicial tenure and would therefore deprive the bench of the benefits of experienced jurists. They predicted that popular election of judges would weaken judicial control over lawyers, since judges would be beholden to the opinion of lawyers for their continuation in office.[46]

Advocates of an elective judiciary, however, contended that it was the continued corporate control of the judiciary that threatened democratic institutions. Crosby argued that the appointed judge who sympathized with corporate interests was "a much greater threat" to "the permanence of free institutions" than the elected judge. Although some advocates of an elected judiciary conceded that election of judges might lead to some abuses, they contended that any such danger would be outweighed by the diminution of corporate influence. Crosby contended that even a judge who was a political hack or indulged in petty corruption would be "far and away the superior of the appointed life judge."[47] Many progressives also argued that an elected judiciary was the natural corollary of courts that had arrogated so much power. If "judges are to act as legislators, they must be elected by the people, and be easily displaced or recalled," an article in the *Yale Review* declared in 1914. "Otherwise democracy is replaced by absolutism."[48]

Proponents of an elected judiciary also contended that popular election would tend to remove the process from political considerations. Clark contended that state judicial elections were less partisan than appointments to the federal bench, which were regarded "as patronage" by presidents, who nearly always named judges from their own party.[49] In an age when the Republican party usually won presidential elections, Clark's argument about patronage may have given his proposal for an elective judiciary an appeal that extended beyond progressives of both parties to attract Democrats who otherwise were not sympathetic toward judicial reform.

---

[45] House Committee on the Judiciary, *Term of Office of Judges of the U.S. Courts: Views of the Minority*, 53rd Cong., 2d sess., Rept. 466, pt. 2, 1894, pp. 3–4; Gray, "Bring Federal Courts Closer," p. 502.

[46] Bausman, "Election of Federal Judges," p. 887.

[47] Crosby, "Jerome and Judges," p. 82.

[48] Yandell Henderson, "The Progressive Movement and Constitutional Reform," *Yale Review* 23 (October 1913): 87.

[49] Walter Clark, "Constitutional Changes Demanded to Bulwark Democratic Government," *Arena*, February 1907, p. 153.

Advocates of an elected federal judiciary further contended that election of judges was consistent with the steady increase in popular democracy that had characterized the history of the Republic. Writing in 1903, Clark denounced the appointment of federal judges as "an anomaly in a country whose government is based upon the principle that it exists only by the consent of the governed."[50] Four years later, Clark declared that "if the people are to be trusted to select the Executive and the Legislature they are also fit to select the judges." In Clark's view, the popular election of federal judges was a natural corollary to the gradual extension of the franchise throughout the nation's history.[51] Similarly, the House report that in 1894 recommended the amendment for ten-year judicial terms pointed out that only four states still retained a life tenure for their judges. Moreover, the provisions for lifetime tenure in those states—Massachusetts, Delaware, New Jersey, and Rhode Island—predated the adoption of the federal Constitution.[52]

Despite the persistent agitation of Clark and other reformers, the movement for an elective federal judiciary and limited judicial tenure never made significant progress. Although the election of qualified and independent state judges belied many of the arguments of the opponents of an elective judiciary, the exigencies of federalism and the strong arm of tradition prevented any precipitate change. In the absence of broad public support for reform of judicial selection and tenure, proponents of change were loath to undertake the arduous efforts necessary to enact measures that would probably have required a constitutional amendment. But although reform of federal judicial selection procedures seemed chimerical in the immediate future, some critics of the judiciary hoped that advocacy of such measures would lay the foundations for future success. As Walter Clark explained in an 1897 letter to Senator Marion Butler, a Populist from North Carolina, "The movement must be begun some time. It can not win at first but the agitation will be educational."[53]

[50] Walter Clark, "Law and Human Progress," *American Law Review* 37 (July–August 1903): 517.

[51] Clark pointed out, for example, that only one state at the time of the Constitution's adoption had permitted the popular election of the governor and that most of the states had selected at least one branch of the state legislature on a restricted suffrage. "The schoolmaster was not abroad in the land, the masses were illiterate and government by the people was a new experiment of which property holders were afraid. . . . The danger to property rights did not then as now come from the other direction—from corporations" ("Supreme Court Unconstitutional?" pp. 725–26).

[52] House Committee on Judiciary, *Term of Office*, pp. 7–8.

[53] Walter Clark to Marion Butler, April 3, 1897, in Brooks, *Papers of Walter Clark*, vol. 1, p. 307.

Many other critics of the courts, however, never supported judicial election or limitation of judicial tenure. Widespread indifference or hostility to these measures among progressives themselves is probably the principal reason there never was any sustained movement for reform of federal judicial selection or tenure. In part, the failure of many progressives to champion these reforms reflected the elitism of the progressive movement and its frustration over the decisions of elected state judiciaries.

The election of judges was only superficially consistent with the progressive faith in direct democracy. Although many progressive reforms such as the direct election of senators, the direct primary, and the initiative, the referendum, and the recall were ostensibly designed to expand popular democracy, progressives were profoundly uneasy about mass participation in government. While pure democracy appealed to certain idealistic strains in the progressive mentality and may have reflected the progressive desire to restore greater individual responsibility and sense of community to an increasingly impersonal society,[54] the elitism of the progressives made them wary of direct democracy. The progressive desire for direct democracy always competed with the recognition that the complexity of government required an expertise that exceeded the capacities of the voters.[55]

Even the most democratic progressives tended to believe that an educated and public-spirited leadership was needed to steer the popular will in a direction that would promote the progressive vision of the commonweal.[56] As Otis L. Graham, Jr., has pointed out, the goal of most progressives was the rationalization rather than the democratization of society; democratization was a means to an end rather than an end in itself.[57] In particular, the distrust by Anglo-Saxon progressives of immigrants made them reluctant to support expansions of democracy. Much of the progressive support for direct democracy was motivated by a desire to circumvent political machines controlled by urban

[54] Richard Hofstadter contended that "the movement for direct popular democracy was, in effect, an attempt to realize Yankee-Protestant ideals of personal responsibility," *The Age of Reform: From Bryan to F.D.R.* (New York: Knopf, 1955), p. 259. Samuel P. Hays argued that direct civic democracy arose "from the hope that a new civic spirit could destroy the particularistic roadblocks to civic growth." *The Response to Industrialism: 1885–1914* (Chicago: University of Chicago Press, 1957), p. 107.

[55] John E. Semonche, *Charting the Future*, p. 272.

[56] James T. Kloppenberg, *Uncertain Victory: Social Democracy and Progressivism in European and American Thought, 1870–1920* (New York: Oxford University Press, 1986), p. 402; Arthur L. Link and Richard L. McCormick, *Progressivism* (Arlington Heights, Ill.: Harlan Davidson, 1983), p. 106.

[57] Otis L. Graham, Jr., *The Great Campaigns: Reform and War in America, 1900–1918* (Engelwood Cliffs, N.J.: Prentice-Hall, 1971), pp. 135, 157–58.

bosses and other political elements whose political and cultural visions were in conflict with the progressives. The elitist cast and Anglo-Saxon character of much of progressivism found expression in the movement's nativistic tendencies, which flowed as an undercurrent during the movement's early years before rising to the surface during the First World War.[58]

Progressive support for direct civic democracy paradoxically reflected a distrust of the electorate.[59] Progressives were willing to use traditional party machinery when it suited their purposes,[60] and many progressives favored measures that actually diminished popular participation in government. Some progressives supported disenfranchisement of African Americans. Even progressive reforms that were ostensibly designed to increase probity in government, such as the Australian ballot and stricter voter registration requirements, had the potential effect of decreasing popular participation in government. Other progressive reforms, such as the introduction of the city-manager form of municipal government, also tended to reduce popular control of government, even though they may have made government more responsive to the broad public interest. The more sophisticated and honest progressives recognized and admitted that direct popular democracy was more a means to an end than an end in itself.[61]

Many progressives therefore recognized that popular election of federal judges was not likely to promote the goals of the progressive movement; the machinery for electing federal judges might fall under the domination of the political machines the progressives so loathed. Professor Albert M. Kales of Northwestern, for example, complained in 1914 that elected judges were "not in fact elected at all" since the selection of judicial candidates was "lodged with the politocrats of the extra-legal government."[62] Since popularly elected state appellate judges during the late nineteenth and early twentieth centuries may have resembled the lower federal judiciary in their professional quali-

[58] See George E. Mowry, *The Age of Theodore Roosevelt, 1900–1912* (New York: Harper, 1958), pp. 92–93; Graham, *Great Campaigns*, pp. 150, 154; Hofstadter, *Age of Reform*, pp. 176–78.

[59] As Samuel P. Hays pointed out, reformers "demanded electoral changes not because they believed in certain political principles but because they hoped that new techniques in politics would enable them to overcome their opposition." *Response to Industrialism*, p. 155.

[60] For example, progressives in Iowa preferred the party caucus to the primary. Ibid., pp. 154–55.

[61] E.g., Herbert Croly, *Progressive Democracy* (New York: Macmillan, 1915), pp. 213–14.

[62] Albert M. Kales, *Unpopular Government in the United States* (Chicago: University of Chicago Press, 1914), pp. 226–27.

fications and class origins,[63] the elite origins of the state judiciary may have enhanced the judiciary's solicitude for corporate business interests. Writing in 1921, Roscoe Pound observed that "the illiberal decisions of which complaint was made so widely at the beginning of the twentieth century were largely, one might say almost wholly, the work of popularly-elected judges."[64]

It is therefore not surprising that many progressives advocated the appointment of state judges.[65] Kales, for example, proposed a plan for an elected head of a consolidated court system to appoint the other state judges from a nonpartisan list of eligible candidates. After serving for a probationary period, voters would cast ballots in a noncompetitive election to decide whether judges would continue in office.[66] This plan and its numerous variations were eventually adopted by a number of states. Kermit L. Hall has pointed out that bar leaders and progressives by the turn of the century "concluded that democratic and professional accountability could be enhanced by eliminating partisanship while giving the increasingly professional bar a greater role in the judicial selection process."[67] As William S. Carpenter, a University of Wisconsin political scientist, argued in 1918, "It is important that the bar be able to make its influence felt by the selecting authority and that judges be given secure tenure," since "the judicial office is one which requires a high degree of expertness."[68]

Although conservatives generally opposed an elective judiciary, some conservatives saw merit in limiting judicial tenure. During the spring of 1910, the *Central Law Journal* discontinued its support for lifetime tenure because it was so alarmed over widespread allegations

[63] Kermit L. Hall, "Constitutional Machinery and Judicial Professionalism: The Careers of Midwestern State Appellate Court Judges, 1861–1899," in Gerard W. Gawalt, ed., *The New High Priests: Lawyers in Post-Civil War America* (Westport, Conn.: Greenwood Press, 1984), pp. 30–46; Kermit L. Hall, "The Impact of Popular Election on the Southern Appellate Judiciary, 1832–1920," in David J. Bodenhamer and James W. Ely, Jr., *Ambivalent Legacy: A Legal History of the South* (Jackson: University Press of Mississippi, 1984), pp. 229–52.

[64] Roscoe Pound, *The Spirit of the Common Law* (Francestown, N.H.: Marshall Jones, 1921), p. 7.

[65] See Bernard Hirschhorn, "Richard Spencer Childs: The Political Reformer and His Influence on the Work of the American Judicature Society," *Judicature* 73 (December 1989–January 1990): 186.

[66] Kales, *Popular Government*, pp. 239–50.

[67] Kermit L. Hall, "Progressive Reform and the Decline of Democratic Accountability: The Popular Election of State Supreme Court Judges, 1850–1920," *American Bar Foundation Research Journal* (1984): 369.

[68] William S. Carpenter, *Judicial Tenure in the United States* (New Haven, Conn.: Yale University Press, 1918), pp. 214–15.

of judicial corruption and "the growing popular antipathy to the federal judiciary." The *Journal* later advocated ten-year terms for district and circuit judges as a condition of increased judicial salaries. Although the *Journal* acknowledged that lifetime tenure sheltered the judiciary from political influences, it concluded that lifetime tenure "frequently promotes disregard of proper criticism," permitted the continued tenure of men who had become "unfit for service," and "promoted an insolent disrespect of state sovereignty." The *Journal* believed that lifetime tenure had "aroused a suspicion of unloyalty to the people's interest" and impaired popular confidence in the courts.[69]

The progressive desire to alter the character of the judiciary without tampering with the character of the judicial function was also manifest in attempts to make judges more aware of the exigencies of a rapidly changing society. The advocates of judicial education attributed much of the conservatism of judges to simple ignorance of social, economic, and industrial conditions. For this they blamed the isolation of jurisprudence from other disciplines. As Pound stated in an article in the *Harvard Law Review* in 1912, "Not a little of the world-wide discontent with our present legal order is due to modes of juristic thought and juridical method which result from want of 'team-work' between jurisprudence and the other social sciences." Pound observed that "the entire separation of jurisprudence from the other social sciences . . . necessitated a narrow and partial view" and was largely responsible for "the backwardness of law in meeting social ends . . . and the gulf between legal thought and popular thought on matters of social reform."[70] Writing in the *Yale Law Journal* in 1912, Theodore Schroeder, a New York attorney, attributed much of the judicial hostility to reform to ignorance and narrowness of vision rather than blatant bias. Schroeder predicted that a "conscious and intelligent application of the scientific method would preclude practically all the evils complained of, and nothing else can give us relief."[71]

The gulf between the law and sociology particularly vexed the progressives because the outcome of so many cases hinged on judicial interpretation of facts concerning social and economic conditions. Ever since the Taney Court had developed the doctrine that the police power permitted state governments to legislate for the protection of public health, safety, or morality, the principal question in most police-

---

[69] "Western Federal Judges Under Fire," *Central Law Journal* (April 1, 1910), p. 248, *Central Law Journal* (April 1910), pp. 266–67.

[70] Roscoe Pound, "The Scope and Purpose of Sociological Jurisprudence," *Harvard Law Review* 25 (April 1912): 510.

[71] Theodore Schroeder, "Social Justice and the Courts," *Yale Law Journal* 22 (November 1912): 26.

power cases had been whether legislative means were properly crafted to achieve legitimate legislative goals. In *Lochner*, for example, the Supreme Court denied not that New York could regulate the baking industry to protect bakery workers but only that the particular limitation of the bakers' hours was necessary to protect the health of the workers. Similarly, the decision of the New York Court of Appeals in *Ives* appears to have turned upon the court's conclusion that the workers' compensation statute did "nothing to conserve the health, safety or morals of the employees."[72] Recognizing that judicial decisions in such cases depended "very much upon the views of the judges and the established public opinion as to what constitutes the liberty guaranteed by our Constitution," a New Jersey attorney argued in 1912 that courts and lawyers should "keep themselves in touch with the facts of life" by knowing "the conditions under which men and women work" and studying "the facts which determine what sort of legislation is needed for the promotion of the public health, safety and welfare."[73]

The potential effectiveness of statistics to persuade a court that a particular measure was needed to protect the health, safety, or welfare of workers was illustrated in *Muller v. Oregon*, in which the Court concluded that Oregon's ten-hour law for women was necessary to protect the safety of Oregon's female laborers. In his celebrated brief in that case, Brandeis presented only two pages of law but offered more than one hundred pages of statistics concerning hours of labor, American and European factory legislation, and the health and morals of women. In his opinion for the Court, Justice David J. Brewer suggested that these statistics had influenced the Court's decision. Brewer's promise that the Court would "take judicial cognizance of all matters of general knowledge" provided an impetus for lawyers to educate judges about the facts of modern industrial life. As Melvin I. Urofsky has observed, *Muller* demonstrated that "lawyers could no longer evade their responsibilities of instructing and advising the courts on the relevant facts."[74] The Court's willingness to consider the social context also encouraged

[72] *Ives v. South Buffalo Railway Co.*, 201 N.Y. 271, 94 N.E. 431, 442 (1911).

[73] Edward Q. Keasbey, "The Courts and the new Social Questions," *Green Bag*, March 1912, pp. 123–24.

[74] Melvin I. Urofsky, *Louis D. Brandeis and the Progressive Tradition* (Boston: Little, Brown, 1981), p. 53. The extent of the influence of Brandeis's brief on the Court in *Muller* is open to question. Fiss has suggested that the Court's reference to the brief "might have been intended not as an expression of admiration or as an acknowledgment of an influence," but rather as a technique for distancing the Court from the views of the progressive Brandeis. Owen M. Fiss, *Troubled Beginnings of the Modern State, 1888–1910* vol. 8 of *Oliver Wendell Holmes Devise History of the Supreme Court of the United States* (New York, Macmillan) (forthcoming), pp. 175–76 (galleys).

progressives to continue to work for the nomination of more liberal judges.

During the years following *Muller*, the Court was sometimes receptive to fact-based arguments by attorneys concerning the need for legislation.[75] State courts also seemed amenable to persuasion by "Brandeis briefs." After striking down a statute prohibiting night work by women in 1907,[76] the New York Court of Appeals upheld a similar statute in 1915 where proponents of the law presented a much more detailed analysis of the need for the legislation. In upholding the statute, Judge Frank H. Hiscock acknowledged that the presentation of such facts had influenced the court.[77]

Like other progressive measures to diminish judicial hostility toward reform legislation, however, the use of social statistics was no panacea.[78] In many cases the Supreme Court had refused to be swayed by statistics presented in support of social legislation.[79] Mere statistics were not likely to persuade a judge to favor legislation that contravened his fundamental social and political philosophies.[80] But by making judges more aware of the exigencies of modern life, social statistics may have helped to alter those philosophies.

Since the analysis of social facts was not a task that the courts were well qualified to perform, some progressives asked whether the ascertainment of social facts should remain within the discretion of the judiciary. In 1913, Walter F. Willcox, a Cornell professor of political economy and statistics, argued that a more "developed system of social statistics" would enable experts to provide objective facts to courts to help judges to reach the "correct" decisions. According to Willcox, "ascertainment and proof of the social facts should not be left to the individual parties to whatever suit may arise. The facts in the case at bar

[75] David Ziskind, "The Use of Economic Data in Labor Cases," *University of Chicago Law Review* 6 (1939): 649–50; Paul L. Rosen, *The Supreme Court and Social Science* (Urbana: University of Illinois Press, 1972), pp. 87–98; John W. Johnson, *American Legal Culture, 1908–1940* (Westport, Conn.: Greenwood Press, 1981), pp. 36–37.

[76] *People v. Williams*, 189 N.Y. 131, 81 N.E. 778 (1907).

[77] *People v. Charles Schweinler Press*, 214 N.Y. 395, 411–13, 108 N.E. 639, 643–44 (1915).

[78] Marion E. Doro, "The Brandeis Brief," *Vanderbilt Law Review* 11 (1958): 792. Writing in 1933 after more than a decade of renewed conservatism in the Supreme Court, Professor Mason remarked that "despite the remarkable encouragement received by the Brandeis type of brief from both state and federal courts, it has not influenced judgments as much as was expected." Alpheus Thomas Mason, *Brandeis: Lawyer and Judge in the Modern State* (Princeton, N.J.: Princeton University Press, 1933), p. 113.

[79] *Stettler v. O'Hara*, 243 U.S. 629 (1916); *Adams v. Tanner*, 244 U.S. 590 (1917); *Adkins v. Children's Hospital*, 261 U.S. 525 (1923).

[80] Mason, *Brandeis*, pp. 113–17; Rosen, *Supreme Court and Social Science*, p. 90.

may be anything but typical and it is by typical, representative or average facts that the court should be guided to a decision." Although Willcox concluded that statisticians seemed "destined to supplement a defect in our judicial system," he offered no specific recommendations about how the courts could tap, refine, and employ the raw data provided by experts.[81]

Other reformers were more precise. In a 1913 *Harvard Law Review* article, John G. Palfrey, a Boston attorney, proposed the creation of a quasi-judicial tribunal composed of experts trained in political science and sociology. Courts would ask the tribunal to conduct investigations to determine whether a law arbitrarily infringed individual rights, and the court would be bound by the tribunal's conclusion. If the tribunal ruled that the statute was arbitrary, its operation would be suspended until further action by the legislature. Palfrey contended that his proposal would have the advantage of relieving courts of the embarrassment of having their judicial mandates "converted into mere temporary checks upon hasty legislative action, or subjected to popular review and reversal."[82]

Progressive efforts to interject scientific methods into the legal process reflected distrust of the corporate bias of lawyers as well as judges. In 1922 Edward A. Ross alleged that legislation to redress social injustices often was rendered nugatory by "ingenious lawyers" hired by special interests, who "proceed by clever sophistication and hairsplittings to befuddle the judges until they have whittled the statute down to the vanishing point." Ross complained that lawyers wasted most of their formidable mental powers in petty wrangling rather than attempting to ascertain the truth, solve problems, and develop law "in the direction of social need." Since lawyers were indifferent or even hostile to the public interest, Ross concluded that the public should listen "more to the advice of the more disinterested and socialized scholars, social workers, sanitarians, school-men, geologists, and economists" who unlike lawyers, had not "trained themselves into taking the private and oftentimes anti-social point of view."[83]

Efforts toward judicial "education" and the introduction of scien-

---

[81] Walter F. Willcox, "The Need of Social Statistics as an Aid to the Courts," *American Law Review* 47 (March–April 1913): 265.

[82] John G. Palfrey, "The Constitution and the Courts," *Harvard Law Review* 26 (April 1913): 507, 525–26, 528. Like Willcox, Palfrey contended that the use of experts would relieve courts of "the opprobrium attending the decision of essentially political questions in which popular feeling often runs high, much as they are now relieved by the jury of the burden of deciding the guilt or innocence of a human being accused of murder" (p. 528).

[83] Edward A. Ross, *The Social Trend* (New York: Century, 1922), pp. 163, 166, 168.

tific expertise into the judicial process were quintessentially progressive. They reflected the progressives' faith that humanity was capable of improving itself through rational and scientific means and that the American political system was sufficiently flexible to accommodate incremental changes based upon discoveries in the social sciences. Progressive attempts to educate judges about the realities of society were also consistent with the progressive predilection for investigation, manifest in the muckraking journalism of the early years of the century, the increasing number of congressional investigations, the establishment of such institutions as the Consumers League and the Russell Sage Foundation, and the literary realism movement.[84] The movement for judicial education tended to discourage support for the election of judges since an appointed judge whose intellect and education enabled him to absorb and appreciate the data presented in a Brandeis brief might be expected to take a more "scientific" view of a legal problem than a judge whose knowledge of social and industrial conditions was based upon his impressionistic experiences at the grass roots of society.

Like many other aspects of progressivism, the judicial education movement was highly conservative. The progressive predilection for judicial fact-finding was consistent with the widespread progressive faith in government by an educated elite—an attitude that clashed with the distrust of experts and bureaucrats that persisted among many Americans, including Jeffersonian agrarians and organized labor.[85] Unlike efforts to secure an elective judiciary, the movement for judicial education required no formal institutional changes and presented no threat to judicial independence. Like other progressive measures, however, the introduction of social science techniques into the judicial process did not lead to the triumph of a "public interest" over narrow partisan and personal interests. As David Danbom has pointed out, the "experts had been correct in believing their expertise was valuable, but they had erred in assuming it would necessarily benefit the public."[86]

Although Brandeis had emphasized in his *Muller* brief that his use of statistics was intended to persuade the Court of the rationality rather than the rightness of the legislation, the use of statistics potentially provided an impetus for judicial activism rather than judicial deference to legislation enacted by the elected representatives of the people. Indeed, the Supreme Court in *Lochner* had used statistics in support of its conclusion that the New York bakers did not need statutory protec-

---

[84] See Hays, *Response to Industrialism*, pp. 90–91.

[85] John Whiteclay Chambers II, *The Tyranny of Change: America in the Progressive Era, 1900–1917* (New York: St. Martin's Press, 1980), p. 139.

[86] David B. Danbom, *"The World of Hope": Progressives and the Struggle for an Ethical Public Life* (Philadelphia: Temple University Press, 1987), p. 143.

tion,[87] and Willcox attributed much of the growing criticism of the courts to judicial fact-finding.[88]

Progressive advocacy of extensive factual inquiries by the judiciary was necessary for the preservation of progressive legislation, however, insofar as the activist courts of the Progressive Era refused to invoke the traditional principle of presumptive constitutionality.[89] But proposals such as those of Willcox and Palfrey for judicial reliance upon expert advice presupposed that the courts could make detailed factual inquiries that might exceed the mere question whether there was a rational basis for legislation. In advocating extensive use of statistics provided by experts, progressives therefore tacitly endorsed the very sort of judicial activism that they ostensibly deplored. Even though the empiricism and pragmatism of the progressives often clashed with the formalistic doctrines that pervaded legal thinking, the progressive goal of efficiency also disposed progressives to favor a high level of judicial independence and power because the courts, more than most other public institutions, had the potential to transcend partisan strife and to make rational decisions untainted by political calculations. In recognizing that a strong judiciary could complement the reform movement, the progressives exalted their political agenda above any principled theory of judicial restraint.

To the extent that social statistics would support progressive arguments and encourage the courts to uphold popular progressive legislation, progressives correctly perceived that the development and use of such statistics would decrease criticism of the judiciary. But advocates of judicial use of social statistics greatly overestimated the degree to which the development of statistics by lay experts would relieve the courts of the need to render politically controversial decisions. Flushed with their faith in the ability of science to solve social problems, progressives failed to appreciate the high degree to which any statistics are subjective.

Forgetting Samuel Clemens's admonition about "lies, damned lies, and statistics," many progressives naively believed that lay experts could provide irrefutable evidence of the need for social legislation. In their ardor to obtain judicial validation of progressive legislation and cleanse the stain of politics from the robes of the judges, advocates of social statistics did not recognize that the creation, interpretation, and application of social statistics inevitably involve elements of political choice. Moreover, they did not perceive that a decision to uphold a

[87] *Lochner v. New York*, 198 U.S. 45, 70–71 (1905).

[88] Willcox, "Need of Social Statistics," p. 260.

[89] Rosen, *Supreme Court and Social Science*, p. 84.

statute could be as much a political act as a decision to strike down a statute. As Benjamin Parke DeWitt observed in 1915, "The great problems . . . of all government . . . are questions of policy, questions on which men disagree even when they know the facts and, in a sense, because they know the facts."[90]

Despite its shortcomings, the judicial education movement demonstrated that judges were willing to consider social realities and would gradually transform the law rather than remaining strictly bound by precedent. Although Arthur L. Corbin acknowledged in 1914 that the "legal profession is now on the defensive" because it had relied upon the precedents of case law "to the exclusion of other sources," he emphasized that the judges had responded to the need to adapt the law to changing social conditions. Corbin remarked that this judicial flexibility had "kept the declared judicial rules within hailing distance of advancing civilization, although occasionally civilization is obliged to send out a loud hail."[91]

Not content with the pace at which judges were adapting the law to the changing needs of an industrial society, many progressives continued to send out a "loud hail." Discouraged by the futility of attempts to secure the election of federal judges and dissatisfied with attempts to change the character of the judiciary through the appointment and education processes, many progressives embraced the expedients provided by the movements for the recall of judges and judicial decisions.

[90] Benjamin Parke DeWitt, *The Progressive Movement: A Non-Partisan, Comprehensive Discussion of Current Tendencies in American Politics* (Seattle: University of Washington Press, 1968), p. 338 (repr., 1915 Macmillan ed.).

[91] Arthur L. Corbin, "The Law and the Judges," *Yale Review* 3 (January 1914): 242.

FIVE

THE JUDICIAL RECALL MOVEMENT

It would seem eminently fair that the men who select the
judge, the men whom the judge is to serve, the men who
pay the judge, should be the men to remove him for
misconduct in office.
(*R. M. Wanamaker, judge of the Ohio Court of Common Pleas,
advocating the recall of judges, 1912*)[1]

The recall of judges . . . invites, even compels, a judge to
keep his ear to the ground and to anticipate the changing
whims of popular passion. He is made a servant, not of the
law, but a mere spokesman of the caprice of majorities.
The system, therefore, is one which tends to eliminate the
protective force of constitutional safeguards.
(*Rome G. Brown, chairman of the American Bar Association
Committee to Oppose the Recall, 1914*)[2]

T HE CONTROVERSY OVER *Standard Oil* and *Ives* occurred at
the very time many critics of the courts were beginning to
advocate and implement a specific measure—the judicial
recall—designed to make the courts more responsive to the popular
will. Unlike other plans that critics had propounded during recent
years, the recall enjoyed widespread support and was enacted into law
by a number of state legislatures. Like other proposals for judicial
reform, however, the recall ultimately failed to provide progressives
with significant relief from judicial hostility to reform legislation. Assiduous and organized opposition from conservatives prevented more
than six states from adopting the recall, and proposals for a federal
recall, like so many other court reform proposals, never received serious consideration. The controversy over the recall was significant,
however, insofar as it intensified public discussion about the role of the
judiciary in American society. Moreover, like other progressive proposals for reform, it may have altered judicial behavior by providing a

---

[1] R. M. Wanamaker, "Recall of Judges—A Judicial Affirmative," *Central Law Journal,*
July 12, 1912, p. 32.
[2] Rome G. Brown, "Judicial Recall," S. Doc. 617, 63rd Cong., 2d sess., 1914 (address to
the Missouri State Bar Association, September 23, 1914), pp. 15–17.

timely reminder of the power of the public to interfere with the independence of a judiciary that was not always responsive to deeply felt public needs.

The first recall statute, in Oregon in 1908, applied to all public officials and was not the culmination of a crusade against conservative judges. It was enacted as a constitutional amendment after voters approved it by a wide margin in an initiative sponsored by the People's Power League,[3] and it attracted little immediate attention. As the debate over judicial reform grew sharper during the next few years, however, many critics of the judiciary perceived that the recall was a politically viable measure that would make courts more responsive to the popular will. As a Minnesota attorney, James Manahan, explained in 1912, "Fear of the stout fist of the people" was "the only antidote" to the "poison injected into the arm of the law" by the "powerful and insidious influence" of big businesses and the wealthy.[4]

The decisions of the New York Court of Appeals in *Ives* and the Supreme Court in *Standard Oil* during the spring of 1911 provided an impetus for the recall movement, since those decisions were handed down at the very time the recall was beginning to attract widespread interest. On the day following the *Standard Oil* decision, Senator La Follette remarked, "This decision puts the movement for the recall of judges ten years ahead. People who never before would have given a thought to such a proposal as the recall of judges, will give it thought now."[5] When Arizona and California considered statutes to permit the recall of judges, the debate over the recall spread eastward and provided a new focal point for the continuing controversy over the courts. The controversy over the Arizona recall attracted much national attention because Arizona's recall provision was part of a constitution that Congress needed to approve before the Arizona Territory could be admitted to the Union as a state.[6]

---

[3] James D. Barnett, *The Operation of the Initiative, Referendum and Recall in Oregon* (New York: Macmillan, 1915), p. 191. For a text of the statute, see Gilbert L. Hedges, *Where the People Rule* (San Francisco: Bender-Moss, 1914), pp. 93–94 160–61.

[4] James Manahan to Edward A. Ross, April 12, 1912, *Manahan Family Papers*, Box 4, Minnesota Historical Society, St. Paul.

[5] William Bayard Hale, "La Follette, Pioneer Progressive," *The World's Work*, July 1911, p. 14600.

[6] "President Vetoes the Statehood Bill," *New York Times*, August 16, 1911, p. 1. Under the proposed Arizona Constitution, all elective officers, including state and county judges, would become subject to a recall by the voters six months after their election. The constitution provided that citizens could initiate the recall of an officer by a petition signed by a number of electors that was equal to 25 percent of the votes cast for all of the candidates for that office at the previous general election. If the officer had not resigned, his name would be placed on a ballot along with other candidates. Both the petitioners

Arizona's recall shocked conservatives throughout the nation. Despite widespread misgivings about the recall, Congress approved statehood for Arizona and New Mexico in 1912 after insurgent Republicans joined with Democrats who were eager for the admission of two heavily Democratic states. However, the congressional resolution that approved statehood required that the state conduct a referendum after admission to allow the voters to decide whether they wished to retain the recall.

This requirement failed to go far enough to satisfy Taft, who vetoed the statehood resolution in August. In a remarkably astringent message to Congress, Taft excoriated Arizona's recall provision as "pernicious" and "injurious to the cause of free Government." He alleged that the recall would encourage hasty action by an electorate inflamed by fleeting passions. Ignoring the likelihood that the collection of petition signatures would ordinarily take a considerable time and that five months were required between the certification of the petition and the recall election, Taft complained that "no period of delay is interposed for the abatement of popular feeling. The recall is devised to encourage quick action, and to lead the people to strike while the iron is hot." A judge, Taft warned, could be "haled before the electorate as a tribunal . . . with no judicial hearing, evidence or defense, and thrown out of office, and disgraced for life" because he had failed, perhaps in a single decision, to capitulate to the caprice of voters. Denying that the recall would protect "the weak and the oppressed," Taft alleged that the recall could enable "unscrupulous political bosses" to control elections and would encourage "the sensational, muckraking portion of the press" to make false charges against just judges.[7]

Although the House voted to override Taft's veto, the Senate passed an amended resolution to admit Arizona on the condition that its constitution strike the judicial recall provision. Arizona was therefore forced to remove the recall provision from its constitution. Proponents of the recall in Arizona, however, warned Taft that

> We will tolerate your gall
> And surrender our recall
> Till safe within the Statehood stall
> Billy Taft, Billy Taft.

---

for the recall and the officer would have the opportunity to appeal to the voters in a two-hundred-word statement on the official ballot. If the incumbent received the highest numbers of votes, he would continue in office. If not, the candidate with the highest tally would succeed him (ibid.).

[7] "Veto Message," in *A Compilation of the Messages and Papers of the Presidents* vol. 16 (New York: Bureau of National Literature), pp. 7636–44; "President Vetoes Statehood Bill."

> Then we'll fairly drive you daft
> With the ring of our horselaugh
> Billy Taft, Billy Taft,
> As we joyfully re-install
> By the vote of one and all
> That ever glorious recall
> Billy Taft, Billy Taft.[8]

The people of Arizona carried out their threat. Shortly after Arizona was admitted to the Union in February 1912, the state amended its constitution to incorporate an even more radical recall provision. In the November 1912 presidential election, the voters took further revenge on Taft, who received only 12 percent of the vote and ranked an ignominious fourth behind Wilson, Roosevelt, and the Socialist Eugene V. Debs.

Arizona adopted its recall measure several months after California voters approved a similar measure in an election in October 1911. The adoption of the recall in California reflected widespread resentment against a conservative judiciary that increasingly seemed out of step with prevalent economic and social opinion in this progressive stronghold. As in so many states, the judiciary in California regularly invoked the Fourteenth Amendment to bludgeon regulatory measures opposed by large corporations. The courts were particularly solicitous of the Southern Pacific Railroad.

When progressives swept the 1910 election in California, electing a liberal Republican legislature and the Republican insurgent Hiram Johnson as governor, their bright hopes for reform were dimmed by the shadow of the courts. Early in his term, Johnson asked the legislature to enact measures for a direct primary, the referendum, the initiative, and the recall of state officials, including judges. Although the proposal for a recall inspired the inevitable howls from conservatives, many progressives also questioned the wisdom of the measure.

Johnson might have been forced to abandon the proposal if California's attorney general had not revealed that a 4–3 state supreme court decision for the retrial of a notorious grafter was rendered under irregular circumstances. In the wake of the resulting public outcry, the legislature approved the recall measure, which was sent to the people for approval in a referendum.[9]

Johnson vigorously campaigned in favor of the recall. Presenting an extreme view of popular sovereignty, Johnson went so far as to argue

---

[8] *Arizona Blade-Tribune* (Florence), August 19, 1911, p. 2.

[9] George E. Mowry, *The California Progressives* (New York: Quadrangle, 1963), pp. 141–42 (repr. 1951 University of California Press ed.).

that the system of checks and balances was hostile toward popular government. When opponents of the recall argued that it would force judges to keep their ears to the ground, Johnson replied, "We would rather that the judges keep their ears to the ground than to the railroad tracks in California."[10] Californians responded to Johnson's appeal by approving the recall measure by a 3–1 vote. Although the electorate also approved other progressive measures, the recall won by a much larger margin than many other reforms, including women's suffrage and the initiative.[11]

While Congress was debating Arizona's recall measure, Senator Robert L. Owen of Oklahoma introduced legislation in July 1911 to permit the recall of federal judges, including Supreme Court justices. Owen's bill provided that a judge's tenure would terminate whenever Congress passed a resolution requesting the president to nominate a successor. Under Owen's bill, Congress would not need to vouchsafe any reason for the judge's removal. Owen explained that to "assign reasons is to discredit the incumbent, while removal without assignment of reasons is the mildest method of dealing with a public servant whose service is no longer desired." Arguing that a free people should "govern themselves without apology," Owen declared that "the mere fact that the people do not like a judge and do not desire him to serve them justifies recall."[12] In August 1912, Democratic senator Henry F. Ashurst of Arizona proposed a constitutional amendment for recall of judges of inferior courts,[13] and an Oregon congressman proposed a similar measure in 1913.[14] Although these measures helped to intensify the controversy over the recall, they received no serious attention in Congress.

By 1912, the enactment of the recalls in Oregon, California, Arizona, Nevada, and Colorado infused the debate over the role of the judiciary with a practical urgency that earlier discussions on the role of the judiciary had lacked. Like Taft in his veto message, conservatives warned that the recall would destroy judicial independence and subject the nation to the tyrannical and unstable rule of arbitrary and shifting majorities.

Opponents of the recall argued that it was premised upon a misun-

---

[10] Ibid., pp. 148–49.

[11] *Statement of the Vote of California at the Special Election held October 10, 1911, on Constitutional Amendments* (Sacramento: State Printing Plant, 1911), p. 9. The recall provision was approved by a vote of 157,596 to 49,345.

[12] S.3112, 62nd Cong., 1st sess., 1911. See 47 *Congressional Record*, 62nd Cong., 1st sess., July 31, 1911, p. 3359 (remarks of Senator Owen).

[13] S. J. Res. 130, 62nd Cong., 2d sess., 1912.

[14] H. J. Res. 26, 63rd Cong., 1st sess., 1913.

derstanding or perversion of the judicial function. As Elihu Root explained in a speech to the New York State Bar Association in 1912, "The judge is confined within the narrow limits of reasonable interpretation. It is not his function or within his power to enlarge or improve or change the law. It is his duty to maintain it, to enforce it, whether it be good or bad, wise or foolish, accordant with sound or unsound economic policy."[15] Similarly, Republican senator George Sutherland of Utah observed that the recall was "based upon a complete misconception of the nature of the relationship . . . between the people and the judge, who is not a political agent to declare the *wishes* of a constituency, but a self-responsible arbitrator to decide the *rights* of contending parties, bound by the most solemn of covenants to consider nothing but the law and the facts and to obey no voice save the compelling voice of his own instructed conscience."[16]

Many progressives argued that the inherent vagueness of such provisions as the due process clause of the Fourteenth Amendment permitted a wide range of judicial discretion and belied the argument that a judge simply applied the "correct" law to a particular set of facts. Since the ambiguity of constitutions and statutes permitted judges to read their own social, political, and economic predilections into the law, the people should have the right to remove a judge whose social and economic philosophies were at odds with the sentiments of a majority of the people. As Manahan told the Minnesota State Bar Association in 1911, "The fact that courts do and can usurp the legislative functions under our system" provided a compelling reason for the recall.[17]

Opponents of the recall in turn argued that the proper remedy for such abuses was to amend state or federal constitutions rather than terrorize the judiciary. Although Professor W. F. Dodd of the University of Illinois did not oppose the recall, he suggested that more effective expedients for judicial abuses would be the deletion of due process clauses from state constitutions and the amendment of the federal judicial code to permit federal courts to review state decisions that invalidated state statutes on federal constitutional grounds.[18] As we have seen, Congress adopted the latter reform in 1914.

Conservatives also argued that the recall contravened the basic character of American government. Pointing out that the American system

[15] "Root Denounces Recall of Judges," *New York Times*, January 20, 1912, p. 7.

[16] George Sutherland, "The Law and the People," S. Doc. 328, 63rd Cong., 2nd sess., 1913, p. 5 (address at annual dinner, the Pennsylvania Society, December 13, 1913).

[17] James Manahan, "Recall of Judges," S. Doc. 941, 62nd Cong., 2d sess., 1912, p. 9 (address before Minnesota State Bar Association, July 19, 1911).

[18] W. F. Dodd, "The Recall and the Political Responsibility of Judges," *Michigan Law Review* 10 (December 1911): 90–91.

of government is republican rather than democratic, conservatives alleged that the recall would violate the spirit, if not the letter, of the Constitution's provision (Art. IV, sec. 4) that the United States shall guarantee to every state a republican form of government and would interfere with the system of checks and balances that provide equilibrium to the American government.[19] "A popular government is not a government of a majority, by a majority, for a majority of the people," President Taft explained in his veto message. "It is a government of the whole people under such rules and checks as will secure a wise, just and beneficent government for all the people." Similarly, Henry Cabot Lodge warned that the recall would confer power upon self-interested and determined minorities.[20]

Conservatives also warned that majority rule was dangerous because any majority was likely to be unstable or tyrannical. During the Senate debate on the Arizona constitution, for example, Republican senator Coe I. Crawford of South Dakota cited statistics on the high incidence of lynching as evidence of the dangers of direct popular participation in the judicial process. In reply to Crawford, Republican senator Moses E. Clapp of Minnesota pointed out that lynch mobs assembled in the very shadow of the courts whose power conservatives defended. Clapp and other proponents of the recall argued that judges had encouraged the recall movement by remaining impervious to changing social conditions.[21]

Opponents also emphasized that the recall would destroy judicial independence since fear of removal would cause some judges to pander to popular caprice. The New York attorney William B. Hornblower, for example, told the graduating class of the Yale Law School in 1912 that the recall would tend "to substitute for the fearless and independent judge a spineless, flabby, cowardly judge, a reed shaken by the wind."[22] Republican representative Samuel W. McCall of Massa-

[19] Albert Fink, "The Recall of Judges," *North American Review,* May 1911, p. 672,678, 683; 47 *Congressional Record,* 67th Cong., 1st sess., August 8, 1911, p. 3712 (remarks of Senator Crawford); Brown, "Recall of Judges," pp. 15–18 and "Argument in Opposition," S. Doc. 649, 62nd Cong., 2d sess., 1912 (an address to the Minnesota State Bar Association, July 19, 1912); Rome G. Brown, "The Judicial Recall a Fallacy Repugnant to Constitutional Government," S. Doc. 892, 62nd Cong., 2d sess., 1912, pp. 8–11, 27–28 (repr. from *Annals of the American Academy of Political and Social Science,* September 1912).

[20] Henry Cabot Lodge, "The Constitution and Its Makers," S. Doc. 122, 62nd Cong., 2d sess., 1911, p. 23 (address to the Literary and Historical Association of North Carolina, November 28, 1911).

[21] 42 *Congressional Record* 62nd Cong., 1st sess., August 8, 1911, pp. 3714–15, 3719.

[22] William B. Hornblower, "The Independence of the Judiciary, The Safeguard of Free Institutions," Address to the Graduating Class of Yale Law School, June 17, 1912, repr. in *Yale Law Journal* 22 (November 1912): 1.

chusetts argued that recall would encourage judges "to consult the popular omens rather than the sources of the law."[23]

Proponents of the recall gleefully pointed out that these arguments proved too much because they tacitly admitted that judges were easily swayed by outside influences. "If it is true that judges will serve the power that controls the tenure of their office to the extent of rendering wrong decisions when that power is the people, is it not true that they will be equally subservient to any other power which controls their official life?" asked New York attorney Gilbert E. Roe in *Our Judicial Oligarchy*, a widely distributed critique of the courts published in 1912.[24] Owen observed that "public opinion is a better and safer influence for judges who may be influenced on the bench than the influence of a political boss or his commercial allies." Manahan contended that judges were already fearful of bosses and influenced by "politicians and the bunco of business men."[25]

Proponents of the recall insisted that the recall would not erode judicial independence. Manahan stated that a "fearless judge would never fear the people. A cowardly judge would fear the people less than he would the political boss and big business men who made him."[26] Republican senator Miles Poindexter of Washington argued that a judge's "knowledge that he is responsible to no power but an intelligent public opinion . . . will be an incentive to any honorable judge to render none but righteous judgments."[27] Hiram Johnson contended that the recall would actually enhance judicial independence by freeing judges from the influence of special interests.[28] Other proponents of the recall went so far as to contend that judicial independence was undesirable to the extent that it protected corruption or permitted judges to render highly political decisions based upon their own predilections. Democratic senator Thomas J. Walsh of Montana, for example, acknowledged that judicial independence was a desirable goal, but he warned that "we may pay too high a price to secure it."[29]

[23] Samuel W. McCall, "Representative as Against Direct Government," *Atlantic Monthly*, October 1911, p. 463, repr. William Bennett Munro, ed., *The Initiative, Referendum and Recall* (New York: Appleton, 1912), p. 185.

[24] Gilbert E. Roe, *Our Judicial Oligarchy* (New York: B. W. Huebsch, 1912), p. 215.

[25] Manahan, "Recall of Judges," p. 12.

[26] Ibid.

[27] Miles Poindexter, "The Recall of Judges," 62nd Cong., 2d sess., S. Doc. 472, 1911, p. 9 (repr. from *Editorial Review*, November 1911).

[28] Hiram R. Johnson to A. H. Heflan, September 9, 1911, *Hiram Johnson Papers*, Bancroft Library, University of California at Berkeley, pt. 2, Box 1.

[29] Thomas J. Walsh, "Recall of Judges" (address to the Washington State Bar Association, July 28, 1911), repr. Sen. Doc. 100, 62nd Cong., 1st sess. 1911, p. 11.

Disputing the contention that the recall would make the judiciary more responsive to the popular will, opponents argued that the recall would merely provide new opportunities for exploitation of the people. Echoing President Taft's warning in his veto message, opponents predicted that political bosses would control the recall process. In an article in the May 1912 issue of *Century Magazine*, Bruce B. McCay predicted that "any powerful organization or interest" would be "in a much better position to initiate the recall than the average man." McCay explained that "the political wirepuller" knew how to manipulate public sentiment, unite minorities into a majority, and plan the most auspicious timing to initiate and effect a recall. He contended that voters would rarely be able to identify "the really competent and uncontrolled judges" and that an honest judge who thwarted powerful interests would be turned out of office "on some fictitious pretext" contrived by those interests before the public could discern the judge's true character. A corrupt judge could retain popular favor by means of an occasional popular political decision, while an honest judge could be removed from office if he rendered one unpopular decision. McCay contended that the recall would expose the judiciary to "the constant menace of political interference" because "the judge will not only be obligated to the political boss for putting him in office, but will remain under a constant obligation to him for keeping him there."[30] Another opponent argued that voters who had succumbed to corporate influence in the election of judges could hardly be expected to resist such influence in recall elections.[31]

Conceding that many judges were already selected for political reasons without regard for professional fitness, the conservative New York attorney Charles A. Boston argued that the most effective antidote to the recall movement would be the selection of better judges. Boston's opinion was based upon an extensive survey that indicated that large numbers of lawyers and laypersons believed that judges were insufficiently competent or excessively partisan. Boston argued that reformers should abandon the recall movement and redirect their energies toward demanding that the president and political bosses select only judges who had eminent intellectual and ethical qualities.[32]

Opponents foretold the dire evils that would flow from the destruction of judicial independence. "A feeble, a timid, an obedient judici-

[30] Bruce B. McCay, "The Judicial Recall," *Century Magazine*, May 1912, p. 16.

[31] Fink, "Recall of Judges," p. 687.

[32] Charles A. Boston, "Some Conservative Views Upon the Judiciary and Judicial Recall," *Yale Law Journal* 23 (April 1914): 525–29; Charles A. Boston and Everett V. Abbot, "The Judiciary and the Administration of the Law," *American Law Review* (July–August 1911): 481–512.

ary . . . has always in the end proven to be an incompetent, a cruel or a corrupt judiciary," Senator Borah of Idaho warned during the debate on the Arizona constitution. Such a judiciary, Borah declared, "leaves human rights uncertain and worthless, unsettles titles, destroys values, leaves the workman and the employer alike without protection or guidance, and has more than once demoralized or destroyed governments."[33] Similarly, Henry Cabot Lodge observed in a speech at Princeton in 1912 that "servile judges are a menace to freedom, no matter to whom their servitude is due."[34] Recognizing that the principal supporters of the recall believed that the courts were excessively solicitous of wealth, opponents were wont to emphasize the danger to personal liberties more than the threat to property. Following the lead of Taft in his veto message, they pointed out that the courts protected minorities from the oppression of the majority and guarded the weak against the mighty. Presaging arguments that conservatives would emphasize during the 1920s, Borah declared, "There is no place in our Government today where those without wealth, influence, or friends are so thoroughly protected as in the courts."[35]

Proponents, however, continued to argue that the courts themselves oppressed the humble and the lowly. Manahan alleged that courts of all ages "have had a tendency if unrestrained to side with the strong and oppress the weak."[36] And the utilities expert and publicist Delos F. Wilcox argued that "courts stand as the bulwark of special interests and spin red tape that binds the poor to their poverty."[37]

Accusing opponents of lacking faith in the people, proponents contended that the recall was the latest development in an ongoing process of democratization.[38] As William Jennings Bryan remarked, "The recall is an evolution rather than a revolution."[39] Opponents continued to insist that the recall would upset the equilibrium that made such a

[35] 42 *Congressional Record*, 62nd Cong., 1st sess., August 7, 1911, p. 3687.

[34] Henry Cabot Lodge, "The Compulsory Initiative and Referendum and the Recall of Judges" (address at Princeton University, March 8, 1912), repr. S. Doc. 406, 62nd Cong., 2d sess., 1912, p. 17.

[35] 42 *Congressional Record*, 62nd Cong., 1st sess., August 7, 1911, p. 3685. Similarly, Senator Knute Nelson of Minnesota pointed out that the Fourteenth Amendment was intended to protect "the meek, the humble and the lowly" and to ensure that "popular outcry may not smother the voice of justice" (ibid., p. 3695). The *New York Times* reminded its readers that "it is not property alone that is sheltered by the guarantees of the Constitution, the rights and the liberties of the citizen are also safeguarded" ("The Courts and the People," January 20, 1912, p. 12).

[36] Manahan, "Recall of Judges," p. 10.

[37] Delos F. Wilcox, *Government by All the People* (New York: Macmillan, 1912), p. 226.

[38] See Roe, *Our Judicial Oligarchy*, pp. 206–10.

[39] William Jennings Bryan, "The People's Law" (address to the Ohio Constitutional Convention, March 12, 1912), repr. S. Doc. 523, 63rd Cong., 2d sess., 1914, p. 38.

democratic process viable. An article in the *North American Review* declared that "lulled to sleep by the unparalleled prosperity we have enjoyed under the Constitution . . . we are prone to believe that human rights and liberties have become so secure as to be in no further need of protection either from the tyranny of a dictator or from that of an unrestrained democracy."[40]

A number of opponents also pointed out that the recall would not express the wishes of the people as a whole but only the small number of persons who voted in a recall election.[41] The vote in recall elections would be light, opponents of the recall predicted, because only one office would be at stake. Accordingly, the power of money interests in such elections would be greatly enhanced.[42]

Opponents argued that the recall would be particularly unjust to a conscientious judge who suffered the ignominy of a recall. It seemed less than fair, William L. Ransom observed, to require the judge to guess about the prevailing public mood concerning the scope of due process and then permit the voters to "chop off his judicial head if he 'guesses' or 'calculates' wrong."[43] Opponents perceived scant likelihood that the electorate would have the ability or the patience to discern the true character of the record of an unpopular judge.

Conservatives predicted that recall campaigns would be tumultuous affairs where the judge's opponents would exploit public ignorance and inflame public passions. Hornblower, for example, warned against the dangers of "stump speeches upon the platform" and "loose declamations and unsworn statements" that would subject a judge "to an indignity and a possible injustice which may blast his reputation for a lifetime."[44] Rome G. Brown, a Minnesota attorney, complained that the power of recall was arbitrary because judges would not be confronted with the charges against them or permitted the privilege of a hearing. Brown, who served for several years after 1912 as chairman of the ABA's Committee to Oppose Judicial Recall, contended that the short statement that the judge was permitted to make on the ballot was a farce because a recall would involve complex issues that a judge could not easily explain.[45]

Similarly, John H. Hazelton, a New York attorney, feared that voters

[40] Fink, "Recall of Judges," p. 677.

[41] Lodge, "Constitution and Its Makers," p. 23.

[42] McCay, "Judicial Recall," p. 18.

[43] William L. Ransom, *Majority Rule and the Judiciary: An Examination of Current Proposals for Constitutional Change Affecting the Relation of Courts to Legislation* (New York: Scribner, 1912), p. 83. Ransom, an advocate of Roosevelt's plan for a recall of judicial decisions, agreed with Roosevelt that a judicial recall might be appropriate under circumstances existing in certain states.

[44] Hornblower, "Independence of the Judiciary," p. 4.

[45] Brown, "Recall of Judges," pp. 13, 22.

would not have access to judicial records and would obtain their information from such biased or unreliable sources as newspapers.[46] Bruce B. McCay complained that "the vote of the swaggering drunk has equal weight with that of the learned judge, and the votes of three hoboes and a ward heeler will contain more judicial power than the votes of any three judges in the country."[47] The *New York Times* further warned that judges could not defend themselves against damaging charges because custom frowned upon extrajudicial explanations of their actions.[48] Hornblower, however, feared that judges might attempt such a defense: "The spectacle of our judges . . . racing up and down their judicial districts haranguing the multitude in defense of their judicial conduct is such a perversion of all judicial proprieties that only the comic opera stage and the genius of Gilbert and Sullivan are adequate to do justice to the situation."[49]

Opponents argued that the recall would therefore debase the quality of the judiciary; talented and honorable persons would be loath to expose themselves to the indignity of the recall or the vulgarity of a recall campaign.[50] "As it is difficult enough now to induce men of high intelligence to accept office, how would it be under this recall system?" the *American Law Review* asked.[51] Brown argued that "no man worthy of a judgeship would be willing to be tried and convicted by public clamor without an opportunity to be heard."[52] Diminution of the quality of the judiciary in turn would merely accelerate the trend toward judicial acquiescence to popular demands.[53] The *Green Bag* stated that law "must of necessity lag behind public opinion; and the moment we attempt to pack our judiciary with 'progressive' judges we run the risk of filling the bench with very bad lawyers, who will render the logical and consistent development of our law impossible."[54]

Proponents of the recall insisted that the electorate would not abuse its right to recall judges. Poindexter, for example, contended that voters would never recall a fearless and fair judge even if they disagreed with his decisions.[55] Samuel Gompers insisted that "no American community will permit a just and upright interpreter of true American

[46] John H. Hazelton, "The Recall of Judges," S. Doc. 723, 62nd Cong., 2d sess., 1912, p. 5.

[47] McCay, "Judicial Recall," p. 17.

[48] "As a Party Wrecker," *New York Times*, March 16, 1912, p. 12.

[49] Hornblower, "Independence of the Judiciary," p. 7.

[50] Ibid., p. 5; *The Nation*, February 27, 1913, p. 194; "Judicial Fitness and the Recall," *The Nation*, July 24, 1913, p. 73; McCay, "Judicial Recall," p. 17.

[51] *American Law Review* 45 (March–April 1911): 303.

[52] Brown, "Argument in Opposition," p. 14.

[53] "Judicial Fitness and Recall."

[54] "The Recall of Judges," *Green Bag*, March 1912, pp. 156–57.

[55] 47 *Congressional Record*, 62nd Cong., 1st sess., August 7, 1911, p. 3673.

principles to be dispossessed of his seat as a jurist in consequence of an occasional unpopular decision."[56] Owen predicted that the "will of the people will not be exercised as by a raging, furious, turbulent mob. It will be exercised, if at all, in the quiet seclusion and safety of the booth in the ballot box."[57] Some proponents, however, argued that the recall was worth the danger of occasional injustices to individual jurists. In a speech to the Ohio Constitutional Convention in 1912, for example, Bryan argued that the "society can better afford to risk such occasional injustice than to put the judge beyond the reach of the people."[58]

Proponents of the recall alleged that conservative misgivings about the procedure reflected their fundamental distrust of democracy. In his address to the Minnesota State Bar Association in 1912, Manahan declared that the "man who believes the people are a mob does not believe in republican form of government. He should leave this country."[59] Roe argued that the "history of patience and forbearance on the part of the masses" in the face of judicial emasculation of social reform belied any argument that the electorate was vulnerable to "momentary gusts of popular passion."[60] Samuel Gompers denounced opposition to the judicial recall as an "argument for monarchical institutions," arguing that conservatives who presumed the voters would not prudently exercise their right to recall judges might as well oppose the popular franchise altogether.[61]

Proponents also argued that properly drafted recall statutes could impose checks on rash action. In 1911, W. F. Dodd proposed various means for minimizing the danger of the recall. He argued that the statutes could allow time for popular passions to cool by requiring a significant interval to pass between the filing of the recall petition and the recall election. Dodd observed that the California statute seemed to provide ample time for reasoned reflection since a recall election would be held between sixty and eighty days after the certification of the recall petition.[62] The statutes could also minimize the politicization of the recall process by requiring first a distinct vote upon the question of removal and a subsequent election for the judge's successor.[63] Dodd

---

[56] Editorial, *American Federationist*, June 1911, p. 463.

[57] 47 *Congressional Record*, 62nd Cong., 1st sess., August, 8, 1911, p. 3725.

[58] Bryan, "People's Law," p. 7.

[59] Manahan, "Recall of Judges," p. 12.

[60] Roe, *Our Judicial Oligarchy*, p. 214.

[61] Editorial, *American Federationist*, June 1911, p. 462.

[62] Dodd, "Recall and Political Responsibility," pp. 83–84. Dodd suggested that shorter periods provided by Arizona and Oregon might not accord sufficient time for prudent consideration.

[63] Ibid. Oregon and Arizona provided that the incumbent judge would compete with other judicial candidates and would be removed from office if he did not receive the

further suggested that the danger of frequent recalls could be reduced by requiring a substantial number of signatures on petitions. He believed that Oregon and Arizona, which required that the number of petitioners be equivalent to 25 percent of the voters at the previous election, would ensure that the recalls would not be too frequent.[64]

Defenders of the recall also pointed out that none of the dire predictions of the recall's opponents had come to pass in Oregon, which had permitted the recall of judges since 1908.[65] Writing in the January 1912 issue of the *Atlantic Monthly*, Republican senator Jonathan Bourne, Jr., of Oregon declared, "Our courts have proceeded with their work as quietly and as deliberately as ever, though possibly with less delay."[66] By 1912, when the recall movement was at its zenith, Oregon had conducted no recall election, and only one serious recall attempt had been made.[67] During the middle of 1913, after national interest in the recall issue had subsided, county judges were recalled in Hood River and Clackamas counties by relatively small margins. At the same time, the county judge in Klamath County was retained in office by an overwhelming majority of votes. Since opposition to all three judges was based upon their actions as members of the county board of commissioners rather than their judicial acts, the recall elections failed to provide the opponents of the recall with useful propaganda.[68]

---

highest vote. Although California required separate votes on the recall and the choice of a successor, both votes were held at the same election.

[64] Ibid., p. 84.

[65] C. F. Taylor, "A Glaring Error in Certain Senate Documents Opposing Popular Government," S. Doc. 651, 62nd Cong., 2d sess., 1912, p. 7; Roe, *Our Judicial Oligarchy*, pp. 214, 217–18; Wanamaker, "Recall of Judges," p. 33.

[66] Jonathan Bourne, Jr., "Initiative, Referendum, and Recall," *Atlantic Monthly*, January 1912, pp. 122, 127.

[67] A recall petition had been widely circulated against a judge who was charged with giving instructions designed to bias a jury in favor of a defendant in a notorious murder case, but proponents of the recall failed to obtain enough signatures to force an election. This recall was vigorously opposed by the press. Even a newspaper that supported the recall amendment opposed the recall of the judge on the ground that the voters were not qualified to assess the legal questions involved in the jury instructions. The newspaper contended that the recall would make the judge a scapegoat for popular disappointment over the verdict. James D. Barnett, "The Operation of the Recall in Oregon," *American Political Science Review* 6 (February 1912): 46–47; Roe, *Our Judicial Oligarchy*, p. 218. In advocating the recall in *Our Judicial Oligarchy*, Roe argued that this case demonstrated that the people would not abuse the recall. Although this case "presented every feature necessary to call forth one of those 'momentary gusts of popular passion' from which the opponents of the recall would protect our judges," Roe believed that the people exercised appropriate restraint.

[68] Hedges, *Where the People Rule*, pp. 97–106. At this time, county judges in Oregon outside Multnomah County sat as probate judges, had some jurisdiction in juvenile cases, and sat as members of the county board of commissioners (ibid., p. 109).

Proponents also argued that the history of judicial elections and tenure and removal mechanisms in the states demonstrated that the people would not expect judges to cater to popular whims. Owen, for example, contended that virtually every state already had a form of recall since thirty-four states elected judges by popular vote for limited terms and forty-three states had established short or limited judicial terms. Owen also pointed out that thirty-two states provided for removal by address of the legislature, a procedure that permitted removal on lesser grounds than those required for impeachment.[69] Defenders of the recall argued that the judiciary's ability to maintain its integrity despite such insecurities demonstrated that the recall would not detract from judicial independence. "Is it customary," the *American Review of Reviews* asked, "for a good judge to spend the last year of an expiring term trying to make decisions that might tickle the popular fancy, just because he is about to come up again for renomination and election?"[70]

Opponents, however, contended that the existing removal procedures provided a sufficient safeguard against abuse of power and that fear of the disgrace of a recall was far more likely to pervert judicial behavior than the prospect of defeat in a general election. Henry Cabot Lodge denied that removal by address of the legislature, at least in Massachusetts, was analogous to the recall, since the legislature conducted quasi-judicial hearings that accorded the judge an opportunity to defend himself.[71]

The organized bar generally opposed the judicial recall. At its 1911 annual meeting in Boston, the American Bar Association adopted a resolution drafted by six of its former presidents that the recall "would be destructive of our system of government."[72] Alton B. Parker, one of the authors of the resolution, later reported that only three of the six hundred delegates voted in opposition to the resolution.[73] At its convention in Milwaukee in 1912, the ABA endorsed a report that denounced all recalls of judges and judicial decisions as "dangerous to the country." The report denied that the recall served the interests of the common people for whom the courts throughout the history of the Republic had acted as "the greatest bulwark" of protection. "Is it any

---

[69] 47 *Congressional Record*, 62nd Cong., 1st sess., July 31, 1911, pp. 3359, 3363–64.

[70] *American Review of Reviews*, April 1912, p. 395. The *Review* favored short judicial terms rather than the recall.

[71] Lodge, "Compulsory Initiative," p. 16.

[72] *Report of the Thirty-Fourth Annual Meeting of the American Bar Association* (Baltimore: Lord Baltimore Press, 1911), p. 51.

[73] Barbara C. Steidle, "Conservative Progressives: A Study of the Attitudes and Role of Bar and Bench, 1905–1912," Ph.D. diss., Rutgers, 1969, p. 342.

reproach upon the courts," the report asked, "that they have extended the same protection to the rich and powerful when assailed by popular prejudice?"[74] In 1911 the ABA established the Committee to Oppose the Judicial Recall, active for nearly a decade, which flooded the nation with literature and deployed a host of speakers to warn audiences about the perils of the recall.[75] The committee included members from every state, who "stood as outposts, each in his own state, to guard against further encroachments."[76]

Many state and local bar associations also denounced the recall. The New York State Bar Association, at a special meeting in April 1912, adopted resolutions condemning the judicial recall and created a committee to cooperate with the American Bar Association in waging a campaign of public propaganda against the recall.[77] A meeting of the Illinois Bar Association in March 1912 condemned the recall of judges by a vote of 549 to 110.[78] Several other state bar associations, including those in Minnesota, Wisconsin, Kentucky, and West Virginia denounced the judicial recall in 1912.[79] By early 1913, a majority of the county bar associations of New York State had adopted resolutions denouncing the recall of judges and judicial decisions.[80]

Meanwhile, professional journals editorialized against the recall and warned against its peril.[81] In July 1912, for example, the editors of the *Central Law Journal* declared that "no lawyer who has given the matter careful attention can see anything but disaster" in the proposals for the judicial recall and the recall of decisions.[82] Opponents of the recalls had to admit, however, that a significant number of attorneys favored some form of the proposal. As the *Green Bag* ruefully observed in October 1912, "It is not without significance . . . that a small minority in the bar associations often comes forward to defend the recall, the

[74] *Report of the Thirty-Fifth Annual Meeting of the American Bar Association* (Baltimore: Lord Baltimore Press, 1912), pp. 574–83; "Meetings of the American Bar Association and Affiliated Bodies," *Green Bag*, October 1912, pp. 468–70. See "Bar Association Denounces Recall," *New York Times*, August 28, 1912, p. 6; "For Reform Instead of Recall," ibid., August 30, 1912, p. 6.

[75] By 1913, the committee had distributed more than 350,000 pamphlets to libraries, newspapers, judges, lawyers, law students, and legislators. *Report of the Thirty-Sixth Annual Meeting of the American Bar Association* (1913), p. 580.

[76] "Report of the Committee to Oppose Judicial Recall," *American Bar Association Journal* 1 (July 1915): 277.

[77] *Green Bag*, May 1912, p. 274.

[78] Steidle, "Conservative Progressives," pp. 356–59.

[79] *Green Bag*, October 1912, p. 498.

[80] *Green Bag*, March 1913, p. 127.

[81] *Green Bag*, April 1911, p. 214; *Green Bag*, March 1912, p. 156; *Central Law Journal*, August 25, 1911, pp. 129–30.

[82] *Central Law Journal*, July 12, 1912, p. 25.

final action not always being secured without debate, even when unanimous in form."[83]

Despite growing bar support for the recall of judges, the recall movement began to wane soon after it had begun to wax. After 1912, only one state—Kansas, in 1914—adopted a provision for a recall of judges during the Progressive Era. The decline of support for the recall was illustrated in Minnesota where the house of representatives adopted a recall measure by a wide margin in April 1911 but overwhelmingly repudiated the recall in June 1912. A proposal for a constitutional recall amendment was defeated at the general election in 1914, and the legislature in 1915 rejected a proposal for the recall of public officials, including judges.[84] Declining enthusiasm for the recall also was discernible in other states. In the progressive stronghold of North Dakota, the house of representatives rejected a recall measure in 1915 even though it had approved such a measure by a wide margin two years earlier. Likewise, the Massachusetts legislature showed no interest in a recall bill introduced in 1915 by that body's only Socialist member.[85]

By August 1912, Brown had observed that the campaign against the recall was beginning to encourage a "spirit of sober reflection" among the public.[86] In an address to the Minnesota State Bar Association in September 1914, Brown explained with satisfaction that the tide of public opinion had turned against the recall because ordinary citizens had discovered that the recall movement was "an attack upon the safeguards established for their protection."[87]

In 1915, the ABA's Committee to Oppose Judicial Recall found that the recall was making no additional progress and predicted that no more states would adopt the recall. The committee resolved, however, to refrain from relaxing its public information campaign, fearing that "neglect of the situation may find us suddenly confronted with a revived antagonist."[88] The vigilance of the ABA appeared to continue to be effective. The committee's report for 1916 concluded that only in the Far West was there "even a remnant of danger" that an additional state would adopt the recall, since recognition of "the viciousness of the judicial recall" had become "prevalent throughout the country." The

[83] *Green Bag*, October 1912, p. 498.

[84] "Report of the Committee to Oppose Judicial Recall," *American Bar Association Journal* 2 (July 1916): 446–47; "Report of the Committee to Oppose Judicial Recall," *American Bar Association Journal* (July 1915): 278; Brown, "Judicial Recall," p. 29.

[85] "Report of the Committee to Oppose Judicial Recall," 1915, p. 278.

[86] Brown, "Judicial Recall," p. 29.

[87] Ibid., pp. 5, 7.

[88] "Report of Committee to Oppose Judicial Recall," 1915, p. 281.

ABA attributed the decline of popular support to the ABA's propaganda campaign. Particularly in the West, where the ABA reported that "local libraries and reading rooms are flooded with Socialist publications," the ABA supplied literature that opposed the recall.[89] In 1917 and 1919, the committee praised itself again for turning public opinion against the recall but warned that the danger had not disappeared.[90] As the recall movement subsided, the committee gradually turned its attention to more general defenses of the Constitution against what the committee perceived as the growing menace of socialism. In particular, the committee monitored the nascent movement to curb the jurisdiction of the courts and began to battle the judicial usurpation theory.[91]

Opponents of the recall were also cheered because the voters were not exercising the recall in the few states that had adopted the recall. The 1916 report of the Committee to Oppose Judicial Recall noted that Californians reported that "the judicial recall in California is in such disrepute as to be practically harmless." Similarly, the report noted that "public sentiment in Arizona is changing to opposition to recall." Only two attempts to invoke the judicial recall, one in California and one in Colorado, had been made during the year prior to the ABA's report. Both attempts had failed.[92]

Although conservative opposition helped to defeat the recall, the movement also suffered from opposition by many progressives. Progressive misgivings reflected the same ambivalence about direct democracy that made many progressives reluctant to support judicial elections. While the recall movement reflected the progressive faith in the wisdom of the disinterested citizen, it conflicted with progressive efforts to make government more orderly and was consistent with the antipopulism of many progressives. Although the recall might have temporarily enabled the progressives to reestablish control over a government that seemed to them to be dominated by self-interested plutocrats and immigrants, astute progressives like Borah recognized that narrow interests ultimately might manipulate the recall. The recall movement demonstrated the tensions between the idealistic and moralistic progressives who sought to restore a pure and individualistic democracy that never really existed and the progressives who sought to

---

[89] "Report of Committee to Oppose Judicial Recall," 1916, pp. 442, 443, 450.

[90] "Report of the Committee to Oppose Judicial Recall," *American Bar Association Journal* 3 (July 1917): 454; "Report of the Committee to Oppose Judicial Recall," *American Bar Association Journal* 5 (1919): 410.

[91] "Report of Committee to Oppose Judicial Recall," 1917, pp. 454–60; "Report of Committee to Oppose Judicial Recall," 1919, pp. 409–14.

[92] "Report of Committee to Oppose Recall," 1916, pp. 443–46.

accommodate democratic values to the exigencies of an increasingly complex and impersonal society. While the former were willing to accept the recall at face value, the latter tended to view the recall more as a tactic to encourage judicial reform. Ultimately, the misgivings of the latter prevailed. As Richard Hofstadter pointed out, much of the political machinery designed to implement the aims of direct democracy was of very limited use since the ethos of individual responsibility was not ideally adapted to the realities of the highly organized society of the Progressive Era.[93]

Some progressives also recognized that the recall was impracticable because it was too radical to enjoy widespread support. Edward A. Ross feared that the recall movement would "offend the conservative instincts of the common people in the states that have had a pretty decent judiciary," and he warned that the progressive movement should not "propose more than it can put through." Ross believed that the direct primary system would encourage the election of better judges in states that elected judges and that the popular demand for more progressive judges would encourage better judicial appointments in states where the governor selected judges.[94]

Even though the recall itself had little impact, the movement for the recall helped to accomplish many of the goals of the progressives. Despite their general opposition to the recall proposals, leaders of the bar recognized that the agitation for recall reflected a profound dissatisfaction with the operation of the legal system. Rather than contenting themselves with condemnations of the recall, many prominent attorneys believed that the bar should take the lead in working for reforms that would restore public confidence in the judicial system. By providing an impetus for procedural reform, the recall movement served a useful purpose, even though only a few states enacted a judicial recall and the possibility of a federal judicial recall was never seriously considered.

The recall also provided a potent reminder to judges that they were responsible to the citizens. Although widespread opposition to the recall demonstrated that Americans cherished judicial independence, the strength of the recall movement indicated that there were limits to public tolerance of judges whose social, economic, and political philosophies were markedly discordant with prevailing public opinion. As George W. Alger observed in 1913, "The recall of judges is in small measure due to a desire to get rid of judges, but more largely to a desire

[93] Richard Hofstadter, *The Age of Reform: From Bryan to F.D.R.* (New York: Knopf, 1981), p. 259.
[94] Edward A. Ross to James Manahan, April 18, 1912, *Manahan Family Papers*, Box 4, Minnesota Historical Society, St. Paul.

to remind them, by its crude potentialities, of their duties to society as well as to the individual."[95] The usefulness of the recall as a reminder rather than as a remedy was demonstrated by the restraint with which it was exercised in those states where it was adopted. As *The World's Work* observed in 1912 with regard to California's judicial recall, "The power is in the people's hands, but they seem conservative in using it against the courts. They no doubt regard it as a gun behind the door."[96]

[95] George W. Alger, "The Courts and Legislative Freedom," *Atlantic Monthly*, March 1913, p. 352.

[96] "The Recall of Judges in California," *The World's Work*, March 1912, p. 494.

SIX

THEODORE ROOSEVELT AND THE
JUDICIAL REFERENDUM

It is the people, and not the judges, who are entitled to say
what their constitution means, for the constitution is
theirs, it belongs to them and not to their servants in
office—any other theory is incompatible with the
foundation principles of our government.
*(Theodore Roosevelt, defending his proposal for popular
referenda on judicial decisions, July 1, 1912)*[1]

This proposed method of reversing judicial
decisions . . . lays the ax at the foot of the tree of well-
ordered freedom and subjects the guarantees of life,
liberty and property without remedy to the fitful impulses
of a temporary majority of the electorate.
*(President William Howard Taft, March 8, 1912, denouncing
Roosevelt's proposal for popular referenda on judicial decisions)*[2]

ALTHOUGH PUBLIC DISCONTENT with the judiciary gathered much momentum between 1906 and 1910, criticism of
the courts remained diffuse. The emergence of the judicial
recall issue during 1911 provided a remedy many critics of the courts
were able to support, but effective reform also required national leadership. Even though many critics of the courts were nationally prominent, none was in a position to lead a politically potent reform movement: Walter Clark's judicial duties circumscribed his political role;
Robert L. Owen's political base was too narrow; and Robert M. La
Follette was too distracted by other issues.

A national spokesman finally emerged when Theodore Roosevelt
took up the cause shortly after he returned to the United States in June
1910 from the triumphal European tour that followed the African
safari on which he had embarked after leaving the presidency in March

[1] Theodore Roosevelt, Introduction to William L. Ransom, *Majority Rule and the Judiciary* (New York: Scribner, 1912), p. 6.

[2] William Howard Taft, "The Judiciary and Progress," address delivered at Toledo,
Ohio, March 8, 1912, repr. S. Doc. 408, 62nd Cong., 2d sess., 1912, p. 9.

1909. Roosevelt burst back into American politics with all of the dazzle of Halley's comet, which began to appear over American skies at the same time that New York City was according a hero's welcome to its returning native son.

Roosevelt assured the Manhattan throngs that greeted him when he landed at the Battery on June 18 that he was "ready and eager" to help the nation solve its problems, and insisted that he would remain aloof from partisan politics. Before long, however, Roosevelt had expressed support for a controversial New York direct-primary law, and he was unable to resist an avalanche of invitations to speak on behalf of progressive causes during the upcoming congressional elections.[3] In his first speech of that campaign, Roosevelt initiated an attack on the judiciary that became one of the cornerstones of a political philosophy and program that Roosevelt developed and articulated during the next two years, and led to the breach in the Republican party that ensured Wilson's election in 1912. Addressing a joint session of the Colorado legislature on August 29, 1910, Roosevelt accused the courts of blocking effective state and federal action to solve urgent national problems. Roosevelt charged that the courts had imposed artificial limits on the powers of the state legislatures and Congress to exercise control over the activities of large corporations. The absence of such control, Roosevelt declared, was "ruinous" to the nation's social fabric. Roosevelt used the Supreme Court's decisions in *Lochner* and the *Sugar Trust Case* as examples of the Court's contravention of popular rights.[4]

Roosevelt's speech created a minor sensation. The reaction was particularly virulent because news reports conveyed the erroneous impression that Roosevelt had devoted his entire speech to an attack on the courts.[5] The speech particularly distressed President Taft, who believed that Roosevelt's proposals would require "a revision of the federal Constitution."[6] Adverse reactions to the speech deeply troubled Roosevelt, who expressed surprise that his proposals would be

[3] See Henry F. Pringle, *Theodore Roosevelt: A Biography* (New York: Harcourt, Brace, 1931), pp. 533–37; Joseph L. Gardner, *Departing Glory: Theodore Roosevelt as ex-President* (New York: Scribner, 1973), pp. 169–72, 182–86; Joseph Bucklin Bishop, *Theodore Roosevelt and His Time*, vol. 2 (New York: Scribner, 1920), pp. 297–300.

[4] Theodore Roosevelt, "Criticism of the Courts," *The Outlook*, September 24, 1910, p. 149.

[5] Oscar King Davis, *Released for Publication: Some Inside Political History of Theodore Roosevelt and His Times, 1898–1918* (New York: Houghton Mifflin, 1925), pp. 208–11. To enable journalists to meet their deadlines, Roosevelt prior to his speech had distributed two typewritten sheets that contained his remarks concerning the courts, the only part of his speech that was in legible form. Ibid.

[6] Taft to Charles P. Taft, September 10, 1910, *Taft Papers*, Series 7, Reel 452, Manuscript Division, Library of Congress.

branded as "revolutionary" and "incendiary" since Justice William H. Moody had suggested its theme and Roosevelt had carefully reviewed the speech with Arthur Hill, a former Boston district attorney.[7] The criticisms so vexed Roosevelt that he defended it in *The Outlook* in September. Complaining that his critics had denounced his speech as "an attack upon the judiciary as a whole, an incitement to riot, and an appeal to the passions of the mob," Roosevelt protested that the speech was as restrained as the legislative audience to which it was addressed and pointed out that his criticism of the Supreme Court was not unprecedented since Abraham Lincoln had publicly denounced the Court's decision in *Dred Scott*. Roosevelt quoted from the stinging dissents of Justice Harlan in *Knight* and Justice Holmes in *Lochner*, which, Roosevelt argued, were more astringent than his speech. Finally, Roosevelt argued that courts should not be above criticism, citing his 1906 message to Congress in support of this position.[8]

No matter how prudently Roosevelt criticized the courts, however, his observations were bound to antagonize conservatives because he had questioned the wisdom of the most reliable bastion of property rights. Conservatives correctly perceived that the speech underscored Roosevelt's growing radicalism. With considerable justification, they feared the ascendancy of a progressive tide led by Roosevelt that would remove barriers to social legislation through the appointment of progressive judges and the enactment of measures to curb judicial power.

Conservative fears about Roosevelt's radicalism were intensified by another forceful speech Roosevelt delivered two days after his Denver address. Speaking in Kansas, he articulated his vision of what he for the first time called the "New Nationalism." Roosevelt called for a broad program of social, political, and economic reform, including extensive regulation of corporate activities, a graduated income tax, an inheritance tax, a revision of the monetary system, and full accounting for campaign expenditures. Although Roosevelt acknowledged that the rights of capital were worthy of protection, he declared that "the true friend of property, the true conservative, is he who insists that property shall be the servant, and not the master, of the commonwealth. . . . The citizens of the United States must effectively control the mighty commercial forces which they have themselves called into being." Roosevelt also explained that the New Nationalism demanded that the judiciary

---

[7] Roosevelt to Henry Cabot Lodge, September 12, 1910, in Elting E. Morison, ed., *Theodore Roosevelt Letters*, vol. 7 (Cambridge, Mass.: Harvard University Press, 1954), pp. 122–23.

[8] Roosevelt, "Criticism of the Courts," pp. 150–53. Roosevelt incorporated these defenses into his next speech criticizing the courts, delivered in Syracuse on September 17.

"shall be interested primarily in human welfare rather than in property."[9]

Roosevelt lowered his political profile only briefly after the 1910 election, in which the Republicans suffered a resounding defeat. By early 1911, however, he had resumed his controversial commentaries on the issues of the day. Roosevelt criticized the judiciary again in February and March 1911 in four articles published in *The Outlook* as part of a series of articles in which he explained his concept of the New Nationalism.[10] Professing great respect for the role of the judiciary in American government, Roosevelt contended that the courts were not too powerful but that they often failed to exercise their power wisely.

Shrewdly recognizing that a powerful judiciary was an indispensable instrument for the achievement of the New Nationalism, Roosevelt declared, "There is no need of discussing the question of whether or not judges have a right to make law. The simple fact is that by their interpretation they inevitably do make the law in a great number of cases. Therefore it is vital that they should make it aright." Although Roosevelt acknowledged that the Founding Fathers had not dreamed of giving the Supreme Court such an exalted status in the political system, Roosevelt praised John Marshall for making "the Constitution march." Marshall's elevation of the Court's status, Roosevelt contended, had provided an impetus for national unity that had prevented the nation's degeneration "into a snarl of jangling and contemptible little independent commonwealths, with governments oscillating between the rule of a dictator, the rule of an oligarchy, and the rule of a mob."[11]

Roosevelt warned, however, that the blindness of some judges to popular needs threatened to undo Marshall's work, arguing that the *Knight* decision invited "industrial chaos" by encouraging each state to act for itself. Similarly, Roosevelt warned that the judicial contempt for popular legislation encouraged the people to curb judicial power. He predicted that the nation would not "permanently tolerate the failure" of government to respond to widespread popular demand for "efficient and genuine control over great corporations." Roosevelt emphasized, however, that the people should not expect the courts to sway with the transient winds of public opinion, since "ordinarily the court knows more than the people can know of any given case." Although he

[9] "Roosevelt out with Platform," *New York Times*, September 1, 1910, p. 1.

[10] Theodore Roosevelt, "Nationalism and the New Judiciary," *The Outlook*, February 25, 1911, pp. 383–85; March 4, 1911, pp. 488–92; March 11, 1911, pp. 532–36; March 18, 1911, pp. 574–77.

[11] Ibid., pp. 490–91.

expressed disapproval of indiscriminate criticism of the courts, he observed that "the men who denounce the free and fair criticism of the judiciary . . . are themselves doing all in their power to render necessary the adoption of some more direct method of popular control."[12]

Even though Roosevelt's articles in the *Outlook* articulated a theory of the proper role of the judiciary, he failed to offer many specific ideas about how to accommodate judicial independence with judicial accountability. Roosevelt opposed the election of federal judges and the popular recall of federal judges. However, he suggested that he approved of allowing both houses of the legislature to remove judges on address by a substantial majority, a system that he noted had been written into law and not abused by New York and Massachusetts. Later in 1911, Roosevelt endorsed a specific proposal for more direct popular control. Speaking in New York on October 20, 1911, Roosevelt declared that the people should be permitted to vote on issues of state constitutional law.[13] He reiterated his proposal for direct popular review of decisions in *The Outlook* of January 6, 1912, urging that the people should have the right to vote on any state or federal constitutional question on which the Supreme Court had not ruled. Accordingly, Roosevelt declared that he hoped that the upcoming New York constitutional convention would approve a measure to "enable the people to decide for themselves, by popular ballot after due deliberation, finally and without appeal, what the law of the land shall be" on constitutional issues when judges had contravened "justice and equity."[14]

Roosevelt's article in *The Outlook* provoked sharp criticism. The *New York Times* declared that it was "the craziest article ever published by a man of high standing and responsibility in the Republic." Warning that Roosevelt's plan was "the simplest and easiest way of tearing the Constitution to tatters," the *Times* suggested that Roosevelt's proposal would destroy republican government.[15] Arthur S. Tompkins, a New York judge, declared that Roosevelt's proposal was "the most radical and revolutionary suggestion ever made under our republican form of government."[16] Republican senator Elihu Root of New York told a meeting of the New York State Bar Association that the plan abandoned the principle that "human nature needs to distrust its own im-

---

[12] Ibid., pp. 536, 576–77.

[13] *Works of Theodore Roosevelt*, vol. 16 (New York: Scribner, 1926), p. 206.

[14] Theodore Roosevelt, "Judges and Progress," *The Outlook*, January 6, 1912, pp. 45–46.

[15] "The Short Way with the Courts," *New York Times*, January 6, 1912, p. 12.

[16] "Queens Bar Hears Recall Discussed," *New York Times*, February 4, 1912, p. 9.

pulses and passions and to establish for its own control the restraining and guiding influence of declared principles of action."[17]

Roosevelt's relations with Taft turned increasingly sour during 1911. Taft was particularly piqued by Roosevelt's endorsement of the Arizona recall provision and criticism of arbitration treaties negotiated by Taft. Meanwhile, Taft's failure to embrace a vigorous progressivism continued to outrage Roosevelt. Although La Follette had announced his candidacy for the presidency and was lining up progressive support, many progressives urged Roosevelt to seek the Republican nomination. Shortly before delivering an address to the Ohio constitutional convention at Columbus on February 21, Roosevelt ended speculation and coined a political phrase when he informed reporters that "my hat is in the ring."

The content of Roosevelt's speech in Columbus created a greater political sensation than his entry into the presidential race. Roosevelt startled the nation by offering a more forceful endorsement of the recall of state judicial decisions than he had given in recent speeches or in *The Outlook* in January. Espousing a highly unorthodox constitutional idea to the constitutional convention, Roosevelt declared, "When the Supreme Court of [a] State declares a given statute unconstitutional, because in conflict with the State or National Constitution, its opinion should be subject to revision by the people themselves." The people, said Roosevelt, "have the right to recall that decision if they think it wrong." In articulating the way such a recall might come about, Roosevelt stated:

> If any considerable number of the people feel that the decision is in defiance of justice, they should be given the right by petition to bring before the voters at some subsequent election, special or otherwise, as might be decided, and after the fullest opportunity for deliberation and debate, the question whether or not the judges' interpretation of the Constitution is to be sustained. If it is sustained, well and good. If not, then the popular verdict is to be accepted as final, the decision is to be treated as reversed, and the construction of the Constitution definitely decided— subject only to action by the Supreme Court of the United States.

Although Roosevelt acknowledged that "we should hold the judiciary in all respect," he contended that "it is both absurd and degrading to make a fetish of a judge or of anyone else." Having announced at the outset of his address that "I believe in pure democracy," Roosevelt declared, "If the courts have the final say-so on all legislative acts, and if no appeal can lie from them to the people, then they are the irrespons-

---

[17] "Root Denounces Recall of Judges," *New York Times*, January 20, 1912, p. 7.

ible masters of the people." Although Roosevelt acknowledged that the people are not infallible, he believed that "the American people as a whole have shown themselves wiser than the courts in the way they have approached and dealt with such vital questions of our day as those concerning the proper control of big corporations and of securing their rights to industrial workers."

In explaining why the need for recall of state judicial decisions was so compelling, Roosevelt delivered a stinging attack on conservative judges and their decisions, alleging that state courts had perpetuated "lamentable injustice" by striking down regulatory legislation. "These foolish and iniquitous decisions have almost always been rendered at the expense of the weak." Although he conceded that many of the judges who handed down such decisions were "entirely well meaning men," he charged that such judges "did not know life as they knew law" and that their "associations and surroundings were such that they had no conception of the cruelty and wrong their decisions caused and perpetuated." Roosevelt accused such judges of preferring "the empty ceremonial of perfunctory legalism" to the "living spirit of justice."

Despite his ringing endorsement of recalling judicial decisions, Roosevelt reiterated his reservations about the recall of judges in his Columbus speech. Although he acknowledged that impeachment was an inadequate remedy and that a "quicker, a more summary remedy is needed," he contended that the recall should be adopted only as a "last resort." He explained that "every public servant . . . at times makes mistakes" and that the recall might inhibit judicial independence. Although he acknowledged that the states would need to adopt provisions that responded to local conditions, he again expressed preference for the more conservative procedure of removal by address of the legislature.

In addition to advocating the recall of judicial decisions, Roosevelt's Columbus speech endorsed a number of other progressive measures, including direct popular nominations, direct election of U.S. senators, the initiative, and the referendum. In an appeal to conservatives, however, Roosevelt argued that the government should regulate rather than dismantle big businesses. Stating that "we are a business people," the erstwhile trust buster declared that "no effort should be made to destroy a big corporation merely because it is big, merely because it has shown itself a peculiarly efficient business instrument." He argued that a fixed government policy of regulation would offer businesses greater stability by enabling them to predict what they could and could not do.[18]

[18] The full text of Roosevelt's address to the Ohio constitutional convention was reprinted in *The Outlook*, February 24, 1912, pp. 390–402.

Roosevelt's defense of robust competition in the marketplace did not diminish conservative outrage over his philippic against the judiciary and his startling proposal for the recall of decisions. The chancellor of Syracuse University declared that "Emma Goldman could not make a more violent assault upon our institutions," and the *Journal of Commerce* described Roosevelt's speech as the "most astonishing episode in the history of the United States," suggesting that Roosevelt's proposal raised "a serious question of his mental balance."[19] Charles Taft reported to his brother that many businesspeople who had admired Roosevelt were "now proclaiming him a faker and a demagogue" and that the "universal theory seems to be that he is crazy."[20] Roosevelt's idea reduced the *New York Times* to editorial apoplexy. The *Times* excoriated proposals for the recall of decisions and the recall of judges in no less than six editorials within three weeks of the Columbus speech.[21] The proposal, the editors insisted, was a "wild scheme" that far from being progressive was "a leap backward toward chaos and black night."[22]

Roosevelt's proposal for the recall of decisions distressed even many progressives. Borah, for example, dismissed it as "bosh," although he noted that the Columbus speech had "more good points than bad ones." Henry Cabot Lodge, who supported Roosevelt's presidential bid, remarked that "the Colonel and I have long since agreed to disagree on a number of points."[23] With some exaggeration, the *New York Times* reported that Roosevelt's proposal "has greatly alarmed the most radical of his followers," who were "manifestly flurried by the lengths they are expected to go" in following his leadership.[24]

Roosevelt's views alarmed no one more than the judge-worshiping

[19] "Has Roosevelt Lost His Mind?" *Current Literature*, April 1912, pp. 371–72.

[20] Charles P. Taft to William Howard Taft, February 26, 1912, *Taft Papers*, Series 8, Reel 452. Similarly, former governor J. N. Gillette of California expressed a widely heard opinion when he denounced the recall as "the craziest proposition I ever heard. It's anarchy" ("'Anarchy,' says ex-Gov. Gillette," *New York Times*, February 28, 1912, p. 3).

[21] "No Longer a Republican," *New York Times*, February 22, 1912, p. 8; "Reversing John Marshall," ibid., February 27, 1912, p. 10; "Progressing Backward", ibid., February 27, 1912, p. 8; "The Lawyers to the Defense," ibid., March 5, 1912, p. 10; "The Road to Despotism," ibid., March 9, 1912, p. 12; "To Make Cowards of Judges," ibid., March 12, 1912, p. 12.

[22] "Progressing Backward," The *Times* snidely suggested that the progressives would next want to allow the people to vote on landmark Supreme Court decisions, thereby unraveling the legal system and creating "horrid confusion," since "every decision abounds with citations from previous decisions." The final step would be the abolition of the Supreme Court and "the transfer of its business to the town meeting" ("Reversing John Marshall," February 25, 1912, p. 10).

[23] "Alarms His Own Followers," *New York Times*, February 22, 1912, p. 5.

[24] Ibid.

Taft. Taft, however, perceived obvious political benefits in Roosevelt's proposal; Roosevelt's alienation of conservatives provided a boon to Taft's bid for renomination. Taft noted with satisfaction that Roosevelt's proposal had benefited his candidacy among "the intelligent and the business community"[25] and that it had "stirred up a veritable hornet's nest of disapproval among the press and the people."[26] Roosevelt's advocacy of a measure that struck at the very bedrock of Taft's principles also eliminated any misgivings that Taft felt about engaging in a political struggle against his former friend and mentor and mitigated Taft's agony over the inevitable conflict. Taft was relieved that the long-dreaded breach with Roosevelt was now complete, although the personal and political implications of the rupture deeply distressed Taft.[27]

Taft made no secret of the intensity of his opposition to Roosevelt's plan. Speaking in fiery terms in Toledo on March 8, 1912, Taft blasted the proposal as "utterly without merit" and "reactionary," and he warned that it would sow "the seeds of confusion and tyranny."[28] Taft predicted that the nation would have the good sense to reject such a nostrum. He told a New Hampshire audience on March 19 that he was confident the American people "will never give up the Constitution, and they are not going to be honey-fugled out of it by being told that they are fit to interpret nice questions of constitutional law just as well or better than Judges."[29]

Roosevelt's reasons for throwing his political bombshell were complex. The most obvious explanation for his advocacy of the recall is that he hoped to win support for his presidential bid by riding the crest of popular dissatisfaction with the courts. James Willard Hurst, for example, has suggested that Roosevelt's proposal was the product of a naive opportunism.[30] In particular, Roosevelt may have advocated the recall as part of his effort to emerge as the unchallenged leader of the progressive movement and to win the Republican nomination.

Even though many progressive Republican leaders had shifted their support to Roosevelt during the early weeks of 1912, La Follette retained a formidable popular following, and La Follette had vowed to remain in the race even if Roosevelt entered it. La Follette's continuation of his campaign threatened to deprive Roosevelt of critical progressive support, particularly in the primaries. Although few of the

---

[25] Taft to Horace D. Taft, March 1, 1912, *Taft Papers*, Series 8, Reel 510.

[26] Taft to Charles P. Taft, February 28, 1912, *Taft Papers*, Series 8, Reel 510.

[27] Ibid.

[28] Taft, "Judiciary and Progress," p. 10.

[29] "All Taft Wants Is a Square Deal," *New York Times*, March 20, 1912, p. 4.

[30] James Willard Hurst, *The Growth of American Law: The Law Makers* (Boston: Little, Brown, 1950), p. 32.

delegates to the Republican national convention would be selected in the primaries, the primary results would influence party leaders who would select the bulk of the delegates. Moreover, a poor showing in the primaries would have embarrassed Roosevelt, who had so vigorously advocated the adoption of primaries and other forms of direct democracy.[31]

Roosevelt's plan for the recall of judicial decisions provided Roosevelt with an opportunity to convince any doubters that he was a true progressive, and it gave him an issue on which he could out-La Follette La Follette. The *Times* reported that many political observers thought that Roosevelt's speech made "La Follette look like a reactionary."[32] Moreover, Roosevelt may have anticipated that the plan would have a compelling appeal since it offered a novel and simple solution to a problem that had increasingly vexed progressives in recent years.

Although Roosevelt may have recognized that the plan would antagonize conservative voters, he may have believed that their support was already lost. Alternatively, he may have hoped that his endorsement of business competition would enable him to attract conservative support at the same time that the recall secured progressive support. Roosevelt may thus have intended to play both ends against the middle by capturing both Taft's support on the right and La Follette's support on the left.

While practical political strategies may account in part for Roosevelt's plan, he may also have been motivated by genuine conviction. His frustration with judicial invalidation of social reform measures was deeply rooted. It antedated his public criticism of the courts during his presidency and may be traced to the New York Court of Appeals' 1885 nullification of the law to prohibit the manufacture of cigars in tenements.[33] As a twenty-four-year-old member of the state assembly, Roosevelt had participated in an investigation of the unhygienic conditions in the cigar industry and had supported the reform legislation. The court's conclusion that the law exceeded the state's police power because it was not needed to protect the health or morals of the workers directly contravened the findings of the investigation and disillusioned the young Roosevelt.[34]

By 1912, Roosevelt was beginning to fear that American democracy could not survive the continuation of arrogant judicial assaults on popularly enacted social legislation and that the recall offered a means of

[31] After entering the race, Roosevelt won nearly all of the primaries he entered. George E. Mowry, *Theodore Roosevelt and the Progressive Movement* (Madison: University of Wisconsin Press, 1946), pp. 230–36.

[32] "Alarms His Own Followers."

[33] *In the Matter of Jacobs*, 98 N.Y. 98 (1885).

[34] Pringle, *Theodore Roosevelt*, pp. 259–61.

averting more radical changes. As Roosevelt told Herbert Croly one week after his Columbus speech, "We cannot permanently go on dancing in fetters. For the last thirty years there has been a riot of judicial action looking to the prevention of measures for social and industrial betterment which every other civilized nation takes as a matter of course, and in some way or other this riot must be stopped."[35] He expressed similar concerns four days after the Columbus speech at a private dinner in Boston with old friends, including the progressive Kansas editor William Allen White and the historian William Roscoe Thayer. When Thayer objected generally to Roosevelt's platform on the ground that it would substitute popular caprice for representative government, Roosevelt replied that he could name forty-six senators who secured their seats and held them at the favor of a Wall Street magnate (probably J. P. Morgan) and his associates. "Do you call that popular, representative government?" Roosevelt asked.[36]

Roosevelt's proposal for the recall of decisions was also consistent with his essential moderation. He explained to Croly that the proposal would offer an alternative to the judicial recall, which he believed might endanger judicial independence.[37] He told Frank B. Kellogg that he regarded the recall of decisions as a more conservative course than the piecemeal amendment of constitutions, which would have unforeseeable consequences.[38] He may also have hoped that the recall would discourage antireform court decisions. Moreover, as he had explained in his Columbus speech, his recall proposal was not intended to supplant the doctrine of judicial review, which Roosevelt strongly favored. As Roosevelt told a New York attorney in April, "It is an advantage that the courts in this country should be able to check the legislature. The trouble is that they have gone too far and that it is now necessary in many cases to recall the ultimate sovereign power—the people—to a position where it can decide between its agents."[39]

Reminding a New York publisher that freedom flourished in lands where no judicial review existed, Roosevelt explained that "so far from asking anything revolutionary I am asking that we take a far more conservative position than every other great civilized state takes."[40] A

[35] Theodore Roosevelt to Herbert Croly, February 29, 1912, *Theodore Roosevelt Papers,* Series 3A, Reel 374.

[36] William Roscoe Thayer, *Theodore Roosevelt: An Intimate Biography* (Boston: Houghton Mifflin, 1919), pp. 351–52.

[37] Roosevelt to Herbert Croly, February 29, 1912, *Roosevelt Papers,* Series 3A, Reel 374.

[38] Roosevelt to Frank B. Kellogg, March 25, 1912, *Roosevelt Papers,* Series 3A, Reel 375.

[39] Roosevelt to Joseph P. Cotton, Jr., April 30, 1912, *Roosevelt Papers,* Series 3A, Reel 375.

[40] Roosevelt to Edward J. Wheeler, February 29, 1912, *Roosevelt Papers,* Series 3A, Reel 374.

week after he spoke in Columbus, Roosevelt conceded that his speech had "frightened a lot of the very timid Conservatives in the East,"[41] but he observed that "any new proposal is sure to cause some fright."[42] He predicted that the conservatives "will get over it in the end" and that "even if they beat me this time, they must eventually come to the principle for which I stand."[43]

As a politician who persistently aimed for national unity though his actions often were divisive, Roosevelt also may have intended that the proposal would have a moderating influence on both radicals and reactionaries. Describing himself as "a man who believes with all fervor and intensity in moderate progress," Roosevelt explained to a British publisher that he had felt a duty to enter the race because "too often men who believe in moderation believe in it only moderately and tepidly and leave fervor to the extremists of the two sides."[44] The recall of judicial decisions might diminish extremism by both sides. It would reduce the opportunities for reactionaries to use the judiciary as a means of striking down progressive legislation. Meanwhile, the survival of more progressive legislation would deprive radical leaders of much of the popular anger on which their movements thrived. As George E. Mowry concluded, Roosevelt "was willing to go far to the left" in order "to stem the ever ascending tide of Socialism" and to prevent the election of a populistic Democrat.[45]

Moreover, Roosevelt may have felt that he had little to lose by advocating the recall. Although the Bull Moose fought hard to win the nomination and election, he was too shrewd a politician to believe that his prospects were favorable. The quixotic quality of his quest for the presidency afforded Roosevelt the luxury of favoring principles over politics. As Roosevelt told a Detroit editor at the end of February, "I made up my mind that I was in this fight to win or lose and I would nail my colors to the mast and make it a fight worth fighting, because I would make it a fight for principles which are essential if our democracy is to persist."[46] Advocacy of so controversial a measure was charac-

---

[41] Roosevelt to George E. Miller, ibid.

[42] Roosevelt to Herbert Croly, ibid.

[43] Roosevelt to George E. Miller, ibid.

[44] Roosevelt to J. St. Loe Strachey, March 26, 1912, *Roosevelt Papers*, Series 3A, Reel 375. Roosevelt lamented that the Republicans were divided into two extreme sides: "the unreasonable or sinister or merely foolish and timid reactionaries under the flabby leadership of President Taft who means well, but means well feebly . . . and, on the other hand, the forces of discontent and of demand for all kinds of . . . impossible progress under the lead of Senator La Follette who is half zealot and half self-seeking demagogue."

[45] Mowry, *Theodore Roosevelt*, p. 214.

[46] Roosevelt to George E. Miller, February 29, 1912, *Roosevelt Papers*, Series 3A, Reel 374.

teristic of Roosevelt, who relished controversy and had built his career around daring maneuvers and histrionic gestures.[47] His advocacy of the recall was merely one of the bolder strokes in a life that was never squeamish.

In an effort to refute the widespread allegation that his proposal was revolutionary, Roosevelt defended and explained his recall proposal in a series of public addresses in which he taunted his critics with characteristic verve and defiance. Paraphrasing Patrick Henry, Roosevelt exclaimed in Boston that "if [recall] is a revolution, make the most of it!"[48] In defending the plan, he first reiterated that his proposal extended only to state decisions that invalidated statutes enacted under the police power to promote the general welfare. Moreover, Roosevelt contended that the recall would not encourage hasty or thoughtless action if recall votes took place at a regular election not less than six months after a recall had been initiated.[49]

Roosevelt also continued to insist that his proposal was consistent with the ideals of American democracy. Rejecting the notion that "the Constitution is a straitjacket to control an unruly patient," he denied that his proposal would subject constitutional issues to the tyranny of a majority. Instead, he argued, his plan would save the nation from the tyranny of a greedy minority that was "grabbing our coal deposits, our water powers, and our harborfronts," adulterating foods and drugs, fostering monopolies and trusts, and perpetuating sweatshops and "the whole calendar of social and industrial injustice."[50]

Roosevelt also tried to explain that the recall would revoke only the principle announced in a judicial decision and would not overturn the court's decision regarding the rights of the parties to the case. Although some opponents of the recall were fair enough to concede this point,[51] Roosevelt confided to the New York attorney William L. Ransom in April that the use of the word *recall* was "unfortunate." He

[47] Willard B. Gatewood, Jr., *Theodore Roosevelt and the Art of Controversy: Episodes of the White House Years* (Baton Rouge: Louisiana State University Press, 1970), pp. 3–31.

[48] "Roosevelt Answers Cry of Revolution," *New York Times*, February 27, 1912, p. 1. Roosevelt had used the same phrase with reference to his criticism of judges in his New York City speech on October 20, 1911 (*Works of Theodore Roosevelt*, vol. 16, p. 198).

[49] By counting the time it takes for a statute to be enacted by a legislature and its constitutionality to be adjudicated by the courts, Roosevelt contended that the entire time for public consideration of a statute would therefore normally exceed two years. *Works of Theodore Roosevelt*, vol. 16, p. 148.

[50] "Roosevelt Hits at Taft Again," *New York Times*, March 21, 1912, p. 1.

[51] T. B. Kelley, "Fallacies of the Recall of Judicial Decisions," *Kentucky Law Journal* 2 (March 1914): 7; William B. Hornblower, "The Independence of the Judiciary, The Safeguard of Free Institutions," address to graduating class of Yale Law School, June 17, 1912, repr. *Yale Law Journal* 22 (November 1912): 9.

explained that he had used the word "as an argument to show men who wanted to recall judges that what they really meant nine times out of ten was that they wanted to change the decision of the judges on a certain constitutional question."[52] He later more accurately referred to his proposed procedure as a referendum.[53]

Despite Roosevelt's attempts to explain his plan and assuage the fears of its critics, apocalyptic predictions about the effects of the recall continued to abound. Andrew D. White declared in March 1912 that Roosevelt's plan was "the most monstrous proposal ever presented to the American people."[54] An article in the *Michigan Law Review* denounced it as "a political heresy, absolutely destructive of the constitution, subversive of civil liberty, damned by history, and a menace to the very existence of government."[55] The Union League Club in New York denounced the recalls of judges and decisions as "dangerous and revolutionary proposals which threaten to overthrow in a common ruin both justice and freedom." Commenting on the resolution, *The Nation* warned that the rhetorical extravagances favored by foes of Roosevelt's plan should not conceal the fact that the plan "does actually strike at a vital part of the organization of our government," even though the deleterious impact would not be immediate.[56]

Opponents of Roosevelt's plan, like opponents of judicial recall, argued that it would degrade the rule of law by permitting the politicization of legal issues. Taft explained in his address in Toledo that the determination of whether a particular statute violated the Constitution often involved technical issues that required "judicial reasoning and far-sighted experience," which the electorate lacked. Taft predicted that in practice the recall would permit "a suspension of the Constitution to enable a temporary majority of the electorate to enforce a popular but invalid act."[57] Alfred P. Thom, a District of Columbia attorney, warned the Alabama State Bar Association that the recall would embroil the electorate in distinctively legal issues and that the election would take place "amid the sympathies, passions, or prejudices aroused by the parties, surroundings, incidents, and perhaps hard-

[52] Roosevelt to William L. Ransom, April 28, 1912, *Roosevelt Papers*, Series 3A, Reel 375.

[53] Roosevelt, Introduction to Ransom, *Majority Rule*, p. 10.

[54] "White Against the Recall," *New York Times*, March 7, 1912, p. 3.

[55] Howard Wiest, "The Recall of Judges and Of Judicial Decisions," *Michigan Law Review* 11 (February 1913): 282.

[56] "A Question of Fundamentals," *The Nation*, March 21, 1912, p. 278. The Union League resolution was not the postprandial bombast of torpid clubmen but the product of the club's committee on political reform, which recommended the resolution in an elaborate report.

[57] "Taft Shows Peril in Roosevelt Policy," *New York Times*, March 9, 1912, p. 1.

ships of a particular case."[58] Another opponent of the recall predicted that masses of voters would fall under the spell of political charlatans and would lack "the stability and wisdom to make a cool clear decision of what is right or what is wrong."[59] Thom believed that "this instability in the Constitution and the subordination of the judicial branch to the legislative power would complete the opportunity for an ambitious executive to obtain and exercise absolute power."[60]

Opponents of the recall of decisions, like the opponents of judicial recall, further contended that it was repugnant to the constitutional requirement that the United States guarantee every state a republican form of government (Art. IV, sec. 4). Like Taft in his Toledo speech, opponents of Roosevelt's plan also argued that the politicization of legal issues would undermine fundamental constitutional freedoms. In particular, they emphasized that the recall of decisions would erode the protections that the law accorded to minorities and the weak.[61] Democratic senator Isidor Rayner of Maryland suggested that Roosevelt was contriving to destroy the judiciary because he wished to become a dictator.[62]

Opponents of the plan also predicted that its enactment by the states would lead to its application to the Supreme Court decisions,[63] especially since the Court's decisions so often created widespread public hostility.[64] But Ransom, a prominent proponent of the recall, explained that there was presently no movement for recall of Supreme Court decisions because the Court had "adopted a reasonable and progressive standard as to what legislation is permitted by the 'due process' clause."[65] Although Roosevelt publicly emphasized that his proposal would not extend to federal decisions, he confided to Croly that he believed the people would ultimately obtain the power to interpret even the federal Constitution.[66]

[58] Alfred P. Thom, "The Pending Revolution," address to the Alabama State Bar Association, July 12, 1912, repr. S. Doc. 883, 62nd Cong., 2d sess., 1912, p. 9.

[59] Kelley, "Fallacies," p. 12.

[60] Thom, "Pending Revolution," p. 10.

[61] Kelley, "Fallacies," pp. 5–6, 10; "Justice Attacks Recall," *New York Times*, February 23, 1912, p. 8; "The Road to Despotism," ibid., March 9, 1912, p. 12.

[62] 48 *Congressional Record*, 62nd Cong., 2d sess., February 27, 1912, pp. 2507–8.

[63] "White Against the Recall"; "Progressing Backward"; Hornblower, "Independence of Judiciary," p. 10.

[64] Hornblower, "Independence of Judiciary," pp. 10–11.

[65] William L. Ransom, *Majority Rule and the Judiciary* (New York: Scribner, 1912), pp. 109, 156–57.

[66] Roosevelt to Croly, February 29, 1912. Roosevelt told Croly that "one way or the other, it will be absolutely necessary for the people themselves to take the control of the interpretation of the constitution. Even in national matters this ought to be, and in my

Other critics of decisions recall predicted that the recall would also be extended to embrace issues beyond the definition of the police power. Ezra Ripley Thayer, the dean of Harvard Law School, warned that "it is not likely that the proposal could be adopted as to one part of the Constitution without its ultimate extension to others." The "'police power' could not be made the line of division," Thayer explained, because that concept was susceptible to infinite expansion.[67]

Despite the widespread outcry over Roosevelt's proposal, the plan found a number of prominent advocates, even at the elite levels of the legal profession. The plan itself was inspired by Professor James B. Thayer of the Harvard Law School and Charles F. Amidon, a federal judge in North Dakota.[68] Amidon told Roosevelt that his plan would "save our court system by making it compatible with popular government."[69] Other prestigious advocates of the recall included William Draper Lewis, dean of the University of Pennsylvania School of Law; Alfred Hays, Jr., of the Cornell Law School; and New York attorneys Ransom and Harold Remington.[70] Ransom published a widely distributed book in August 1912 defending Roosevelt's plan.[71]

One recent study has concluded that support and sympathy for Roosevelt's recall plan among lawyers indicates that opposition to social reform among the middle and upper levels of the bar was not so monolithic as has sometimes been supposed.[72] But support for the recall by the bar was probably exceptional. The sheer volume of writings and recorded remarks by lawyers tipped sharply in opposition to the plan, and bar associations overwhelmingly registered their disapproval. Like Roosevelt, the attorneys who favored the recall must have had complex reasons for advocating such a singular innovation. Since lawyers tended to revere the judiciary, many of the lawyers may have wished only to serve a warning on conservative judges. Personal ambitions may also have influenced their views. Lewis, for example, had

---

opinion will be eventually done. But there the problem is different. As regards the States the difficulty is very much less."

[67] Ezra Ripley Thayer, "Recall of Judicial Decisions," S. Doc. 28, 63rd Cong., 1st sess., 1913, pp. 8–9.

[68] Kenneth Smemo, *Against the Tide: The Life and Times of Federal Judge Charles F. Amidon, North Dakota Progressive* (New York: Garland, 1986), pp. 56–63.

[69] Ibid., p. 61, n. 34.

[70] Harold Remington, "Mr. Roosevelt's 'Recall of Judicial Decisions,'" *American Review of Reviews*, May 1912, p. 567. Remington defended Roosevelt's proposal as "sound in legal principle and essentially right in political philosophy and in economics."

[71] Ransom, *Majority Rule.*

[72] Stephen Stagner, "The Recall of Judicial Decisions and the Due Process Debate," *American Journal of Legal History* 24 (1980): 259.

long admired Roosevelt and became a Roosevelt advisor after he defended Roosevelt's plan.

Proponents of the recall disparaged the notion that the recall of decisions was revolutionary in theory or would be dangerous in practice. Like the defenders of the judicial recall, advocates of the recall of decisions contended that the reform would not unduly impinge upon the judicial function or erode judicial independence because decisions subject to the recall would involve broad questions of constitutional interpretation rather than technical points of law. Advocates argued that the public was often better qualified than judges to define vague phrases such as *due process* in cases involving social legislation. Ransom argued that popular determination of the "prevailing morality" and "preponderant opinion" accorded with the traditional procedures of the courts themselves, which permitted laypeople to decide questions of fact.[73] Ransom explained that "judges are chosen because they are upright and know the law, not because they know or can ascertain, when they are sitting in a busy appellate court, whether unclean and tubercular conditions in underground bakeries could affect the bread after it is baked."[74]

Proponents of the recall said that respect for judicial institutions was so deeply ingrained in the American character that the people would not abuse the recall. Far from subjecting the nation to a tyranny of the majority, Ransom argued, the recall would rescue the nation from the tyranny of the minority of political bosses and business interests who kept the courts in what Ransom called "the grasp of privilege."[75]

Advocates of Roosevelt's proposal also contended that it was superior to the recall of judges. One proponent argued that recall of decisions was "more precise and effective" because the "question is shifted from men to principles and the issue is made impersonal and concrete."[76] Proponents likewise agreed with Roosevelt that the plan was preferable to the enactment of constitutional amendments, which would simply raise new issues of law that would lead to protracted litigation, placing the poor at a disadvantage.[77] They also feared that federal amend-

[73] Ransom, *Majority Rule*, p. 128. According to Ransom, "The public needs as to social legislation should not be matters of *legal precedent* at all—they depend on *conditions of fact* which change with the time, the locality, the industrial or economic environment, the conscience and moral standards of the people, their habits of life and thought, and a thousand other factors as complex and variable as American life itself" (p. 132).

[74] Ibid., p. 135.

[75] Ibid., p. 22.

[76] Karl T. Frederick, "The Significance of the Recall of Judicial Decisions," *Atlantic Monthly*, July 1912, p. 48.

[77] Daniel W. Baker, "The Recall of Judicial Decisions," *Georgetown Law Journal* 1 (January 1912): 11.

ments would have unforeseen consequences[78] and that amendment of state constitutions would reduce state bills of rights into what Ransom called "a patchwork of exceptions and provisos" that might enable legislatures to enact exceptionally broad statutes that the courts would be powerless to invalidate. In contrast, Roosevelt's plan would merely allow the people to reinstate a particular statute and leave the courts free to strike down any more drastic statute.[79] Accordingly, proponents of the recall contended that it was essentially conservative.[80]

Opponents often argued that Roosevelt's plan was far more radical than the judicial recall because it permitted ordinary citizens to decide specific points of law. Gilbert E. Roe, a La Follette adviser, argued that the "recall of decisions means that the wholly untrained layman shall undertake to do, personally, the highly specialized and technical work of a judge."[81] Similarly, the *Central Law Journal* argued in 1921 that "the recall of judges is conservatism itself" compared with the recall of decisions, which would transfer "intricate, delicate and difficult problems" to the hustings.[82]

Opponents of Roosevelt's plan also expressed fear that the recall would destroy the law's consistency and predictability. Arguing that the recall of judges was innocent compared with "this giant of destruction," an article in the *Michigan Law Review* stated, "It may make but little difference whether one man or another . . . sits on the bench, so far as we know what the law is."[83] Taft explained that the "majority which sustains one law is not the majority which comes to consider another" and that the recall would produce "application of constitutional guaranties according to popular whim."[84] Lodge warned that

---

[78] William Draper Lewis, "A New Method of Constitutional Amendment," *Annals of the American Academy of Political and Social Sciences* 43 (September 1912): 313; Ransom, *Majority Rule*, p. 32.

[79] Ransom, *Majority Rule*, pp. 151–52; Lewis, "New Method," pp. 317–19.

[80] As a 1913 *Atlantic Monthly* article observed, "Instead of attempting to terrorize the judge by the threat of personal punishment through the recall, instead of repealing the due-process clause, instead of adopting amendments to our constitutions, necessarily broad and general, and conferring large and possibly dangerous powers on legislators in advance of legislation, it proposes to refer to the people a specific law, with the "due-process' objections of the courts to its constitutionality" (George W. Alger, "The Courts and Legislative Freedom," *Atlantic Monthly*, March 1913, p. 352).

[81] Gilbert E. Roe, *Our Judicial Oligarchy* (New York: B. W. Huebsch, 1912), p. 219. The contrast between Roe's ardent support for the recall of judges and his bitter opposition to the recall of decisions perhaps may be explained more in terms of politics than principles since Roe was one of La Follette's closest advisors.

[82] "Recall of Judicial Decision Held to Be Constitutional," *Central Law Journal*, June 17, 1921, p. 425.

[83] Wiest, "Recall of Judges," p. 282.

[84] "Taft Shows Peril in Roosevelt Policy," *New York Times*, March 9, 1912, p. 1.

the "majority of one year may be the minority of the next."[85] Opponents also contended that it would create inconsistencies among the laws of the different states. In one of its plethora of editorials in opposition to Roosevelt's plan, the *New York Times* warned that the recall of decisions would create "a hopeless mess and muddle" because voters in different states might interpret the Constitution in different ways.[86] Similarly, Thom warned that the recalls would be adopted "without a comprehensive view of the effect on the constitutional system."[87]

Ransom replied that these arguments were based upon conjecture and that no popular vote could reverse an earlier vote more completely than the Court did in its cases involving legal tender and the income tax. Also, the laws of various states were in sharp conflict about the constitutionality of such social welfare measures as workers' compensation and the limitations on hours for women in factories.[88]

Although the furor over Roosevelt's proposal subsided during the summer and autumn of 1912, judicial issues remained prominent throughout the presidential campaign. The emphasis placed on the issue, however, varied widely among the parties. While Roosevelt continued to call for judicial reform, he devoted less attention to judicial issues during the autumn campaign when he needed to appeal to a broader and more conservative element of the electorate in the general election. Roosevelt's reticence may indicate that he believed the issue had cost him support during the spring and had hindered his effort to secure the Republican nomination. In his speech accepting the Progressive party's presidential nomination, however, Roosevelt staunchly defended the recall and emphasized the importance of popular participation in government. In words that made conservatives wince, Roosevelt declared that the "people themselves must be the ultimate makers of their own Constitution."[89]

The Progressive platform adopted Roosevelt's proposal in general terms, demanding "such restriction of the power of the courts as shall leave to the people the ultimate authority to determine fundamental questions of social welfare and public policy." The platform also endorsed the reform that came to be embodied in the Judiciary Act of 1914 and urged the states to adopt the initiative, referendum, and recall, although it did not explain whether this was intended to em-

---

[85] "Lodge Is Strongly Against the Recall," *New York Times*, March 9, 1912, p. 8.

[86] "The Road to Despotism," *New York Times*, March 9, 1912, p. 12.

[87] Thom, "Pending Revolution," p. 9.

[88] Ransom, *Majority Rule*, pp. 14–15.

[89] Theodore Roosevelt, "Purposes and Policies of the Progressive Party," address before the Progressive convention in Chicago, August 6, 1912, repr. S. Doc. 904, 62nd Cong., 2d sess., 1912, p. 9.

brace the recall of judges. The platform further called vaguely for "a more easy and expeditious method of amending the Federal Constitution."[90]

In contrast to Roosevelt and Wilson, Taft emphasized the constitutional issue throughout the campaign. He set the tone in his speech accepting the GOP nomination when he declared that the preservation of the Constitution was "the supreme issue" of the election. Although Taft acknowledged that the Constitution permitted governmental action to promote "the comfort of the people" and to encourage greater "equality of opportunity in respect of the weaker classes," he made it clear that he would support reforms only within the existing constitutional framework. "The Republican Party stands for the Constitution as it is," Taft declared, although he acknowledged that changing conditions might justify amendments. Taft bitterly assailed "hostility to the judiciary and the measures to take away its power and its independence," including the judicial recall and measures to restrict the use of the injunction against secondary boycotts and to confer the right to a jury in contempt proceedings. Taft also bitterly excoriated Roosevelt's "grotesque proposition" for recall of decisions. He chided Progressives for asking for a restoration of popular government, "as if this had not been a people's Government since the beginning of the Constitution."[91]

While the Republican platform did not explicitly mention Roosevelt's proposal or denounce the Progressives for their views concerning the judiciary, the GOP promised to maintain the "authority and integrity" of the state and federal courts, which the platform portrayed as the guardians of civil liberties, political stability, and orderly progress. The platform advocated "legislation to prevent long delays and the tedious and costly appeals" in both civil and criminal cases. Although the platform derogated the recall of judges as "unnecessary and unwise," it called for "such action as may be necessary to simplify the process by which any judge who is found to be derelict in his duty may be removed from office."[92]

Although Taft did not conduct a vigorous campaign for re-election, he continued to warn in public and private about the Bull Moose threat to constitutionalism. In particular, Taft warned that the Progressives would transfer power from the courts to the legislative branch of gov-

[90] Donald Bruce Johnson, ed., *National Party Platforms* vol. 1, *1840–1956* (Urbana: University of Illinois Press, 1978), p. 176.

[91] "Speech of William Howard Taft Accepting the Republican Nomination for President of the United States," August 1, 1912, S. Doc. 902, 62nd Cong., 2d sess., 1912, pp. 5–6, 9–11.

[92] Johnson, *National Party Platforms*, p. 184.

ernment, which would trample upon the personal and economic liberties of the people.[93] Roosevelt's defeat in the election did little to allay Taft's concerns. Although Taft believed that Wilson's views on the Constitution were relatively sound,[94] he feared that Roosevelt's strong showing might enable Roosevelt's faction to take control of the Republican party. In his concession address, Taft declared that the large vote for Roosevelt and Debs was "a warning that their propaganda . . . has formidable support."[95] Privately, Taft expressed fear that Roosevelt would take control of the Republican party or retain enough influence to persuade it to accept some of his views on the Constitution.[96] Taft's decision to accept a professorship at Yale was heavily influenced by his desire for a platform from which to proclaim his views concerning constitutionalism.[97]

Unlike Taft, Wilson was reticent in his discussions of the court issue. When the judicial recall had begun to emerge as an important issue during 1911, Wilson publicly expressed tepid opposition. Although Wilson supported some measures to permit the recall of nonjudicial officials, he stated that the recall of judges encouraged the heresy that "determinations of what the law is must respond to popular impulse."[98] In private, Wilson somewhat more emphatically stated that he always had been "absolutely against" the recall of judges.[99] He believed that the recall of judges would merely treat a symptom rather than the malady in a political system that had permitted special interests to determine the selection of judges. During the spring of 1912, Wilson publicly expressed emphatic opposition to the recall of judges,[100] telling the Maryland legislature that "the way to purify the

[93] See, for example, statement by Taft to *Boston Advertiser* dated October 24, 1912, in Taft Papers, Series 8, Reel 515, and clipping from *Springfield Union*, October 6, 1912, ibid., Reel 514. For a general account of the 1912 election campaign, see Francis L. Broderick, *Progressivism at Risk: Electing a President in 1912* (Westport, Conn.: Greenwood Press, 1989).

[94] Taft to Clarence H. Kelsey, November 8, 1912, *Taft Papers*, Series 8, Reel 515.

[95] Statement given to the press by Taft in Cincinnati, November 5, 1912, *Taft Papers*, Series 8, Reel 515.

[96] Taft to Charles Hopkins Clark, November 8, 1912; Taft to William Barnes, Jr., November 8, 1912; Taft to Herbert Parsons, November 8, 1912; *Taft Papers*, Series 8, Reel 515.

[97] Taft to Elihu Root, November 20, 1912; Taft to J. G. Schurman, December 5, 1912; *Taft Papers*, Series 8, Reel 515.

[98] Arthur S. Link, ed., *The Papers of Woodrow Wilson*, vol. 23, *1911–1912* (Princeton, N.J.: Princeton University Press, 1977), pp. 362, 370.

[99] Woodrow Wilson to Richard Heath Dabney, November 16, 1911, in Link, *Papers of Wilson*, p. 551.

[100] "Wilson Opposes Recall of Judges," *New York Times*, April 28, 1912, p. 6.

judiciary is to purify it at its roots, if it needs purification, in the process of selection."[101] Wilson expressed the same idea the following month in a speech in Savannah.[102]

Wilson virtually ignored the judicial issue during the autumn campaign. His only major discussion of the issue occurred in September when he repeated his earlier assertions that reform of the judicial selection process was the only way to purge the bench of judges beholden to special interests. Wilson explained that the recall of judges selected by powerful corporate interests would accomplish no good if those same interests were permitted to select new judges. Wilson averred that the corruption of the judicial selection process was a "canker in our vitals" that "must be cut out," but he warned that the operation required surgical skill not to "disturb the vital tissues to which this ugly thing is attached."[103] Like Wilson, the Democratic platform was reticient about judicial issues. It had far less to say about the courts than the Republican, Progressive, and Socialist platforms.[104]

It is not surprising that the Socialists advanced the most radical proposals concerning the courts during the 1912 campaign. The Socialists, who garnered an all-time high of 6 percent of the popular vote, called for a raft of reforms, including abolition of the Supreme Court's power to review the constitutionality of federal statutes, abolition of all federal district and circuit courts, the "election of all judges for short terms," popular referenda on the repeal of federal laws, popular votes on federal constitutional amendments, and a federal constitutional convention. The platform also advocated measures to permit the recall of state and federal judges.[105]

The split in the Republican party ensured Wilson's victory. Although the impact of the judicial issue on the actual vote tallies is impossible to calculate, the fact that Roosevelt, despite his lack of a major party nomination, placed second in the race and received 28 percent of the

---

[101] Link, *Papers of Wilson*, vol. 24, *1912*, pp. 235–36.

[102] Ibid., pp. 350–51.

[103] Ibid, pp. 240–41.

[104] Johnson, *National Party Platforms*, pp. 172, 174, 176–77, 183–84, 190–91. The Democratic party reiterated its 1908 platform's allegations that the Republicans had raised "a false issue respecting the judiciary" and that "it is an unjust reflection upon a great body of our citizens to assume that they lack respect for the courts" (Ibid., 172). As in 1908, the Democratic party called for vigilance against abuse of judicial processes and expressed support for reform of federal contempt proceedings. The Democratic platform also recognized "the urgent need of reform in the administration of civil and criminal law" and recommended the enactment of measures to "rid the present legal system of delays, expense, and uncertainties" (ibid., p. 174).

[105] Ibid., pp. 190–91.

popular vote and eighty-eight electoral votes suggests that Roosevelt's reform proposal did not unduly shock large numbers of Americans. Roosevelt's defeat, however, spelled the end of the recall as a serious issue in American politics. With the election of Wilson, advocates of judicial reform turned their attention to more viable expedients.

After Roosevelt's defeat in the 1912 presidential election, his proposal for a recall of decisions withered on the vine of practical politics. Even the progressive strongholds that had adopted the initiative, referendum, and recall of judges showed little interest in enacting Roosevelt's proposal.[106] Colorado was the only state to enact a provision for recall of decisions, and even in that state no recall election was ever conducted. The Colorado measure was approved by 57 percent of the voters in an initiative that appeared on the ballot in the November 1912 election.[107] The initiative enacted a constitutional amendment providing that the state supreme court was the only court that could declare that any state or municipal law violated the state or federal constitutions and that voters could disapprove any such decision.[108] The amendment created disparity in trial court opinions and confused the bar. One lawyer complained at the 1913 annual meeting of the state bar that the recall statute had so confused the state's constitutional law that "the stability of the government of Colorado is being seriously threatened."[109] Similarly, a Colorado judge expressed fear that the amendment would create "an astounding conflict" among the laws of different jurisdictions in the state.[110]

In 1920, the Colorado Supreme Court ruled that the recall measure was unconstitutional to the extent that it prevented the lower state courts from adjudicating issues under the federal Constitution and permitted the voters to review state supreme court rulings involving the federal Constitution. The court declared, "There is no sovereignty in a state, to set at naught the Constitution of the Union, and no power in its people to command their courts to do so. That issue was finally settled at Appomattox."[111] In a companion case, the high court of

[106] In Oregon, for example, there was a futile attempt during the 1913 legislative session to embody a slightly modified version of Roosevelt's plan in a constitutional amendment. James D. Barnett, *The Operation of the Initiative, Referendum and Recall in Oregon* (New York: Macmillan, 1915), pp. 174–76.

[107] Duane A. Smith, "Colorado and Judicial Recall," *American Journal of Legal History* 7 (July 1963): 202–3.

[108] Session Laws of Colorado, 1913, pp. 678–79.

[109] Smith, "Colorado and Judicial Recall," p. 201.

[110] Jesse G. Northcutt, "The Recall in Colorado," *Green Bag*, September 1913, pp. 372, 381, 382.

[111] *People v. Western Union*, 70 Colo. 90, 97–98, 198 P. 146, 149 (1921).

Colorado also invalidated the amendment's application to state decisions. The court ruled that the amendment would deny procedural due process to criminal defendants since the trial court was deprived of jurisdiction to hear a defendant's defense that the statute under which he was being prosecuted was unconstitutional.[112]

Although the court's decisions were rendered at a time when judicial activism was reemerging as a public issue, the movement for direct democracy had long since faded, and the decisions attracted little attention. The *Rocky Mountain News* dryly observed that the people were not likely to rise in revolt in the belief that the court had invaded their rights.[113] The *Central Law Journal* observed that "the steadier and clearer light of the present period" permitted the court to render decisions "which a few years ago would have raised a storm of indignation all over the country."[114]

The movement for the recall of decisions made no headway at the federal level either. In December 1912, Senator Joseph L. Bristow, a Kansas Republican, sponsored a joint resolution for an amendment that would have permitted Congress to refer to the people for approval or disapproval any federal law the Supreme Court had nullified.[115] In introducing the measure, Bristow declared that the "courts did not make the Constitution. They simply interpret what they think it means. It is the people's law, enacted by them, and if they do not desire the interpretation placed upon it by the courts . . . this provision gives them the opportunity to so declare."[116] Bristow's bill was tabled, as was a similar bill that he introduced in April 1913.[117] Similarly, Congress took no action on a measure introduced by Republican senator Fred S. Jackson of Kansas in August 1912 that would have permitted the legislatures of three-fourths of the states to override any decision of a federal court that struck down a federal law.[118]

The movement for the recall of judicial decisions, like the judicial recall movement, did not reemerge during the controversy over the judiciary in the 1920s. One of the few proposals for electoral reevalua-

---

[112] *People v. Max*, 70 Colo. 100, 105–9, 198 P. 150, 153–55 (1921). The court also reasoned that the provision on state decisions could not be severed from the part of the amendment concerning federal decisions and that the former must therefore fall with the latter (70 Colo. 104, 198 P. 152).

[113] Smith, "Colorado and Judicial Recall," p. 209.

[114] "Recall of Judicial Decision Held to be Constitutional," *Central Law Journal*, June 17, 1921, p. 425.

[115] S. J. Res. 142, 62d Cong., 3rd sess., 1912.

[116] 49 *Congressional Record*, 62nd Cong., 3d sess., December 5, 1912, p. 83.

[117] S. J. Res. 8, 63d Cong., 1st sess., 1913.

[118] H. J. Res. 351, 62d Cong., 2d sess., 1912.

tion of judicial decisions during that decade was made by Representative Fiorello H. La Guardia of New York, who included such a proposal in his draft of a proposed platform for the Republican party of New York in 1922.[119] The proposal for both forms of recall were peculiarly part of the clamor for direct popular democracy that reached its zenith during the height of the Progressive Era.

[119] *Papers of Fiorello H. La Guardia*, Box 4157, Municipal Archives, New York City. La Guardia's proposed plank, closely resembling Roosevelt's 1912 proposal, stated: "When an act passed under the police power of the State is held unconstitutional under the State Constitution by the highest court of the State, the voters, after ample interval for deliberation, shall have the opportunity of expressing their preference at the polls; if they vote for the affirmation of such law, it shall become law, notwithstanding such judicial decision."

SEVEN

EBB AND FLOW, 1913–1921

Had the judges ever adhered strictly to the doctrine that
precedents are the only source of the common law and are
of binding effect, surely those precedents would have been
overthrown in short order and the judges along with them.
But precedents have been forgotten, have been
disregarded and evaded, have been flatly disapproved and
overruled. We must not forget this fact, even though at
times the judges did not move as fast as other people.
Arthur L. Corbin, (Yale Law Professor, 1914)[1]

T HE FUROR OVER judicial power abated for several years
after the election of Wilson in 1912. Although many progressives and trade unionists continued to advocate limitations on
judicial power, their voices were muted, and their arguments received
less attention from politicians and the press. This period of calm, however, proved to be a lull in a continuing tempest. Events from 1913 to
1921 precipitated a sharp revival in the controversy over the courts
from 1922 to 1924. When widespread protests over judicial power
began to erupt again in 1922, critics of the courts propounded reforms
that were different and in many respects more radical than those they
had advocated before 1913. Since these new proposals germinated
during the years when criticism of the courts had faded from public
view, those years marked an important period of transition in the ongoing controversy over the role of the courts in a free society.

It was no accident that criticism of the courts declined sharply after
the 1912 election, for the defeat of the Progressive party banished its
proposals for judicial reform to political oblivion for the foreseeable
future. Although the Progressive party survived the 1912 election and
began to develop a permanent organization, its widespread defeats in
the 1914 election ensured its rapid demise. The reunification of the
Republican party made radical judicial reform even more difficult to
attain since reunification required compromises from both sides and
judicial reform was one of the issues on which Old Guard Republicans
were least likely to make concessions.

[1] Arthur L. Corbin, "The Law and the Judges," *Yale Review* 23 (January 1914): 242.

Moreover, Wilson's vigorously progressive "New Freedom" program promised to ameliorate some of the conditions that had fanned the flames of the judicial reform movement. Samuel Gompers hailed the Clayton Antitrust Act of 1914 as labor's "Magna Carta," since it curtailed the extent to which courts could impose sanctions against the activities of labor unions. The limitations of the statute, however, were immediately obvious to sophisticated observers and gradually became apparent to everyone.[2] Until 1917, however, when the Supreme Court began again to frustrate labor's aims, the AFL's professed belief that the statute afforded substantial protection from judicial interference helped to mute the AFL's criticisms of the judicial system.

The triumphs of the New Freedom program demonstrated that progressive goals could be achieved through legislative measures that did not fundamentally curb judicial power. Such measures as tariff reduction and the creation of the Federal Trade Commission and Federal Reserve Board, which did not directly address judicial issues, may have distracted attention from quixotic plans for curbing judicial power and directed progressive energies toward more constructive measures. By helping to restore progressive confidence in government, such measures abated criticisms of the courts.

The constitutional amendment process also demonstrated that fundamental reforms could be achieved without abrogating judicial

---

[2] See William Letwin, *Law and Economic Policy in America: The Evolution of the Sherman Antitrust Act* (New York: Random House, 1965, repr. Westport, Conn.: Greenwood Press, 1980), pp. 274–75; Philip S. Foner, *History of the Labor Movement in the United States*, vol. 5, The AFL in the Progressive Era, 1910–1915 (New York: International, 1980), pp. 130–39; Arthur S. Link, *Woodrow Wilson and the Progressive Era: 1900–1917* (New York: Harper and Row, 1954), pp. 72–73. Although the statute declared that labor unions were not to be construed as illegal combinations or conspiracies within the meaning of the antitrust laws, the statute did not expressly prohibit the application of the antitrust laws to union activities. The statute's declaration that union activity itself was not illegal merely codified well-established common law, and its provision that peaceful strikes and primary boycotts were not illegal did not render unions immune from judicial attack. Moreover, the statute failed to define the meaning of *property* for its provision that federal courts could not issue injunctions in labor disputes except where necessary to prevent irreparable injury to property that money damages could not compensate. Although the statute required that the application for an injunction describe with particularity the property or property right the applicant sought to protect, the statute's failure to offer definition of *property* left judges with almost unbounded discretion to determine that a property right was at stake. The statute's provision for a right to trial by jury in criminal contempt proceedings may have been its most useful reform. For a study of the background of the Clayton Act, see Daniel R. Ernst, "The Labor Exception, 1908–1914," *Iowa Law Review* 74 (July 1989): 1151–73. Ernst argues that the Clayton Act's labor provisions were also significant because they recognized that labor relations involved distinctive problems that could not be resolved by analogies from the individualistic legal doctrines that governed business enterprises, ibid., pp. 1172–73.

power. Nearly fifty years after the enactment of the last constitutional amendment, the Constitution was amended twice during 1913—to permit a federal income tax and to require the direct election of U.S. senators. Prior to the adoption of those amendments, criticism of the courts had been stimulated by a widespread belief that the constitutional amendment process was too cumbersome to be practicable.[3] Writing in 1912, William D. Guthrie contended that public faith in the government required that this notion be dispelled.[4] Meanwhile, several members of Congress introduced measures for constitutional amendments to simplify methods of amending the Constitution.[5] For example, Robert M. La Follette of Wisconsin proposed an amendment that would have initiated the amendment process by a majority in Congress or the application of ten states and would have permitted ratification by a majority of the electors in a majority of the states.[6]

By erasing the legacy of two of the Supreme Court's most unpopular decisions, the income tax amendment demonstrated that constitutional amendments provided a viable remedy for judicial abuses. In the opinion of *The Nation*, the ratification of the income tax amendment put "an end to the notion that the Constitution of the United States is virtually unamendable."[7] Shortly before the enactment of the Sixteenth and Seventeenth amendments, *The Nation* had argued that the "quiet progress" of the movements for those amendments belied the notion that the Constitution was an "iron-bound" charter that necessarily impeded political reform and social progress.[8]

The enactment in May 1913 of the Seventeenth Amendment for the direct election of senators further demonstrated the viability of the amendment process as a vehicle for reform. Moreover, it strengthened the influence of the people in the federal judicial selection process because it made the senators directly accountable to the electorate for their votes on judicial nominees. The enactment of the amendment was followed by a marked, if sporadic, increase in organized efforts by individuals and groups to cajole senators during the confirmation process. The advent of the direct election of senators may account in part for the high level of public activity by supporters and opponents of

[3] William D. Guthrie, "Constitutional Morality," *North American Review*, July 1912, p. 172; *The Nation*, November 7, 1912; *The Nation*, February 6, 1913, p. 117.

[4] Guthrie, "Constitutional Morality," p. 172.

[5] S. J. Res. 138, 61st Cong., 3d sess., 1911; H. J. Res. 350, 62nd Cong., 2d sess., 1912; H. J. Res. 375, 62nd Cong., 3d sess., 1913; S. J. Res. 20, 63rd Cong., 1st sess., 1913; S. J. Res. 26, 63rd Cong., 1st sess., 1913; H. J. Res. 60, 63rd Cong., 1st sess., 1913; S. J. Res. 26, 63rd Cong., 1st sess., 1913.

[6] S.J. Res. 24, 63rd Cong., 1st sess., 1913.

[7] *The Nation*, February 6, 1913, p. 117.

[8] "Progress and the Constitution," *The Nation*, November 7, 1912, p. 424.

Louis Brandeis in 1916, Pierce Butler in 1922, and Charles Evans Hughes and John J. Parker in 1930. Although those nominations might have attracted widespread public involvement under any circumstances, the ability of the voters to retaliate against senators at the polls increased public participation in the confirmation process. By providing voters with a higher degree of leverage over federal judicial nominations, the Seventeenth Amendment may also have mitigated demands for the direct election of federal judges.

But although the enactment of the Sixteenth and Seventeenth Amendments helped to discourage proposals to abrogate judicial power, the impact of the amendments was not so great as both reformers and conservatives may have hoped. Those amendments provided a vivid reminder that the ultimate power to shape the Constitution rested in the hands of the people, but the practical difficulties of amending the Constitution were so great that the availability of the amendment remedy could provide only limited solace to frustrated reformers.

Even if progressives could rely on widespread public support for amendments, the amendment process would remain cumbersome. The requirement of ratification by three-quarters of the state legislatures or conventions in three-quarters of the states would force progressives to conduct a nationwide campaign on behalf of a constitutional amendment. Such a campaign would be time-consuming and expensive, especially since big-business groups and other special interests could be expected to fight such measures on Capitol Hill and at the statehouses.

The circumstances surrounding the enactment of the Sixteenth Amendment demonstrated the perils of the amendment process. Nearly two decades had passed between the Court's decision in the *Income Tax Case* and the enactment of the Sixteenth Amendment, and the amendment might not have been enacted if conservative members of Congress had not so badly miscalculated the likelihood that the requisite number of state legislatures would ratify the amendment. Moreover, progressives recognized that the widely held belief that the Constitution should be amended only under extraordinary circumstances would continue to impede efforts to use the amendment process as a means of overturning Supreme Court decisions. The Sixteenth, Fourteenth, and Eleventh amendments were the only ones that nullified Supreme Court decisions, and there was little hope that the requisite majorities of Congress and state legislatures would invoke the process to overturn decisions that involved issues of less magnitude than state judicial power, black citizenship, and the income tax. Likewise, the enactment of the Seventeenth Amendment offered little precedent for the availability of the amendment process as an antidote to judicial abuse of power since it had effected a reform that could only have been made through the amendment process at the national level.

Many progressives recognized that the amendment process had limited utility as a vehicle for achieving the often mundane reforms that provided the grist of the progressive movement. Complaining that the amendment process had converted democracy into "a golden hoard, to which access could be obtained only at rare intervals and after heroic effort," Herbert Croly in 1914 joined La Follette and other progressives in advocating a liberalization of the process.[9] Meanwhile, progressives in Congress continued to introduce measures to ease the amendment process.[10]

Criticism of the courts during the early years of the Wilson administration might also have been diminished by the perception that both state and federal courts were becoming more receptive to progressive legislation. Shortly before the 1912 election, for example, the New York Court of Appeals held that public policy precluded an employee from assuming a risk created by his employer's violation of a statute or from waiving his employer's liability for his injuries.[11] Early in 1913, George Alger detected a "slow but sure change, under the pressure of formulated public opinion, in the character and scope of the constitutional limitation of due process of law."[12] Similarly, *The Nation* observed in November 1912 that "there is evidence that the judges are awake to the need of modifying old rules of law in order to make them better fit modern conditions." Praising the decision of the New York Court of Appeals in the employer's liability case, *The Nation* declared that the court's willingness "to take cognizance of a visibly rising public sentiment and to make old rules bend to new conditions is a good thing for the country and a good thing for the judges." Only a few more liberal decisions, *The Nation* believed, would banish the "absurd conception" that a judge was "a sort of unnatural monster without either knowledge of his struggling fellows or a flicker of pity for them."[13]

Meanwhile, between 1911 and 1914 the Supreme Court sustained

---

[9] Herbert Croly, *Progressive Democracy* (New York: Macmillan, 1914), pp. 237, 243, 230–44. Croly believed that La Follette's plan was the best that had been drafted (p. 231).

[10] E.g., H. J. Res. 315, 64th Cong., 2d sess., 1916; S. J. Res. 8, 65th Cong., 1st sess., 1917; H. J. Res. 12, 66th Cong., 1st sess., 1919; H. J. Res. 306, 66th Cong., 2d sess., 1920; H. J. Res. 12, 67th Cong., 1st sess., 1921; H. J. Res. 21, 67th Cong., 1st sess., 1921; H. J. Res. 29, 67th Cong., 1st sess., 1921; S. J. Res. 14, 67th Cong., 1st sess., 1921; H. J. Res. 118, 67th Cong., 1st sess., 1921; H. J. Res. 162, 67th Cong., 1st sess., 1921; S. J. Res. 271, 67th Cong., 4th sess., 1923; H. J. Res. 34, 68th Cong., 1st sess., 1923; H. J. Res. 37, 68th Cong., 1st sess., 1923; S. J. Res. 17, 68th Cong., 1st sess., 1923.

[11] *Fitzwater v. Warren*, 206 N.Y. 355, 99 N.E. 1042 (1912).

[12] George W. Alger, "The Courts and Legislative Freedom," *Atlantic Monthly*, March 1913, p. 351.

[13] "Judges Do Move," *The Nation*, November 14, 1912, p. 449.

the constitutionality of a number of progressive measures, including the Pure Food and Drug Act of 1906,[14] the White Slave Act,[15] and a federal employers' liability act that had been revised to meet the Court's objections in the controversial *First Employers' Liability Cases* in 1908.[16] The Court declined an invitation to rule that the initiative and referendum violated the guarantee of the Constitution[17] and upheld the power of the Interstate Commerce Commission to regulate intrastate rates when they directly affected interstate commerce.[18] In July 1914, *The Outlook* declared that the Supreme Court had never been more worthy of veneration.[19]

Despite the diminution of judicial antagonism against progressive legislation, many state and federal decisions continued to frustrate reform. Judicial conservatism was particularly pronounced in cases involving the rights of organized labor. In 1915, for example, the Supreme Court in *Coppage v. Kansas* struck down a state statute that prohibited yellow-dog contracts.[20] The Court antagonized workers two years later by sustaining an injunction that had restrained the United Mine Workers from attempting to unionize West Virginia miners who had entered into a yellow-dog contract.[21] And although the Court in January 1917 sustained the controversial federal statute that mandated an eight-hour day for railroad workers,[22] the dissents of four justices presented an ominous portent.[23]

[14] *Hipolite Egg Co. v. United States*, 220 U.S. 45 (1911); *McDermott v. Wisconsin*, 228 U.S. 115 (1913).

[15] *Hoke v. United States*, 227 U.S. 308 (1913).

[16] *Second Employers Liability Cases*, 223 U.S. 1 (1912).

[17] *Kiernan v. Portland*, 223 U.S. 151 (1912). The Court ruled that whether a state had ceased to have a republican form of government within the meaning of the guaranty in the Constitution was a political question solely for Congress to determine.

[18] *Houston, East and West Texas Railway Co. v. United States*, 234 U.S. 342 (1914) (the *Shreveport Rate Case*).

[19] "A Great Court," *The Outlook*, July 4, 1914, p. 508. Similarly, another publication stated in 1914 that "the Supreme Court . . . once regarded as the very stronghold of extreme constitutionalism, has been steadily setting an example of liberal construction" and that the decision of the New York Court of Appeals in *Ives* was widely regarded as "a survival of a past attitude of mind than typical of the present temper of the courts of last resort in our leading states" ("The Majority Juggernaut," *Unpopular Review*, January 1914, p. 23).

[20] 236 U.S. 1 (1915). Relying upon the Court's invalidation of a similar federal statute in *Adair v. United States*, 208 U.S. 161 (1908), the Court held that the Kansas law violated the due process clause of the Fourteenth Amendment because it was not needed to protect the health, morals, or welfare of the community.

[21] *Hitchman Coal & Coke Co. v. Mitchell*, 245 U.S. 229 (1917).

[22] *Wilson v. New*, 243 U.S. 332 (1917).

[23] Gompers also complained that the Court's reasoning was too narrow, and he criticized the Court for its gratuitous remarks in support of compulsory arbitration. Samuel Gompers, "5 To 4 on Slavery," *American Federationist*, April 1917, pp. 290–91.

The prestige of the federal judiciary also suffered a potential blow in June 1916 when Hughes resigned from the Supreme Court to accept the Republican presidential nomination. Even though Hughes had actively opposed efforts to draft him for the nomination, his immediate transformation from an ostensibly apolitical Supreme Court justice to a partisan standard-bearer seemed to belie the argument that judges stood above politics. In resisting Republican attempts to nominate him in 1912, Hughes had warned that his resignation from the Court might weaken the independence of the judiciary and impair public confidence in the incorruptibility of the courts.[24]

Although Hughes left the bench with the blessings of his colleagues, Chief Justice White believed that the nomination of Hughes was a great blunder from which it would take the Court years to recover.[25] The *New York Times*, which had so assiduously disparaged the notion that political currents influenced the Court, was especially indignant about the nomination. Declaring that the "robe of the Justice on that bench, like the priest's tonsure, sets him apart, dedicates him," the *Times* contended that Hughes's candidacy threatened to corrupt the "integrity and reputation" of the Court.[26] The *Times* interpreted Hughes's defeat as "a guarantee that the freedom of the Supreme Court from playing to the galleries . . . is to be maintained."[27]

Senate Democrats also expressed righteous indignation. Three days after Hughes's resignation, Senator William Joel Stone of Missouri, the chairman of the upcoming Democratic convention's Committee on Resolutions, proposed a constitutional amendment to incapacitate Supreme Court justices from becoming candidates for office within five years after their service on the bench.[28] At the same time, Democratic senator Charles S. Thomas of Colorado advocated an amendment to disqualify federal judges from eligibility for any elective federal office

[24] In a statement issued through Rabbi Stephen S. Wise, Hughes in 1912 had expressed fear that a political party might exploit the judicial record of a judge who became its nominee and that the opposing party might make the same record the object of partisan strife. Hughes also explained that the election of former federal judges to political office might encourage judges to skew their decisions with an eye to popular approval. Merlo J. Pusey, *Charles Evans Hughes*, vol. 1 (New York: Macmillan, 1951), p. 300; 51 *Congressional Record*, 63rd Cong., 2d sess., July 31, 1916, p. 11851.

[25] Pusey, *Charles Evans Hughes*, p. 332, quoting James E. Watson, *As I Knew Them* (Indianapolis: Bobbs-Merrill, 1936), p. 164.

[26] Editorial, "The Supreme Court and the Presidency," *New York Times*, June 15, 1916, p. 10. The *Times* later lamented that Hughes's candidacy had broken the "great tradition which permitted us to assume that the Justices upon that bench were altogether and permanently removed from the brawls of partisan politics" ("The Judge in Politics," September 28, 1916, p. 8).

[27] "The Supreme Court and the Presidency," *New York Times*, November 11, 1916, p. 8.

[28] "Stone Raps Hughes and the Platforms," *New York Times*, June 13, 1916, p. 1.

during their judicial terms and for two years after their departure from the bench. During a debate over the amendment that Democrats contrived to coincide with Hughes's formal acceptance speech on July 31, Senator Walsh declared that the election of Hughes would forever cause Americans to distrust the motives of federal judges in rendering their decisions. Walsh warned that the election of Hughes would undermine public support for life tenure and the appointive system and would trigger a demand for radical changes that even the Thomas amendment might fail to arrest.[29]

The issue receded into the background of the campaign after Wilson refused to permit the Democratic platform to condemn Hughes for his resignation. The AFL attacked Hughes's judicial record, and workers in Indianapolis and Toledo heckled Hughes over the Court's decision in the *Loewe v. Lawlor*,[30] but Hughes's judicial record did not emerge as a major campaign issue. The Democrats were probably wise to avoid attacks on Hughes for forsaking the bench. Such attacks might have seemed hypocritical since Alton B. Parker had resigned from the New York Court of Appeals to accept the Democratic presidential nomination in 1904.[31]

More significantly, however, Hughes's irreproachable conduct during his last days on the bench and the widespread recognition that the Republican party had turned to Hughes as the one man who could unite the party relieved Hughes of any significant appearance of impropriety.[32] The peculiar circumstances that spared Hughes from personal criticism also shielded the Court from any major attack. In the opinion of the *Nation*, "No argument can ever be drawn from his career that the way to political preferment lies through the courts."[33] Republican senator Charles E. Townsend of Michigan observed during the debate on the Thomas amendment that the circumstances of the Hughes nomination were unique. Townsend noted that it was ironic that Hughes's critics did not question the presidential practice of nominating judges whose chief qualification was partisan fealty. "It would be

[29] 51 *Congressional Record*, 63rd Cong., 2d sess., July 31, 1916, p. 11851.

[30] "The Judge in Politics," *New York Times*, September 28, 1916, p. 8.

[31] "Leaders Plan Lure For Progressives," *New York Times*, June 13, 1916, p. 2. Although the *Times* contended that Parker's resignation was different because Parker was an elected judge and the New York high court is less sacrosanct than the Supreme Court, few voters were likely to comprehend or care about such nuances ("The Supreme Court and the Presidency," *New York Times*, November 11, 1916, p. 8).

[32] As *The Nation* observed, the Republicans had nominated Hughes the public man rather than Hughes the judge: "No man can point to a single decision, a single gesture, of his on the bench, and say that it was animated by political ambition" ("The Nomination of Hughes," *The Nation*, June 15, 1916, p. 635).

[33] Ibid.

better for the country to have a great judge for President than a time-serving politician for judge," Townsend declared.[34]

As Alexander Bickel observed, the hazards that the candidacy of Hughes candidacy presented to the Court were "negotiated with singular success and luck."[35] It is unlikely that his candidacy significantly intensified the antagonism of the judiciary's critics or increased their ranks. Indeed, his candidacy may have diminished support for plans for an elective federal judiciary and limited terms since it called attention to the dangers of politicization of the bench. Nevertheless, the episode proved again that judges often wore partisan labels beneath their judicial robes and that politics was never far from the bench. Although the episode provided no major impetus for the court reform movement, it may have had a subtle impact upon public opinion toward the judiciary that helped to lay a foundation for the imminent revival of attacks upon the courts.

Even though criticism of the courts subsided during the early years of the Wilson administration, the most implacable antagonists of judicial activism continued to assail the courts for thwarting the popular will. As the optimism with which progressives hailed the early reforms of the Wilson administration gave way to disillusionment because the New Freedom program had failed to foster community values[36] and tailored many reforms to fit the needs of big businesses, progressives began to renew their search for nostrums for the nation's ills. Looking for scapegoats, they naturally were loath to spare their old bête noire, the courts, from their wrath.

While progressive complaints against the courts remained much the same, their proposed remedies began to change. During the years following 1913, critics of the courts turned away from remedies that would have increased popular control over the selection and retention of judges and began to advocate the curtailment or abolition of judicial review. As so often in the past, Walter Clark was the harbinger of the trend. Clark had long favored the abolition of judicial review, but he had at first preferred to work for more feasible goals, particularly the election of judges for limited terms. Beginning about 1913, however,

[34] 51 *Congressional Record*, 63rd Cong. 2d sess., July 31, 1916, p. 11853.

[35] Alexander M. Bickel and Benno C. Schmidt, Jr., *The Oliver Wendell Holmes Devise History of the Supreme Court of the United States*, vol. 9, *The Judiciary and Responsible Government, 1910–1921* (New York: Macmillan, 1984), p. 397.

[36] As David B. Danbom has observed, the basic error of the progressives was their assumption that society could be changed without fundamental alterations in the capitalist system; the main motivation of business remained profit and could never be the public interest. *"The World of Hope": Progressives and the Struggle for an Ethical Public Life* (Philadelphia: Temple University Press, 1987), pp. 171, 232.

Clark's calls for the abolition of judicial review grew more strident, and he seemed to lose faith in the practicability of less draconian measures. In a speech at Cooper Union in New York on January 27, 1914, Clark suggested that the outright abolition of judicial review by congressional legislation was the only really effective means of curbing judicial usurpation. He favored legislation rather than the "slow process of constitutional amendment," which special interests would have fought in every state legislature. Although Clark reiterated his call for the election of federal judges, he warned that judicial election would "not cure the evil entirely as long as the judges retain their assumed power of an irretrievable veto upon legislation." Clark also reiterated his opposition to the judicial recall on the ground that it would permit the removal of conscientious judges for decisions that did not involve constitutional issues, although he favored the recall of judicial decisions.[37] He attacked judicial review again in 1915 and 1916 in articles urging Americans to "go 'back to the Constitution' as it is written."[38]

Clark's views appealed to Senator Robert L. Owen, who wrote to Clark in July 1916 that Congress should impeach or summarily remove any Supreme Court justice who attempted to nullify federal legislation. Like Clark, Owen believed that Congress should be the ultimate arbiter of the Constitution because the people could "exercise their sovereignty better through the legislative branch than through a Court not amenable to the direct control of the people."[39] Owen, born and raised in Virginia, shared Clark's innate southern antipathy toward federal judicial power, although he was willing to use federal legislative power to achieve populistic and progressive reforms. Owen's misgivings about the federal judiciary were particularly intense since the reforms he supported during his representation of Oklahoma in the Senate from 1907 to 1925 were threatened and sometimes thwarted by the federal judiciary.

In January 1917, Owen embodied his judicial views in two joint resolutions to forbid federal judges from declaring any act of Congress unconstitutional. The resolutions further provided that any federal judge who presumed to nullify an act of Congress would be deemed to have violated the constitutional requirement of judicial 'good behavior'

[37] Aubrey Lee Brooks and Hugh Talmage Leflar, eds., *The Papers of Walter Clark*, vol. 2, *1902–1924* (Chapel Hill: University of North Carolina Press, 1950), pp. 572, 589–94.

[38] Walter Clark, "Back to the Constitution," *Virginia Law Review* 3 (December 1915): 214–26; Walter Clark, "Back to the Constitution," *American Law Review* 50 (January–February 1916): 14. The articles are identical.

[39] Robert L. Owen to Walter Clark, July 11, 1916, Brooks and Leflar, *Papers of Clark*, pp. 305–6.

and would automatically forfeit his office.[40] Clark approved of Owen's proposals.[41]

Owen's proposal alarmed many conservatives, who feared a revival of public interest in attempts to curb the courts. In a speech to a joint session of the Oklahoma legislature two weeks after Owen introduced his proposal, Judge C. B. Stuart of Oklahoma City declared that Owen's proposal would destroy the Constitution, leaving the nation "without anchor and without compass." Stuart further suggested that the proposal for depriving judges of their offices violated the constitutional provisions that judges serve for life and suffer no diminution of compensation during their tenure.[42] In a rejoinder to Stuart in Oklahoma City four days later, Owen declared that "the judicial veto" had "been proven highly mischievous" and had become "unendurable" since the justices allowed their allegedly plutocratic predilections to influence their decisions. Near the end of Owen's address, nearly all the 1,250 people in his audience rose when he asked for a show of support for his proposal. Only about ten rose in opposition.[43]

The entry of the United States into the First World War in April 1917 abated criticism of the courts. The exigencies of the war distracted energy and attention from domestic reform movements, including efforts to make judicial power subject to popular restraints. Moreover, the Wilson administration's attempt to portray the war as a crusade for democracy created an environment where attempts to call attention to undemocratic features of American government were made to seem unpatriotic or even seditious. A nation that professed to fight for the destruction of autocracy abroad did not wish to hear that it suffered from a judicial oligarchy at home. Moreover, such criticism often explicitly or implicitly derogated the Constitution, which along with the flag was one of the nation's great patriotic symbols.

Although the war provided a sharp reminder that the courts could provide protection against the tyranny of the majority, the record of the judiciary during the war belied the arguments made by opponents of the recall during the prewar period that the courts were a bulwark of civil liberties. Juries, trial judges, and appellate courts meted out harsh

[40] S. J. Res. 193, S.J. Res. 195, 64th Cong., 2d sess., 1917; *Congressional Record*, January 9, 1917, p. 1068.

[41] Robert L. Owen to Walter Clark, June 23, 1917, Brooks and Leflar, *Papers of Clark*, p. 346.

[42] C. B. Stuart, "Power of the Supreme Court to Declare Acts of Congress Unconstitutional," an address to the joint session of the legislature of Oklahoma, Oklahoma City, January 23, 1917, repr. S. Doc. 708, 64th Cong., 2d sess., 1917, p. 14.

[43] Robert L. Owen, "Withdrawing Power from Federal Courts to Declare Acts of Congress Void," an address delivered in Oklahoma City, January 27, 1917, repr. S. Doc. 737, 64th Cong., 2d sess., 1917, p. 24.

justice to opponents of the war. More than one thousand convictions were obtained in the more than two thousand cases arising under the broadly drafted Espionage Act of 1917 and Sedition Act of 1918,[44] and countless more convictions were obtained in state courts under a multitude of local laws. Only a few federal judges, notably Charles A. Amidon of North Dakota and Learned Hand of New York, refused to impose penalties for mere criticism of the war effort. Hand's declaration that the state must tolerate any speech that does not directly incite unlawful action[45] was overruled by the court of appeals.[46]

Few of the judiciary's traditional critics among progressives and organized labor criticized judicial suppression of dissent during the war. Most judicial outrages passed unnoticed,[47] although there was some murmuring over the more extreme decisions such as the ten-year prison sentence one federal judge in Missouri gave to a woman for suggesting in a letter to a newspaper that the government abetted war profiteers.[48]

The courts escaped criticism in part because the wartime repression had originated with the executive and legislative branches. The courts' decisions on subversion were genuinely popular with many who had disagreed with many conservative judicial decisions prior to the war. Ironically, judicial willingness to exercise the deference to the legislature urged by the judiciary's prewar critics facilitated during wartime the very repression that the judiciary's prewar defenders had contended that the courts would prevent.

The intense progressive faith in democracy that had motivated reforms prior to the war was now transformed into a less benign crusade for democracy that had little patience with dissent. The ranks of the progressives included many Anglophiles, businessmen, and militarists who had strong personal motives for supporting the war. Progressives, who had responded to Roosevelt's ringing declaration at the 1912 convention—"we stand at Armageddon, and we battle for the Lord"— now diverted their energies to a different type of battle. Like the bellicose Roosevelt, many progressives were unwilling to waste sympathy on dissenters who refused to enlist categorically in the crusade to make the world safe for democracy.

[44] Paul L. Murphy, *World War I and the Origin of Civil Liberties in the United States* (New York: W. W. Norton, 1979), pp. 210–11.

[45] *Masses Publishing Co. v. Patten*, 244 F. 535, 540 (S.D.N.Y. 1917).

[46] *Masses Publishing Company v. Patten*, 246 F. 24 (2d Cir. 1917).

[47] Professor Murphy has observed that "by and large, the civil libertarians failed in their attempts at wartime consciousness-raising and agenda-setting. At no time, from April 1917 to November 1918, did the civil liberties issue emerge as a legitimate public policy question" (Murphy, *Origin of Civil Liberties*, pp. 173–74).

[48] "Ten Years for Criticism," *Literary Digest*, June 15, 1918, p. 13.

The AFL had no interest in criticizing the courts for repressing wartime dissent since the AFL was anxious to achieve social respectability and material concessions in return for its support of the war. The AFL also recognized that the war afforded labor moderates with an opportunity to purge the labor movement of its more radical elements.[49] At its 1918 convention, the AFL endorsed the Espionage and Sedition acts.[50]

Judicial decisions during the war years, however, provided the basis for renewed assaults on the federal judiciary after the war. In 1917, the Court invoked substantive due process to strike down a Washington law prohibiting an employment agency from charging fees to employees,[51] upheld workers' compensation and wage-and-hours legislation by ominously narrow margins,[52] and sustained an injunction against attempts by the United Mine Workers to unionize the West Virginia coalfields.[53] Commenting on one of the wage decisions, the *New Republic* declared, "Nothing could bring more strikingly to light the constant peril of leaving to the courts their present power of reviewing legislation under the Fifth and Fourteenth amendments."[54] After the Supreme Court struck down Washington's employment agency law, the *New Republic* observed that "decisions of this sort emphasize a situation that is fast becoming intolerable."[55] Bitterly stung by the Court's decision in the West Virginia case, the *American Federationist* proclaimed that the decision was "of greater significance to Labor than any other court decision" because it involved "the existence of the organized labor movement."[56]

Although the war distracted attention from the judiciary, a broader surge of antagonism arose against the Court in 1918 when it invalidated the first federal child-labor law in *Hammer v. Dagenhart*.[57] Enacted in 1916, the law had prohibited the interstate shipment of the products of mines that employed children under age sixteen and mills

[49] Ibid., pp. 144–45.

[50] *Report of Proceedings of the Thirty-Eighth Annual Convention of the American Federation of Labor* (Washington, D.C.: Law Reporter, 1918), pp. 118–19.

[51] *Adams v. Tanner*, 244 U.S. 590 (1917).

[52] *Mountain Timber Co. v. Washington*, 243 U.S. 219 (1917); *Bunting v. Oregon*, 243 U.S. 426 (1917); *Stettler v. O'Hara* and *Simpson v. O'Hara*, 243 U.S. 629 (1917). In two decisions earlier in 1917, the Court had unnimously upheld workers' compensation laws enacted by New York and Iowa. *New York Central Railroad v. White*, 243 U.S. 188 (1917); *Hawkins v. Bleakly*, 243 U.S. 210 (1917).

[53] *Hitchman Coal & Coke Co. v. Mitchell*, 245 U.S. 229 (1917).

[54] Editorial, *New Republic*, April 14, 1917, p. 305.

[55] Editorial, "A Reactionary Decision," *New Republic*, June 30, 1917, pp. 234–35.

[56] "That Supreme Court Decision," *American Federationist*, March 1918, p. 225.

[57] 247 U.S. 251 (1918).

that employed children under fourteen. The statute also prohibited interstate shipment of articles produced by mills that employed children between the ages of fourteen and sixteen for more than eight hours in one day, for more than six days per week, or before dawn or after dusk. Although the legislation had encountered vigorous opposition from mining and manufacturing interests and was enacted only after long and tireless efforts by progressives, the measure enjoyed widespread popular support. The Court's objection to the statute was simple, but the logic of its brief opinion no doubt eluded many Americans. According to the Court, the statute transcended Congress's power to regulate interstate commerce and permitted Congress to exercise a power over a local matter to which Congress's power did not extend. Any contrary ruling, the Court warned, would practically destroy the American form of government by ending freedom of commerce and eliminating the power of the states over local matters.

The force of the Court's reasoning was badly undercut by Justice Holmes's dissenting opinion, joined by Justices McKenna, Brandeis and Clarke. Pointing out that earlier decisions of the Court had established that Congress enjoyed broad powers to regulate interstate commerce, Holmes declared that the statute did not impinge upon any right of the states to regulate their internal affairs. To the extent that the statute contravened the domestic policy of "some self-seeking State," the state must bend to the will of Congress since the "public policy of the United States is shaped with a view toward the benefit of the nation as a whole." Going beyond the doctrine of the case, Holmes chided the Court for allowing its political predilections to override congressional discretion.

Holmes's views were echoed throughout the nation by critics of the Court's decision. The *New Republic* blasted "the unwarranted distortion of the Constitution by five men governed by well-defined intellectual bias,"[58] and *The Outlook* predicted that the Court's opinion would help to persuade advocates of social reform that the Constitution and the courts impeded justice.[59] Samuel Gompers said that the decision was "a shock to the American people" since it came "at a time of world upheaval . . . when principles and methods of human welfare and betterment are given greater consideration than ever before."[60] Despite the disappointment over the Court's decision, reactions were at first muted by distraction over the war and a failure to discern that the decision augured a change of direction by the Court in cases involving economic

[58] "States' Rights vs. the Nation," *New Republic*, June 15, 1918, p. 194.
[59] "Child Labor Law Invalid," *The Outlook*, June 12, 1918, p. 248.
[60] "Child Life Must Be Conserved," *American Federationist*, August 1918, p. 693.

issues.[61] Since the Court had so often taken a step backward before it took a few more steps forward in its march toward acceptance of social legislation, it is hardly surprising that progressives could not have foreseen that *Dagenhart* marked the start of two decades of greater judicial hostility to social legislation.

Many progressives expressed confidence that the setback was temporary.[62] As Thomas Reed Powell contended, decisions "which are out of joint with the times . . . and which meet with strong dissent from some of the ablest of the judges, are not likely long to remain unmodified."[63] Since the Court's opinion did not suggest that a federal child-labor law would contravene the due process clause, progressives hoped that Congress could find a way to frame a law that the Court would uphold. Powell and other progressives believed that the congressional taxing power provided the most promising alternative to the commerce power. Although a constitutional amendment provided a means of overturning the decision, reformers quailed at the delays, expenses, and uncertainties of the amendment process. An official of the National Child Labor Committee, which preferred to work for a new statute rather than an amendment, explained that Americans were "not disposed to change their Constitution unless they feel themselves forced to do it."[64]

Dagenhart marked a turning point in the controversy over judicial power since it provided an impetus for specific proposals to curb the Court's power. *Dagenhart* was the spark that ignited new fires that raged from 1922 to 1924. The *New Republic*, that bellwether of progressive opinion, presaged the trend when it declared that the decision would damage the Court's prestige and that "in the long run American opinion will not consent to have social legislation invalidated and its social progress retarded by the necessarily accidental and arbitrary preference of one judge in a court of nine."[65]

Shortly after the Court handed down its decision, members of Congress began to sponsor new child-labor measures. Although most of those bills were designed to avoid the constitutional objections on which the *Dagenhart* decision was based, Senator Owen introduced legislation that defied the decision and challenged the Court's power.

[61] Stephen B. Wood, *Constitutional Politics in the Progressive Era: Child Labor and the Law* (Chicago: University of Chicago Press, 1968), p. 179.

[62] Thomas Reed Powell, "The Child-Labor Decision," *The Nation*, June 22, 1918, p. 731; "The Child-Labor Defeat," *Literary Digest*, June 15, 1918, p. 16 (quoting the New York *Evening Mail*); "Child Labor Law Invalid," p. 248.

[63] Powell, "Child Labor Decision," p. 731.

[64] Wood, *Constitutional Politics*, p. 187.

[65] *New Republic*, June 8, 1918, pp. 158–59.

Owen's bill provided for the reenactment of the original law he had sponsored in the Senate and forbade the federal courts to review the constitutionality of the new law. Like the measure that Owen had introduced in 1917, the bill also provided that any judicial officer who impugned the constitutionality of the statute would forfeit his office.[66]

In defending his measure during a Senate debate on June 6, 1918, Owen urged the Senate to defy the doctrine of judicial review. Denouncing the "mischievous, dangerous, unconstitutional" precedent established by *Marbury v. Madison,* Owen contended that such defiance was supported by the precedent established by Congress in the limitation of habeas corpus jurisdiction that the Court had upheld in *McCardle.* Responding to questions, Owen acknowledged that the Supreme Court had the power to review the constitutionality of state statutes and suggested that there was more justification for state courts to review the constitutionality of state legislation because most state judges were elected and were thus answerable to the people. In response to Republican senator Frank B. Kellogg's contention that the abrogation of judicial review of federal legislation would invite congressional tyranny, Owen declared that congressional power could not "lead to tyranny" because members of Congress had to seek reelection.[67]

Although *Dagenhart* did not immediately rekindle progressive efforts to curb judicial powers, the decision greatly helped to transform the AFL's attitude toward the federal judiciary. As recently as the spring of 1918, when the AFL was still smarting over the Court's decision in *Hitchman Coal,* Gompers had continued to express faith that courts "can not indefinitely bar progress."[68] Until *Dagenhart,* AFL leaders had continued to urge such palliatives as judicial education and reforms in equity jurisdiction.[69] In an editorial after *Dagenhart,* however, Gompers finally asserted that the time had come to consider measures for curbing the Court's powers. Explaining that "our nation must think further than curative methods," Gompers declared that the nation

[66] S. 4671, 65th Cong., 2d sess., 1918. Unlike Owen's previous bill, this measure provided that executive officers would also forfeit their offices if they presumed to deny the constitutionality of the statute.

[67] 66 *Congressional Record,* 65th Cong., 2d sess., June 6, 1918, pp. 7430–35 (emphasis deleted). Another critic of Owen's proposal alleged that it would destroy "the equilibrium which marks with regular precision the working and harmony of the three great branches of government," thereby jeopardizing "the rights of property and the safety of individuals." C. A. Hereshoff Bartlett, "The Co-Ordinate Powers of Government," *American Law Review* 52 (September–October 1918): 670–79.

[68] Samuel Gompers, "That Supreme Court Decision," *American Federationist,* March 1918, p. 227.

[69] See, e.g., W. B. Rubin, "A Judicial 'And-You-Too-Brutus' Stab at Unionism," *American Federationist,* March 1918, p. 220.

"must regulate the veto power of the Supreme Court and eliminate an intolerable situation that enables five men to defeat the will of the nation."[70]

In a report submitted to the Senate Committee on Education and Labor in January 1919, the AFL called for legislation to permit Congress to reenact any legislation that the Supreme Court had declared unconstitutional. The AFL also urged the adoption of legislation to permit the state legislatures to reenact a statute that the Supreme Court had nullified. Five months later, Jackson H. Ralston, the AFL's general counsel, published a more detailed report that proposed similar measures. Ralston concluded that no court, including the Supreme Court, should have the power to pass upon the constitutionality of congressional enactments. Ralston's plan would also have divested the state courts of the power to review the constitutionality of state legislation, except to the extent that it contravened the federal Constitution or federal laws or treaties. Ralston's plan would have permitted the Supreme Court to retain its jurisdiction to rule on the constitutionality of state legislation, although the Court's nullification of a state statute would have required the concurrence of "considerably more than a bare majority of its members."[71]

At its annual convention in June 1919, the AFL unanimously voted to adopt a report that denounced judicial review as "a most flagrant usurpation of power" that was a "blasphemy on the rights and claims of free men in America." The report, which referred to Jackson's study, did not specifically recommend Jackson's detailed remedies, but it urged the "early enactment of laws to deny the further usurpation of these unwarranted powers" and urged Congress to impeach all judges who exercised authority that was not expressly delegated to them.[72]

The AFL's abandonment of much of its traditional caution toward judicial issues reflected the effects of the war and volatile postwar conditions. The war had increased the assertiveness of the AFL because the union had thrived during wartime when the government had made many concessions to organized labor and had taken union leaders into its councils. Low unemployment and high wages improved the conditions of workers, and AFL membership nearly doubled between 1916 and 1920.[73] By refraining from strikes and providing other

[70] Gompers, "Child Life," p. 692.

[71] *Report of Proceedings of the Thirty-Ninth Annual Convention of the American Federation of Labor* (Washington, D.C.: Law Reporter, 1919), pp. 97–99; Matthew Woll, "American Labor in Convention," *American Federationist*, July 1919, p. 610.

[72] *Report, AFL*, 1919, pp. 361–62; "American Labor's Greatest Convention," *American Federationist*, August 1919, p. 690.

[73] Philip Taft, *The A.F. of L. in the Time of Gompers* (New York: Harper, 1957), p. 362.

support for the war effort, the AFL had proved its patriotism. At last the trade union movement seemed to have achieved the respectability for which Gompers had so persistently striven. Although the end of the war ushered in a period of reaction, the unions originally hoped that the end of the war would provide the occasion for renewed dedication to reform.

The AFL's 1919 proposal for judicial reform was one of eighteen proposals for a postwar "Reconstruction Program" that the AFL advocated for the adjustment of postwar economic and industrial problems. The AFL's report to Congress urged the adoption of such measures as shorter work hours, public housing, improved workers' compensation laws, and the abolition of private employment agencies.[74] However, since the AFL believed, that courts were likely to disfavor any legislation that arose out of its proposals, the AFL began to call for restraints on judicial power.

Although the AFL's attacks on the courts reflected its new confidence and growing assertiveness, the union's increasing antipathy toward the courts also arose from labor's disillusionment with the political reaction against labor during the postwar years, which seemed to jeopardize the gains achieved during the New Freedom and the war and threaten the very existence of the trade union movement. Although Gompers was more inclined to support governmental activism during the war, he remained profoundly suspicious of the state.[75]

Organized labor's fears about repression of unionism were especially aggravated by the labor troubles of 1919 when the eruption of more than two thousand strikes involving four million workers led to widespread use of the injunction and encouraged business leaders to begin a campaign for the nonunion shop. The success and barbarity of the Bolshevik revolution and the violence of many members of the radical International Workers of the World (IWW) provided labor's foes with an opportunity to amplify their dire warnings about the dangers of workers' movements. Fed by fears of revolution, the Department of Justice under Attorney General A. Mitchell Palmer brutally suppressed the IWW and other radical labor unions and zealously deported aliens, many active in the labor movement. This repression provided a painful reminder of the precarious legal status of trade unionism.[76] Facing a possible fight for its very existence, the AFL

[74] "Labor Advocates Drastic Policies," *New York Times*, January 16, 1919, p. 5; Taft, *A.F. of L.*, pp. 369–72.

[75] William M. Dick, *Labor and Socialism in America: The Gompers Era* (Port Washington, N.Y.: Kennikat Press, 1972), pp. 139–40.

[76] Ibid., pp. 156–61; John E. Semonche, *Charting the Future: The Supreme Court Responds to a Changing Society: 1890–1920* (Westport, Conn.: Greenwood press, 1978), pp.

lashed out at the courts, which threatened to continue to thwart the aspirations of labor.

Having provided crucial support for the nation's fight for democracy, the AFL could no longer abide the seemingly undemocratic character of judicial review. Just as prewar reformers had denounced the courts as an oligarchy, so the AFL began to equate judicial review with autocracy. In the resolution adopted at its 1919 convention, the AFL alleged that courts "freely and uninterruptedly exercise powers which even the monarchs and kaisers dared not exercise with all their claims to power by inherent divinity." The resolution excoriated judicial review as a "repudiation and denial of the principle of self-government recognized now as a world doctrine." The AFL concluded that "it is inconceivable that such an autocratic, despotic, and tyrannical power can long remain in a democracy."[77]

The willingness of the AFL to call for curbs on judicial power also reflected a growing power struggle within the AFL. During the early postwar years, the AFL's conservative leadership faced increasing opposition from both Socialists and non-Socialist opponents of the AFL's traditional antipathy to governmental activism. Although the AFL's Reconstruction Program represented a concession to statist goals, many elements in the AFL favored even greater governmental activism to develop solutions to the myriad problems of postwar life. The large membership increases of the war years brought more radicals into union ranks, and the growing hostility of employers toward labor encouraged greater union militancy.[78]

Gompers feared that the triumph of the Bolsheviks in Russia and the growing power of the British Socialists might produce a recrudescence of the radicalism that the AFL leadership had successfully repressed. Aged and ailing, Gompers faced his first serious challenge in a decade for the leadership of the AFL when John L. Lewis of the AFL-affiliated United Mine Workers mounted a challenge from the left in 1921.[79] Although Gompers prevailed in that contest, he could not ignore the growing restiveness over his conservatism. The AFL's attacks on the Court provided an opportunity for the AFL to pacify its growing left-wing factions. Matthew Woll, the vice president of the AFL, asserted in August 1919 that the AFL was "entirely earnest" about its proposal to curb judicial review, and he averred that the AFL

374–75; Frederic L. Paxson, *American Democracy and the World War*, vol. 3, *Postwar Years: Normalcy, 1918–1923* (New York: Cooper Square, 1966), (repr. 1948 University of California ed.), pp. 88–89.

[77] *Report, AFL*, 1919, p. 361.

[78] Taft, *A.F. of L.*, p. 363; Dick, *Labor and Socialism*, p. 163.

[79] Taft, *A.F. of L..*, pp. 367–68.

firmly intended "to put forth every legitimate effort to secure ratification of what it believes to be evils of the most grievous character in the judicial machinery of the country."[80]

During 1919, unionist suspicions about the incorrigibility of the federal judiciary grew when a federal court of appeals judge affirmed a judgment under the Sherman Antitrust Act against the United Mine Workers Union for damages caused during a strike.[81] In June 1919, Woll declared that the North Carolina decision illustrated "the urgent need" for legislation to curb the Supreme Court's power.[82]

The AFL proposal attracted vehement criticism. The *New York Times* predicted that the nation "will prefer the judicial interpretation of the statutes to the edicts of the unions."[83] But although the AFL's proposal offended conservatives, it attracted the support of many progressives. The *New Republic*, for example, declared that Ralston's recommendations were "fully worthy of liberal support" and hailed the AFL for putting its weight "behind a fundamental and urgent reform." Predicting that the coming decades would "require more than ever drastic interferences with vested property rights," the *New Republic* observed that reform would make slow progress as long as the Court had "the final word as to the compatibility of legislation with the public welfare." It concluded, that "Even conservatives will admit that it is better to act moderately and sanely today than to wait until popular resentment over such decisions as the child labor case lead to more drastic and subversive measures."[84]

The hostility of progressives and labor to judicial review was aggravated during 1920 by a series of 5–4 decisions in which the Supreme Court offended nearly every stripe of liberal opinion. The Court could not have provided better grist for the mill of its critics, for the decisions exemplified the judicial arrogance and hostility toward social reform of which progressives and trade unionists had so bitterly complained about in recent years. Although the fact that the cases were decided by a one-vote margin may have given some hope to liberals, the effect of the narrowness of the decisions was exactly the opposite since the four dissents in each case provided a vivid reminder that Supreme Court decisions were often dictated by political proclivity rather than compelled by law. Even though the Court's decisions in these cases did not

[80] Matthew Woll, "Courts Should Not Make or Unmake Our Laws," *American Federationist*, August 1919, p. 712.

[81] *United Mine Workers v. Coronado Coal Company*, 258 F. 829 (8th Cir. 1919).

[82] Matthew Woll, "Judges' Autocratic Power Must Go," *American Federationist*, June 1919, p. 511.

[83] "Labor and the Courts," *New York Times*, June 21, 1919, p. 14.

[84] "The Supreme Court and the A.F. of L.," *New Republic*, July 30, 1919, pp. 409–10.

attract widespread attention, alert progressives recognized that they confirmed the Court's shift toward conservatism.

The Court's solicitude for the wealthy was illustrated by its decision in *Eisner v. Macomber* on March 8, 1920, where the Court invalidated the portion of the Revenue Act of 1916 that had imposed an income tax upon stock dividends.[85] The Court's arrogance was illustrated in *Evans v. Gore* in June 1920 when the Court held that the salaries of federal judges were not subject to the income tax.[86] The contrast between the Court's solicitude for preserving the weal of the wealthy, including the justices themselves, and its insensitivity to the woes of the poor was graphically illustrated in August 1920 when the Court in *Knickerbocker Ice Co. v. Stewart* invalidated a provision of the Federal Judicial Code that had permitted workers' compensation claims for maritime workers to be litigated in state court rather than under the general federal admiralty jurisdiction.[87] The decision had the practical effect of forcing maritime workers to litigate all injury claims under federal law, which had no workers' compensation statute, and to litigate those claims in federal courts. In commenting on *Knickerbocker*, the *New Republic* observed that "'petty decisions' make a petty Constitution and swell the tide of discontent against its petty and rigid restrictions more than all the diatribes of the 'agitators.'"[88]

Liberals had reason to worry about confidence in the judiciary since the Bolshevik revolution had demonstrated what could happen to a government that frustrated widespread demands for reform. Ironically, however, conservative alarm over the Russian revolution may have fueled the reaction that was reflected in judicial decisions such as *Knickerbocker*. Taft, who became chief justice in 1921, equated many

---

[85] 252 U.S. 189 (1920). The Court reasoned that the tax was not within the scope of the Sixteenth Amendment because it was a tax on property rather than income and therefore was a direct tax prohibited by Article I of the Constitution. The dissenters—Holmes, Brandeis, Day, and Clarke—believed that the Sixteenth Amendment was clearly intended to embrace stock dividends.

[86] 253 U.S. 245 (1920). The Court reasoned that the tax would violate the constitutional provision that prohibits diminution of the compensation of federal judges during their tenure of office. In a dissent joined by Justice Brandeis, Justice Holmes contended that the tax violated neither the original Constitution nor the Sixteenth Amendment. Holmes denied that the tax would erode judicial independence and contended that federal judges should not be a "privileged class, free from bearing their share of the cost of the institutions upon which their well-being if not their life depends" (p. 265).

[87] 253 U.S. 149 (1920). Justice McReynolds's opinion for the Court reasoned that the statute had unconstitutionally delegated the admiralty power that the Constitution had conferred upon the federal courts and that application of the laws of different states would create inconsistencies in the outcome of like cases (ibid., p.164).

[88] "Another Case of Five to Four," *New Republic*, June 9, 1920, p. 38.

liberal reforms with bolshevism and expressed eagerness for a square confrontation between the forces of discontent and those of reform, for he believed that the essential conservatism of the American people would ensure the triumph of the latter.

One year after the 1920 decisions that so dismayed the liberals, the Court in *Newberry v. United States*, another 5–4 decision, gutted another congressional enactment, section 8 of the Corrupt Practices Act, which had limited expenditures by candidates for the U.S. Senate.[89] Since many progressives had worked to banish big spending from the election process and business interests regularly outspent labor unions in election contests, the *Newberry* decision was bound to offend many of the Court's critics. Moreover, as Benno C. Schmidt, Jr., has observed,

> In its narrow literalism and historical rigidity, in its commitment to qualitative, categorical, conceptual principles of constitutional interpretation, in its candid rejection of functional measures of national interest, and in its overriding of a recent, considered congressional judgment on a matter peculiarly within the ambit of legislative concern, Justice McReynolds' *Newberry* opinion was a window on the troubled course of constitutional adjudication in the decade of the twenties and beyond.[90]

Progressive hostility toward the Court during the immediate postwar period was also aggravated by the Court's lack of judicial solicitude for civil liberties. During the first few years after the end of the war, the Court pioneered the development of theories of free speech. The results did not cheer liberals.

In the first three cases that came before the Court, in 1919, the Court upheld convictions under the Espionage Act. The Court found that the defendants' activities had created a "clear and present danger" to the government.[91] Civil libertarians objected to the standard used by the Court and to its application to the facts of the cases: the speech of the defendants in the three cases did not appear to present any real threat to the government, and the "clear and present danger" standard seemed excessively broad.[92] Later in the year, the Court upheld a

---

[89] 256 U.S. 232 (1921). The Court reasoned that the constitutional provision that confers on Congress the power to regulate congressional elections does not extend to primary elections since such contests were unknown to the Framers. The Court reversed the conviction of Senator Truman H. Newberry, a conservative Republican senator from Michigan who had flagrantly exceeded the statute's spending limitations in a primary election.

[90] Bickel and Schmidt, *Responsible Government*, p. 969.

[91] *Schenck v. United States*, 249 U.S. 47 (1919); *Debs v. United States*, 249 U.S. 211 (1919); *Frohwerk v. United States*, 249 U.S. 204 (1919).

[92] Civil libertarians complained that the speech of the defendants presented no imminent danger to the government's conduct of the war. Although Schenck's distribution of

conviction under the Sedition Act on the ground that the distribution of leaflets opposing the American Expeditionary Force to Russia might have interfered with the war against Germany.[93]

Justices Holmes and Brandeis dissented in that case, adopting the more liberal position that a court should impose penalties only on speech that was reasonably calculated to create a direct and imminent threat to the government. They dissented again in subsequent cases where the Court upheld the convictions of a German-American editor and three Socialists on the ground that their dissemination of antiwar writings might have a "tendency" to provoke civil disobedience.[94] The Court's adoption of the "bad tendency" test, which was even broader than the "clear and present danger" doctrine, further distressed many of the Court's critics.

Even though few progressives had deplored judicial repression of dissent during the war, the Court's encouragement of repression during the postwar years distressed at least some progressives, who deplored the irony that the courts were willing to accord a deference to the legislature in free speech cases that they were not willing to grant in economic cases. As the *New Republic* observed in January 1921, "With increasing recklessness our Courts are writing 'unconstitutional' across legislation—except legislation restrictive of speech."[95] Numerous progressives criticized the courts for their disdain of free speech. Gerard C. Henderson saw ominous portents in the Court's willingness in *Abrams* to define broadly the key questions of dangerousness and intent. On both of these issues, Henderson pointed out, "the Supreme Court has . . . definitely cast its weight . . . on the side which fears the free interchange of opinion, and relies on force rather than reason to preserve the authority of the state and the stablility of our institutions."[96]

Despite their disappointment with free-speech decisions, progressives and civil libertarians commended the courts for insisting that the

---

circulars that urged draftees to resist induction might directly have encouraged some draft resistance, it was less likely that the articles of the newspaper in *Frohwerk* that had attacked the draft and challenged the constitutionality of the war would have any discernible impact on the war effort. Moreover, it was not clear that the newspaper had intended to interfere with mobilization. Similarly, civil libertarians could not agree with the Court that an antiwar speech by Debs was intended to interfere with mobilization or that it would have that effect.

[93] *Abrams v. United States*, 250 U.S. 616 (1919).

[94] *Schaefer v. United States*, 251 U.S. 466 (1920); *Pierce v. United States*, 252 U.S. 239 (1920).

[95] "'Preventive Justice' Balked," *New Republic*, January 19, 1921, p. 219.

[96] Gerard C. Henderson, "What Is Left of Free Speech," *New Republic*, December 10, 1919, p. 52.

government accord basic procedural protections to suspected political radicals who were prosecuted by the Justice Department during the "Red Scare" instigated by Attorney General Palmer during 1919 and 1920. In a 1920 decision, for example, the Supreme Court barred the government from using as evidence at trial various documents it had seized in an illegal warrantless raid.[97]

Civil libertarians also found much to praise in a number of federal district court decisions. In releasing twenty suspected radicals who were arrested upon insufficient cause during one of the most spectacular of the Palmer raids, Judge George W. Anderson of Massachusetts castigated the Justice Department for its lawless procedures.[98] Similarly, Judge George M. Bourquin of Montana, in granting a writ of habeas corpus to a foreign-born member of the IWW, declared that the federal agents who had perpetrated "a reign of terror, violence and crime" were a greater threat to American freedom than the radicals they persecuted.[99] The *New Republic* observed that a "few more decisions like this one of Judge Bourquin will go far toward restoring the faith of the American citizen in the moral integrity, the vision and the courage of the American judiciary."[100]

During the next several years, however, there were few decisions that helped to restore the faith of progressives and trade unionists in the judiciary. Some of the most bitter episodes in the protracted struggle between social reformers and the courts would occur in the 1920s.

[97] *Silverthorne Lumber Company v. United States*, 251 U.S. 385 (1920). The *New Republic* observed that the Court's "stinging rebuke" to the government "condemns as unconstitutional and illegal the whole series of nation-wide raids with which the Attorney General has sought to entertain a jaded electorate" (*New Republic*, February 18, 1920, p. 326).

[98] *Colyer v. Skeffington*, 265 F. 17 (D. Mass. 1920).

[99] *Ex parte Jackson*, 263 F. 110, 112–14 (D. Mont. 1920).

[100] "A Federal Judge Speaks Up," *New Republic* March 31, 1920, p. 135.

EIGHT

THE TAFT COURT AND THE RETURN

OF "NORMALCY"

Chief Justice Taft deals with abstractions and not with the
work-a-day world, its men and its struggles. For all the
regard that the Chief Justice of the United States pays to
the facts of industrial life, he might as well have written
this opinion as Chief Justice of the Fiji Islands.
(*Editorial, The* New Republic, *January 18, 1922,
commenting on* Truax v. Corrigan)[1]

Judges are liable to error. The judgments of the Supreme
Court have stirred bitter opposition. The people have,
however, properly appraised the inestimable value . . . of
the settlement of critical and threatening questions of law
by a tribunal as far removed as is possible from politics
and partisan and personal interest. Where, however, Jove
nods and the tribunal has fallen into error in the
considered judgment of the people, they have preferred to
abide the necessary delay and to change by amendment
the effect of the Constitution as construed by the court,
rather than to abolish the power of judicial settlement.
(*Chief Justice Taft, speech at Philadelphia, May 2, 1922*)[2]

FACED WITH increasing hostility from the courts and decreasing political influence, the progressives and trade unionists became more strident in their denunciations of the judiciary after
1920. In contrast to the willingness of prewar critics to explore various
methods for mitigating state and federal judicial hostility toward social
and labor legislation, the critics of the courts during the 1920s were
more inclined to advocate dramatic but ultimately chimerical proposals to curtail judicial power. Progressive proposals more often involved only the Supreme Court and ignored the possibility of reform at
the state or lower federal levels.

The growing conservatism of the Supreme Court helps to explain

[1] "The Same Mr. Taft," *New Republic,* January 18, 1922, p. 193.
[2] "Chief Justice Taft's Address," *American Bar Association Journal,* June 1922, p. 334.

why the Court now became the focus of progressive criticism of the judiciary, for the Court continued to issue decisions that offended the labor and progressive movements. During the half century between the adoption of the Fourteenth Amendment in 1868 and the end of 1920, the Court invoked the due process clause to invalidate state and local acts in only 13 out of 195 cases in which a due process challenge was raised. During the six years from 1921 to 1926, however, the Court agreed with fifteen out of fifty-three due process arguments in striking down federal and state statutes.[3] As the most powerful and visible court in the nation, the Court also provided a convenient target for progressives and trade unionists.

The growing hostility of the progressives toward the Court also represented an attempt to find an issue that would unify the increasingly fractured progressive movement. Progressivism during the 1920s suffered from deep divisions between its urban and rural and its labor and agrarian components, and it began to lose much of its support in the urban middle classes and professionals. Having achieved many of its original objectives during the Wilson administration, the progressive movement was also afflicted by what Arthur S. Link has called "a substantial paralysis of the progressive mind." Progressives were especially uncertain whether to continue to work for business regulation and social reform within capitalism or to move toward socialism.[4]

Progressivism also suffered from the retreat from reform that characterized postwar politics. Weary of the swift pace of the changes that had transformed the nation during recent years, voters in 1920 presaged a decade of conservatism when they favorably responded to Warren Harding's promise to replace "nostrums" with "normalcy." Yet although the progressives never recovered their prewar élan, the progressive movement remained remarkably resilient during the 1920s. A vigorous current of reform stirred beneath the tide of reaction. Unions also continued to prosper, even though they lost many of their members and much of their influence in the White House and Congress. The conflict between an ascendant conservatism and a still energetic but now troubled social reform movement created tensions that were inevitably reflected in judicial decisions and in the attitude of the reformers toward the courts.

Troubled by internal divisions, loss of support among their core constituencies, and uncertainties about their goals, both the unions and the progressives found that proposals to curtail the Supreme Court's

[3] Ray A. Brown, "Due Process of Law, Police Power, and the Supreme Court," *Harvard Law Review* 40 (May 1927): 944–45.

[4] Arthur S. Link, "What Happened to the Progressive Movement in the 1920's?" *American Historical Review* 64 (July 1959): 841.

power of judicial review provided a simple and dramatic issue by which they could attempt to rally both internal and external support for their causes. Moreover, opposition to the courts also provided a common denominator for cooperation between progressives and unionists. The defection of many of the middle-class and eastern progressives also tended to encourage attacks on the courts, for the workers and middle western farmers who composed the core of the progressive movement during the 1920s came out of a cultural milieu in which deference to the judiciary was not so deeply rooted as it was among the middle classes of the East Coast.

Labor's growing animus toward the Court was intensified in January 1921, two months after the election of Harding, when the Court held in *Duplex Printing Press Company v. Deering* that the antitrust laws did not prohibit injunctions to restrain secondary boycotts.[5] The *Duplex* decision produced a paroxysm of outrage among unionists and progressives and stiffened the AFL's resolve to seek measures to curtail the powers of the Court. Dissenting members of the Court led the chorus of criticism. In a dissent joined by Holmes and Clarke, Justice Brandeis explained that he could not find that secondary boycotts were prohibited either by statute or the common law and that it was not for the courts to prescribe the limits of permissible industrial activity.[6] Robert M. La Follette declared that the decision constituted a "body blow" to labor that placed unions "at the mercy of every employer and combination of employers who may seek injunctions from the federal courts."[7] Similarly, Samuel Gompers declared that the decision was "thoroughly in accord with the most ardent wishes of predatory greed and should be highly satisfactory to those who exalt profits and deny the aspirations of humanity."[8]

Perceiving that judicial hostility toward labor was unremitting, the Conference of Representatives of National Trade Unions urged Congress in January 1921 to remove "the usurped power" of judicial review and endorsed outright defiance of injunctions. Although the Conference recognized that this was a radical proposal, it contended that

[5] *Duplex Printing Press Co. v. Deering*, 254 U.S. 443 (1921). The Court determined that secondary boycotts were not protected by either section 20 of the Clayton Act, which prohibited the use of injunctions in labor disputes except to prevent irreparable injury to property and forbade injunctions against picketing or primary boycotts, or section 6, which had provided that the antitrust laws did not apply to union activities (pp. 466–68).

[6] Ibid., p. 488.

[7] Editorial, "Supreme Court Strikes Labor A Body Blow," *La Follette's Magazine*, January 1921, pp. 1–2.

[8] Samuel Gompers, "Rights Judicially Purloined," *American Federationist*, February 1921, p. 135.

judicial activism imperiled American freedom.[9] At its convention in Denver in June 1921, the AFL reiterated its support for the curtailment of the Supreme Court's power to review the constitutionality of statutes. The convention endorsed a specific joint resolution to be presented in Congress for a constitutional amendment to provide that any duly enacted federal statute "shall be deemed and held to be valid under the Constitution wherever called in question."[10] This proposal was consistent with Ralston's recommendation and the AFL's call in 1919 for the abolition of judicial review. Like so many other AFL proposals, this was never embodied in legislation introduced in Congress.

Despite their growing antagonism toward the Supreme Court, trade unionists and progressives did not present any challenge to the nomination of William Howard Taft to the chief justiceship in 1921.[11] In contrast to the vigorous efforts by progressives to dissuade Wilson from placing Taft on the Court, progressives failed to attempt to discourage Harding from nominating Taft. Although Harding received a number of letters opposing Taft's nomination, most came from the Right rather than the Left.[12] Only four senators voted against the nomination: Republican progressives Hiram Johnson of California, William E. Borah of Idaho, and La Follette of Wisconsin, and the Democratic populist Thomas E. Watson of Georgia. The opposition of

[9] "The Challenge Accepted: Labor Will Not be Outlawed or Enslaved," (report of the Conference of Representatives of National Trade Unions), *American Federationist*, April 1921, pp. 293, 296.

[10] *Report of the Proceedings of the Forty-First Annual Convention of the American Federation of Labor, 1921* (Washington, D.C.: Law Reporter, 1921), p. 125; Samuel Gompers, "The Denver Convention—Action and Review," *American Federationist*, August 1921, p. 634.

[11] Alpheus Thomas Mason, *William Howard Taft: Chief Justice* (New York: Simon and Schuster, 1964), pp. 84–87; Henry Abraham, *Justices and Presidents: A Political History of Appointments to the Supreme Court*, 2d ed. (New York: Oxford University Press, 1985), pp. 184–85.

[12] National Archives (NA), General Records of the Department of Justice, Record Group 60, File 348, "Records Relating to Members of the Supreme Court 1853–1932," Box 5, Taft folder. Many opponents of Taft's nomination objected to Taft's support for American entry into the League of Nations. Although progressives had been divided on the issue of American membership in the League, letters objecting to Taft's nomination on this ground had a distinctly right-wing flavor; for example, L. H. Wheeler to Henry M. Daugherty, June 15, 1921 (ibid.). Other opponents of the nomination objected to Taft's tolerance toward Roman Catholicism and his Unitarian faith (Taft folder, ibid.). One of the few liberal groups to oppose Taft's nomination was the Boston branch of the National Equal Rights League, which alleged that Taft was content to allow the South "to go on in her mad career, which is one of mob lawlessness, peonage and disfranchisement, thereby making America a burning disgrace to civilization." National Equal Rights League, Greater Boston Branch, office of the Secretary, to Warren G. Harding, June 11, 1921 (ibid.).

the Senate's three leading progressive Republicans was prophetic, however, since it presaged the progressive criticism of the Court during the coming years.

Moreover, the near unanimity with which the Senate confirmed Taft's nomination may have masked deeper opposition to the appointment. Republican senator Philander C. Knox of Pennsylvania had roundly denounced the possibility of Taft's nomination on the day before Taft's name was sent to the Senate, and Republican senators Frank B. Kellogg of Minnesota and Frank B. Willis of Ohio had told Johnson that they opposed the nomination. Johnson reported to his sons, however, that when the nomination was received, "What a bustle there was! Every sycophant in the Senate rushed about to obtain immediate consideration and unanimous confirmation."[13] During the Senate's consideration of the nomination in executive session, Johnson declared that Taft was unfit for the chief justiceship by education and temperament, and that he might provide crucial votes in favor of reactionary decisions in cases that had far-reaching political consequences.[14] Johnson, who was already deeply discouraged over the decline of progressivism, told Harold Ickes that he found Taft's nomination "most depressing."[15] To another friend, Johnson wrote, "When I think of the industrial disputes that are coming, of imperiled humanity in the next few years, and of the possibilities of a decision of the United States Supreme Court, then my heart grows sick."[16]

[13] Hiram Johnson to Hiram W. Johnson, Jr., July 2, 1921, in Robert E. Burke, *The Diary Letters of Hiram Johnson 1917–1945, vol. 3, 1919–1921* (New York: Garland, 1983), p. 5. Johnson told his sons that Willis delivered a eulogistic speech and that Knox, who "slobbered as only a sycophant could do," explained later to Johnson that he had decided to "gracefully acquiesce" to Taft's nomination.

[14] Ibid., pp. 5–6. Johnson complained to his sons that Taft was "crooked, both intellectually and otherwise" and that Taft was "a traitor to his country" because he had championed American membership in the League of Nations. Johnson also charged that Taft had chosen "to become a cheap talker for cheap fees at chautauqua, and a petty scribbler for small remuneration, rather than practice his profession when he had the opportunity of living his life in the dignity befitting an ex-President" (ibid., p. 6).

[15] Johnson to Harold L. Ickes, July 2, 1921, Johnson Papers, Part 3, Box 3, Bancroft Library, University of California at Berkeley.

[16] Johnson to Raymond Robins, July 1, 1921, Johnson Papers, Part 3, Box 1. Some contemporary observers believed that Taft's participation in the League of Nations controversy may have provided the decisive factor in the decision of Johnson, La Follette, and Borah to oppose Taft, since they could not have forgotten or forgiven Taft's harsh remarks about Borah and other opponents of the League in addresses that Taft delivered at a pro-League conference in St. Louis in February 1919. "Purely Political," *Joplin Globe*, July 2, 1921, in *Taft Papers*, Series 3, Reel 229, Manuscript Division, Library of Congress. Although Borah, Johnson, and La Follette had differed sharply with Taft on many political issues long before they locked horns with Taft over the League of Nations issue, the bitterness engendered by Taft's cutting remarks about senatorial opponents of

Unlike Johnson, most progressive opponents of the nomination did not question Taft's character. *The Nation*, which had taken a sharp turn to the left when Oswald Garrison Villard became editor in 1918,[17] conceded that Taft had a "high character" and that "few politicians long preserve as much of the milk of human kindness." Like Johnson, however, the *New Republic* questioned his professional qualifications, observing that no one would think of Taft primarily as a lawyer.[18] Oliver Wendell Holmes, Jr., had expressed similar doubts in May 1921, telling Harold Laski, "I never saw anything that struck me as more than first-rate second rate."[19]

Since Taft had served as a court of appeals judge, taken a lifelong interest in the judiciary, watched the workings of the government from the vantage point of the presidency, and served eight years as professor of constitutional law at Yale, criticisms of his legal talents were not altogether justified. Indeed, Holmes came to admire Taft's abilities. A more serious objection was that Taft's conservative political philosophy would govern his performance as chief justice. As the *New Republic* observed, "Taft has made his political character visible to the whole people. It is a conservative character, and the decisions of the Supreme Court will be shifted toward conservatism by it."[20] *The Nation* likewise expressed the belief that Taft would carry his political biases to the bench.[21]

The progressive criticisms of the nomination were nearly drowned out, however, by the widespread acclaim that greeted the nomination. The *Literary Digest* observed that "seldom has the robe of office been

---

the League during his 1919 tour in support of the League may indeed have persuaded those progressives to oppose the nomination. In his St. Louis speech, Taft had named Senators Borah, Poindexter, and Reed as "destructive critics" who had "utterly fail[ed] to tender any constructive suggestions . . . for a method by which peace can be maintained and the just results of war can be secured." "Taft Challenges League Opponents," *New York Times*, February 26, 1919, p. 2. In other speeches, Taft had denounced senatorial crtics of League membership as "small Americans" and had accused them of deliberately misrepresenting the League's principles. "'Small Americans' Condemned by Taft," ibid., February 21, 1919, p. 2; "Taft Assails Senators," ibid., March 13, 1919, p. 2, col. 2.

[17] Michael Wreszin, *Oswald Garrison Villard: Pacifist at War* (Bloomington: Indiana University Press, 1965), pp. 87–90.

[18] Editorial, *New Republic*, July 13, 1921, p. 177. Although the *New Republic* conceded that Taft had been a good judge, it complained that he was not a great judge, that he had not served on the bench for two decades, and that he had "contributed practically nothing to legal thought" during his years at Yale. "Mr. Chief Justice Taft," *New Republic*, July 27, 1921, p. 231.

[19] Oliver Wendell Holmes to Harold Laski, May 27, 1921, in Mark DeWolfe Howe, ed., *Holmes-Laski Letters: The Correspondence of Mr. Justice Holmes and Harold J. Laski, vol. 1, 1916–1925* (Cambridge, Mass.: Harvard University Press, 1953), p. 339.

[20] Editorial, *New Republic*, July 13, 1921, p. 177.

[21] "The Chief Justice—A Mistaken Appointment," *The Nation*, July 13, 1921, p. 32.

adjudged a perfect fit by so numerous a body of citizens as when . . .
Taft donned the gown of Chief Justice." The plaudits cut across sectional and party lines, with the nomination receiving praise even from
Democrats. Indeed, Taft's nomination appears to have been particularly popular in the South, which was grateful to Taft for favors during his presidency.[22]

The nomination of the conservative Taft seemed to fit the temper of
the times by promising "normalcy" rather than innovation. As the
Democratic New Orleans *Times-Picayune* observed: "There have been
times in our history when we might have been prepared to welcome . . . a man of more original views . . . but just now we are surfeited with thrills and for some time to come will be satisfied to have the
nation's judicial touring-car held strictly to the middle of the road and
not allowed to hug the cliff or skirt the precipice too closely."[23] The *New
Republic* agreed that Taft fit the temper of the times, even though it did
not regard this as a cause for joy, observing that the popular acclaim for
the Taft nomination demonstrated "the present temporary triumph of
reaction. Labor is cowed, liberalism is confused, and the country's
thinking generally is done in the storm-cellar."[24]

The dire predictions by liberals that Taft would have a baneful influence upon the Court were borne out before the year was ended when
Taft cast the deciding vote and wrote the majority opinion in *Truax v.
Corrigan*, a decision that invalidated an Arizona statute prohibiting
courts from enjoining peaceful picketing.[25] In dissent, Holmes bluntly
declared, "There is nothing that I more deprecate than the use of the
Fourteenth Amendment beyond the absolute compulsion of its words
to prevent the making of social experiments that an important part of
the community desires, in the insulated chambers afforded by the
several states, even though the experiments may seem futile or even
noxious to me and to those whose judgment I most respect."[26]

---

[22] "Chief Justice Taft," *Literary Digest*, July 16, 1921, p. 13. A group of Mississippi
lawyers unanimously adopted a resolution commending the appointment and lauding
Taft for "his high character, ripe experience, and eminent professional attainments." T.
G. Birchett to William Howard Taft, July 5, 1921 and accompanying resolution, *Taft
Papers*, Series 3, Reel 229. The *Houston Post* declared that Taft had "earned the genuine
affection of Southern people" through "his liberal treatment of the South during his
term as president" and that Taft had subsequently "on so many occasions shown himself
in sympathy with Southern ideals." In the *Post*'s opinion, only the appointment of an
eminent southern Democrat could have more pleased the South (*Houston Post*, July 2,
1921).

[23] "Chief Justice Taft."

[24] "Mr. Chief Justice Taft," p. 231.

[25] *Truax v. Corrigan*, 257 U.S. 312 (1921).

[26] Ibid., p. 344. Holmes also argued that the selection of the class of employers and
employees for special treatment was permissible since the law treated each class alike and
that the legislature could properly deny injunctive relief to the class without legalizing

Truax was especially frustrating to proponents of the rights of organized labor, who were still smarting over *Duplex Printing* and another decision in which the Court had reaffirmed that the Clayton Act offered only limited protection against injunctions.[27] The Socialist *Call* of New York complained that *Truax* was "one more decision placing property rights above human rights."[28] The *American Federationist* alleged that the Supreme Court was "moving with unusual speed toward the destruction of liberty" by seeking to broaden the use of the injunction and to destroy the right to picket.[29]

Since the injunction was one of the most potent of employers' weapons and was the traditional remedy by which courts had suppressed union organizations, these decisions seemed to represent an ominous threat to the viability of a union movement that was afflicted by a postwar depression in which unemployment had risen and union membership had declined. The decisions provided an impetus for the growing use of the injunction in labor disputes. William E. Forbath has estimated that 25 percent of all strikes were enjoined during the 1920s, compared with only 5 percent from 1914 through 1919. The proportion of secondary strikes and boycotts enjoined increased from 23 percent during the 1910s to 46 percent during the 1920s.[30]

In a message to the AFL's Executive Council in February 1922, Gompers warned that the "injunction menace is growing rapidly" because both federal and state courts were issuing injunctions more frequently and were "occupying new ground and constantly widening the scope of their orders so as to make them cover a very wide classification of acts." Gompers complained that "scarcely a day passes that does not witness the issuance of an injunction against workers somewhere in the country, either ordering them to do things which they have a lawful right not to do or ordering them not to do things which they have a lawful right to do."[31]

---

the conduct of which the employer had complained. "Legislation may begin where an evil begins," Holmes declared. "If, as many intelligent people believe, there is more danger that the injunction will be abused in labor cases than elsewhere I can feel no doubt of the power of the legislature to deny it in such cases" (ibid., p. 343).

[27] *American Steel Foundries v. Tri-City Central Trades Council*, 257 U.S. 184 (1921). In this case, the Court invalidated as overly broad an injunction which had prohibited picketing, but the Court reaffirmed *Duplex*'s application of the antitrust laws to the rights of organized labor.

[28] "When Picketing Is Illegal," *Literary Digest*, January 7, 1922, p. 14.

[29] Samuel Gompers, "The Supreme Court at It Again," *American Federationist*, January 1922, p. 44, 46.

[30] William E. Forbath, "The Shaping of the American Labor Movement," *Harvard Law Review* 102 (April 1989): 1252–53. Forbath points out that these proportions reflect in part the decreasing number of total strikes and the increasing number of large strikes.

[31] Samuel Gompers to Executive Council, American Federation of Labor, February 8,

Truax and *Duplex Printing* intensified the outcry among progressives and presaged the imminent national debate over the Court's jurisdiction. The *New Republic* alleged that *Truax* justified the worst fears about Taft "more quickly than the sturdiest skeptic was entitled to fear"[32] and that the decision was "fraught with more evil" than any the Court had rendered in a generation.[33] The journal declared that *Truax* offered a challenge "to all who find intolerable authoritarian rule by five men in contested fields of social policy," which failed to accommodate "the varying needs and purposes of each of the forty-eight states."[34] In another denunciation of the decision, the *New Republic*'s editors stated that they knew of "no problem in the institutional life of this country which calls for a more courageous searching and fundamental scrutiny than the nature of the power which the majority of the Court exercises in the Arizona case and the manner in which that power is wielded."[35] But the editors recommended no specific solution for the dilemma beyond urging that Congress and the public should take a more active role in the process of selecting and confirming federal judges.[36]

An editorial in *The Nation* sounded an even more ominous tone. Entitled "Does Mr. Taft Want Direct Action?" it observed that "once again, a matter of the gravest importance to the public good has been determined by the vote of one of the men who by the more or less fortuitous chance of human affairs happen to occupy the bench of the Supreme Court." Since the Court's decision was not subject to reversal by the legislature, *The Nation* warned, the decision might eventually engender "defiance of the courts."[37]

Continued judicial hostility to liberal legislation was further underscored by the decision of a federal district court in December 1921 to invalidate the child-labor law that Congress had enacted in the wake of *Hammer v. Dagenhart*. The court declared that Congress had improperly attempted "to regulate a purely internal affair of the states."[38]

1922, *American Federation of Labor Records: The Samuel Gompers Era* (Microfilm ed., 1979), Reel 106.

[32] "The Political Function of the Supreme Court," *New Republic*, January 25, 1922, p. 236.

[33] "Same Mr. Taft," p. 192.

[34] "The Political Function of the Supreme Court," *New Republic*, January 25, 1922, p. 236.

[35] "Same Mr. Taft," p. 192.

[36] "The Political Function of the Supreme Court," *New Republic*, January 25, 1922 pp. 237–38.

[37] *The Nation*, January 11, 1922, pp. 32–33. Taft professed to remain unperturbed by such criticism. He told one acquaintance that he did wish to see *The Nation*'s editorial and that he would regard Villard's approval of the *Truax* opinion "as evidence of its wrongful tendency." Taft confessed that "I entertain a contempt for Oswald Villard that it grieves me to have to express." Taft to Frederick L. Hoffman, January 11, 1922, *Taft Papers*, Series 3, Reel 238.

[38] *George v. Bailey*, 274 F. 639 (W.D. N.C. 1921); *Drexel Furniture Co. v. Bailey*, 276 F. 452 (W.D. N.C. 1921).

Although the trend toward judicial activism dismayed the Court's critics, few responsible people were willing to call for a frontal attack on the jurisdiction of the federal courts. Republican senator George W. Norris of Nebraska continued to stand out as a notable exception. During a debate in April 1922 on a bill to increase the number of federal judges, he reiterated his support for the abolition of the lower federal courts, although he acknowledged that this reform lacked political viability. Contending that the danger of local prejudice that had led to the creation of federal courts no longer existed, Norris argued that the maintenance of a double system of courts imposed an unnecessary burden on the taxpayers and that the expense of travel to distant federal courts had bankrupted many ordinary citizens. Norris further contended that the federal judges were "held aloof by their positions." In contrast to state judges, they were unfamiliar with local conditions, and their secure tenure caused them to "forget too often the toiling masses who are struggling for an existence."[39]

Five months after the *Truax* decision, the Court decided two more cases that provided the catalyst for attacks that would besiege the Court for the next two and a half years. Like *Truax*, both involved labor issues, and both confirmed the widespread fear that the Court was an inveterate defender of the economically mighty. In *Bailey v. Drexel Furniture*, decided on May 15, 1922, the Court affirmed the district court decision that invalidated the second child-labor law.[40] Three weeks later, in *United Mine Workers of America v. Coronado Coal Company*, the Court held that labor unions were liable for damages in suits for torts committed by unions during strikes.[41]

Bailey engendered widespread surprise since Congress had carefully drafted the second child-labor law to immunize it from constitutional objections. In contrast to the first law, enacted as an exercise of the commerce power, the second child-labor law was premised on Congress's taxing power. While the first law had prohibited the transportation in interstate commerce of goods from factories that utilized child labor, the second imposed heavy duties on goods introduced into interstate commerce by firms that employed children. Although the Court had determined in 1918 that Congress's regulation of child labor was beyond the scope of the commerce power, Congress believed that the Court would uphold a law that imposed a tax rather than a prohibition

[39] *Congressional Record*, 67th Cong., 2d sess. April 6, 1922, p. 5108. Norris was surprised that he received letters from several lawyers commending his proposal for the abolition of the lower federal courts. George W. Norris to Albert F. Coyle, July 20, 1923, *Norris Papers*, Box 31, Manuscript Division, Library of Congress.

[40] *Bailey v. Drexel Furniture*, 259 U.S. 20 (1922).

[41] *United Mine Workers of America v. Coronado Coal Co.*, 259 U.S. 344 (1922).

on the interstate movement of such goods. In various cases, the Court had broadly construed the taxing power and had refrained from considering whether the principal purpose of the tax was to regulate industry rather than raise revenue.

In *Bailey*, however, the court held that the statute invaded the reserved powers of the states in violation of the Tenth Amendment because the levies imposed for violation of the statute operated as a penalty rather than a true tax.[42] The Court distinguished other cases in which the Court had upheld allegedly excessive taxes on state bank notes, oleomargarine, state corporations, and narcotics.[43]

In his opinion for the Court, Taft emphasized that it was the Court's "high duty and function" to ensure that Congress did not regulate matters solely within the control of the states. The Court could not avoid that duty, Taft declared, even though it forced the Court to strike down legislation "designed to promote the highest good." Any other result would create a serious breach in "the ark of our covenant."[44] According to Taft, validation of the child-labor law would have had the most dire consequences for federalism since it would have permitted Congress to regulate any activity over which the states presently exercised exclusive jurisdiction.[45] The Court's opinion in *Bailey* was rendered more plausible because even Justices Brandeis and Holmes joined it.[46] Only Clarke dissented, and he did so without writing an opinion.[47]

[42] *Bailey*, 259 U.S., 38–39.

[43] Ibid., pp. 41–43.

[44] Ibid., p. 37.

[45] Ibid., p. 38. Taft echoed the same concerns about federalism in his private correspondence. He told the New York attorney Frederic Coudert, "Certainly the time had come to call a halt in recognizing the efforts of Congress to usurp state functions by the use of the name 'tax.'" In a letter to his brother Horace, Taft dismissed the child labor law as a "mere effort of good people, who wish children protected throughout the country, to compel certain States to conduct their police powers in accord with the views of the good people, as well as an effort by the manufacturers of Connecticut and Massachusetts to increase the cost of production of commodities in which they compete with the Southern States, by depriving them of child labor. Unfortunately, we can not strain the Constitution of the United States to meet the wishes of good people or yankee competitors." Taft to Frederic R. Coudert, May 17, 1922, *Taft Papers*, Series 3, Reel 242; Taft to Horace Taft, May 15, 1922, ibid.

[46] Clarke probably would have written a dissenting opinion if the bachelor justice had not been distracted by the illness of one of his sisters. Mason, *Taft*, p. 248. In a letter to Woodrow Wilson, Clarke declared that he could have made a very convincing argument based on the oleomargarine and narcotic drug cases (ibid., citing *McCray v. United States*, 195 U.S. 27 [1904], *United States v. Doremus*, 249 U.S. 86 [1919]). Taft, however, contended that "Clarke dissents, not because he knows why, but just on general principles. Clarke is a good fellow, but he has such prejudices that he decides quite a number of cases as he reads the title to the case" (Taft to Horace Taft, May 15, 1922, *Taft Papers*, Series 3, Reel 242).

[47] 259 U.S., p. 44.

Bailey was tolerantly received, even by many reformers, who conceded that the law was vulnerable under established principles of federalism. Felix Frankfurter pointed out that "humanity" is not the "test of constitutionality," even when Congress has sought "to redress monstrous wrongs." Declaring that "we must pay a price for federalism," Frankfurter averred that there "will be occasions, from time to time, when a good law will not be a 'just' law, because it will violate the bond of union."[48] Similarly, the St. Louis *Post-Dispatch* declared that the Court had upheld "a good political principle at the temporary expense of a good social cause."[49]

Opponents of child labor who supported *Bailey* predicted that the decision would provide an impetus for action by the states. Fabian Franklin predicted that public opinion would continue to force states to enact child-labor statutes.[50] The St. Louis *Post-Dispatch* predicted that states that had not yet abolished child labor would "acquire a new virility" now that the Court had determined that "they are dependent upon themselves and not upon a Federal overlord for their social and political advancement."[51]

Despite its widespread support, the *Bailey* decision did not lack critics. Arguing that the Court's attempts to distinguish the oleomargarine and bank-notes cases was unconvincing, the constitutional scholar Edward S. Corwin argued that tariffs were likewise regulatory in nature and that such regulation inhered in the sovereignty of the federal government.[52] Corwin contended that *Bailey* was "fatally at variance" with the broad vision of federal power enunciated by Chief Justice Marshall in *McCulloch v. Maryland*.[53] Corwin alleged that *Bailey* made the Court "the supervisor of the purposes for which Congress may exercise its Constitutional powers."[54] Similarly, *The Nation* argued that the apparent inconsistency between *Bailey* and the oleomargarine and narcotics decisions suggested that *Bailey* was motivated by political prejudices rather than logic. *The Nation* explained:

> The reconciliation of progress with the rigidity of a written constitution is a matter of politics and not of law. And political matters are decided, not by a strict attention to realities or even to logic, but by a complicated mixture of data, belief, pressure, and public opinion. By such consider-

[48] "Child Labor and the Court," *New Republic*, July 26, 1922, p. 248.
[49] Editorial, "Restoring the State Power," St. Louis *Post-Dispatch*, May 16, 1922, p. 16.
[50] Fabian Franklin, "Why the Supreme Court Rejected the Child-Labor Law," *The Independent*, June 10, 1922, p. 508.
[51] "Restoring State Power."
[52] "The Child Labor Decision," *New Republic*, July 12, 1922, p. 179.
[53] 17 U.S. (4 Wheat.) 316 (1819).
[54] "Child Labor Decision," p. 177.

ations are the justices of the Supreme Court subconsciously moved when deciding political questions. When they deem the matter sufficiently urgent they permit the framework of the Constitution to relax. When they think otherwise they call it "the ark of our covenant," as did the Chief Justice, and refuse to let it budge. Decisions like this on the child-labor law make the unsatisfactory nature of such a situation cry out to high Heaven.[55]

Although the *Bailey* decision attracted widespread discontent with the Court among the general public, the *Coronado* decision inspired deeper antagonism in labor circles. Labor journals from coast to coast denounced the decision with particular vehemence. *The Call* described the decision as the "most staggering blow ever aimed at the organized working class." In Chicago, the *New Majority* declared that it had laid "the legal groundwork for the attempted destruction of the unions and enslavement of the workers by practical and effective denial of their right to strike." And the Seattle *Union Record* predicted that the decision "will go a long way toward nullifying the fine work of the American Federation of Labor in the past few years in forwarding labor advances through orderly methods." Morris Hillquit, a leading labor lawyer, predicted that the ruling would hasten the day when the nation's six million union members would form a labor party. Others made similar forecasts. Samuel Gompers, who had long opposed the creation of a class-based party, made no such prediction, but he also made no attempt to conceal his bitterness about the decision. Reiterating the need to curtail the Court's jurisdiction, Gompers pointed out that "there is a latent power over and above the Supreme Court . . . and that is the power of Congress and the people of the United States."[56]

However, the decision was popular among many conservatives and moderates, who hailed it as an evenhanded application to labor of the principles already applicable to capital. *The Independent*, for example, observed that "labor monopoly is just as unlawful under the Sherman Act as is capitalistic monopoly, and on precisely the same ground— that it endangers the welfare and safety of the people of the United States. If you believe in *inequality* before the law, you will dislike this decision: if you believe in *equality*, we see no sound reason for not approving it."[57]

In recognition of the growing criticism of the Court and apparent

[55] "Child Labor and the Constitution," *The Nation*, May 31, 1922, p. 639.

[56] "Labor Unions Liable to Pay for Strike Damages," *Literary Digest*, June 17, 1922, p. 7.

[57] "Labor and the Supreme Court," *The Independent*, June 24, 1922, p. 540 (emphasis in original).

anticipation of the storm over the *Bailey* and *Coronado* decisions, Taft offered a rare public defense of the Court. Speaking in Philadelphia on May 2, 1922, Taft defended the doctrine of judicial review, the life tenure of federal judges, and the lower federal courts. After presenting a brief argument in support of the historical legitimacy of judicial review, Taft observed that the Court's exercise of the power of judicial review had inevitably embroiled the Court in political controversy and inspired criticism "by those unfavorably affected by the judgment." Pointing out that it "would be remarkable if the court could thus discharge its functions without encountering misconstruction of its motives or of its judicial attitude from time to time," Taft explained that the "questions decided are often close ones, and develop conscientious differences of view by the different members of the court, and lead to strong dissents by a minority." Although Taft observed that "criticism of judicial judgments is most wholesome," he warned that popular government would be "foredoomed to failure" if judges were forced "to follow popular clamor and the inconstancy of mob opinion."[58]

Although Taft's defense of the federal courts and judicial review was eloquent and able, his words could not hold back the tide of animosity against the Supreme Court and the lower federal judiciary. The period of most active hostility and criticism lay just ahead.

[58] "Chief Justice Taft's Address," pp. 333–35.

NINE

THE LA FOLLETTE PROPOSAL

The time has come when we must put the ax to the root of
this monstrous growth upon the body of our government.
The usurped power of the Federal courts must be taken
away at one stroke and the Federal judges must be made
responsive to the basic principle of this government.
*(Robert M. La Follette, addressing the AFL convention in
Cincinnati, June 14, 1922)*[1]

The Supreme Court . . . is dreadful enough: with Taft at
its head it has sunk to the lowest estate ever reached in its
history. But if it were ten times worse it would still be
better than government by undisguised and unmitigated
scoundrels. . . . a Congress free to work its wicked will
upon the Treasury and the people, absolutely unimpeded
by checks or balances, would be a curse almost too horrible
to contemplate. In ten years every citizen who was not a
Government spy and licensed blackmailer would be
bankrupt and in jail.
(H. L. Mencken, "The Supreme Court," Baltimore Evening
Sun, *November 19, 1923*, p. 17)

T HE COURT'S RULINGS in the *Bailey* and *Coronado*
cases were handed down when the progressive movement was
beginning to show signs of renewal. The prospects for a progressive revival seemed bright as the conservative Republicans who
dominated the Harding administration and Congress began to lose
public favor. Many Americans who had agreed with Harding's 1920
campaign slogan that the nation needed "not nostrums but normalcy"
were disappointed when Harding failed to restore a prewar normality
that never really existed, and they began to wish that he would dispense
some nostrums for the problems that beset postwar life. The principal
cause of public discontent was a recession that grew increasingly severe
during 1921 and 1922. In February 1922, railroad brotherhoods organized a convention in Chicago to form a coalition that would help to

---

[1] *Report of Proceedings of the Forty-Second Annual Convention of the American Federation of
Labor* (Washington, D.C.: Law Reporter, 1922), p. 241.

elect progressives to public offices and influence public policy. The delegates included union officials, members of the Non-Partisan League and other farm leaders, Socialists, and representatives of other organizations and viewpoints who were united primarily in their opposition to conservative Republicans. The convention established a permanent organization, the Conference for Progressive Political Action (CPPA), which set up branches in most states.[2]

The Supreme Court's rulings in the *Bailey* and *Coronado* cases a few months after the formation of the CPPA seemed to ensure that the Court would continue to be political issue. In addition to the grumbling of intellectual reformers and the unions, prominent progressives in Congress were becoming increasingly vocal in their criticisms of the Court. Until now, however, rage against the Court had been largely inchoate. Although the AFL had proposed various measures for abridging the Court's jurisdiction, those plans had received little attention or support outside labor circles and had not been embodied in a bill introduced in Congress. For the Court's critics to undertake any realistic effort to counteract the Court's baneful influence, they needed a specific plan, a prominent leader, congressional support, and the backing of a powerful lobby. Organized opposition to the Court, so long in developing, finally crystallized during the late spring of 1922 when Senator Robert M. La Follette and the AFL announced a plan to curb the Court's jurisdiction.

In the wake of the *Bailey* and *Coronado* decisions, the AFL had given court reform a prominent place on the agenda of the AFL's upcoming convention in Cincinnati. Appearing as the principal speaker at the convention's "child labor protest session" on Flag Day, La Follette unveiled a proposal for a constitutional amendment to permit Congress to reenact any federal statute that the Court had declared unconstitutional and to prohibit any federal judge of a lower federal court from nullifying an act of Congress.[3] La Follette announced his plan during the course of a rousing diatribe against the federal judiciary. The AFL members, still outraged over the Court's recent decisions, provided an ideal audience. After greeting La Follette with a torrent of applause, they stood on chairs, pounded tables, and shouted throughout his

[2] Kenneth C. MacKay, *The Progressive Movement of 1924* (New York: Columbia University Press, 1947), pp. 60–66.

[3] The full text of Senator La Follette's address was published in the *Congressional Record* and the report of the proceedings of the AFL convention. See 62 *Congressional Record*, 67th Cong., 2d sess., June 21, 1922, pp. 9076–82; *Report, AFL*, 1922, pp. 232–43. Although La Follette's proposal would presumably have permitted Congress to reenact the law by a majority vote, LaFollette eventually came to advocate the AFL's proposal to permit reenactment only by a two-thirds vote of both houses.

philippic. His proposal for a constitutional amendment provoked an uproar of approval.[4]

La Follette contended that the federal judiciary's lack of responsiveness to the popular will had created a crisis in government that could be remedied only by curtailing the jurisdiction of the courts. Borrowing the phrase that Gilbert E. Roe had given currency a decade earlier, La Follette alleged that the nation was ruled by "a judicial oligarchy" that had "wrested sovereignty from the people." La Follette averred that the Supreme Court, often by a bare majority of five, had "construed the Constitution to mean whatever suited their peculiar economic and political views." This "judicial usurpation," La Follette declared, "is now a supreme issue."

The Court's decision in the second child-labor case provided La Follette with a particularly pungent example of the usurpation he decried. Alleging that this decision had imperiled popular faith in democracy, La Follette explained that "it is a great task to overcome the loss of enthusiasm, the disappointment and discouragement on the part of those who have given years of life and service to a cause when it is defeated. The people are made to feel helpless and hopeless. Their Government appears to be an autocracy instead of a democracy."

La Follette disparaged the utility of piecemeal measures such as an amendment to prohibit child labor. "We cannot live," he declared, "under a system of government where we are forced to amend the Constitution every time we want to pass a progressive law." Accordingly, he announced that the time had come to face the "fundamental issue of judicial usurpation squarely with a determination to make an end of it once and for all."

Like so many revolutionaries and reformers throughout history who have appealed to first principles, La Follette denied that his plan was radical. He explained that it "merely aims to restore to the lawmaking branch of the Government the power which the Constitution in express terms confers upon it." The real revolutionaries, La Follette alleged, were the federal courts. Although he contended that the nation had created "a Frankenstein which must be destroyed or it will destroy us," La Follette denied that his plan would destroy the fundamental powers of the Supreme Court. He could not resist a barb at Taft, contending that the voters, who had repudiated Taft as president in 1912, would not have elected him to the chief justiceship.

La Follette's attacks on the judiciary were echoed by labor leaders at sessions of the AFL convention during the following week.[5] In endors-

---

[4] "La Follette Lashes Federal Judiciary," *New York Times*, June 15, 1922, p. 1.

[5] *Report, AFL*, 1922, pp. 260, 275, 291–96, 371–90, 391–98.

ing La Follette's proposed amendment, the AFL's Special Committee on Court Decisions declared that a "judicial oligarchy" threatened the nation's "very existence as a democracy."[6] Following the recommendation of the Special Committee on Court Decisions, the AFL convention voted by an overwhelming margin to endorse a constitutional amendment to permit Congress to reenact by a two-thirds vote of both houses any federal law the Supreme Court had declared unconstitutional. The AFL also endorsed amendments for the prohibition of child labor and the prohibition of any law or judicial determination denying workers the right to organize, deal collectively with employers, or engage in a strike or boycott. The AFL also called for repeal of the Sherman Antitrust Act and a constitutional amendment to make amendment of the Constitution easier, although the proposal offered no specifics.[7] True to the lifelong principles of Samuel Gompers, the convention reaffirmed the AFL's fundamental conservatism by refusing to consider the creation of a labor-based political party.[8]

La Follette's plan won few plaudits beyond the frenzied cheers of the AFL delegates. *The Nation*'s observation that LaFollette's proposal came "at a moment psychologically well timed for its favorable consideration"[9] was accurate only insofar as there could were few times when it would have received a better reception. George Norris offered a more perceptive analysis of the political winds when he privately observed on the day after La Follette's speech that members of Congress would "hesitate to start in on a fight that they know will take years, and for which the sentiment of the country is perhaps not yet ready." Norris affirmed his belief, however, that "the sentiment of the entire country is crystallizing with regard to some change in the Supreme Court."[10]

Since conservatives controlled the judiciary committees in both houses, it was virtually certain that La Follette's measure would not receive consideration by the current Congress. While La Follette perhaps foresaw that the upcoming election would return a more liberal Congress and that his own power would be enhanced in a Senate in which a reduced Republican majority needed progressive support, he was too seasoned a politician to entertain serious hopes that the election would so transform Congress that his plan could win the support

[6] Ibid., p. 371; "Labor Urges Veto on Supreme Court," *New York Times*, June 22, 1922, p. 19.

[7] "Labor Would Curb the Supreme Court," *New York Times*, June 22, 1922, p. 17; *Report, AFL*, 1922, pp. 372–73.

[8] "Labor Would Curb Supreme Court."

[9] Editorial, *The Nation*, June 28, 1922, p. 761.

[10] George W. Norris to A. B. Cox, June 15, 1922, *Norris Papers*, Box 31, Manuscript Division, Library of Congress.

of the requisite two-thirds of the members of both houses, even though he could have not have foreseen the extent of the conservatism that pervaded the middle and late 1920s. Moreover, La Follette could not even depend upon the support of leading progressives, who were characteristically divided on the issue of judicial reform. Although Hiram Johnson observed privately that the merits of La Follette's plan were at least "debatable" and that allegations that the plan would subvert liberties were "the veriest rot,"[11] Johnson was unwilling to endorse the plan or to work with La Follette and other progressives for the development of an alternative measure. As we shall see in chapter 10, Borah advocated a rival measure.

The probability that La Follette did not view his plan as a viable legislative measure is demonstrated by his failure to sponsor legislation in support of his proposal. Athough he sought advice from Walter Clark and Roe concerning the exact wording of the proposal, no technical question impeded La Follette from expeditiously introducing his legislation. Clark proposed a simple amendment providing that no decision invalidating a statute would take effect if the statute was reenacted by a two-thirds vote of both houses of Congress.[12] Roe drafted two similar measures.[13] Neither can La Follette's inaction be attributed to his preoccupation with other matters. Although La Follette fought a difficult renomination contest during 1922, traveled in Europe for three months during 1923, suffered from pneumonia during early 1924, and campaigned for the presidency during most of the remainder of 1924, this dynamic man surely could have found time to frame a bill on a matter he professed to believe was so important.

La Follette's failure to embody his plan in legislation suggests that his proposal, like so many other progressive proposals for court reform,

[11] Johnson to C. K. McClatchey, September 17, 1924, *Hiram Johnson Papers*, Bancroft Library, University of California at Berkeley, Part 3, Box 7.

[12] Walter Clark to Robert M. La Follette, January 8, 1924, *La Follette Family Papers*, Series B, Box 58, Manuscript Division, Library of Congress.

[13] Roe proposed to La Follette's son Robert, Jr., that the amendment should provide that any Supreme Court decision invalidating an act of Congress should not take effect unless Congress failed to enact the measure again within a prescribed period of time. Roe pointed out that La Follette's original plan would have permitted the decision to take effect and therefore would have allowed rights to arise under a decision that Congress might later nullify. As Roe explained, if "the time is left unlimited, property rights which were affected by the decision of the Supreme Court would be in hopeless confusion, for no one could tell when the Congress might decide to repass the law." Roe also proposed that the Supreme Court be required to certify its decision to the Senate and House. Roe presented two alternative drafts containing only a few dozen words. If La Follette had been serious about sponsoring a bill, he could easily have incorporated Roe's suggestions into a bill. Gilbert E. Roe to Robert M. La Follette, Jr., January 7, 1924, *La Follette Family Papers*, Series B, Box 101.

was largely tactical. As a champion of organized labor and a principal leader of what remained of the progressive movement, La Follette hardly could ignore the growing tendency of the Court to invalidate progressive legislation and make rulings that antagonized the unions. He therefore needed to respond to the growing dismay over the Court by denouncing the Court's recent decisions. There was at least some truth to what a Wisconsin banker knowledgeable about his state's politics told Taft about La Follette late in 1922: "Of course, he doesn't believe that Supreme Court decisions should be reversed by action of Congress. . . . He only talks that kind of stuff for political effect. It is popular with his followers." The banker correctly predicted that La Follette would not press Congress for court reform.[14]

It would be a mistake, however, to dismiss La Follette's proposal as no more than cynical posturing. Even though he did not see fit to introduce legislation to curb the Court's power, his advocacy of a constitutional amendment demonstrates that he recognized that the widespread public rage against the Court demanded that progressives translate their grievances against the Court into a specific proposal. If he had merely railed against the Court without offering a reform proposal, his rhetoric would have amounted to no more than impotent bombast, and he would have tacitly acquiesced to judicial review. Accordingly, La Follette needed to propound a remedy, even if he did not wish to take the time to sponsor an actual bill. He was genuinely outraged by the Court's hostility toward progressive measures, and he wished to remind the Court that it ultimately wielded its immense powers at the sufferance of the people. Since Theodore Roosevelt's attacks on the courts were widely credited with having encouraged greater judicial liberalism during the heyday of progressivism in the 1910s, La Follette probably hoped that his proposals for reform would have a salutary impact on the Court's decisions.

Moreover, La Follette may have hoped to provide a focus for criticism of the Court that would stimulate public discussion about the Court's role. He may also have intended that his proposal would provide a starting point for the formulation of legislation to restrict judicial review if public outrage over the Court's decisions intensified. There is no reason to suppose that La Follette had any genuine philosophical objections to such legislation. His lifelong dedication to the expansion of direct popular democracy and his longtime frustration over the conservatism of the judiciary suggests that he would have had no qualms about restricting the scope of judicial review.

[14] George W. Burton to William Howard Taft, December 14, 1922, *Taft Papers*, Reel 248, Library of Congress.

Like La Follette, the AFL did not formulate a practical program for enacting legislation that would have embodied its Court-curbing plan.[15] The AFL, like La Follette, may have recognized that its proposed constitutional amendment would face virtually insurmountable obstacles in Congress and the state legislatures.[16] By registering its profound discontent with the courts and stimulating widespread discussion about the role of the judiciary in government, the AFL reminded judges that there was a practical remedy for curtailing their power if they continued to render decisions that offended significant segments of public opinion. For now, this was all the AFL could hope to accomplish.

Although the AFL's active support for judicial reform was muted by pessimism about its practicability, the AFL's inaction may also have reflected the optimism that continued to lie at the heart of the labor movement, even during the bleak days of the early 1920s. Despite his public fulminations against the courts, Gompers continued privately to express confidence that labor was inexorably making permanent advances. Although Gompers acknowledged that he was impatient with the labor movement's progress, he believed that labor finally had "broken the back of industrial autocracy" and that "a return to the old days of absolute domination by the employer" was "forever impossible." While he warned that "every gain by the people in higher standards requires the greatest vigilance to retain," he declared that "even in the darkest hour I have never failed to be optimistic of the future."[17]

Even though La Follette never introduced a measure to permit Congress to override judicial nullification of legislation, a measure that embodied part of the plan advocated by La Follette and the AFL was introduced in the House by Republican James A. Frear of Wisconsin in

[15] Despite the convention's ringing endorsement of the proposal to permit Congress to override Supreme Court decisions, Gompers turned the proposal over to the AFL's attorneys for further study at an executive council meeting in November, stating that no action should be taken "until there is a fair interchange of views." AFL Executive Council Records/Minutes, November 20, 1922, pp. 7, 14, *American Federation of Labor Records: The Samuel Gompers Era* (microfilm ed., 1979), Reel 7.

[16] Matthew Woll, the vice president of the AFL, stated at the 1922 AFL convention that "to undertake a constitutional amendment under our present form and procedure for amending our Constitution will require years of struggle, years of propaganda, years of sincere and honest fight." Accordingly, Woll proposed that the AFL meanwhile secure the reintroduction of legislation to redress labor's grievances. Judicial nullification of such legislation, he predicted, would "hasten the day when there will be a real reform . . . in the proper relations of the various departments of government." *Report, AFL*, 1922, p. 395.

[17] Samuel Gompers to Thomas A. French, March 7, 1922, *AFL Records*, Reel 107; Gompers to W. E. Remington, September 26, 1922, ibid., Reel 106; Gompers to James J. Bingham, June 1, 1923, ibid., Reel 107.

February 1923. Frear proposed an amendment that would have permitted Congress to enact a law to set aside by a two-thirds vote any Supreme Court decision that invalidated a federal statute. Unlike La Follette's proposal, Frear's would also have permitted Congress to set aside any Supreme Court decision that invalidated a state court decision.[18]

The criticisms of the Court by La Follette and the AFL do not appear to have greatly perturbed Taft or other members of the Court. To Taft, the ire of Gompers and La Follette over the Court's recent decisions demonstrated that those decisions were "right and useful."[19] Taft observed that attacks on the Court were inevitable since the Court's power of judicial review "is a power which when exercised must be contrary to the views of the temporary majority."[20] A judge could not expect to decide anything of importance, especially in cases involving class conflict, without encountering such attacks.[21] Taft derived solace from the knowledge that "Chief Justice Marshall was very roundly abused from time to time"[22] and that attacks on the Court in the past had been unsuccessful.[23] Although Taft conceded that he could not predict the virulence of the present movement for a constitutional amendment, he nonetheless told his son Robert, "I have an abiding conviction that when the issue is squarely presented, the supporters of an amendment to the Constitution will find arrayed against them a conservative strength that in their blatant mouthings they do not realize the existence of."[24] Similarly, Taft wrote to the chief justice of Ontario in August: "I am abundantly satisfied that fundamental public opinion of the United States is very conservative and entirely opposed to radical and communistic notions. It needs a good deal to rouse the expression of such fundamental opinion, but it is a bulwark against any real injury to the Court and its jurisdiction by constitutional amendment."[25]

Taft also noted that recent acts of violence by union members in labor disputes and the apparent growth in militancy by union leaders were likely to detract from the movement to curb the Court's jurisdiction. "The daily vaporings of Gompers and the open declaration of war

[18] H. J. Res. 436, 67th Cong., 4th sess., 1923. Frear's resolution also granted Congress the power to enact a statute for the recall of federal judges and would have given Congress the power to impose supermajoritarian requirements upon Supreme Court decisions. See chapter 10.

[19] Taft to George Benjamin Edwards, August 23, 1922, *Taft Papers*, Series 3, Reel 244.

[20] Taft to William R. Meredith, August 19, 1922, *Taft Papers*, Series 3, Reel 244.

[21] Taft to J. H. Trowin, July 19, 1922, *Taft Papers*, Series 3, Reel 243.

[22] Ibid.

[23] Taft to William E. Meredith, August 19, 1922, *Taft Papers*, Series 3, Reel 244.

[24] Taft to Robert A. Taft, July 29, 1922, *Taft Papers*, Series 3, Reel 244.

[25] Taft to William R. Meredith, August 19, 1922, *Taft Papers*, Series 3, Reel 244.

by Debs are calculated to arouse all the conservative feeling that there is in the country," Taft declared.[26] Taft confided to Justice Day that La Follette and Gompers were more troubled by *Coronado* than by the child-labor decision, and he observed that they did not dare to test public feeling over *Coronado* by attempting to reverse it by legislation.[27]

Taft's confidence that La Follette's plan would not succeed does not mean that members of the Court were unaffected by the criticisms of the Court. Taft was too good a politician to ignore public opinion, and his frequent references to La Follette in his correspondence betray at least a modicum of anxiety over his criticism. The justices must have been aware that the movement to curb the Court's jurisdiction, while presenting no immediate threat, would gather momentum if the Court continued to render decisions that were unpopular with a large segment of the population. They recognized that dissatisfaction with the Court's decisions might grow if political winds began to shift to the left. They also recognized that a continuation of highly unpopular decisions could significantly erode the Court's institutional prestige and lay the foundation for a more potent movement against its prerogatives. With his keen appreciation of the Court's history and his profound respect for the role of the judiciary in American government, Taft must have been particularly cognizant of this danger and especially eager to avert it.

Even though no measure to permit Congress to reenact legislation that the Court had overturned received serious consideration by Congress, the proposal that La Follette and the AFL had endorsed inspired spirited discussions among lawyers, judges, academicians, politicians, polemicists, and the public that continued after the 1924 presidential election. Critics of the plan argued that it would completely transform American government since it would confer congressional supremacy over the coordinate branches of the federal government and the states. The plan would therefore destroy the system of checks and balances among the three federal branches and would annihilate federalism. Indeed, the plan would eradicate popular sovereignty itself since Congress could violate the Constitution with impunity.

Even the process of constitutional amendment would not afford any protection from this congressional tyranny; La Follette's plan would permit Congress to disregard any such amendment, just as it could capriciously interpret any other part of the Constitution. As the constitutional scholar Charles Warren declared in a 1923 *Saturday Evening Post* article, the La Follette amendment "would ipso facto constitute the

---

[26] Taft to Robert A. Taft, July 29, 1922, *Taft Papers*, Series 3, Reel 244.
[27] Taft to William R. Day, August 18, 1922, *Taft Papers*, Series 3, Reel 244.

entire Constitution, and all the rest of that document would be a scrap of paper, whenever the Congress chose so to regard it."[28] In another typical denunciation of the La Follette plan, Lewis H. Smith told the California Bar Association in 1923 that curtailment of judicial review would "remove the foundation stone of the Constitution, and cause the whole structure of our government to totter."[29] In addition to threatening civil liberties, the new order would also create political instability. As the New York *Evening Post* argued, the proposal would cause the Constitution to "fluctuate as tariff policies, taxation policies, and foreign policies have fluctuated."[30]

Critics of the La Follette plan argued that Congress was particularly ill suited to act as an arbiter of constitutional questions. As Chief Justice Robert von Moschzisker of the Supreme Court of Pennsylvania observed in 1924, members of Congress were heavily influenced by the political "expediencies of the moment."[31] Likewise, the attorney and constitutional scholar Thomas J. Norton argued that "[a] Congress dominated by agricultural and industrial groups cannot be expected to consider profoundly the Constitutional bearings of a bill" since much legislation was designed "to aid a 'bloc,' or to curry favor with a highly-organized minority which is powerful and often insolently dominating as a lobbyist." Norton and von Moschzisker also pointed out that few members of Congress were known for their erudition in constitutional issues.[32]

In response to these arguments, supporters of the plan pointed out that two-thirds of the members of Congress were lawyers and former judges and that many legislators were at least as competent and conscientious as federal and state judges. Former Democratic representative John J. Lentz of Ohio declared that members of Congress "are just as well qualified to think and vote on such questions of general welfare as the income tax or child slavery or other forms of slavery, as are the men who wear the gown and sit on the bench." Lentz pointed out that mem-

---

[28] Charles Warren, "Borah and La Follette and the Supreme Court of the U.S.," (National Security League, 1923), p. 15, repr. from *Saturday Evening Post*, October 13, 1923).

[29] Lewis H. Smith, "The Right of the Supreme Court to Declare Acts of Congress Unconstitutional," address, convention of the California Bar Association, Stockton, October 13, 1923 (San Francisco: Recorder Printing, 1923), in *Papers of Albert J. Beveridge*, Box 253, Manuscript Division, Library of Congress.

[30] "Is the Supreme Court Too Supreme?" *Literary Digest*, July 1, 1922.

[31] Robert von Moschzisker, "Judicial Review of Legislation by the Supreme Court," *Constitutional Review* 9 (1924): 80.

[32] Thomas J. Norton, "The Supreme Court's Five To Four Decisions," *American Bar Association Journal*, July 1923, p. 418; von Moschzisker, "Judicial Review," p. 80.

bers of Congress had better means of acquiring information on public questions and that they constituted "the safest exponent and barometer of the hopes, and ambitions and highest aims" of the people.[33]

In defending the Court, opponents of the La Follette plan exploited public distrust of Congress. Warnings that a Congress unchecked by the Court could erode civil liberties became the principal theme of many attacks on the LaFollette plan. In his *Saturday Evening Post* article, for example, Charles Warren listed twenty-five examples of tyrannical actions that he alleged Congress could undertake under La Follette's plan. Warren included violations of all of the guarantees of the Bill of Rights, together with violations of such other constitutional guarantees as the prohibitions against involuntary servitude, taking private property for public use without just compensation, and ex post facto laws. Warren concluded that "under Senator La Follette's proposal, no man, woman or child in the country would have a single right of any kind which Congress would be obliged to respect or of which Congress might not deprive him or her at any time."[34]

Critics of the La Follette proposal frequently pointed out that Congress and the state legislatures generally ranked low in public esteem and that the Supreme Court enjoyed broader popular respect, even though many of its individual decisions might be unpopular. As *The Outlook* observed, "It is a curious anomaly of popular government that the representative branch of government should so often have failed in reputation as compared with the judicial branch."[35] Similarly, the New York *World* contended that "the American people have had, as a rule, more confidence in their Supreme Court than in their average Congress."[36] As a writer in the Jesuit publication *America* observed in November 1924, "Any citizen whose life, liberty and property were in jeopardy would rather have his case tried before nine lawyer-judges whom he could look in the eye, than before that vast, miscellaneous, political throng at Congress, responding or not to the roll call as they saw fit."[37] Accordingly, Elihu Root advised Taft not to be worry about attacks on the Supreme Court because "its impregnable defense is that it furnishes the only agency through which limitations can be imposed

[33] John J. Lentz, Leaflet 15, La Follette-Wheeler National Committee, Publicity Bureau, *La Follette Family Papers*, Series B, Box 205.

[34] Warren, "Borah and La Follette," pp. 11–12.

[35] "The Attack of Senator La Follette on the Supreme Court," *The Outlook*, June 28, 1922, p. 368.

[36] "Supreme Court Too Supreme?" p. 21.

[37] Robert A. Shortall, "The Supreme Court and Congress," *America*, November 8, 1924, p. 95.

on the power of Congress and state legislatures, all of which are much more unpopular than the court."[38]

The Court's defenders insisted that the danger of congressional tyranny was more than hypothetical. "Congress would pass Acts it would not now attempt," argued a writer in the *North American Review*.[39] With characteristically deliberate hyperbole, H. L. Mencken warned that Congress would certainly exercise its new power to enact tyrannical laws, "for every new invasion of the citizen's rights means thousands of new jobs for loafers and criminals, and every new job for a loafer or a criminal makes some Congressman's seat that much more secure." Although Mencken understood why many people believed that "it would be hopeless to try to ram any feeling for common justice or even for common sense into a group of men so obviously prejudiced" as the Supreme Court justices, he warned that Court-curbing plans were "a great deal worse than the disease." Unlike most other critics of the plans, however, Mencken emphasized that the transfer of power to the legislature would pose a far more imminent threat to economic freedom than to personal liberty. "As things stand today," Mencken declared, "the rights of the citizen are nearly all gone, but his property, if he has any, remains safe." But "all security would vanish," Mencken warned, if the Court's jurisdiction was curbed.[40]

In seeking to appeal to a mass audience, most defenders of the Court's jurisdiction emphasized the Court's role as a protector of personal liberties rather than property. Although subsequent history may demonstrate the verity of the contention that the Supreme Court offers effective protection against infringement of personal liberties, the Court's history at the time La Follette introduced his proposal afforded scant support for the contention that the Court was an effective restraint against legislative encroachments upon personal liberties. Only rarely had the Court upheld individual liberties against federal intrusions. And cases in which the Supreme Court had upheld personal liberties against state intrusion were even rarer. Not until 1923, when the Court invalidated statutes that restricted the teaching of foreign languages, did the Court invoke the due process clause of the Fourteenth Amendment against infringement of personal liberties in a context not involving race or property. And it was not until 1925 that the Court began to apply to the states the specific guarantees contained in the Bill of Rights. Far from standing as a palladium of personal liber-

[38] Elihu Root, Jr., to Taft, November 5, 1923, *Taft Papers*, Series 3, Reel 258.

[39] Frank R. Savidge, "Five to Four Supreme Court Decisions," *North American Review*, April 1924, p. 471.

[40] H. L. Mencken, "The Supreme Court," *Evening Sun*, November 19, 1923, p. 17.

ties, the Court had consistently upheld restraints in cases involving free speech and freedom of the press.

Only in cases involving property rights had the Court consistently acted as a check upon legislative infringements of personal liberties. And in those cases the freedom that the Court had protected had nearly always been the freedom of corporations and the rich. As Mencken observed in 1923, "The general tendency of all the recent decisions of the sapient and puissant Nine is toward shoving the man down and lifting the dollar up." The government, Mencken pointed out, "may grab a poor yokel out in Iowa and send him to Siberia to serve in an army of bandits making war upon a nation with which the United States is at peace, but it may not pass a law shortening the 12-hour day of his brother in the steel mill."[41]

Critics of the Court argued that Congress would protect civil liberties and property because its members were answerable to the electorate. They pointed out that parliamentary supremacy had not prevented individual freedom from flourishing in Great Britain.[42] To many of the Court's critics, the British parliamentary system provided an attractive model of government. An article in *The Forum* in 1924 argued that British government was autocratic in form but democratic in substance, while the situation in the United States was the opposite.[43] Although recognizing that the adoption of a parliamentary system was not presently feasible, *The Nation* in 1924 declared that such a drastic change was desirable. In expressing its approval of the La Follette plan, *The Nation* stated that "until the voters insist upon the supremacy of their will, and that of their representatives, there can be no development of modern and progressive democracy in the United States." Disparaging the view that the supremacy of Congress would erode civil liberties, *The Nation* declared, "Congress will continue to reflect majority sentiment, as the court has often reflected minority prejudices."[44]

Opponents of the court plan argued that judicial review offered a more certain foundation for individual liberties than legislative supremacy. As one political scientist argued, "Life, liberty, and property may be as safe in England as in the United States, but they are safe only by the grace of the sufferance of the majority that happens at the

---

[41] Ibid.

[42] Charles Grove Haines, "Shall We Remake the Supreme Court? II. The Practice of Other Countries," *The Nation*, May 14, 1924, pp. 553–56.

[43] Jackson Harvey Ralston, "Shall We Curb the Supreme Court? I. Labor and Law," *The Forum*, May 1924, pp. 568–69.

[44] "Courts or People—Which Shall Rule?," *The Nation*, May 21, 1924, pp. 575–76.

moment to be in control of the government. . . . It is only tradition that restrains it, and tradition may not always prove a safe restraint."[45]

Aside from the argument that Congress would trample on personal liberties, the most widely circulated argument against the La Follette plan was its threat to federalism. The plan, its opponents contended, would permit and indeed encourage Congress to violate the rights of the states.[46] As Charles Warren argued, the La Follette proposal would sweep away "all the boundary lines" between national and state powers, and the states would "exist only at the sufferance of Congress."[47]

Although La Follette appears to have been at a loss to explain how his plan could protect the states from congressional tyranny,[48] its defenders argued that it would preserve federalism to the extent that it did not abridge the Court's power to adjudicate the constitutionality of state statutes. Arguing that the plan was really not so radical since it extended only to congressional enactments, they echoed the celebrated observation by Justice Holmes: "I do not think that the United States would come to an end if we [the Supreme Court] lost our power to declare an act of Congress void. I do think the Union would be imperiled if we could not make that declaration as to the laws of the several States."[49] But the protests of the plan's advocates often were drowned out by the cries of opponents, who willfully or negligently mischaracterized the plan or argued that the plan in practice would extend to state statutes.

Opponents also emphasized that the Court's power to nullify acts of Congress had been used very sparingly. Again and again, the Court's defenders explained that the Court throughout its entire history had invalidated only about fifty federal statutes.[50] Since the Court had adjudicated nearly thirty thousand cases and Congress had enacted nearly forty-five thousand statutes during the 135 years of the Republic,[51] the Court's record hardly justified portrayals of the Court as a

---

[45] James Frederick Peake, "Power of the Supreme Court to Nullify Acts of Congress," *Constitutional Review* 8 (April 1924): 96.

[46] See Ira Jewell Williams, "The Attack Upon the Supreme Court," *Constitutional Review* 7 (July 1923): 149.

[47] Warren, "Borah and La Follette," p. 10.

[48] Williams, "Attack Upon Supreme Court," p. 149.

[49] Ralston, "Shall We Curb?" p. 569, quoting Oliver Wendell Holmes, Jr., *Collected Legal Papers* (New York: Harcourt, Brace, 1920), pp. 295–96.

[50] Peake, "Power of Supreme Court," p. 94; Warren, "Borah and LaFollette," p. 4; von Moschzisher, "Judicial Review," p. 71.

[51] See, for example, William Marshall Bullitt, "The Supreme Court and Unconstitutional Legislation," *American Bar Association Journal*, June 1924, p. 419; George E. Sloan, "The Supreme Court and Five-to-Four Decisions," *Central Law Journal*, December 5, 1923, pp. 405–6.

veto-wielding tyrant. Similarly, they alleged that the record regarding state legislation was similarly benign. Of the hundreds of thousands of state and local statutes enacted since the dawn of the Republic, the Court had killed only about three hundred state statutes and a few dozen municipal ordinances.[52] Although the more honest defenders admitted that nullifications of congressional acts had become increasingly common—the Court invalidated only three federal statutes during the first 75 years of its existence and had voided more than twenty during the past two decades—they contended that the volume of legislation and the number of cases reaching the Court also had increased considerably during the past half century. Accordingly, the actual rate of nullification had not significantly increased.[53] Opponents of the La Follette plan and other measures to curb the Court's jurisdiction also pointed out that very few of the fifty statutes nullified by the Court conferred any significant right or privilege upon individual citizens and that most of the cases protected citizens from the power of the government.[54]

Although the principal critics of the La Follette plan were political conservatives who probably feared congressional interference with property rights more than they feared encroachment upon personal liberties, criticism of the plan also came from the Left. The Socialist *Call* of New York predicted that the Supreme Court's "reaction would be transferred to Congress itself" if the Court was shorn of its power. "And Congress," *The Call* added, "is reactionary enough; this would make it still more so."[55] Writing in *The Nation* shortly before La Follette announced his plan, Raymond Leslie Buell warned that such a plan would "remove a desirable check on the domination of Congress by special interests, whether they be Agricultural blocs, American Legions, or Anti-Saloon Leagues." Like more conservative critics of the La Follette plan, Buell also observed that such a plan "would deprive the country of the services of the one branch of our Government where learning and intellect are conspicuous."[56] Other progressives expressed concern that the plan would upset the balance of powers. Professor Edwin M. Bouchard of Yale Law School privately informed La Follette in 1924 that the "breadth of your proposal has frightened many lawyers, and I think perhaps justly so, for as between the competing claims of State and Federal government in the exercise of power, it

52 Von Moschzisker, "Judicial Review," p. 71; Bullitt, "Supreme Court," p. 419.
53 Von Moschzisker, "Judicial Review," p. 72.
54 Bullitt, "Supreme Court," pp. 419–25.
55 "Supreme Court Too Supreme?" p. 21.
56 Raymond Leslie Buell, "Reforming the Supreme Court," *The Nation*, June 14, 1922, p. 715.

is proper that an umpire determine the line between them and not leave this determination to one of the parties to the issue." Borchard urged LaFollette to limit his proposal to legislation nullified on due process grounds.[57]

Despite their antagonism toward the prevailing conservatism of the Court, the Court's critics made no effort to prevent the Court from becoming even more conservative when Harding nominated former Utah senator George Sutherland to succeed Justice Clarke, who resigned from the Court on September 4, 1922.[58] The Senate unanimously confirmed Sutherland on the following day.[59]

Clarke's resignation from the Court was a real loss to progressives and labor unions, even though Clarke had sided with the conservative majority in a number of key cases. With the exception of Brandeis and possibly Holmes, he was the Court's most liberal voice. Although Clarke was outnumbered by conservatives in many cases, his vote could have made a difference in close cases. Clarke, who lived until 1945, could also have spared the country and the Court much agony during the 1930s if he had remained on the Court to support New Deal legislation that was often invalidated in 5–4 votes. Like Brandeis and Holmes, Clarke could also have had influence by writing dissenting opinions and by persuading his colleagues to moderate the language of opinions in which he joined. He might have influenced the thinking of his colleagues, although Clarke's influence on such determined men as McReynolds and Taft would no doubt have been slight. Recognizing the significance of Clarke's departure, the New York *Globe* explained that Clarke "occupied a strategic place. He is a liberal among conservatives. . . . Without him during the Harding Administration the Court

[57] Edwin M. Borchard to LaFollette, October 20, 1924, *People's Legislative Service Papers*, Box 1, Manuscript Division, Library of Congress.

[58] Clarke's departure was a surprise since he had served but six years on the Court and was only sixty-five. Clarke had been increasingly unhappy on the Court. The death of his sister, a prominent physician in Youngstown, Ohio, had placed Clarke, a bachelor, in a melancholy frame of mind that made the Court seem particularly oppressive. Clarke found the Court's routine boring, and his inability to alter its conservative course frustrated him. The unremitting antagonism of the irrepressible McReynolds also was a source of misery to the sensitive Clarke, who lacked the will to fight bullies. Clarke finally decided that he could be more useful to his country by working for America's entry into the League of Nations and other causes of world peace. He also may have harbored presidential ambitions. John H. Clarke to Willis Van Devanter, March 7, 1922; July 13, 1922; Aug. 23, 1922; Aug. 31, 1922; *Willis Van Devanter Papers*, Box 32, Manuscript Division, Library of Congress. Taft to Warren G. Harding, August 31, 1922; Taft to Elihu Root, September 13, 1922; John H. Clarke to Taft, August 31, 1922; Taft to Elihu Root, September 13, 1922; *Taft Papers*, Series 3, Reel 245.

[59] 62 Cong. Rec., 67th Cong., 2d sess., Sept. 5, 1922, p. 2190; *New York Times*, September 6, 1922, p. 19.

will inevitably be more conservative at a time when liberalizing influences are sorely needed."[60]

Progressive protests against Sutherland's nomination were little more than perfunctory, and there was no serious effort to block Sutherland's confirmation. Much of this acquiescence may be attributed to the progressives' recognition that Harding could hardly be expected to appoint a liberal to the Court and that Sutherland's record as a conservative was not noxious. Moreover, the Court's critics recognized that conservative strength in the Senate would make opposition futile. Progressives may have preferred to bide their time until after the upcoming election in which they expected to gain strength that might enable them to mount a viable fight against the nominees Harding would name if Day and Holmes retired. The distraction of those elections also discouraged progressives from opposing the Sutherland nomination. La Follette, who might have been expected to lead the opposition to the nomination, was engaged in the final stage of a bitter primary campaign when Sutherland was nominated. Voting in Wisconsin was on September 5, the same day the Senate received and confirmed Sutherland's nomination.[61]

Although many progressives failed to grasp the full significance of Clarke's departure, the perspicacious Taft was well aware that the replacement of Clarke with Sutherland was a boon to conservatism. Taft remarked privately that "Sutherland is a safe and good appointment,"[62] and he expressed satisfaction that Sutherland had "a very different view of the Constitution and its limitations from that which Clarke entertained." Although Taft personally admired Clarke, Taft believed that Clarke was unduly influenced by his political predilections.[63]

Although Sutherland bolstered the dominance of the Court's conservative majority, La Follette's triumph in the Wisconsin primary seemed to strengthen the position of the Court's opponents and to augur progressive victories in the November election. An attempt by the Republican National Committee to defeat the GOP maverick ended in embarrassing failure when La Follette captured 72 percent of the vote in the primary and went on to receive 83 percent in the election.[64]

[60] *Literary Digest*, September 16, 1922, p. 15. *The Nation*, however, contended that Clarke's departure did not alter the complexion of the Court because Sutherland was no more conservative than Clarke (September 20, 1922, p. 267).

[61] *New York Times*, September 6, 1922, p. 19.

[62] Taft to George W. Wickersham, September 18, 1922, *Taft Papers*, Series 3, Reel 245.

[63] Ibid.; Taft to Clarence H. Kelsey, September 12, 1922, *Taft Papers*, Series 3, Reel 245.

[64] David P. Thelen, *Robert La Follette and the Insurgent Spirit* (Boston: Little, Brown,

The size of La Follette's landslide in the primary and the virtual certainty of a similarly lopsided result in the general election triggered considerable speculation about La Follette's future role in national politics. Since voters were expected to pare the Republican majority in Congress, many political observers pointed out that La Follette might lead a group of progressives who could hold the balance of power in the next Congress. La Follette's victory in the primary also invigorated speculation that La Follette might run for president in 1924 as an independent.[65] La Follette's victory distressed Taft, who predicted that it would embolden foes of constitutionally protected property rights and persons who "are radically hostile to the existence of the Supreme Court."[66] Taft told his brother Charles that La Follette's victory and recent attacks on the Court by labor unions presaged "an active agitation against the Court, and an effort to reduce its functions so as to prevent its nullification of statutes enacted by Congress. This will probably last a decade."[67]

However, Taft continued to believe that attacks on the courts were destined to fail. He accurately observed that "one of the safeguards of the existing status is the personal ambition of the various would-be leaders of radicalism. La Follette must be first or he will not play at all. Johnson has the same feeling, and hates La Follette with a perfect hatred; and Borah is disgusted with both." Taft also perceived that the Left was hopelessly divided by fundamental differences between its industrial and agrarian components: "The farmers really have no use for the labor unions, and the labor unions no use for the farmers." Taft believed that conservative Democrats would oppose any abridgement of the Court's power, and he hoped that the defenders of the Court could "isolate the real Progressive radicals, and when they are isolated, I am quite sure their number will not seem so formidable." Taft believed that "the sooner the fight comes, the better," for it would jolt conservatives into more vigorous defenses of the Court.[68]

Taft's only real worry was that a radical Congress "might take steps either to abolish or to practically destroy much of the useful jurisdiction of the inferior Federal courts." Although he believed that such a Congress "would frighten the country into a reaction, which would teach a permanent lesson," justice would suffer while the radicals held sway. Taft concluded that meanwhile "there is nothing for the Court to

---

1976), p. 171; Belle Case La Follette and Fola La Follette, *Robert M. La Follette* (New York: Macmillan, 1953), pp. 1055–64.

[65] "La Follette for President?," *Literary Digest*, September 23, 1922, pp. 11–12.

[66] Taft to George Sutherland, September 10, 1922, *Taft Papers*, Series 3, Reel 245.

[67] Taft to Charles P. Taft, September 10, 1922, *Taft Papers*, Series 3, Reel 245.

[68] Ibid.

do but to go on about its business, exercise the jurisdiction it has, and not be frightened because of threats against its existence."[69]

The victory of La Follette that Taft believed would embolden radicals was only one of many progressive triumphs in the primary elections during 1922. Borah declared that the primaries represented "a political revolution" and predicted that a formidable third-party movement would arise in 1924 unless there was "a complete change in the program of the Republican Party." Gompers claimed that the primaries had "stunned the reactionists so effectively as to make certain that the next Congress will be unable to enact any piece of important reactionary legislation."[70]

The general election in 1922 suggested a progressive revival. In addition to reelecting La Follette, voters elected Smith W. Brookhart in Iowa and Lynn J. Frazier in North Dakota and reelected Johnson in California and Charles L. McNary in Oregon. One of the most impressive victories for insurgency occurred in Minnesota, where the voters elected Henrik Shipstead, the Farmer-Labor candidate. Although progressives still held only a small number of seats in Congress, their strength exceeded their numbers since they held the balance of power in Congress in the wake of shrunken Republican majorities.[71]

In contrast to the gloom with which Taft received the news of La Follette's triumph in September, Taft was not unduly discouraged by the results of the November election. On New Year's Day 1923, Taft observed that the "late election was very misleading. It was affected by so many currents that it is altogether unfair to attribute it to a permanent tendency of our people to anything Bolshevistic." Taft expressed confidence that "the forces in this country looking to preserve our present civilization under our present Constitution may be counted on to cooperate to resist the Bolshevistic tendency."[72]

Recognizing the difficulty of curbing judicial power, critics of the courts continued to try to influence the judicial selection process. Writ-

[69] Taft to Sutherland, September 10, 1922.

[70] William English Walling, "Labor's Attitude Toward a Third Party," *Current History*, October 1924, p. 35. Gompers warned "reactionary politicians" that labor "has a militant progressive organization in every State in the Union."

[71] The new Senate had 51 Republicans, 43 Democrats, and 2 independents, compared with 59 Republicans and 37 Democrats in the previous Congress. The House elected in 1922 contained 225 Republicans, 207 Democrats, and 3 independents, a loss of more than 75 seats for the Republicans.

[72] Taft to Mrs. Bellamy Storer, January 1, 1923, *Taft Papers*, Series 3, Reel 249. Taft attributed the decline in Republican fortunes to bad farming conditions, continued high taxes, disappointment over the defeat of a soldiers' bonus measure, the recession, and "a general discontent because the Republicans had not made everything perfect" (William Howard Taft to A. I. Vorya, November 13, 1922, *Taft Papers.*, Series 3, Reel 247).

ing in *America* in May 1924, a Roman Catholic priest argued that the remedy for declining public confidence in judicial decisions was "to select judges who have manifested correct principles and views on the great social questions."[73] Recognition of the importance of the judicial selection process was reflected in the controversy that arose late in 1923 when President Harding nominated Pierce Butler, a conservative corporation attorney, to replace William R. Day on the Court. Butler's appointment was a victory for Taft, who had worked relentlessly to secure his appointment.[74] Taft explained to Max Pam, a Chicago lawyer, that Butler "is a man who could pull his weight into the boat. He is young, strong, clear-headed, courageous, and he has come up from the bottom by his own exertions."[75] For Taft, however, Butler's most appealing characteristic was the reliability of his fealty to the constitutional principles espoused by Taft.

The broad center of the political spectrum reacted favorably to Butler's nomination, announced on November 23.[76] On the left and the right, however, Butler's nomination was unpopular and it inspired more public and senatorial opposition than any nomination since that of Brandeis. Although Butler's Roman Catholicism stirred resentment among nativists[77] and the Ku Klux Klan was reported to have flooded the Senate with mail against Butler,[78] right-wing opposition never galvanized.

Opposition by trade unionists and progressives was a more serious threat.[79] Butler's record as an attorney for railroads and utilities made him an obvious target of progressive senators and union leaders, who correctly perceived that Butler would aggravate rather than mitigate the Court's conservative tendencies. As Taft wrote to Butler on Decem-

[73] Philip H. Burkett, "Five to Four Decisions," *America*, May 31, 1924, p. 170.

[74] Taft to Elihu Root, Nov. 19, 1922, *Taft Papers*, Series 3, Reel 247.

[75] Taft to Max Pam, October 28, 1922, *Taft Papers*, Series 3, Reel 246.

[76] David J. Danelski, *A Supreme Court Justice Is Appointed* (New York: Random House, 1964), repr. (Westport, Conn.: Greenwood Press, 1980), pp. 90–92; "Another Supreme Court Shift," *Literary Digest*, December 9, 1922, p. 15; *New York Times*, November 25, 1922, p. 12.

[77] See e.g., M. B. Grace to Warren Harding, December 9, 1922; W. D. Jones to Warren Harding, December 10, 1922; C. L. Case, secretary, Women's Auxiliary of the Ohio State Good Government Association, to Warren Harding, November 25, 1922; E. E. Cunningham to Warren Harding, November 15, 1922; NA, General Records of Department of Justice, Record Group 60, Series 348 Box 1.

[78] Danelski, *Supreme Court Justice*, p. 92.

[79] "For Associate Justice," *New York Times*, November 25, 1922, p. 12. See e.g., Resolution of International Brotherhood of Electrical Workers, Local Union No. 134, December 16, 1922, NA, General Records of Department of Justice, Record Group 60, Series 348, Box 1.

ber 12, "You have the misfortune of being appointed to the Bench at a time when there is a radical flare-back, and a movement to attack the Supreme Court and to attack Harding." Taft warned Butler that the attack would be led by La Follette, "a master of dirty publicity," and Norris, "an ugly kind of individual, at odds with the world generally." But although Taft told Butler that the progressives might "make a great noise" that would delay Butler's confirmation, he assured Butler that "your nomination has been received with such wide approval that I think their effort will recoil on themselves."[80]

Butler's opponents denounced the nominee as a "big business fanatic," a "reactionary," and an "enemy of the common man."[81] In the opinion of Indiana University law professor Hugh E. Willis, Butler was "unfitted for judicial duties by the very characteristics by which he has won success as a trial lawyer."[82] By a vote of 12 to 6, the Socialist-dominated Minneapolis City Council approved a resolution denouncing the appointment as "a crime against the people."[83] The *New Republic*, one of the most vocal opponents of the nomination, declared that Harding's appointment of a "reactionary of the most pronounced type" was "almost astonishing" since it came "on the heels of a most vigorous protest by the people against the reactionary policies of the present administration." To add insult to injury, the administration had chosen a nominee from a state that had registered an outstanding progressive victory in the midterm elections by electing Shipstead to the Senate.[84]

As Taft had predicted, La Follette and Norris were the principal opponents of the nomination. Their suspicions that Butler was a rigid reactionary who lacked judicial temperament grew as they began to receive reports concerning Butler's performance as a member of the Minnesota Board of Regents. A professor at the University of Minnesota alleged that Butler had bullied the administration, and four former professors alleged that Butler was responsible for their wrongful dismissal or demotion. The most serious allegations were made by John Schaper, former chairman of the political science department, who had been summarily dismissed in 1917 for his alleged pro-German views. Butler's record as a regent helped to crystallize opposi-

[80] Taft to Pierce Butler, December 5, 1922, December 12, 1922, *Taft Papers*, Series 3, Reel 248.

[81] Danelski, *Supreme Court Justice*, pp. 92–93.

[82] Hugh E. Willis to Warren G. Harding, Dec. 12, 1922, NA, General Records of Department of Justice, Record Group 60, Series 348, Box 1.

[83] *New York Times*, November 25, 1923, p. 13.

[84] "A Reactionary for the Supreme Bench," *New Republic*, December 13, 1922, pp. 65–66.

tion to Butler and convince progressives that the nomination was worth a fight, even though defeat was likely.[85]

Although La Follette succeeded in preventing a vote on the nomination during the special session of Congress that adjourned on December 4,[86] progressives mounted an attack on the nomination during the first days of the regular session that met later in the month. Leading the opposition to the nomination, Senator-elect Shipstead averred that Butler's decisions on the Court would "necessarily and inevitably be influenced by his past interests and associations" and that attempts to place Butler on the Court would "arouse bitter resentment and criticism."[87] Although the Judiciary Committee conducted hearings that substantially confirmed Butler's intense solicitude for corporations and his authoritarian record as a regent, a majority seem never to have wavered in firm support for Butler. Indeed, Butler's views probably appealed to most of the members of the committee. Leaving nothing to chance, Taft attempted to ensure that Butler's supporters on the Judiciary Committee would be present on December 18 to recommend his nomination.[88] With Borah, Norris, and two other members absent, the committee unanimously recommended Butler's confirmation.[89]

Although the fight against Butler's confirmation seemed increasingly hopeless during mid-December, opponents continued to attack Butler. Gompers wryly declared that Butler's nomination was "one of the longest steps yet taken by President Harding back to what he calls 'normalcy,'" since Butler "belongs in the class called reactionary." Like Shipstead, Gompers argued that Butler's close ties to the railroads would inevitably influence Butler's opinions on the Court.[90] The *New Republic* declared on the eve of the Senate's vote that "he is the kind of man who would assuredly use a warped or doubtful interpretation of a phrase in the Constitution to prevent needed experiments in economics and government."[91]

When the Senate met in executive session to consider the nomination on December 21, La Follette spoke for an hour in a futile attempt

[85] Butler's record as a regent enraged the *New Republic*, which fumed that Butler behaved during the war "in the manner of a blind and bumptious bigot." "Pierce Butler and the Rule of Reason" (December 20, 1922, p. 82).

[86] Danelski, *Supreme Court Justice*, p. 106.

[87] A copy of Shipstead's letter to the Committee on the Judiciary is found in *Papers of George W. Norris*, Box 41, Library of Congress. See also "Shipstead Attacks Butler on 4 Points," *New York Times*, December 9, 1922, p. 5.

[88] Taft to Pierce Butler, December 17, 1922, *Taft Papers*, Series 3, Reel 248.

[89] "Favors Butler Nomination," *New York Times*, December 19, 1922, p. 14.

[90] "Why Pierce Butler?" *American Federationist*, January 1923, pp. 76–77; "Butler 'Reactionary,' Gompers Declares," *New York Times*, December 18, 1922, p. 4.

[91] "Pierce Butler and the Rule of Reason," *New Republic*, December 20, 1922, p. 82.

to persuade his colleagues to remand the nomination to the Judiciary Committee. Citing Butler's record as a railroad attorney, he argued that Butler's nomination had further shaken public confidence in the Court and contributed to the growing perception that the Court was a citadel of privilege rather than a temple of justice. La Follette also argued that Butler's a economic biases and his actions as a regent demonstrated that he lacked a judicial temperament.[92]

After La Follette's motion to send the nomination back to committee was defeated by a vote of 63 to 7, the Senate voted 61 to 8 to confirm Butler. La Follette, Norris, and Peter Norbeck of South Dakota were the only progressives who opposed the nomination, although Brookhart announced his pair with New York's Republican senator William M. Calder. Hiram Johnson, who had so vociferously opposed Taft's nomination, voted in favor of Butler. Borah, who had raised no protest against the nomination, was not present. The other dissenters, five southern Democrats, appear to have succumbed to Ku Klux Klan influence or anti-Catholicism.[93]

Taft believed that Butler's confirmation reproached the Court's critics and revealed "the weakness of La Follette and his gang."[94] Opponents of the appointment, however, continued to insist that Butler's presence on the bench would hasten the erosion of public confidence in the Court. In a column in *La Follette's Magazine*, La Follette declared, "The selection of attorneys of the Pierce Butler type will do much to confirm and intensify the conviction in the public mind that our federal courts are becoming more and more the bulwark of the special interests." La Follette argued that disrespect for the courts extended far beyond demagogues and "has become the settled conviction of millions of worthy citizens of the Republic."[95]

Similarly, The *New Republic* warned that Harding's nomination of Butler was "an extraordinarily stupid mistake" because it jeopardized public faith in the Court, which was "peculiarly dependent for its sufficient functioning upon general popular confidence." The appointment of other reactionaries, the editors warned, would provide an excuse for the disaffected classes to make "the very appeal to force

[92] Danelski, *Supreme Court Justice.*, pp. 137–38.

[93] 64 *Congressional Record*, 67th Cong., 4th sess., December 21, 1922 p. 813; John P. Frank, "The Appointment of Supreme Court Justices, III," *University of Wisconsin Law Review* 1941 (July 1941): 487; see also Danelski, *Supreme Court Justice*, p. 165.

[94] Taft to Anson B. Jackson, Jr., December 26, 1922, *Taft Papers*, Series 3, Reel 248.

[95] *La Follette's Magazine*, January 1923, p. 1. Since La Follette often published his Senate speeches as editorials in his magazine, the editorial probably was based upon La Follette's Senate speech in the closed session of December 21, 1922. See Danelski, *Supreme Court Justice*, pp. 136–39.

which all sensible and humane people are most anxious to avoid." The *New Republic* explained that it opposed Butler's nomination "not because we dislike and disbelieve in the preservation by the Supreme Court of its existing political functions but because we believe in them and would much prefer to see them continued."[96]

Ten days after Butler's confirmation, a new Court vacancy occurred when the ailing Pitney resigned. Although Taft may have discouraged Harding from appointing various nominees, he failed to persuade him to nominate his first choices for the seat[97] and finally threw his political weight behind U.S. district judge Edward T. Sanford. The idea of appointing Sanford, which originated with Attorney General Harry M. Daugherty,[98] appealed to Taft because he believed that the appointment of a federal district judge would raise the prestige of the lower federal courts.[99] Taft's support of Sanford was widely credited with persuading Harding to nominate Sanford on January 24, 1923.[100]

Although Sanford was conservative, his reputation as an urbane and open-minded man helped to make him palatable to progressives. In contrast to Butler, Sanford had no notable ties to large corporations, and his record as a judge did not reveal any antilabor or corporate bias. A Harvard Law School graduate, Sanford had worked as a general practitioner, law lecturer, and assistant U.S. attorney general prior to his elevation to the federal bench. A Tennessee editor reported that Sanford lacked "the dogmatism of a Butler. He is not a professional patrioteer, 'hundred per center,' nor labor-baiter."[101] Even *The Nation* hailed Sanford's appointment, contending that Harding's selection of the Tennessean was "the best of his several judicial appointments" since Sanford was reputed to be a man of moderate instincts, had not served as a corporation attorney, and was not a friend of the president's.[102]

After the Senate Judiciary Committee favorably reported the nomination by a unanimous vote, the Senate confirmed the nomination without opposition on January 29, four days after Harding sent Sanford's name to the Senate.[103]

---

[96] "Pierce Butler and Rule of Reason," pp 81–83.

[97] Taft to Warren G. Harding, December 4, 1922, *Taft Papers*, Series 3, Reel 248; Taft to Henry W. Taft, January 16, 1923, Series 3, Reel 249; Taft to Horace Taft, January 26, 1923, Series 3, Reel 250.

[98] Taft to Warren G. Harding, December 13, 1922, *Taft Papers*, Series 3, Reel 248; Taft to Charles C. Burlingham, January 16, 1923, *Taft Papers*, Series 3, Reel 249.

[99] Taft to Henry W. Taft, January 16, 1923, *Taft Papers*, Series 3, Reel 249.

[100] "Nominates Sanford for Supreme Bench," *New York Times*, January 25, 1923, p. 5.

[101] George F. Milton, Jr., "Sanford—Neither Radical nor Reactionary," *The Outlook*, February 14, 1923, p. 299.

[102] *The Nation*, February 7, 1923, p. 137.

[103] 64 *Congressional Record*, 67th Cong., 4th sess., January 29, 1923, p. 2677.

Satisfied with the soundness of the two new justices, Taft remained optimistic that the progressives lacked the power to curb the Court. Their thin ranks in the new Congress, he believed, would enable them to do no more than to block or modify legislation.[104] "The truth is that the so-called radicals are vastly more noisy than they are important," Taft observed on New Year's Day, 1923.[105] Since the progressive leaders could not agree upon what they wanted and they all had presidential ambitions, any constructive plan was likely to dissolve into "innocuous confusion."[106] Taft also predicted that optimism inspired by the election would "lead them into extravagances, which will cause a further reaction,"[107] and he was encouraged that court reform was absent from the legislative agenda that progressives prepared following the election.[108]

Although Taft accurately assessed the bleak prospects of the anti-Court measures, he may not have entirely foreseen that the progressive outcry against the Court would intensify before it began to subside. During the coming year, the Court was subjected to a more intense protest against its powers than had occurred for a century, and vituperation against the Court was more widespread than at any time in the Court's history.

---

[104] Taft to Anson B. Jackson, December 5, 1922, *Taft Papers*, Series 3, Reel 248.
[105] Taft to Mrs. Bellamy Storer, January 1, 1923, *Taft Papers*, Series 3, Reel 249.
[106] Taft to Helen Manning, November 26, 1922, *Taft Papers*, Series 3, Reel 247.
[107] Taft to George W. Burton, November 22, 1922, *Taft Papers*, Series 3, Reel 247.
[108] Taft to George W. Burton, December 13, 1922, *Taft Papers*, Series 3, Reel 248.

TEN

THE BORAH PROPOSAL

*Five to four decisions have caused more criticism of the
our Supreme Court than any other one thing.
(William E. Borah, 1923)[1]*

THE DEBATE over judicial power grew more intense early in 1923 when Senator Borah proposed legislation to require the concurrence of at least seven members of the Court in any decision that invalidated an act of Congress.[2] Borah's proposal of a remedy that rivaled LaFollette's plan was characteristic of the disunity that hobbled progressive efforts to restrain judicial power. Like other Court-curbing measures, Borah's proposal lacked political viability and never received serious consideration, although it stimulated much discussion.

Borah's proposal also lacked originality. Almost exactly one century earlier, critics of the Marshall Court had introduced analogous measures,[3] and the House had approved a similar proposal in 1868.[4] The concept had been revived by a number of court critics during the two decades before Borah proposed his measure. As we have seen, William Trickett advocated such a measure in 1906. In 1911, Senator Jonathan Bourne, Jr. introduced a bill that would have required unanimity in any Supreme Court decision involving the constitutionality of federal or state legislation,[5] and Carl Hayden of Arizona had embodied a

[1] Borah to W. P. Hamilton, February 8, 1923, *Borah Papers*, Box 144, Manuscript Division, Library of Congress.

[2] See S. 4483, 67th Cong., 4th sess. 1923, 64 *Congressional Record*, 67th Cong., 4th sess., February 5, 1923, p. 3004; *New York Times*, February 6, 1923, p. 4.

[3] Senator Richard M. Johnson of Kentucky had sponsored a bill to require unanimity in decisions invalidating state or federal statutes, and Senator Martin Van Buren of New York and other critics of the Court had advocated requiring the concurrence of at least five of the seven justices in decisions invalidating state laws. At least three similar measures were proposed in the House. Charles Warren, *The Supreme Court in United States History*, vol. 1, *1789–1835* (Boston: Little, Brown, 1926); pp. 663–67; Maurice S. Culp, "A Survey of Proposals to Limit or Deny the Power of Judicial Review by the Supreme Court of the United States," *Indiana Law Journal* 7 (March 1929): 392–95.

[4] The bill, which provided that the Supreme Court could not invalidate any part of any federal law without the concurrence of two-thirds of the justices, was defeated by the Senate (S. 163, *Congressional Globe*, 40th Cong., 2d sess., 1868, pp. 477–89).

[5] S. 3222, 62nd Cong., 1st sess., 1911. For Bourne's defense of the proposal, see 47 *Congressional Record*, 62nd Cong., 1st sess., August 14, 1911, pp. 3877–78.

supermajoritarian proposal in an amendment introduced in the House on three occasions between 1917 and 1921.[6] As recently as 1922, Democratic representative John J. McSwain of South Carolina had introduced a similar measure.[7] Borah's bill attracted more far attention than these other proposals since it was introduced when the Court was under widespread attack, the progressives occupied a strategic position in Congress, and Borah was widely viewed as presidential timber. Borah's proposal therefore significantly intensified public debate over the role of the Supreme Court.

Borah's proposal was more moderate than La Follette's plan since it did not permit Congress to override the Court's nullification of a statute. The plan suffered, however, from the same myopic expediency that characterized the La Follette plan and most other proposals to circumscribe the powers of the Court. Designed to ensure the survival of progressive legislation, it would also have protected reactionary legislation. Like the plans of La Follette and others, it failed to envision a time when the Court might be more progressive than Congress. Moreover, like La Follette's plan, Borah's proposal would not necessarily have offered much immediate assistance to progressives. Just as a heavily conservative Congress was unlikely to muster a two-thirds vote to overturn a Court decision, more than two members of the Court could not be expected often to support the kind of legislation that Borah's measure was designed to protect. With the departure of Clarke from the Court in 1922, Brandeis and Holmes were the only members who were likely to look favorably on the constitutionality of important progressive legislation. And, as the Court's decision in *Bailey* had demonstrated, progressives could not always depend upon the votes of Brandeis and Holmes.

The contrast between the relative radicalism of La Follette's plan and the relative moderation of Borah's proposal reflected the political differences between Borah and La Follette. Despite many points of agreement between these two progressive Republican senators, Borah's views on most issues were generally less extreme than La Follette's. Borah also maintained much closer ties with mainstream party organizations and leaders. Moreover, as a Borah biographer has pointed out,

---

[6] H. J. Res. 39, 65th Cong., 1st sess., 1917; H. J. Res. 16, 66th Cong., 1st sess., 1919; H. J. Res. 15, 67th Cong., 1st sess., 1921. The Hayden Collection at the Department of Archives and Manuscripts, Arizona State University, Tempe, contains few papers for this period of Hayden's service in Congress and provides no clues about Hayden's reasons for sponsoring these three resolutions. Although Hayden (1877–1972) was primarily interested in local issues during his fifty-seven years in Congress, his sponsorship of legislation to curb the Court may have reflected his strong ties to Arizona labor.

[7] H. J. Res. 9755, 67th Cong., 2d sess., 1922.

Borah "had always opposed suggestions that threatened the concept of a government based on separation of powers."[8] Borah, who may have aspired to a seat on the Court,[9] had a profound appreciation of the role of the Supreme Court in the American constitutional system. Accordingly, Borah's bill offered a means of protecting the Court from the more fundamental assaults of La Follette and other opponents of federal judicial power while helping to ensure that the Court would not strike down progressive legislation unless there was widespread agreement on the Court that the legislation was unconstitutional. These dual goals assisted Borah in his continuing and often precarious efforts to straddle mainstream Republicanism and progressive insurgency. As Steven F. Lawson has pointed out, Borah's measure was designed to appeal more to conservatives than to progressives.[10]

In public and private remarks concerning his bill, Borah always emphasized that the measure was designed to strengthen the Court. Borah publicly explained that 5–4 decisions inspired "deep regret" among the general public and that such decisions "seem to breed an atmosphere of distrust" about the federal judicial system. Borah warned that unless Congress acted to ensure that the Court's opinions would enjoy greater credibility and permanency, "we shall have to meet the situation after it becomes more serious."[11]

Similarly, Borah explained privately that closely divided decisions encouraged a baneful "want of respect and faith in the Court" among both laypeople and professionals.[12] Borah told Philadelphia attorney Ira Jewell Williams that 5–4 decisions detracted from the government's stability and that his bill was intended "to add strength and respect to the Court rather than to derogate from its dignity and power."[13] He told a Spokane attorney that "the evil which now confronts us is one which is going to more and more attract the attention of the country and will be dealt with in some way." Borah professed to believe that it

---

[8] LeRoy Ashby, *The Spearless Leader: Senator Borah and the Progressive Movement in the 1920's* (Urbana: University of Illinois Press, 1972), p. 32.

[9] Ibid., pp. 239–40.

[10] Steven F. Lawson, "Progressives and the Supreme Court: The Case for Judicial Reform in the 1920s," *The Historian* 42 (May 1980): 425–26.

[11] Although Borah never defended his plan on the floor of the Senate, he discussed it in a *New York Times* article that was later published in the *Congressional Record*. See William E. Borah, "Five to Four Decisions as Menace to Respect to Supreme Court," *New York Times*, February 18, 1923, p. 1; *Congressional Record*, 67th Cong., 4th sess., February 19, 1923, pp. 3959–60.

[12] Borah to W. P. Hamilton, February 8, 1923, *Borah Papers*, Box 144.

[13] Borah to Ira Jewell Williams, September 24, 1923, *Borah Papers*, Box 144. Similarly, Borah wrote to an Idaho attorney that "if these five to four decisions could be avoided, it would add much to the respect, both of the profession and of the layman, to the decisions of the Court (Borah to J. Ward Arney, January 2, 1924, ibid., at Box 168).

was "utterly inconceivable that we will go on indefinitely permitting five judges to overrule the action of both Houses of Congress, of the Chief Executive, and four Members of the Court as to what constitutes constitutional law."[14]

Borah's concerns about the effects of close decisions were echoed by other critics of the Court, who predicted that the multiplication of such decisions endangered the existence of judicial review. The *New Republic* observed in March 1923 that the growing perception that the Court's decisions turned upon the judges' personal political predilections was placing "a great strain upon the political capacity of the country." Although the editorial acknowledged that the "prestige of the court is very great and the country will accept a great deal of guidance from it," it warned that "a house divided against itself cannot stand." Accordingly, the *New Republic* could "see little harm and much virtue" in a constitutional requirement that the Court "act with some degree of unanimity" in cases involving sensitive constitutional issues.[15] Six months later, the *New Republic* warned again that Americans would "eventually deprive the Supreme Court of its supreme function" if the Court continued to "erect the Constitution into a barrier against orderly social adjustment."[16]

Other critics of the Court argued that the Court's decisions encouraged disrespect for the law itself and invited revolution or anarchy. AFL counsel Jackson Harvey Ralston, who opposed any form of judicial review of acts of Congress, suggested that the decisions that had "condemned thousands to stinted lives or to death, to unrequited injuries, to earnings too scanty to sustain a decent living," might "at some inopportune moment supply the explosive element that may shatter our institutions."[17] In more measured terms, Senator George W. Norris expressed a similar view in a letter to a union official in June 1923. Norris explained that he favored some sort of limitation on the Court's power to invalidate acts of Congress since the Court's 5–4 decisions had encouraged a general disrespect for the law that extended far beyond the decisions themselves. According to Norris, frustration over judicial decisions created among ordinary citizens "a feeling of injustice" that had "a tendency to create anarchy and communalism."[18]

Similarly, former justice Clarke warned in November 1923 that 5–4

---

[14] William E. Borah to O. C. Moore, November 12, 1923, *Borah Papers*, Box 144.

[15] "The Supreme Court Again," *New Republic*, March 14, 1923, p. 60.

[16] "Judges as Statesmen," *New Republic*, September 12, 1923, p. 63.

[17] Jackson Harvey Ralston, "Shall We Curb the Supreme Court? I. Labor and Law," *The Forum*, May 1924, p. 568.

[18] George W. Norris to Albert F. Coyle, June 2, 1923, *Norris Papers*, Box 31, Library of Congress; *Norris Papers*, MS 3298, Box 1, State Archives, Nebraska State Historical Society, Lincoln.

decisions were helping to create formidable opposition to the Court since ordinary citizens instinctively resented "an implication of one-man power." To restore public confidence in the Court, Clarke proposed that the Court itself voluntarily refuse to invalidate a statute when two or more justices believed that the statute was constitutional. Like other critics of 5–4 decisions, Clarke pointed out that the dissent of two or more justices raised "a rational doubt" about the invalidity of the statute.[19] Although Clarke's proposal was characteristic of this gentle and conciliatory man, his difficult years of service on a deeply divided Court must have made him aware of the proposal's impracticability. To the justices who composed the Court's conservative majority, no "rational doubt" was raised by the dissents of their brethren. Like Clarke, William Allen White believed that the Court should take the initiative to avoid narrow decisions. Observing that "the people are weary beyond words of five to four decisions," White predicted that "if the court doesn't make its own rule, if it doesn't stop of its own motion, a rising indignation might force a constitutional amendment taking great powers necessary to good government away from the courts."[20]

In addition to Borah, other members of Congress likewise advocated legislation to impose a supermajoritarian requirement upon the Supreme Court. During the week that Borah unveiled his proposal, Republican representative Roy O. Woodruff of Michigan sponsored an identical measure, and Representative James A. Frear, a Wisconsin Republican, introduced a bill that would have allowed Congress to determine how many members of the Court were required to join in any decision striking down or limiting any federal or state law.[21] In late March, Senator Simeon D. Fess informally proposed that the concurrence of at least six justices be required to invalidate a federal statute.[22]

Advocates of the Borah plan believed that it was more viable than the La Follette plan since it would not require a constitutional amendment; section 2, Article III, of the Constitution provides that the Court's appellate jurisdiction shall exist "with such Exceptions, and under such Regulations as the Congress shall make." But opponents of the Borah plan and many of its supporters disputed the validity of this simple reasoning, contending that section 2 does not permit Congress to interfere with the Court's manner of exercising its appellate jurisdiction after Congress confers that jurisdiction. Although the *New Republic* was

[19] John H. Clarke, "Judicial Power to Declare Legislation Unconstitutional," *American Bar Association Journal*, November 1923, pp. 691–92.
[20] William Allen White to Albert J. Beveridge, January 16, 1924, *Albert J. Beveridge Papers*, Box 253, Manuscript Division, Library of Congress.
[21] H.R. 14209, 67th Cong., 4th sess., 1923; H. J. Res. 436, 67th Cong., 4th sess., 1923.
[22] *Congressional Digest* 2 (June 1923): 271, 278, 282.

sympathetic to a reform along the lines proposed by Borah, it argued that such a reform would be "an unequivocal interference with the judicial power and beyond the powers delegated by the Constitution to Congress."[23]

From the other side of the political divide, Charles Warren argued that the plan would unconstitutionally interfere with the separation of powers because it would substitute the command of Congress for judicial discretion.[24] Borah himself conceded that his bill raised constitutional questions and suggested that the reform might be accomplished only by a constitutional amendment.[25] Another critic of the measure pointed out that the Court itself would have to rule on the constitutionality of legislation that imposed a supermajoritarian requirement.[26]

Opponents contended that the measure would erode rather than bolster public confidence in the Court and the governmental process because it would contravene the principle of majority rule that underlies the American system of government. "Every time six out of the nine justices pronounced a law unconstitutional and the law nevertheless went into effect, the country would witness a spectacle far more damaging to the court's prestige than any that is now presented," one opponent argued.[27] A *Georgetown Law Journal* article declared that "one must have a strange idea of administrative justice to advocate that . . . the minority opinion is to govern."[28] Similarly, a Roman Catholic priest warned that Borah's proposal, like other Court-curbing measures,

[23] "The Supreme Court Again," *New Republic*, March 14, 1923, pp. 59–60.

[24] Charles Warren, *Congress, the Constitution and the Supreme Court* (Boston: Little, Brown, 1925), pp. 181–82.

[25] Two days after he introduced his measure, Borah admitted in a private letter to the editor of the *Wall Street Journal* that Congress's power to enact such a measure was not clear but that "the more I investigate that power, the more I think we have the power. And if we have the power, I think we ought to use it." In a *New York Times* column later in February, Borah acknowledged that the line between the Court's judicial power and its appellate jurisdiction was not always "clear and distinct" and couched in rather timid language his conclusion that his measure did not invade the Court's judicial power. Seven months later, Borah betrayed a similar lack of certitude in a letter to Ira Jewell Williams, although he continued to defend the measure's constitutionality. Acknowledging that Congress could not invade the Court's constitutionally ordained "judicial power," Borah said that he entertained "very grave doubts" that majority rule in the rendition of an opinion was part of the judicial power. Borah to Hamilton; Borah, "Five to Four Decisions as Menace," p. 1; Borah to Williams.

[26] Alexander Sidney Lanier, "Congress and the Supreme Court," *North American Review*, November 1923, p. 37.

[27] Fabian Franklin, "Five to Four in the Supreme Court," *The Independent*, April 14, 1923, p. 247.

[28] Joseph D. Sullivan, "Curbing the Supreme Court," *Georgetown Law Journal* 11 (May 1923): 13.

would expose the rights of minorities to the tyranny of the majority. "We cannot afford," he declared, "to weaken the practically impregnable position of individual liberty as guaranteed by the . . . Court, and other checks and balances of our Government, even to achieve very desirable social ameliorations."[29]

Opponents of the Borah plan also denied that a decision by a majority of one constituted a form of one-man rule that contravened democratic ideals. As one opponent of the plan observed, "It is just as erroneous to say that a five to four decision is a one man decision . . . as it is incorrect to say that an Act of a branch of Congress passed by a majority of one is a one man Act of that branch of Congress."[30] The anomaly of minority-rule decisions vexed Walter Clark, who told La Follette that such a prospect "cannot be defended." Clark also privately disparaged the plan as "child's play" because Clark believed that special business interests would have no serious difficulty in obtaining the appointment of two additional justices who would favor their point of view.[31]

Pointing out that the Court does not decide abstract issues but adjudicates actual controversies to which individual citizens or institutions are parties, opponents of the Borah bill argued that the plan would be manifestly unjust to a litigant whose position was rejected by the Court even though a majority of its members supported that position.[32] Another practical question was whether a decision by a minority vote would provide a precedent binding upon the Court.[33] The bill as drafted further failed to take account of the fact that one or two justices were often absent from the Court. If one member was absent, a litigant asserting a constitutional right would need to convince all but one justice of the applicability of that right and would need to obtain unanimous assent if two justices were absent.[34]

Critics of the plan observed that the government might have difficulty enforcing a statute that had been upheld by a minority vote. Charles Warren pointed out that such disrespect could have serious consequences if such laws were unpopular measures such as the recent

[29] Daniel M. O'Connell, "Five to Four Decisions," *America*, October 27, 1923, p. 46.

[30] Frank R. Savidge, "Five to Four Supreme Court Decisions," *North American Review*, April 1924, p. 472.

[31] Walter Clark to Robert M. La Follette, January 9, 1924, *La Follette Family Papers*, Series B, Box 58, Library of Congress.

[32] Lewis H. Smith, *The Right of the Supreme Court to Declare Acts of Congress Unconstitutional*, address delivered at the convention of the California Bar Association, Stockton, Calif., October 13, 1923 (San Francisco: Recorder, 1923).

[33] Ira Jewell Williams, "The Attack Upon the Supreme Court," *Constitutional Review* 7 (July 1923): 147.

[34] Robert von Moschzisker, "Judicial Review of Legislation by the Supreme Court," *Constitutional Review* 9 (April 1925): 73.

wartime measures on alcohol consumption and compulsory military service.[35] Chief Justice Robert von Moschzisker of Pennsylvania warned that "minority control cuts both ways, and . . . a day may come when it will be hard to get the body of the people to accept . . . the upholding, by the vote of less than a majority of the Supreme Court of what may happen to be unpopular national legislation."[36]

Although critics of the Borah measure acknowledged that legislative enactments carry a presumption of constitutionality, they argued that the Supreme Court already accorded such a presumption to statutes and that it did not lightly invalidate laws enacted by Congress. As one lawyer stated, the imposition of a heavier presumption of constitutionality by requiring a 7–2 vote "is really a proposal to weight the scales against the Constitution" since it would create a presumption similar to the heavy presumption of innocence in criminal trials, based upon the theory that it is better to allow many guilty men to go free than to permit one innocent man to suffer. He argued that this theory was inapplicable to constitutional cases "unless we are prepared to say that it is better that ninety and nine unconstitutional laws should go into effect than that one constitutional law should be nullified."[37]

Opponents of the measure further suggested that close decisions actually might enhance public respect for the Court. "Unanimity of opinion does not always indicate a result above criticism," one attorney observed. "Personally, I prefer an opinion by a divided court. Then I feel sure that the case has been heard with attention, has been studied by the opposing groups of judges with a view to swaying the minds of those inclined to waver, and perhaps has been the subject of an earnest argument in the council chamber."[38] Similarly, another attorney observed that "sharp differences of belief have always appeared whenever the question has been worth while."[39]

Discussions of the Borah bill did not need to rely entirely upon abstract arguments, hypothetical cases, and surmises. The state of Ohio, which had adopted a similar measure, provided a laboratory to test its merits. Ohio's new constitution, adopted in 1912, required the concurrence of six of the seven judges of the state supreme court to strike down any law unless the judgment was an affirmation of a decision of the court of appeals declaring the law constitutional. At the time Borah introduced his plan, the supreme court of Ohio had issued a

[35] Warren, *Congress, Constitution*, p. 193.
[36] Von Moschzisker, "Judicial Review," p. 78.
[37] Franklin, "Five to Four," p. 247.
[38] Sullivan, "Curbing Supreme Court," p. 12.
[39] Thomas J. Norton, "The Supreme Court's Five to Four Decisions," *American Bar Association Journal*, July 1923, p. 420.

minority decision upholding the constitutionality of a statute in only one case. In 1918, four members of the court had contended that an election law that imposed certain election expenses upon county governments was unconstitutional, but the law was upheld because three members voted to sustain it.[40] Although opponents of Borah's plan suggested that this demonstrated the statute's absurdity,[41] the case did not provide the plan's advocates or opponents with compelling argument since it did not involve the assertion of a fundamental constitutional right.

The supreme court of Ohio provided better ammunition for both the opponents and the proponents of Borah's plan in November 1923 when by minority vote it upheld a section of the Ohio Workmen's Compensation Act that subjected employers who had not subscribed to state insurance to a 50 percent penalty on any award rendered against them if they failed to pay the award within ten days.[42] Although von Moschzisker and Warren cited this case as an example of how a court minority had thwarted a due process right claimed by a private individual,[43] the outcome provided proponents of Borah's bill with a perfect example of the potential benefits of such a measure. By preventing the Ohio court's conservative majority from thwarting a legislative attempt to protect employees, the Ohio constitutional provision had vindicated the expectations of its progressive framers.

Just as opponents of the La Follette proposal often pointed out that the Supreme Court had rarely nullified acts of Congress, the opponents of the Borah bill emphasized that only eight of those fifty-three cases were decided by a 5–4 vote.[44] And in only four other cases did more than two justices dissent.[45] To a certain extent, however, the

[40] *Barker v. City of Akron*, 98 Ohio St. 446, 121 N.E. 646 (1918).

[41] Charles Warren, "Borah and La Follette vs. the Supreme Court," *Saturday Evening Post*, October 13, 1923, pp. 31, 192.

[42] *De Witt v. The State*, 108 Ohio St. 513, 141 N.E. 551 (1923).

[43] Warren, *Congress, Constitution*, pp. 186–87; von Moschzisker, "Judicial Review," p. 78.

[44] Warren, *Congress, Constitution*., p. 183; Savidge, "Five to Four," p. 460; James Frederick Peake, "The Power of the Supreme Court to Nullify Acts of Congress," *Constitutional Review* 8 (April 1924): 94. Those cases were *Ex parte Garland*, 4 Wallace 333 (1867); *Pollock v. Farmers' Loan & Trust Co.*, 157 U.S. 429 (1895); *Fairbank v. United States* 181 U.S. 283 (1901); *First Employers' Liability Cases*, 207 U.S. 463 (1908); *Hammer v. Dagenhart*, 247 U.S. 251 (1918); *Knickerbocker Ice Co. v. Stewart*, 253 U.S. 149 (1920); *Eisner v. Macomber*, 252 U.S. 189 (1920); *Newberry v. United States*, 256 U.S. 232 (1921).

[45] Warren, *Congress, Constitution*., pp. 183–84. As with the other cases where the Court had invalidated acts of Congress, opponents of curbing the Court's jurisdiction argued that the facts of most of those cases did not necessarily result in the erosion of individual liberties or the aggrandizement of powerful economic interests. The first 5–4 decision, *Ex Parte Garland* in 1868, actually upheld the rights of an individual against the state. The

argument about the rarity of 5–4 decisions proved too much, since four of the eight decisions had been rendered since 1918, and the eight decisions struck down significant legislation involving the income tax, child labor, and campaign financing.

Despite the growth of public concern over the increasing frequency of 5–4 decisions that nullified federal statutes, the Borah plan did not perturb the conservatives on the Court. In his copious missives to far-flung correspondents, Taft had little to say about the plan, and his few remarks about it suggested that the Borah plan worried him no more than the La Follette plan. In March 1923, Taft remarked to his brother Horace that the recent adjournment of Congress had made everyone breathe more easily and that "there is no cloud in the sky unless we hear a yawp from Borah who is filling empty heads with a . . . supply of emptiness."[46] In December, Taft supposed that Borah would press his bill, but he expressed doubt that the measure would pass. Taft was confident that Coolidge would veto the measure and that its proponents would fail to muster the votes to override his veto.[47]

Other members of the Court also appear to have been unintimidated by the Borah proposal, for the Court on April 9, 1923, handed down another controversial close decision, *Adkins v. Children's Hospital.* In *Adkins*, the Court struck down a federal statute that permitted a government board to establish minimum wages for women and children in the District of Columbia.[48] This decision provoked an intensification of the controversy over judicial power because it represented judicial review in its boldest form and economic Darwinism in its rawest incarnation. In contrast to the *Bailey* decision, which rested on well-established doctrines of federalism, *Adkins* was based upon the Court's contention that due process permitted only a narrow range for governmental regulation of private economic relations. In ruling that the statute violated the Fifth Amendment's due process clause by interfering with the freedom of workers and employers to enter into contracts of employment upon mutually agreeable terms, the Court once again seemed determined to substitute its ideas for those of Congress and to use the Constitution as a means of protecting wealth and privilege. Although the Court conceded that every worker had an "ethical right" to a living

---

Court's 5–4 decision in the *Income Tax Case* was cured by the Sixteenth Amendment, the decision of the *First Employers Liability Act* was cured by an act of Congress, and the decision in *Knickerbocker Ice* could probably be cured by a properly drawn federal statute.

[46] Taft to Horace Taft, March 27, 1923, *Taft Papers*, Series 3, Reel 252, Library of Congress.

[47] Taft to Robert A. Taft, December 2, 1923, *Taft Papers*, Series 3, Reel 259.

[48] 261 U.S. 525 (1923).

wage, the Court denied that Congress had a power to establish a minimum wage to help an employee attain that right.

The Court's decision in *Adkins* went too far even for William Howard Taft, who joined Holmes and Sanford in dissent. If Brandeis had not disqualified himself from the case because his daughter, Elizabeth Brandeis Raushenbush, was a member of the District of Columbia Wage Board, he almost certainly would have joined in the dissent, making the decision another of the 5–4 decisions which the Court's critics singled out for special execration. Explaining that Congress could reasonably have determined that employees do not enjoy equality of bargaining power with employers, Taft declared, "It is not function of the court to hold congressional acts invalid simply because they are passed to carry out economic views which the court believes to be unsound."

Despite the firmness of Taft's dissent, Taft privately expressed little distress over the decision, and he does not appear to have worried much about its impact upon the movements to curtail the Court's jurisdiction. Although Taft told Clarke that "some of my brethren went too far," and that "there are expressions in Sutherland's opinion that will merely return to plague us," he emphasized that the members of the Court were "getting along very well, and I have no reason to complain of the brethren."[49]

Other opponents of the *Adkins* decision, however, did not hesitate to complain about the brethren. The decision aroused anguished outcries and provided ammunition to the advocates of curtailment of the Court's jurisdiction. Like the dissenters on the Court, the critics heaped scorn on the Court's sanguine assumption that poorly paid women enjoyed an ideal freedom of contract. *The Nation* declared that the Court's naiveté and ignorance about industrial conditions was particularly shocking since the Court occupied a "pivotal position in determining the economic policy of the country."[50] Similarly, the *New Republic* declared that "the Supreme Court does not know that democracy and wage-slavery are incompatible. . . . The Supreme Court does not know that every worker must feel his moral position weakened by the fact that his death or disability may thrust his wife or daughter or sister into a position where she has to make a choice between slow starvation and moral degradation."[51]

More fundamentally, the decision's critics argued that the Court had

[49] Taft to John H. Clarke, May 3, 1923, *Taft Papers*, Series 3, Reel 253. Taft wryly observed that his only possible complaint about his colleagues was "that one [Holmes] has passed his usefulness, and as to another of them [Brandeis]. . . there is some question as to how much of usefulness ever existed."

[50] "The Supreme Court Supplants Congress," *The Nation*, April 25, 1923, p. 484.

[51] "An Appeal from the Supreme Court," *New Republic*, April 25, 1923, p. 228.

read its own political biases into the Constitution and ought to have accorded greater deference to legislative discretion. *The Nation* declared, "The people ought to be entitled to decide such matters for themselves, free from the shadow of the potential veto of the odd justice of the Supreme Court. Until this power of judicial review is limited or eliminated, the people of the United States will neither be wholly free nor will they have the opportunity to test the vital principles of government of, for, and by the people."[52]

The decision further eroded confidence in the Court among progressives and encouraged them to despair about their ability to effect durable social reforms. *La Follette's Magazine* observed that the decision was "a hard blow to those who have spent a generation of time in securing legislation to cope with and humanize modern industrial conditions. Such laws are secured only by tremendous effort and in response to the great need and demand which can no longer be denied. To have such hard-won reforms defeated by hair splitting decisions of a divided court is a cause of wide-spread dissatisfaction on the part of plain, commonsense folks."[53]

Similarly, the director of the Women's Bureau of the Labor Department declared that the decision was "nothing short of a calamity to the women workers of this country."[54] Speaking at a conference sponsored by the National Women's Trade Union League, Gompers declared that the opinion likened "the labor of a woman to the purchase of a shinbone over the counter to make soup."[55] Similarly, the *American Federationist* stated, "The brutality of the majority decision can beget nothing but wrath. . . . The court declares that this labor power, this contribution of human service, this giving of self and soul in the doing of humanity's most poorly requited tasks, is nothing less than the bartering of commodities."[56]

Defense of the opinion came from predictable quarters. The *New York Journal of Commerce* went a step beyond the Court's reasoning to declare that wage earners not only could defend their interests when they bargained with employers but were "in a position to wring from industry the last farthing in wages that it can pay under existing conditions."[57] Other defenders of the decision cleaved to traditional legal

[52] "Supreme Court Supplants," p. 485.
[53] "The Minimum Wage," *La Follette's Magazine*, May 1923, p. 70. To the extent that the law lacked particularly broad legislative support, however, one could argue that the Court had greater justification for submitting the law to careful constitutional scrutiny.
[54] "Woman's Right to Low Wages," *Literary Digest*, April 21, 1923, p. 12.
[55] *New York Times*, May 16, 1923, p. 21.
[56] "Take Away Its Usurped Power," *American Federationist*, May 1923, p. 399.
[57] "Woman's Right to Low Wages."

doctrine concerning freedom of contract. A New York attorney complained to Justice Sutherland that the critics of the decision failed "to distinguish between a legal principle and a social hope."[58]

But not all conservative and moderate opinion lauded the decision. Just as *Adkins* had shattered the consensus that had prevailed on the Court in *Bailey*, *Adkins* distressed many who had been willing to defend or at least tolerate *Bailey*. For example, the St. Louis *Post-Dispatch*, which had won praise from Taft for its editorial defense of *Bailey*, declared that "theoretically the wage earner has freedom of contract, but the necessities of life and employment far removed from the soil force unorganized and unskilled labor to accept whatever wages are offered."[59] The *New York Law Journal* denounced the decision as "unsound and unfortunate."[60]

Many opponents of *Adkins* advocated a constitutional amendment to permit states to regulate hours and wages for women.[61] The *New Republic* favored a less legalistic remedy, calling upon labor unions to "formulate a national conception of the minimum wage below which no class of labor should be permitted to fall" and to use its muscle to force employers to accept such a standard. "Determined action by the unions would go far toward deterring employers from taking advantage of the exploiting privilege conferred upon them by the Supreme Court."[62]

Even though many critics of *Adkins* preferred to work around the Court, the decision naturally invigorated calls for curtailment of the Court's jurisdiction. Pointing out that "the Income Tax Law, the Ten-hour Law of New York, the Child Labor Law, and now this law, have all been held invalid by five-to-four decisions," Borah observed that "these five-to-four decisions are forcing constant agitation for Constitutional amendments."[63] The *Baltimore Sun* predicted that *Adkins* would "serve to mobilize further strength" for Borah's bill, but the same editorial suggested that the decision was not likely to increase support for La Follette's more radical measure, which it contended had support only among extremists.[64]

The decision, however, appears to have increased the fervor of the advocates of both measures. In May 1923, Gompers reiterated his call

[58] Ernest E. Baldwin to George Sutherland, April 16,1923, *Sutherland Papers*, Box 5, Manuscript Division, Library of Congress.

[59] Editorial, "Freedom of Contract," St. Louis *Post-Dispatch*, April 10, 1923.

[60] "The Minimum Wage Law Decision," *New York Law Journal*, April 16, 1923, p. 192.

[61] "Woman's Right to Low Wages."

[62] "Appeal from Supreme Court," pp. 228–29.

[63] "Woman's Right to Low Wages."

[64] Editorial, "The Minimum Wage Decision," *Baltimore Sun*, April 11, 1923, p. 10.

for the adoption of a constitutional amendment to give Congress the power to override decisions of the Supreme Court.[65] At its convention in October, the AFL reiterated its support for an amendment to permit Congress to reenact federal legislation that the Court had nullified.[66] Expressing dismay over *Adkins*, The *American Federationist* declared, "There appears to be no other effective avenue of relief from reactionary Supreme Court decisions" than to strip the Court of its power "to write such ugly pages as this into the history of a great democratic civilization."[67] Matthew Woll, the vice president of the AFL, told the National Women's Trade Union League conference that "the most revolutionary thing we have today is the power of five men to cast aside the law of the land. No other country in the world has vested in nine men so far removed from the source of their selection such power as is in the United States Supreme Court." Another speaker at the conference, the Reverend John A. Ryan, director of the Social Action Department of the National Catholic Welfare Council, advocated the adoption of a constitutional amendment to require the concurrence of seven or eight Supreme Court justices to declare a federal law unconstitutional.[68]

Meanwhile, Senator Edwin F. Ladd, a North Dakota Republican, stated in Los Angeles that no act of Congress should be declared unconstitutional except by a vote of eight members and that the Supreme Court should have no power to invalidate the act of any state legislature unless at least seven members concurred. Ladd suggested that the change could be effected by legislation rather than by a constitutional amendment and predicted that the Court would uphold such a statute.[69] Samuel Untermyer, a prominent New York attorney, told the Political Club at Columbia University that Congress should have the power to overrule Supreme Court decisions by a three-quarters vote.[70]

The uproar over the *Adkins* decision had abated considerably by the time Congress reconvened late in 1923 and Borah reintroduced his measure in the Senate.[71] Fiorello H. La Guardia, who embodied Borah's proposal in a bill he introduced in the House early in the new session,[72] was one of the few members of Congress who actively

---

[65] "Labor Leaders Hit Wage Law Decision," *New York Times*, May 16, 1923, p. 21.

[66] *Report of Proceedings of the Forty-Third Annual Convention of the American Federation of Labor* (Washington, D.C.: Law Reporter, 1923), pp. 35–36, 265.

[67] "Take Away Its Usurped Power," pp. 399, 401.

[68] "Labor Leaders Hit Decision."

[69] "Ladd Sees Danger in Supreme Court," *New York Times*, May 23, 1923, p. 22.

[70] "Favors Check on Courts," *New York Times*, April 18, 1923, p. 23.

[71] S. 1197, 68th Cong., 1st sess., 1923.

[72] H. J. Res. 721, 68th Cong., 1st sess., 1923. Republican Roy O. Woodruff introduced a virtually identical measure at the same time (H.R. 697, 68th Cong., 1st sess., 1923).

session,[72] was one of the few members of Congress who actively worked for supermajoritarian requirement. The New York City congressman told the Idaho senator that the support of an easterner for Borah's proposal might "shock some of our stand-pat reactionary friends," and he apparently hoped that such shock might help them to recognize the seriousness of public outrage against the Court's recent decisions.[73] La Guardia, who had been advocating a similar remedy for a number of years, assured Borah that the "measure will be extremely popular in this City and State, although the desire of the people may not be reflected in the vote of their delegation in the House."[74]

The New York delegation, however, never voted on the measure. Like other legislation to curb the Court's powers, the Borah-La Guardia measure never reached a vote in any committee, much less a vote in either house of Congress. Conservatives remained too tightly in control of Congress, and public support for the Court remained too resilient. The success of the Court was by no means inevitable, however, and Chief Justice Taft himself took the initiative to help deflect rising public sentiment in favor of curtailing judicial power.

[72] H. J. Res. 721, 68th Cong., 1st sess., 1923. Republican Roy O. Woodruff introduced a virtually identical measure at the same time (H.R. 697, 68th Cong., 1st sess., 1923).

[73] Fiorello La Guardia to Borah, November 9, 1923, *Borah Papers*, Box 144.

[74] Fiorello H. La Guardia to Borah, October 31, 1923, *Borah Papers*, Box 144.

ELEVEN

THE SUPREME COURT CALMS THE TEMPEST

Public opinion throughout the United States is beginning
to rally to the defense of the Supreme Court, and to
express itself in organized and formal protests."
(The Constitutional Review, *April 1924*)[1]

EVEN BEFORE the rage over the Court's decision in *Adkins* had
subsided, there were signs that the Court would emerge from
the tempest with its powers unimpaired. As in earlier and later
periods of agitation against the Court, the Court demonstrated a remarkable resilience. Once again, however, the preservation of judicial
power was not inevitable. Much depended upon the shrewdness of the
justices and their propagandists, and the failings of their opponents.
Carefully planned and vigorous defenses of the Court by lawyers, academics, and publicists were buttressed by decisions of the Court that
helped to restore it to popular favor. Meanwhile, the disorganization of
the Court's opponents, particularly their chronic inability to unite behind any specific reform, ensured that the institutional obstacles im-
peding any legislation or constitutional amendment would prevent the
enactment of a measure to curtail power.

Organized efforts by conservatives to bolster public support for judicial review were already well under way by the time public agitation
against the Court reached its peak between 1922 and 1924. As Michael
Kammen has pointed out, the National Security League and other
conservative organizations had since 1916 promoted the celebration of
an annual "Constitution Day" on September 17 to promote public
awareness of the role of the Constitution and the courts in providing a
barrier against unrestrained democracy that could threaten personal
and economic liberties. By the mid-1920s, organizations like the American Legion, Sons of the American Revolution; Chambers of Commerce; and the Rotary, Kiwanis, and Lions clubs were sponsoring a
plethora of activities, programs, and publications to inculcate reverence for the Constitution and to increase public knowledge and
understanding about the judiciary.[2]

[1] "Public Opinion Defends the Supreme Court," *Constitutional Review*, April 1924,
p. 119.
[2] Michael Kammen, *A Machine That Would Go of Itself: The Constitution in American
Culture* (New York: Knopf, 1986), pp. 219–54.

Although veneration of the Constitution did not necessarily translate into support for judicial review, the emergence of what Kammen has called a "cult of the Constitution"[3] helped to shore up support for the powers of the federal courts, which were the special guardians of the ark of the constitutional covenant. Meanwhile, the appearance of Albert J. Beveridge's four-volume biography of John Marshall between 1916 and 1919 capped an apotheosis of the architect of judicial review that had been gathering strength for nearly two decades.[4] Beveridge's veneration of Marshall is particularly significant since Beveridge was a prominent progressive.

The resilience of public support for the Court was demonstrated by the failure of a diligent attack that William Randolph Hearst launched against Chief Justice Taft in the wake of *Adkins*. Even though Taft had dissented in that decision, the popular uproar that followed it provided an ideal occasion for the Hearst newspapers to attack an old foe. A few days after the Court handed down its decision in *Adkins*, the Hearst newspapers alleged that Taft's acceptance of an annual annuity of ten thousand dollars from the estate of Andrew Carnegie made Taft beholden to the United States Steel Company from whose bonds the annuity was paid. Even though public sentiment generally favored Taft's acceptance of the legacy, the controversy created by the attack probably caused Taft more anguish than any other event during his chief justiceship.

The Hearst reports about the legacy in April 1923 were not really news since the terms of Carnegie's will had been published after Carnegie died in 1919. Carnegie's provision for Taft was not surprising since Taft's politics and personality appealed to Carnegie. The steel magnate and the Republican politician shared a profound social conservatism and an idealistic humanitarianism. In their personal contacts, the genial Taft had charmed Carnegie just as he had won the devotion of Roosevelt. Taft's work to promote world peace and the betterment of African Americans particularly impressed Carnegie.[5]

---

[3] Ibid., pp. 208, 213.

[4] Albert J. Beveridge, *The Life of John Marshall*, 4 vols. (Boston: Houghton Mifflin, 1916–1919); Kammen, *Machine*, pp. 210–13, 251.

[5] The two men had first become well acquainted when they attended a commencement at the Tuskegee Institute while Taft was secretary of war. Taft later became chairman of the board of the trustees of the Hampton Institute, of which Carnegie was a large benefactor. While Taft was president, Carnegie took an intense interest in Taft's sponsorship of arbitration treaties with France and Great Britain and called several times at the White House to discuss Senate ratification. Carnegie also sought Taft's advice concerning his establishment of what became the Carnegie Endowment for International Peace. Taft to Thomas W. Shelton, June 23, 1923, *Taft Papers*, Series 3, Reel 254, Manuscript Division, Library of Congress.

Fearful that Taft's devotion to public service would impoverish Taft's purse, Carnegie in 1912 made provision for Taft in his will.[6] Although Carnegie later created a trust to pay retired presidents and their surviving widows an annual pension of $25,000,[7] Carnegie revoked the trust after Taft expressed doubts about the propriety of the trust following his defeat in the 1912 election.[8] According to Taft, he was unaware that he was a legatee of Carnegie's will until he read about Carnegie's will in a newspaper after Carnegie's death.[9] Taft told Thomas W. Shelton that he did not believe that the annuity created any conflict of interest since "the security is so substantial and so sure to meet the obligations that the business condition of the Steel Company does not affect the value of the bonds."[10]

Upon learning of the attack on April 15, Taft immediately informed the president of Yale, Arthur T. Hadley, that he would assign to the Yale Law School his income from the annuity during his lifetime. Although Taft emphasized that the legacy had not clouded his judicial impartiality, he acknowledged that "persons who wish to alter the functions and jurisdictions of the Court" would use his receipt of the annuity income as "an argument against the impartiality of the Court."[11] Taft later concluded, however, that he could not "give up the annuity under fire, because that would be an admission that I never should have taken it."[12]

Although Taft toyed with the idea of resigning, he decided that his resignation would be misconstrued as a tacit admission of wrongdoing.

---

[6] Taft to J. D. Brannan, November 25, 1912, Taft to Arthur T. Hadley, November 29, 1912, *Taft Papers*, Series 8, Reel 515; Taft to Thomas W. Shelton, June 25, 1923, *Taft Papers*, Series 3, Reel 254.

[7] Ibid; Taft to Thomas W. Shelton, June 23, 1923.

[8] Taft to Thomas W. Shelton; Taft to Brannan; Taft to Hadley. Taft explained to Hadley that he could not perceive any "difference between the proposal of a private benefactor to increase the Presidential salary during the term and to pay a pension for the service after the term. In either case it furnishes a motive for divided allegiance."

[9] Taft to Shelton.

[10] Taft to Shelton.

[11] Taft to James Rowland Angell, April 15, 1923, *Taft Papers*, Series 3, Reel 252. In one of the two letters that he drafted to Yale's president, Taft explained that he was "profoundly concerned that the usefulness and influence of the Court should not be lessened on this account and wish to do every thing I can to remove the slightest semblance of foundation for the charge, however unjust."

[12] Taft to Charles Taft, April 17, 1923, *Taft Papers*, Series 3, Reel 252. Similarly, Taft told his son Robert, "I would be quite willing now to give it up or to assign it to some good purpose, but I don't like to do it under fire, so that I suppose I shall have to stand the battering, which is quite nerve straining when one is engaged in work that should command all his faculties and all his attention" (Taft to Robert A. Taft, April 16, 1923, *Taft Papers*, Series 3, Reel 252).

In considering whether he ought to renounce the legacy or resign from the Court, Taft professed to worry primarily about how his decision would affect the Court. Shortly after learning of the first Hearst articles, Taft told Horace that "Resignation would be like suicide. It is confession and would demoralize the Court greatly." Although Taft confided to Horace that the "use of me and my record to attack the Court cuts me to the heart," he resigned himself to the need to "sit tight and take my medicine of mental suffering." With a fatalism that would have done credit to his Puritan forebears, Taft consoled himself with the thought that the "crosses and burdens" that he now bore were the just price he must pay for the intense satisfaction that he had derived from his judicial duties.[13]

Although Taft no doubt wished to avoid any suggestion of an admission that he had committed an impropriety, his decision to keep the legacy was also dictated by financial expediency.[14] The charges particularly galled him since he had passed up the opportunity to make a large fortune in private practice after he left the White House.[15] Although he decided to keep the annuity, he continued to worry that the charges would abet the movement to restrict the Court's jurisdiction.[16]

The Hearst attack on Taft was amplified by the Socialist party's National Executive Committee, which on April 30 adopted a resolution calling for Taft's resignation on because of the legacy.[17] In two ad-

---

[13] Taft to Horace Taft, *Taft Papers*, Series 3, Reel 259. Although this undated letter is marked with the notation "[ca Dec. 1923?]," the text of the letter reveals that it was written shortly after Taft learned about the attack in the Hearst newspapers. Taft's decision may have been influenced by some of his closest confidants, who advised Taft to hold firm. For example, Henry Taft warned his brother that renunciation of the legacy would imply that Taft had acted wrongfully (Henry W. Taft to William Howard Taft, May 22, 1923, *Taft Papers*, Series 3, Reel 253).

[14] The legacy substantially improved the finances of Taft, whose income in 1919 consisted of his $6,000 salary from Yale, a few thousand from lectures, and about $10,000 from interest on capital of about $250,000. (Taft to Shelton, June 23, 1923, June 24, 1923). As Taft explained to Shelton, "At the scale upon which I am now living, this annuity is an important part of my income, from which I am not saving anything at all now" (Taft to Shelton, June 24, 1923).

[15] Taft to Shelton, June 24, 1923. Taft told Shelton that he had decided to forego such lucre because "there were then bitter attacks upon the Judiciary, as now, and my appearance in Court would be a source of embarrassment" since he had appointed six Supreme Court justices and 30 percent of the lower federal judiciary. Although Taft dismissed the possibility that any judge would be influenced by the fact that Taft had appointed him, he believed that "it would be difficult to convince the defeated party, if I won, that this fact did not have weight."

[16] Taft to Mrs. Frederick J. Manning, April 16, 1923, Taft to Charles P. Taft, April 17, 1923, *Taft Papers*, Series 3, Reel 252; Taft to Henry S. Pritchett, April 25, 1923, *Taft Papers*, Series 3, Reel 253.

[17] "Socialists Assail Taft," *New York Times*, May 1, 1923, p. 44.

dresses in Newark in mid-May, Eugene V. Debs insisted that the Socialists would press for Taft's impeachment if he refused to resign. "Think of a pensioner of such an institution as the steel trust being Chief Justice of the highest court of the land!" exclaimed Debs, who averred that he lacked any respect for the Supreme Court.[18] A week later, Debs demanded Taft's impeachment when he addressed an audience of fifteen thousand at Madison Square Garden. "Taft is on the payroll of the Steel Corporation," Debs declared to applause. "The $10,000 given to him was for services rendered."[19] As Debs continued to excoriate Taft in speeches, various local chapters of the Socialist party adopted resolutions denouncing the chief justice and calling for his resignation or impeachment.[20]

The Socialist attacks wearied Taft, but they encouraged him insofar as they suggested that the Carnegie issue might become identified with the political fringe.[21] Taft nevertheless recognized that he would "have to go through the discomfort of having the matter discussed in Congress, and just await the action of those two bodies."[22]

The seriousness of the attacks, however, was less than Taft than feared. As Horace Taft correctly perceived at the outset of the onslaught, the "people that swallow Hearst already condemn your Court and most courts." Horace accurately predicted that "this thing will amount to nothing except as a very slight addition to the unpopularity of the Supreme Court, an unpopularity which, according to all precedents, will die down and then flame up again according to the approval or disapproval with which the public regards a decision on important questions."[23] The Hearst attack began to wither when other newspapers ignored the charges or staunchly defended Taft.

Taft's defenders roundly disparaged the suggestion that Taft's ac-

---

[18] "Debs Attacks Taft," *New York Times*, May 14, 1923, p. 17. Debs assured his audience that he was not motivated by any personal desire for revenge against Taft, even though Taft had expressed the view that Debs had been properly incarcerated in federal prison for criticizing American participation in the war.

[19] "Launch Debs Boom for Presidency," *New York Times*, May 23, 1923, p. 23.

[20] A resolution of the Salt Lake City chapter of the Socialist party, for example, declared that Taft's continued acceptance of the annuity was unethical and incompatible with the high ideals of the Supreme Court. Similarly, the resolution of the Socialist party in Connecticut stated that Taft's "acceptance of this annuity coming indirectly from the Steel Trust, the most powerful and predatory corporation in the United States is not only unethical but a menace to the integrity of our courts and detrimental to the best interests of the American people." Resolution of Local Salt Lake City of the Socialist Party, May 22, 1923, *Taft Papers*, Series 3, Reel 253; Resolution Demanding Removal of William Howard Taft from the Supreme Court, June 10, 1923, *Taft Papers*, Series 3, Reel 254.

[21] Taft to Horace Taft, May 16, 1923, *Taft Papers*, Series 3, Reel 253.

[22] Taft to Mrs. Frederick J. Manning, May 20, 1923, *Taft Papers*, Series 3, Reel 253.

[23] Horace Taft to William Howard Taft, April 17, 1923, *Taft Papers*, Series 3, Reel 252.

ceptance of the annuity was likely to prejudice his views. The *Chicago Daily Tribune* argued that Hearst's logic would preclude any judicial, legislative, or executive official from investing in any standard security and would preclude any judge from owning any property "except, perhaps, his clothes."[24] The ABA *Journal* argued that no litigation involving U.S. Steel would affect the value of the annuity because the income from which the annuity was paid was derived not from stock but from bonds secured by a first mortgage on the company's property.[25] Taft's defenders also pointed out that the legacy did not make Taft beholden to any interest since it was irrevocable. Indeed, the legacy helped to immunize Taft from corporate influences to the extent that it afforded him a measure of financial independence.[26]

Like Taft himself, the defenders of the chief justice discerned that the brouhaha over the legacy was part of a broader effort by the Hearst press to win support for the movement to curb the Court's jurisdiction.[27] The *New York Times* argued that the Hearst press had impugned Taft's integrity because the Borah plan was too dry "to fire the hearts of excitable but ignorant people."[28]

Even though the attack on Taft was largely confined to the Hearst press and the Socialist party and Taft was gratified by the widespread editorial support, he continued to worry about the possible effects of

[24] *Chicago Daily Tribune*, April 18, 1923, p. 8.

[25] "An Unfounded Aspersion," *American Bar Association Journal*, May 1923, p. 304: A "decree for the dissolution of the corporation or for its separation into its original constituents would affect only the value of its stocks and indirectly perhaps the amount of its earnings, but no court would or could by judicial decree destroy the property on which the bonds were secured."

[26] As the *Fort Worth Star-Telegram*, May 14, 1923, p. 8, argued "Mr. Carnegie's purpose was quite the opposite of what the propagandists are trying to make it appear. It was to render Mr. Taft to some degree independent of money-making and to enable him to devote his great talents to the public interest." Similarly, a West Virginia newspaper suggested that the amount of money that Taft derived from the Carnegie legacy was paltry compared to what he could have earned if he had chosen to practice law rather than teach and later return to public service (*The Advertiser*, May 3, 1923, p. 6).

[27] *Chicago Daily Tribune* contended that "Hearst wishes to assist the movement to do away with five to four decisions by discrediting the chief justice" and that the "end object of that attack is to shake the confidence of the American people not merely in an individual but in an institution. It is the Supreme Court that Hearst is after" ("Rats at the Foundation," April 23, 1923). Likewise, the *Fort Worth Star-Telegram* declared that criticism of Taft was "simply part of a campaign against the Supreme Court itself" by persons who wanted "to destroy that tribunal" (*Fort Worth Star-Telegram*, May 14, 1923, p. 8).

[28] The *New York Times* observed that Borah "must be mortified at the way in which his original suggestion has been degraded by this vile association with it of motives and methods which he must abhor, but that is the sort of thing to be expected when a beginning is made in breaking down an established institution" ("The New Attack," May 20, 1923, p. 2.6).

the attack. Although he refused to make any public comment about the issue, he assisted ABA officials, particularly Shelton, who orchestrated public defenses of Taft. In late June, Taft wrote three letters to Shelton carefully explaining the background of his acceptance of the legacy so that Shelton could better coordinate his activities.[29] Although Taft disavowed any intention of suggesting any action or form of action to be taken by any bar association, he admitted that he was "anxious . . . that some one who knew the facts should advise those who were interested to inquire."[30]

In coordinating the ABA's efforts to rally public support for the chief justice, Shelton devoted particular attention to the South, which had given Taft its heart if not its electoral votes. Shelton, a Virginian, concentrated on the South because he had strong personal connections there and believed that defense of Taft from Democrats would have greater credibility. Shelton also recognized that many southern editors would be amenable to his conservative appeal and that their support could counteract the populistic tendencies of many southerners. Taft's popularity in the region assured that Shelton's appeals would fall upon sympathetic ears.[31]

Working with Robert C. Alston, an Atlanta attorney, Shelton succeeded in persuading newspaper editors throughout the South to publish editorials supporting Taft.[32] By June, Shelton could inform Taft that every major southern newspaper would publish between one and three editorials supporting Taft's acceptance of the Carnegie legacy and criticizing efforts to curtail the Court's jurisdiction.[33] He explained, "Our program has been to organize the Southern Press and afterwards the Press of the country in defense of the Courts." The editors would explain that Hearst was "using an innocent incident to attack the Courts" and that there was no good reason why Taft should not enjoy the bequest. Shelton advised Taft that clippings of the editorials would be sent to southern senators and representatives.[34] Shelton's description of the editorials was apt, for many offered florid praises of Taft and bitter denunciations of Hearst without providing

[29] Taft to Thomas W. Shelton, June 23, 1923; June 24, 1923; June 25, 1923, *Taft Papers*, Series 3, Reel 254.

[30] Taft to Thomas W. Shelton, June 28, 1923, *Taft Papers*, Series 3, Reel 254.

[31] As the editor of the Harrisonburg, Virginia, newspaper observed in an editorial defending Taft, southerners had an affection for Taft because he had appointed to the Court two southerners, Horace H. Lurton and Joseph R. Lamar, and had elevated a Louisianan, Justice Edward D. White, to the chief justiceship ("A Rebuke of Reckless Journalism," *Daily News-Record*, July 6, 1923, p. 4).

[32] Thomas W. Shelton to Taft, June 7, 1923, *Taft Papers*, Series 3, Reel 254.

[33] Thomas W. Shelton to Taft, June 27, 1923, *Taft Papers*, Series 3, Reel 254.

[34] Thomas W. Shelton to Taft, June 28, 1923, *Taft Papers*, Series 3, Reel 254.

many facts concerning the character of the legacy or the background of its creation.[35] In July, the ABA also helped to maneuver the Georgia Senate and the Virginia Bar Association into approving resolutions in support of Taft.[36]

Although Taft repeatedly insisted that he would remain publicly silent about the storm over the Carnegie legacy[37] and proposals to curb the Court's jurisdiction, he tacitly defended the Court in a speech delivered at the unveiling of a monument to Chief Justice Salmon P. Chase in Cincinnati on May 30, 1923. Since the Court during Chase's tenure had been much maligned, Taft believed that the dedication of the monument would provide an ideal occasion to remind the nation of the Court's resilience.[38] "There is nothing new under the sun," Taft remarked to an editor shortly before he went to Cincinnati, "and certainly the proposals of Mr. La Follette and Mr. Borah and others are not lacking in novelty, however they may be lacking in wisdom."[39]

In his speech, Taft recalled that Chase guided the Court through the turbulent years of Reconstruction and rather pointedly emphasized that Chase found himself at odds with a Congress dominated by radical Republicans. Taft recounted that "in the heat of the feeling against the Court, bills were proposed limiting its power to declare laws invalid by a majority, and there were serious proposals made to abolish this power of the Court altogether." Although he acknowledged that "mistakes were made by the Court in those days, as at other times, for it was and is a human institution," he declared that history had vindicated the fortitude of the Court during those stormy years. The "people now are glad that the guarantees of personal liberty were maintained by the Court against the partisan zeal of the then majority. The Court survived the inevitable attacks upon its jurisdiction as it had survived them so many times before." Observing that the animus of the Chase years were followed by "a judicial calm of twenty-five years," Taft tacitly admitted that the Court had again been the subject of much criticism during the

[35] See "When Gutter Scribes Assail the Nation's Highest Court," *Atlanta Journal,* June 22, 1923.

[36] Resolution Approving the Legacy of Andrew Carnegie to Honorable William Howard Taft, *Taft Papers,* Series 3, Reel 259; "Georgians Indorse Taft," *New York Times,* July 27, 1923, p. 13; Taft to Shelton, June 28, 1923, *Taft Papers,* Series 3, Reel 254; *Daily News-Record* (Harrisonburg, Virginia), July 26, 1923. The Georgia resolution expressed the Senate's approval of the Carnegie bequest and declared that Taft's life and character had been "a blessing and a benefaction to the nation."

[37] For example, Taft to Horace Taft, May 16, 1923; Taft to William D. Johnson, May 23, 1923, *Taft Papers,* Series 3, Reel 253.

[38] Taft to Frank Irving Cobb, May 24, 1923, *Taft Papers,* Series 3, Reel 253.

[39] Taft to Rollo Ogden, May 24, 1923, *Taft Papers,* Series 3, Reel 253.

years since 1895. Even though he did not directly mention the present controversy, his message for the present was unmistakable:

> From time to time, by reason of its jurisdiction and a proper exercise of it, the Court cannot help becoming the stormy petrol of politics. It is the head of the system of Federal Courts established avowedly to avoid the local prejudice which non-residents may encounter in State courts, a function often likely to ruffle the sensibilities of the communities, the possibility of whose prejudice is thus recognized and avoided. More than this, the Court's duty to ignore the acts of Congress or the State Legislatures, if out of line with the fundamental law of the Nation, inevitably throws it as an obstruction across the path of the then majority who have enacted the invalid legislation. The stronger the majority and the more intense its partisan feeling, the less likely it is to regard constitutional limitations upon its power and the more likely it is to enact laws of questionable validity.

Taft declared, "It is convincing evidence of the sound sense of the American People in the long run and their love of civil liberty and its constitutional guarantees that, in spite of hostility thus frequently engendered, the Court has lived with its powers unimpaired until the present day."[40]

In an editorial praising Taft's account of the tribulations of the Chase Court, the *New York Times* predicted that the present chorus against the Supreme Court "will die into silence, as it has died before. In the end, the people never fail to see that the Supreme Court is the faithful and necessary, if by no means infallible guardian of their liberties and rights. Congresses have their little hour of strut and rave. The Court stays."[41]

Apart from his Philadelphia address in May 1922, delivered before attacks on the Court had become so direct and persistent, Taft's Cincinnati address was the nearest he ever came to responding publicly to proposals to curb the Court's jurisdiction. On numerous occasions, he declined invitations to make any further public defense of the Court because he believed that defenses of the Court should be left to members of the bar.[42]

---

[40] "Address of Chief Justice Taft," *American Bar Association Journal*, June 1923, pp. 348–52. See also "Taft Lauds Record of Supreme Court," *New York Times*, May 31, 1923, p. 14.

[41] Editorial, "The Supreme Court and Partisan Passion," May 31, 1923, p. 14.

[42] In June 1923, for example, he turned down an opportunity to present his views to some of the Court's most outspoken critics when he declined an invitation to write an article for the *Brotherhood of Locomotive Engineers Journal*. Taft also refused opportunities

Although Taft refused to make any more public defenses of the Court, politics was so ingrained in him that a passive role for the beleaguered chief justice would have been unthinkable. Even though he cleaved in theory to a creed of legal formalism, in practice he was the consummate legal realist. Despite Taft's public reticence, the chambers of the Supreme Court were no cloister but the center of the former president's active political network. Taft carried on the efforts that he had begun during the storm over the Carnegie legacy to help coordinate support for the Court. To ensure wide coverage of his Cincinnati address, for example, Taft sent advance copies to editors of major newspapers in New York, Philadelphia, and Washington.[43]

In his attempts to generate defenses of the Court, Taft's principal agent was the American Bar Association. As the largest professional organization of attorneys, the ABA could not have remained aloof from the controversy over the Court, and its mainstream conservatism ensured that it would defend the status quo. Taft's maneuvers, however, may have embroiled the ABA even more intensely in the defense of the Court. Taft's far-flung political connections and his long association with the ABA, of which he served as president during 1913, guaranteed the success of his efforts to ensure that the ABA would not slacken in its defense of the Court.

At the same time, Taft used the attacks on the Court as a means of eliciting support from the organized bar for his cherished program of procedural reform. Shortly before he left Washington for the annual meeting of the ABA in August 1923, Taft explained to his Yale classmate Clarence Kelsey that he sought "to organize the Bench and the Bar into a united group in this country dedicated to the cause of the improvement in judicial procedure and in the defense of the constitutional provisions for the maintenance, through the judiciary, of the guarantees of the Constitution." Taft stated that there "is no reason

---

to address more friendly audiences when he declined an offer to write articles for the *American Legion Weekly* and the American Legion magazine in Washington State. Taft suggested that the *American Legion Weekly* editor solicit an article from Attorney General Wickersham. Taft also turned down invitations from the American Security League and Temple Beth El of Detroit. Taft to Albert F. Coyle, June 11, 1923; Albert F. Coyle to Taft, June 8, 1923; *Taft Papers*, Series 3, Reel 254; Taft to Ira Jewell Williams, August 4, 1923, Series 3, Reel 255; Taft to L. B. Schwellenbach, August 5, 1923, ibid.; Taft to E. L. Harvey, September 11, 1923, E. L. Harvey to Taft, September 5, 1923, Series 3, Reel 256; Taft to Jacob Nathan, September 24, 1923, Series 3, Reel 257.

[43] Taft to Rollo Ogden (editor, *New York Times*), Taft to Frank Irving Cobb (editor, New York *World*), Taft to Theodore W. Noyes (editor, *Evening Star*, Washington, D.C.), Taft to David E. Smiley (editor, *Public Ledger*, Philadelphia), Taft to John J. Spurgeon (managing editor, *Washington Post*), May 25, 1923; *Taft Papers*, Series 3, Reel 253.

why the Bar should not exert a tremendous influence through the country." He warned, however, that proper organization was necessary to achieve this result.[44]

In addition to his work through the national structure of the ABA, Taft was always willing to lend encouragement to the activities of state bar associations and to offer suggestions for coordination of defenses of the Court. In February 1923, for example, Taft wrote to thank the secretary of the Massachusetts Bar Association for writing an article in opposition to curbing the Court's power, expressing satisfaction "that answers to these attacks are taking form."[45] After Lewis H. Smith informed Taft that Smith's widely reported October 1923 address to the California State Bar Association was being distributed to all attorneys in California, Taft urged Smith to send the address to every member of Congress if possible and at least to every member of the California congressional delegation.[46]

As part of its campaign to rally support for the Court, the ABA tried to take advantage of every opportunity to direct favorable publicity toward the Court and Constitution. For example, when David Lloyd George toured the United States during the autumn of 1923, Shelton tried to arrange for the former British prime minister to make a pilgrimage to John Marshall's tomb, but he apparently preferred to visit Civil War sites. "Whether it was because Lloyd George was more interested in the late War Between the States or less interested in judicial matters one cannot even speculate," Shelton reported to Taft.[47]

At the behest of Taft and on their own initiative, more and more defenders of the Court came forth to sound the alarm against proposals to curtail judicial powers. Within a few weeks of La Follette's address to the AFL in June 1922, Rome G. Brown, who had so assiduously opposed the judicial recall, drafted a resolution condemning La Follette's proposal. The Hennepin County Bar Association in Minnesota adopted the resolution and sent four thousand copies of it to the press, judges, and lawyers. Brown warned Taft that constant vigilance was necessary to quelch La Follette's plan.[48] As in the fights against the recall of judges and the judicial referendum, the organized bar was highly vigilant and became the most aggressive defender of judicial

[44] Taft to Clarence Kelsey, August 17, 1923, *Taft Papers*, Series 3, Reel 256.

[45] Taft to F. W. Grinnell, February 16, 1923, *Taft Papers*, Series 3, Reel 250.

[46] Lewis H. Smith to Taft, October 25, 1923, *Taft Papers*, Series 3, Reel 257; Taft to Lewis H. Smith, November 1, 1923, *Taft Papers*, Series 3, Reel 258.

[47] Thomas W. Shelton to Taft, October 30, 1923, *Taft Papers*, Series 3, Reel 258.

[48] Rome G. Brown to Taft, July 5, 1922, *Taft Papers*, Series 3, Reel 243; *American Law Review* 56 (July–August 1922): 617–20.

power. Throughout 1923, various bar associations endorsed resolutions opposing any abridgment of the Court's powers.[49] It is not surprising that the elite bar would work to protect the power of the courts since the judiciary had been such a staunch defender of property rights. Lord Bryce contended that the power and influence of the legal profession in America had been a major factor in maintaining the power and influence of the federal courts, since the bar's support for the courts "ensured the obedience of the people."[50]

One of the most tireless and influential defenders of the Court was Charles Warren, whose works spanned audiences of lawyers, scholars, and the general public. In October 1923, Warren reached millions of Americans with his *Saturday Evening Post* article attacking the Borah and La Follette proposals.[51] Published two months before the convocation of a Congress in which the progressives who held the balance of power were expected to push for court reform, the appearance of Warren's article was masterfully timed to have maximum impact. Warren's article was reprinted and widely distributed by the National Security League. Shelton also arranged for the ABA to distribute many thousands of copies of Warren's article to the state bar committees.[52]

Here again, Taft's hidden hand was operating. Taft commended Shelton for distributing the article and told Shelton, "It is quite important especially to send it to the members of the Senate and House."[53] He congratulated Warren for publishing the article in "a place where it will have such wide circulation" and thanked him for having "pricked the bubble" of the Court's critics.[54] After Warren defended the Court before the Maryland State Bar Association in an address on 5–4 decisions during the spring of 1923, Taft urged him to send a copy of his speech to every member of Congress. "No one can overestimate the value of your work in this regard," he told Warren, "because I conceive that there will be a decided majority in each House against any such change as that proposed, if only you make them understand what the question is." Meanwhile, Holmes praised Warren as "the bulwark of the Court."[55]

[49] "Public Opinion Defends Supreme Court," pp. 119–22.

[50] James Bryce, *The American Commonwealth*, 2d ed., vol. 1 (London: Macmillan, 1891), pp. 259–61.

[51] Charles Warren, "Borah and LaFollette vs. the Supreme Court," *Saturday Evening Post*, October 13, 1923, p. 31.

[52] Shelton to Taft, October 30, 1923.

[53] Taft to Shelton, November 1, 1923, *Taft Papers*, Series 3, Reel 258.

[54] Taft to Charles Warren, October 12, 1923, *Taft Papers*, Series 3, Reel 257.

[55] Taft to Charles Warren, April 2, 1924, *Charles Warren Papers*, Box 2, Manuscript Division, Library of Congress; Oliver Wendell Holmes, Jr. to Mrs. Charles Warren, November 10, 1924, (ibid.).

Warren also defended the Court's power in his magnum opus, *The Supreme Court in United States History*, published in three volumes during the spring of 1922. Warren's study was the first comprehensive history of the Court since George Ticknor Curtis's work of 1889, and it was widely praised for its thoroughness. Drawing heavily upon primary sources, Warren's book traced the history of criticism of the Court and attempts to curb its powers. Warren pointed out that the Court had repeatedly withstood the slings of myopic detractors who failed to appreciate the Court's contributions to the Republic's stability, prosperity, and freedom. Although Warren acknowledged that the Court had made mistakes, he argued that the history of the Court demonstrated that the liberties of Americans were "safer in the hands of the Judiciary than in those of the Legislature, and that if either body is to possess uncontrolled omnipotence, it should be reposed in the Court rather than in Congress, and in independent Judges rather than in Judges dependent on election by the people in passionate party campaigns and on partisan political issues."[56]

Warren explained to Taft that he had intended to provide "an arsenal of weapons for the defenders of the Court as an institution," for he had foreseen that the Court would "pass through another of the recurrent tides of criticism which have occurred at variously recurring periods in American history."[57] Taft appears to have found the book useful. Although he privately noted that Warren was "inaccurate and his judgment is not reliable in certain respects," he praised Warren for demonstrating that the "Court has lived through a great many attacks at every stage of its history" and that the failure of frequent efforts to curb its power showed that public opinion "insists on the maintenance of the jurisdiction of the Court." Taft remarked that he had not known that attacks upon the Court during the tenures of Marshall, Taney, and Chase had been so virulent.[58]

Warren reiterated his defense of judicial review in a highly polemical book published a decade later in 1935. Meanwhile, Beveridge declared in a December 1923 *Saturday Evening Post* article that "the Supreme Court has been far harder on capital" than on labor, and that the Supreme Court had been "far more liberal than state supreme courts."[59] During this period, James M. Beck, who served as solicitor

---

[56] Charles Warren, *The Supreme Court in United States History* (Boston: Little, Brown, 1926), pp. 754–55.

[57] Charles Warren to Taft, November 7, 1922, *Taft Papers*, Series 3, Reel 247.

[58] Taft to Charles P. Taft, II, September 4, 1922, *Taft Papers*, Series 3, Reel 245.

[59] Charles Warren, *Congress, the Constitution and the Supreme Court* (Boston: Little Brown, 1935); Albert J. Beveridge, "Common Sense and the Constitution," *Saturday Evening Post*, December 15, 1923, p. 122.

general from 1921 to 1925, published widely distributed treatises on the Constitution that extolled judicial review.[60]

Although the warnings by opponents of court reform about the dangers of legislative tyranny did not lack resonance, their insistence that the Court was a palladium of personal liberties rang rather hollow. As we have seen, the liberties of the Bill of Rights had not yet been applied to the states, and the Court had only rarely protected non-economic liberties against infringements by the federal government.

As Steven F. Lawson has pointed out, Warren's contention that the Court was a guardian of civil liberties was a shrewd but cynical argument "aimed at appealing to a wide audience." Despite Warren's appeal to the need for the preservation of civil liberties, Warren had advocated a plan for prosecuting civilians by military courts in espionage and sedition cases when he served as assistant attorney general during the war. Lawson aptly observed that "In reality, conservative spokesmen valued the judiciary more as the defender of private property interests than as a protector of free speech for radicals or the right of workers to strike."[61]

Two weeks after Taft's speech in Cincinnati, however, the Supreme Court handed down *Meyer v. Nebraska*, a major decision that provided support for defenders of the Court who argued that the Court was a bulwark against legislative tyranny. By a 7–2 vote, the Court nullified statutes in Nebraska, Iowa, and Ohio that prohibited instruction in foreign languages to elementary school students in private and parochial schools.[62] They had been challenged by German Lutheran parochial schools, which alleged that the statutes interfered with property rights, parental freedom, and liberty of religion.

In striking down the statutes, the Court articulated a broad vision of personal freedom. Although the Court based its rulings partly on the ground that the statutes violated the economic rights of the appellants, the Court also for the first time invoked the Fourteenth Amendment to uphold personal liberties in a case that did not involve racial discrimination. Although the Court acknowledged that "the state may do much, go very far, indeed, in order to improve the quality of its citizens, physically, mentally and morally," the Court declared that "the individ-

---

[60] James M. Beck, *The Constitution of the United States: A Brief Study of the Genesis, Formulation and Political Philosophy of the Constitution of the United States* (New York: George H. Doran, 1922); James M. Beck, *The Constitution of the United States: Yesterday, Today—and Tommorrow?* (New York: George H. Doran, 1924); Kammen, *Machine*, p. 252.

[61] Steven F. Lawson, "Progressives and the Supreme Court: A Case for Judicial Reform in the 1920s," *The Historian* 42 (May 1980): 424.

[62] *Meyer v. Nebraska*, 262 U.S. 390 (1923); *Bartels v. Iowa, Bohning v. Ohio, Pohl v. Ohio, Nebraska District of Evangelical Lutheran Synod v. McKelvie*, 262 U.S. 404 (1923).

ual has certain fundamental rights which must be respected."[63] Since the Court found that no emergency justified restrictions on foreign-language instruction, the Court determined that the state could not infringe the rights of the individuals. The Court declared that the Fourteenth Amendment "denotes not merely freedom from bodily restraint but also the right of the individual to contract, to engage in any of the common occupations of life, to acquire useful knowledge, to marry, establish a home and bring up children, to worship God according to the dictates of his own conscience, and generally to enjoy those privileges long recognized at common law as essential to the orderly pursuit of happiness by free men."[64]

The breadth of the Court's language, which went far beyond what was necessary to justify its decision, suggests that the Court was consciously attempting to demonstrate its primacy as the guardian of personal liberties. In rendering its decision, however, the Court had not impaired its ability to continue to act as the watchdog of economic legislation and to uphold legislative restrictions upon radical groups. By tying personal freedom to economic freedom, the Court had actually buttressed the doctrine of economic due process. And the liberties that the Court had enumerated were not likely to be invoked by political radicals. Freedom of speech, the liberty most frequently relied upon by radicals, was conspicuously absent from the Court's list. Ultimately, however, the decision provided a precedent for further judicial expansion of fundamental rights. In particular, it helped to prepare the way for the long process by which the Court would incorporate into state law most of the specific guarantees of the Bill of Rights.[65]

Despite its fecund implications, the *Meyer* decision received little attention among progressives and trade unionists. Although the decision had the effect of invalidating restrictions on teaching foreign languages in approximately twenty states, the beneficiaries of the decision were mostly conservative farming people and urban ethnic workers who presented no challenge to the political, social, or economic order. The impact of the decision may help to explain why liberals tended to ignore the decision. The strain of nativism that infected substantial elements of the progressive movement also explains why the decision received little attention, since progressives were not likely to hail a decision that enabled ethnic Americans, particularly German Americans, to preserve their distinctive heritages.

[63] Ibid., p. 401.
[64] 262 U.S. at 399.
[65] William G. Ross, "A Judicial Janus: Meyer v. Nebraska in Historical Perspective," *University of Cincinnati Law Review* 57 (1988): 125, 185–203.

But although middle-class progressives scarcely noticed *Meyer*, the decision helped to rally support for the Court among millions of ethnic Americans. The statutes that were nullified in *Meyer* were part of a broader recrudescence of nativism that threatened the culture of ethnic Americans. Wartime efforts to encourage "100 percent Americanism" had continued during the unsettled and anxious postwar years when many Anglo-Americans blamed ethnic Americans for the problems of an increasingly complex society. As John Higham has pointed out, the widespread feeling that "things had gone terribly wrong at home and abroad" and the enervation of the progressive spirit of reform "transferred energies into negative and destructive programs."[66]

In addition to trying to suppress the use of foreign languages, many nativists waged a vigorous campaign against parochial education. The movement for compulsory public education received active support from a number of fraternal lodges, civic organizations, and the Ku Klux Klan, which attracted millions of members in every corner of the nation during the early 1920s. Although voters in Michigan defeated a compulsory public school initiative by 2–1 margins in 1920 and 1924 and a similar measure was defeated more narrowly in Washington in 1924, Oregon approved a compulsory public education law in 1922. The movement to require compulsory public education caused deep anxiety among Roman Catholics and many Lutherans, who believed that parochial education was necessary for the preservation of their distinctive religious beliefs. Throughout their struggle to preserve their schools, the leaders of these churches expressed confidence that compulsory public education was unconstitutional and that the courts would ultimately vindicate the right to parochial education.

The *Meyer* decision, handed down only seven months after the victory of the Oregon initiative, seemed to justify the confidence of Roman Catholic and Lutheran leaders, for the Court's broad language about parental rights strongly suggested that the Court would disfavor the Oregon legislation. Arthur F. Mullen, a Roman Catholic attorney who had successfully argued against the language laws before the Court, believed that *Meyer* struck a blow at the "whole brood of laws that are aimed at the citizen because of his religion, his nationality and his condition in life."[67] *Meyer* breathed life into the argument that the

[66] John Higham, *Strangers in the Land: Patterns of American Nativism, 1860–1925*, 2d ed. (New Brunswick, N.J.: Rutgers University Press, 1988), p. 282.

[67] Arthur F. Mullen to John J. Burke, June 14, 1923, Records of the United States Catholic Conference, Box 14, Department of Archives and Manuscripts, The Catholic University of America.

judiciary was the guardian of personal liberties. After *Meyer*, the defenders of judicial power directed their arguments heavily toward ethnic Americans, who were struggling to prevent the extinction of their parochial schools and the suppression of their cultural identities. The Court's invalidation of the Oregon school law in 1925 consolidated ethnic support for the federal judiciary.

One week after the Court announced its decision in *Meyer*, the Court handed down another decision that had broad appeal to both liberals and conservatives. In *Wolff Packing Co. v. Court of Industrial Relations*,[68] the Court struck down a Kansas statute that had established a three-person commission to settle disputes involving wages and working conditions in key industries. In a unanimous opinion, the Court held that the state could not regulate most of those industries because they did not sufficiently affect the public interest. Although the statute had been enacted at the behest of Henry J. Allen, a progressive governor of Kansas, the statute was widely opposed by many progressives. For example, Felix Frankfurter believed that compulsory arbitration was ineffective and unjust as long as trade unionism was not widely accepted and there was no recognized body of industrial standards that industrial commissions could apply.[69]

The Kansas statute was also strongly opposed by many labor leaders, especially Samuel Gompers. The AFL had denounced the statute as an "an act to establish involuntary servitude for the workers of Kansas," and an "act to protect the financial interests of the owners of public utilities at the expense of the employers."[70] Gompers, who had been convinced that the courts would not invalidate the statute, was delighted by the Court's decision. Conservative organizations such as the National Manufacturers' Association, which had resented the commission's restrictions on the autonomy of employers, also hailed the decision.[71]

Amid the jubilation over the invalidation of the Kansas statute, only a few progressives and trade unionists seemed bothered that the same theory of limitations on legislative power the Court had relied upon in *Wolff* had been invoked by the Court in striking down statutes that liberals supported. Frankfurter, one of the few progressive commentators to notice this contradiction, contended that "it was for the legislature of Kansas, and not for the Supreme Court, to kill" the Kansas

[68] 262 U.S. 522 (1923).

[69] "Exit the Kansas Court," *New Republic*, June 27, 1923; (Editorial), pp. 112–13, repr. Philip B. Kurland, ed., *Felix Frankfurter on the Supreme Court: Extrajudicial Essays on the Court and the Constitution* (Cambridge: Harvard University Press, 1970), pp. 141–42.

[70] Philip Taft, *The A. F. of L. in the Time of Gompers* (New York: Harper, 1957), p. 413.

[71] Frankfurter, "Exit Kansas Court," pp. 140–41; Taft, *AFL.*, p. 417 n. 59.

law.[72] Frankfurter also warned that the Court's benign use of judicial power did not outweigh its malign uses.[73] Few critics of the courts were as consistent or principled as Frankfurter. Although some opponents of judicial review could justify decisions like *Meyer* by a distinction between review of economic regulations and review of legislation involving personal liberties, most critics of the courts, as the reaction to *Wolff* suggests, were opposed to the way the courts exercised their power rather than to the power itself.

Although *Meyer* and *Wolff* and the propaganda campaigns waged by defenders of the judiciary helped to diminish criticism of the Court, the practical exigencies of congressional politics contributed more significantly to the waning prospects for court reform during 1923. The inability of progressives to agree on any single measure assured the failure of any plan to abridge the Court's power to review legislation. Even if the progressives had united in support of a particular measure, however, such a measure would probably have failed to survive the treacherous shoals of congressional scrutiny.

Contrary to the hopes of liberals and the expectations of many political observers, progressives failed to dominate the Sixty-eighth Congress even though they ostensibly held the balance of power. As La Follette ruefully conceded late in 1923, progressives lacked the strength to secure the enactment of significant reform legislation.[74] Moreover, the progressives lacked representation on key congressional committees that would decide the fate of reform legislation. No proponent of judicial reform sat on the House Judiciary Committee. Although Borah and Norris were members of the Senate Judiciary Committee, other members were indifferent or hostile to court reform. The House Rules Committee would have buried the measures even if the Judiciary Committee had approved them.[75]

The strength of congressional support for the federal judiciary was demonstrated by the enactment of judicial reform statutes in 1922[76] and 1925[77] for which Taft and his fellow justices had vigorously lobbied. Motivated by Taft's desire to make the federal judiciary more efficient and reduce its growing workload, both statutes augmented the power of the federal judiciary, particularly the Supreme Court and especially the chief justice. The 1922 statute created two dozen new

[72] "Exit Kansas Court," p. 141.

[73] Editorial, "Can the Supreme Court Guarantee Toleration?" *New Republic*, June 17, 1925, pp. 85–87, repr. *Frankfurter on Supreme Court*, pp. 174–78.

[74] *La Follette's Magazine*, December 1923, p. 178.

[75] Lawson, "Progressives and Supreme Court," p. 429.

[76] Act of September 14, 1922, 42 Stat. 837.

[77] Act of February 13, 1925, ch. 229, 43 Stat. 936.

district court judgeships and permitted the chief justice to assign district judges to overworked circuits. It also created a judicial conference, headed by the chief justice, to oversee the work of the federal courts and to promote legislation, particularly the revision of procedural rules. The 1925 statute, the so-called Judges' Bill, sharply decreased the number of appeals that the Supreme Court was obliged to hear by greatly enlarging the scope of the Court's discretionary certiorari jurisdiction.

Both statutes encountered considerable opposition from progressives, the AFL, and other critics of the federal judiciary. AFL leaders, for example, predicted that the annual convocation of the judicial conference would "permit those who believe in judge-made laws to sow the seed that will bring about a unanimity of decisions against labor and the people."[78] Southern congressmen who distrusted the federal judiciary succeeded in defeating Taft's proposal for eighteen judges who would serve at large, to be deployed by the chief justice to any court in the country. Senator John K. Shields of Tennessee warned against the "political influence and power over the judiciary of which a designing man could avail himself in times of great political turmoil."[79] Other senators also objected to the provision to permit the chief justice to assign judges to overworked districts since it would unduly aggrandize the chief justice's power and would send judges to remote districts with which they were unfamiliar.[80]

Antagonists of the judiciary also alleged that the judicial conference would transfer power from the lower federal courts to the Supreme Court[81] and that its annual meetings in Washington would provide the occasion for profligate social activities and expose the judges to the blandishments of lobbyists for large corporations.[82] During a Senate debate in 1922, Norris warned that the judges would "be killed with social favoritisms before they get down to business." He predicted that favor seekers would lavish special attention on "the genial Chief Justice we have, who dines out somewhere every night." In one of the most stinging public attacks on Taft during his years as chief justice, Norris

[78] *Report of Proceedings of the Forty-Second Annual Convention of the American Federation of Labor* (Washington, D.C., 1922) p. 95.

[79] 62 *Congressional Record*, 67th Cong., 2d sess., March 31, 1922, pp. 4861–63; ibid., April 5, 1922, pp. 5097–98 (remarks of Senator Overman, North Carolina).

[80] Ibid., March 31, 1922, p. 4849 (remarks of Senator Thaddeus H. Caraway, Arkansas); ibid., April 6, 1922, p. 5107 (remarks of Senator John Sharp Williams, Mississippi).

[81] 62 *Congressional Record*, 67th Cong., 2d sess., March 31, 1922, pp. 4863–64 (remarks of Senator Shields); ibid., March 31, 1922, p. 4853 (remarks of Senator Overman).

[82] *Report of Proceedings of the Forty-Second Annual Convention of the American Federation of Labor* (Washington, D.C.: Law Reporter, 1922), pp. 93–95, 339–40.

went on to declare, "I do not believe there is any man who can stick his legs under the tables of the idle rich every night and be fit the next day to sit in judgment upon those who toil."[83]

Vigorous lobbying by the ABA and the justices hepled to convince Congress that the measures were needed. The provision for a judicial conference passed the House without a division and was approved by the Senate 36–29. Although the Judges' Bill at first encountered intense opposition from Senator Thomas J. Walsh of Montana, who alleged that it verified the maxim "that a good court always seeks to extend its jurisdiction,"[84] the Senate approved the measure by a 76–1 vote, with Norris, La Follette, and Shields absent. Walsh and Borah voted for the measure.

Despite its enactment of the 1922 and 1925 judicial reform acts, Congress balked at Taft's proposal for a uniform code of federal procedure, to be formulated by the Supreme Court with the approval of Congress. Opponents of the rules believed that Taft's proposal would concentrate greater power in the federal courts at the expense of state courts, whose procedures were followed by federal courts. They also feared that the rules would transfer power to the Supreme Court at the expense of Congress, since the Court would propose the rules and would presumably wield considerable influence over congressional approval. Although Taft worked tirelessly for the rules throughout his tenure, a uniform code of procedure was not authorized by Congress until 1934 and did not take effect until 1938.[85]

Although the refusal of Congress during the 1920s to authorize federal rules of procedure reflected tensions between Congress and the Court, congressional approval of the 1922 and 1925 statutes demonstrated that Congress generally remained amicable toward the federal courts. Congress was willing to increase the efficiency of the federal courts, even if the new reforms risked the aggrandizement of the Supreme Court's power. The enactment of the two judicial reform acts

[83] 62 *Congressional Record*, 67th Cong., 2d sess., April 6, 1922, pp. 5113–14. Although Norris received many letters condemning his biting remarks about the chief justice, some of his correspondents praised him. An Alabamian, for example, thanked Norris for having the courage to speak the truth in "audible, understandable, language." He explained that "grave fears. . . beset me when I see the heads of the institutions that I must rely upon for protection against injustice, contracting debts, the payment of which, might seriously affect, and retard my chances of obtaining justice" W. L. Varner to Norris, April 13, 1922, *Norris Papers*, Box 31, Library of Congress.

[84] "The Overburdened Supreme Court," address by Thomas J. Walsh delivered at Lynchburg, Virginia, June 8, 1922, 62 *Congressional Record*, 67th Cong., 2d sess., June 12, 1922, p. 8547.

[85] Alpheus Thomas Mason, *William Howard Taft: Chief Justice* (New York: Simon and Schuster, 1964), pp. 114–20.

was particularly noteworthy since congressional consideration of the measures could have inspired a debate about the courts that would have increased the momentum for curtailment of federal judicial power. Yet despite a few volleys against the courts by Norris, Walsh, Shields, and a handful of other senators, the consideration of these bills did not provide the occasion for any serious or sustained congressional scrutiny of judicial power. It is ironic that Congress increased the power of the federal courts at the very time that agitation by progressives and labor leaders for curtailment of judicial power was reaching a new intensity. In view of such resilient congressional support for the federal judiciary, it is no wonder that progressives and trade unionists did not make more serious efforts to fight for legislation to curb the federal judiciary.

TWELVE

THE JUDICIAL ISSUE IN THE 1924 ELECTION

Every minority body that may be weak in resources or
unpopular in the public estimation, also nearly every race
and religious belief, would find themselves practically
without protection if the authority of the Supreme Court
should be broken down and its powers lodged
with the Congress.
*(President Calvin Coolidge, speech in Baltimore,
September 6, 1924)*[1]

In all the history of this world, no people has ever looked
to the courts as the guardian of its liberties. The liberties
of the people rest with the people.
*Robert M. La Follette, presidential campaign speech in Omaha,
October 20, 1924)*[2]

THE RESILIENCE of public support for the power of the Supreme Court was tested and demonstrated by the 1924 election in which Calvin Coolidge and Charles G. Dawes won a landslide victory after a shrill campaign in which they and their fellow Republicans sedulously attacked La Follette's proposal to curb the Court's power. Republican warnings that any diminution of the Court's power would threaten civil liberties and prosperity helped to drain votes from La Follette, who mounted an initially formidable third-party bid for the presidency. The election helped to vindicate Taft's belief that the nation was too conservative to countenance any tampering with the Supreme Court, and it chilled the anti-Court movement for a decade.

La Follette's candidacy grew out of a mild revival of political liberalism that was reflected in the formation of the Conference for Progressive Political Action (CPPA) in 1922; the success of progressive candidates in the 1922 congressional elections; and the growing disenchantment of farmers, intellectuals, and the labor movement with the

---

[1] "Coolidge Assails La Follette Views on Supreme Court," *New York Times*, September 7, 1924, p. 1.

[2] *La Follette Family Papers*, Series B, Box 228, Manuscript Division, Library of Congress.

Republican and Democratic parties. After Borah rejected overtures from progressives to lead a third-party ticket,[3] La Follette emerged as the most likely third-party candidate. Insisting that he would not lead a separate movement if either major party adopted a progressive platform, La Follette urged Republicans to endorse his proposals for popular consideration of a constitutional amendment to permit Congress to reenact statutes the Supreme Court had invalidated and the direct election of federal judges for terms of not more than ten years.[4] In early July, after the GOP convention rejected La Follette's platform and it became clear that the Democrats would not endorse a progressive program, La Follette announced that he would run for president as an independent.

La Follette's first choice for a running mate was Justice Brandeis. Although Brandeis rejected an overture from La Follette, he may have given it some serious consideration.[5] Predicting that La Follette would mount a "grand fight," Brandeis told his brother that "if I had several watertight compartment lives, I should have liked to be in it. The enemies are vulnerable and the time ripe."[6] Taft told a friend, "I know enough about Brandeis to know that that is the last position which he would accept." Taft acknowledged, however, that "his sympathies may be with La Follette, though I should not think he would go so far as La Follette with reference to the abolition of the power of the Court."[7] After Brandeis's rejection of the nomination, La Follette turned to Senator Burton K. Wheeler of Montana. As a Democrat, Wheeler helped to lessen the reluctance of Democrats to vote for La Follette, who remained a Republican. Wheeler's blunt populism and energetic campaign style were also expected to help the ticket.[8]

La Follette received the endorsements of the CPPA, the Socialist

---

[3] LeRoy Ashby, *The Spearless Leader: Senator Borah and the Progressive Movement in the 1920s* (Urbana: University of Illinois Press, 1972), pp. 124–36.

[4] "Delegates Worried About La Follette," *New York Times*, June 9, 1924, p. 1. The proposal did not specify the size of the majority by which the measure would need to be reenacted. In addition its call for Court reform, the platform advocated nationalization of the railroads, repeal of the Esch-Cummins railroad law, prompt ratification of the child-labor amendment, removal of legal discriminations against women that would not prejudice legislation for their protection, and elimination of the injunction in labor disputes.

[5] Belle Case La Follette and Fola La Follette, *Robert M. La Follette*, vol. 2 (New York: Macmillan, 1953), p. 1115.

[6] Louis D. Brandeis to Alfred Brandeis, July 19, 1924, in Melvin Urofsky and David W. Levy., eds., *Letters of Louis D. Brandeis*, vol. 5 (Albany: State University of New York Press, 1978), p. 134.

[7] Taft to Max Pam, September 12, 1924, *Taft Papers*, Series 3, Reel 267, Manuscript Division, Library of Congress.

[8] "What Wheeler Brings to La Follette," *Literary Digest*, August 2, 1924, pp 9–11.

party, and the AFL. The AFL reluctantly endorsed La Follette only after the major parties had refused to endorse the AFL's proposals for various reforms, including a constitutional amendment to permit Congress to reenact by a two-thirds vote any measure that the Supreme Court had nullifed.[9] Although the AFL could hardly have expected the Republican platform to accommodate such measures, the Democratic party's complete lack of encouragement came as a bitter disappointment. As Samuel Gompers ruefully observed, the Democratic and Republican parties "are owned body and soul by the same interests."[10] Despite its endorsement of the La Follette campaign, the AFL continued to hew to Gomper's long-standing opposition to the creation of a labor-based political party.[11] Even though the AFL promised to support La Follette with its full resources,[12] it failed to use its full muscle in the campaign.[13]

Although the CPPA did not formally adopt La Follette's platform, the CPPA platform embraced many of the reforms he advocated, including curtailment of judicial power. The CPPA's nebulous court plank called for "abolition of the tyranny and usurpation of the courts, including the practice of nullifying legislation in conflict with the political, social or economic theories of the judges." The platform also advocated election of all federal judges for "limited terms."[14] The

[9] Kenneth C. MacKay, *The Progressive Movement of 1924* (New York: Columbia University Press, 1947), pp. 151–52. The AFL had also called for restriction of injunctions in labor disputes, ratification of the child labor amendment, membership in the League of Nations and the World Court, and various other liberal measures.

[10] Gompers to Dr. J. S. Brandt, October 28, 1924, Reel 300, p. 688, Samuel Gompers MSS, Manuscript Division, Library of Congress.

[11] Accordingly, the AFL endorsement was carefully worded to make it plain that the AFL was supporting the Republican La Follette and the Democratic Wheeler as independent candidates for president and that the AFL was not abandoning its traditional stance of nonpartisanship to endorse the Progressives or any other third party. MacKay, *The Progressive Movement of 1924*, pp. 153–54.

[12] American Federation of Labor National Non-Partisan Political Campaign Committee, letter from Executive Committee to All Organized Labor, August 13, 1924, in *La Follette Family Papers*, Box B-58; "La Follette Silent on U.S. Ownership," *Baltimore Sun*, September 4, 1924, p. 4.

[13] It contributed only about $25,000 to the campaign, about one-tenth of the expenditures of the La Follette-Wheeler effort and a paltry sum indeed compared to the vastly greater sums spent by the Republicans. Taft correctly guessed that "these labor men, after having paid their regular dues, are likely to confine their contributions to shouting and voting." Moreover, the ailing Gompers was too ill to provide the active and inspired leadership that might have rallied greater enthusiasm among workers. Taft to Gus Karger, Oct. 20, 1924, *Taft Papers*, Series 3, Reel 268; MacKay, *Progressive Movement*, pp. 152, 184–89.

[14] Donald Bruce Johnson, ed., *National Party Platforms*, vol. 1, *1840–1956* (Urbana: University of Illinois Press, 1978), p. 256. At its second convention in December 1922, the

vagueness of both platforms suggested that progressives continued to recognize that judicial reform was controversial and that explanation of details would make their proposals even more vulnerable to attack. Moreover, the failure of progressives to explain their proposals more clearly suggests that progressives did not entertain serious hopes for their enactment.

In addition to the support of the CPPA, the Socialists, and the AFL, La Follette also enjoyed considerable support among three other constituencies: farmers, intellectuals, and German Americans. La Follette's support among farmers stemmed from his appeal to their widespread belief that finance capitalists were cheating them out of a fair return on their investments. La Follette had long enjoyed considerable support among intellectuals, whom *The Outlook* described as being first in noise but last in numbers among La Follette's constituents.[15] Intellectuals admired La Follette's civics book approach to government and his accomplishments in Wisconsin. La Follette received the endorsement of *The Nation* and the *New Republic*, and his supporters included such luminaries as Felix Frankfurter, Jane Addams, and Helen Keller. German Americans admired La Follette's courage in risking political ruin by opposing American entry into the war, and they were grateful to him for defending their civil liberties during the war.[16]

La Follette also enjoyed the advantage of having the liberal field largely to himself, since the Republicans adopted a stand-pat platform and nominated the conservative Coolidge and his running mate, Charles G. Dawes, a banker and brigadier general. Progressive ideals fared little better at the Democratic convention. Bitterly divided by sectional and cultural cleavages, the convention remained deadlocked for fifteen days before the delegates finally nominated John Davis on the 103d ballot.

Davis, the Wall Street attorney par excellence, provided an ideal foil

---

CPPA had adopted a platform that called for Congress to terminate judicial review of legislation (ibid., p. 71).

[15] Stanley Frost, "La Follette's Mixed Army," *The Outlook*, October 29, 1924, p. 321.

[16] La Follette's appeal to German Americans, however, was politically parlous insofar as it reminded other Americans of his opposition to the war. The Steuben Society's endorsement may have cost him more than it won (MacKay, *Progressive Movement*, p. 216). Nevertheless, La Follette recognized the importance of his German support and made special attempts throughout the campaign to appeal to German Americans. Virtually all of the cities where La Follette campaigned had heavy German populations, and La Follette emphasized his opposition to the war in speeches in heavily German Cincinnati and St. Louis (*La Follette Family Papers*, Series B, Box 228). Villard reported in mid-October that "there isn't a single audience that does not applaud enthusiastically references to his war record" (Oswald Garrison Villard, "The Prairies Catching Fire," *The Nation*, October 15, 1924, p. 413).

for the Court's critics. Although Davis had supported progressive measures as a member of Congress from 1911 to 1915 and had argued the government's cases for progressive measures as solicitor general from 1915 to 1918,[17] he had emerged as a stalwart advocate for corporate interests after he returned to the private practice of law in 1921 following a stint as ambassador to Great Britain. In seven cases he argued before the Supreme Court, Davis advocated positions that most progressives opposed.[18] His law firm was almost solely devoted to the service of powerful captitalistic enterprises, including large banks, railroads, and public utilities. Its work for J. P. Morgan particularly provoked the indigation of Davis's opponents.[19] Davis had made little attempt to conceal the essential harmony between his personal views and those of his corporate clients. While serving as president of the ABA in 1923, Davis had denounced attempts to curtail judicial power as "an attack upon our theory of government under a written constitution."[20]

Davis's combination of professional brilliance and pragmatic but tenacious conservatism strongly appealed to Taft, who wanted Davis to join him on the bench. Unwilling to leave his lucrative private practice, Davis in 1921 and again in 1922 had discouraged Taft and Van Devanter from trying to persuade the pliable Harding to nominate him to the Court.[21] Aside from his brief return to national politics in 1924, Davis remained in Wall Street for the remainder of his life.

Davis's nomination for president cheered Taft because it relieved his "fear that we shall have a radical in the White House to initiate a change of our constitutional system, and especially to bring about an interference with the function and usefulness of the Federal Judiciary and our Court." Taft predicted that "such nostrums as those advocated by Borah . . . will find no countenance from him."[22] He believed that

[17] William H. Harbaugh, *Lawyer's Lawyer: The Life of John W. Davis* (New York: Oxford University Press, 1973), esp. pp. 70–73, 77–78.

[18] As *The Nation* pointed out, "Almost every one of these cases cuts into an important social issue. To summarize them is to summarize the choice John Davis made when he faced the question of the character of the practice which he would enter" (August 20, 1924, p. 173).

[19] "A Lawyer for President? What Lawyer?" *The Nation*, October 1, 1924, p. 324.

[20] John W. Davis, "Present Day Problems," *American Bar Association Journal*, September 1923, p. 557.

[21] John W. Davis to Willis Van Devanter, October 31, 1922, *Van Devanter Papers*, Box 32, Manuscript Division, Library of Congress; Harbaugh, *Lawyer's Lawyer*, pp. 190–93. Taft conceded that Davis was "entitled to look after his household," but he predicted that Davis would live to regret his decision. Taft feared that if Davis waited, he would "have become so identified with the Morgan interests that no President would feel like taking him right from the center of Wall Street and putting him on the Bench" (Taft to Willis VanDevanter, November 2, 1922, *VanDevanter Papers*, Box 32).

[22] Taft to Henry Taft, July 11, 1924, *Taft Papers*, Series 3, Reel 266, Library of Con-

Davis would act with "energy and courage" to preserve "the Constitution and the Government as now established."[23] Taft also predicted that Davis would "appoint the best Judges" that he could find,[24] "having a view to the preservation of constitutional principles and the dignity and influence of the Court."[25] But although Davis's nomination pleased Taft, the chief justice wanted Coolidge to win the election,[26] although he did not publicly endorse Coolidge.[27]

Like other third-party movements in American history, the La Follette campaign encountered formidable obstacles that ensured its failure. The underfinanced and hastily assembled La Follette organization could not shake deeply entrenched party loyalties. In retrospect, this idealistic crusade against a highly popular president in the midst of an era of extraordinary prosperity and political cynicism seems quixotic. Throughout most of the campaign, however, La Follette seemed to have a very real chance of depriving the Republicans of a majority in the Electoral College and throwing the election into the House of Representatives, since La Follette seemed likely to carry several midwestern and western states and Davis had a lock on the votes of the Solid South.[28] Republicans feared that a deadlocked election would enable a coalition of Democrats and progressive Republicans in the House to block the election of Coolidge.[29] Unlike Coolidge and Davis, La Fol-

---

gress. Similarly, Taft later told his son Robert that Davis "will be a friend of the Court. He certainly will not consent to any increase in the number or any proposal that the majority in the Court shall be increased in order to declare invalid an invalid law" (Taft to Robert A. Taft, July 14, 1924, *Taft Papers*, ibid.).

[23] Taft to Mary E. Patten, July 16, 1924, *Taft Papers*, Series 3, Reel 266.

[24] Taft to Harry Taft, July 11, 1924, *Taft Papers*, Series 3, Reel 266.

[25] Taft to Mary E. Patten, July 16, 1924, *Taft Papers*, Series 3, Reel 266.

[26] Taft to Calvin Coolidge, September 16, 1924, *Taft Papers*, Series 3, Reel 267.

[27] Taft to C. S. Thompson, September 21, 1924, Taft to Charles P. Taft, September 21, 1924, *Taft Papers*, Series 3, Reel 267.

[28] In July the political correspondent for *The Independent* predicted that La Follette would carry Wisconsin, Minnesota, Iowa, Idaho, the Dakotas, possibly Washington, Nebraska, and Wyoming, and perhaps Indiana, Illinois, and Ohio (Benjamin Stolberg, "La Follette Crosses the Rubicon," *The Independent*, July 19, 1924, p. 56). In a nationwide presidential poll by the Hearst newspapers on September 11, La Follette outpolled Coolidge by a small margin and received more than twice the votes of Davis ("First Returns in 'The Digest's' Election Poll," *Literary Digest*, September 20, 1924, p. 7). Although the polling methods were primitive and the Hearst organization's support for La Follette may have biased the results, the poll still indicated that La Follette had remarkable strength. Not until late October did Davis begin to catch up with La Follette in the *Literary Digest's* poll ("Davis Overtaking La Follette in the Big Poll," October 25, 1924, p. 5). Despite La Follette's strength, few political observers at any time forecast a La Follette victory.

[29] "The Conspiracy to Make Bryan President," *Literary Digest*, November 1, 1924, p. 12.

lette enjoyed a loyal personal following, and his lack of an established party label was partly offset by the dismal fortunes of the major parties. The Republicans continued to suffer from the stigma of Teapot Dome, and the Democrats' internecine battle at the convention had crippled their party.

In an effort to find an issue that would broaden their appeal beyond their core constituents, the Progressives declared that monopoly was the "supreme issue" of the campaign. The selection of this issue was a tactical mistake since the trust-busting days of the 1910s were over and monopoly no longer aroused widespread public indignation. Moreover, La Follette's proposal spoke the language of the old progressivism, which had sought to open up the system and ignored the growing liberal support for state intervention to protect the health and safety of citizens.[30] The issue of monopoly was also too abstract and complex to appeal to the mass of voters.

Lacking a positive issue that might have placed the Republicans on the defensive, the Progressives were vulnerable to Republican attacks. Many Republicans were eager to conduct a vigorous offensive against the Progressives since the race in many midwestern and western states was a contest between Coolidge and La Follette, with Davis reduced to virtual third-party status. Moreover, although it became increasingly plain as the campaign progressed that La Follette was draining more support from the Democrats than the Republicans, GOP strategists originally feared that the Republican La Follette would woo more votes from his own party. A virulent campaign against La Follette seemed to provide the best means of keeping Republican voters within the fold.

The phlegmatic Coolidge was hardly the man to lead such a crusade. Consistent with his carefully cultivated image of taciturnity, Coolidge sought to enhance his reputation as a leader by remaining preoccupied with affairs of state.[31] With Coolidge remaining above the battle, the duty of sounding the alarm against the dangers of progressivism fell to Dawes. The feisty and blunt-spoken Dawes relished this role and may have carried it beyond the bounds that many Republicans preferred. With the connivance of party leaders, Dawes decided to portray La

[30] See F. E. Hayes, "La Follette and La Follettism," *Atlantic Monthly*, October 1924, p. 541; William Hard, "LaFollette's Strategy," *The Nation*, September 10, 1924, p. 260. MacKay's study of the 1924 campaign observed that "monopoly was not the torch word La Follette expected it to be" and that "as he denounced monopoly, La Follette was . . . reiterating the battle cries and suggesting the panaceas of an earlier day" (*Progressive Movement*, p. 251).

[31] As Hiram Johnson accurately predicted late in 1923, Coolidge would be "the mysterious, silent man in the White House, for whom big business of the country . . . will speak" (Hiram R. Johnson to Charles K. McClatchey, December 12, 1923, *Johnson Papers*, Bancroft Library, University of California at Berkeley, Part 3, Box 6).

Follette as a dangerous radical. Although La Follette's advocacy of public ownership of railroads and utilities and his endorsement by the Socialists provided grist for Dawes's mill, Dawes made La Follette's proposal for curbing the Supreme Court's jurisdiction the focal point of his attacks. Even though the Court plank may have been one of the least viable parts of La Follette's platform and the one about which La Follette may have been the least serious, it was the proposal that Dawes shrewdly sensed was the most likely to alarm American voters. Moreover, the issue had important symbolic importance and broad implications since it helped to support Dawes's more general thesis that the socialistic elements of La Follette's program would subvert the Constitution and lead to communism. At the urging of Coolidge and other party leaders, Dawes inaugurated this theme in his acceptance speech on August and continued to exploit it throughout the campaign.[32]

In his acceptance speech, Dawes declared that "La Follette, leading the army of extreme radicalism, has a platform demanding public ownership of railroads and attacking our courts, which are a fundamental and constitutional safeguard of American citizenship." Blasting the Progressives for permitting the Socialists to enroll beneath their banner, Dawes excoriated the La Follette movement as "a heterogenous collection of those opposing the existing order of things, the greatest section of which, the Socialists, flies the red flag." La Follette, Dawes declared, would lead the nation into "war upon those fundamental principles of human liberty and the inalienable rights of men which are giving in this country safety and opportunity to the humblest."[33]

It is somewhat ironic that Coolidge's first choice for the vice-presidential nomination was William E. Borah, an outspoken critic of the Court and the author of one of the principal plans to limit the power of judicial review.[34] Even though Borah's proposal was much

---

[32] As Dawes stated in his autobiography:

In my speech of acceptance I announced the constitutional issue precipitated by Senator La Follette as the dominant one. Chairman Butler was adverse to this course, feeling that the issue of economy should be the one to be stressed. I sent my speech before delivery to President Coolidge, who returned it without suggestion as to change, except that he substituted 'an important issue' for 'the predominant issue' as a caption to that portion of my address devoted to the La Follette position on the Constitution. From the time of delivery of the acceptance speech . . . until the end of the campaign, during which I travelled fifteen thousand miles . . . and made one hundred and eight speeches, I endeavored to keep that issue in the minds of the people. (Charles G. Dawes, *Notes as Vice President 1928–1929* (Boston: Little, Brown, 1935), pp. 19–20)

[33] "Text of Dawes's Speech Accepting Nomination," *New York Times*, August 20, 1924, p. 2.

[34] Leroy Ashby, *The Spearless Leader: Senator Borah and the Progressive Movement in the 1920s* (Urbana: University of Illinois Press, 1972), pp. 151, 154–56.

more moderate than La Follette's plan, the GOP might not have transformed La Follette's court plank into a major election issue if Borah had run with Coolidge. Coolidge's willingness to run with a prominent critic of the Court helps to demonstrate the tactical character of Republican attacks on La Follette's court plan. While Coolidge's offer to Borah cannot be construed as an indication of sympathy of Borah's views concerning the Court, Coolidge's overture represented an attempt to achieve some rapprochement with progressives and to win support in the West, an area of Republican weakness.

The Republican strategy of emphasizing the Court issue received hearty praise from Taft, who wrote to Coolidge in September to commend the "wisdom and courage" of the Republican decision "to force consideration of the issue of the Constitution and the Court."[35] But Dawes's charges drew stern criticism from Democrats and liberals, who dismissed his rhetoric as a transparently cynical election maneuver that was unlikely to deceive many voters. Frank R. Kent, of the pro-Davis *Baltimore Sun*, declared that Dawes underestimated the intelligence of the American people in his "effort to make it seem that if La Follette carries a few Republican States the stage is set for Trotzky, and the Supreme Court, along with the Constitution, will be sunk in a sea of chaos."[36]

Like many other election observers, the *New Republic* argued that Dawes's use of the court issue was designed to distract attention from Republican corruption and favoritism to the wealthy.[37] Early in the campaign there was widespread speculation that this strategy would not succeed. *The Nation* observed in early September that "the country shows as yet no signs of alarm" since voters recognized that "no fundamental change in the Constitution can be made except by the slow and weary process of amendment."[38]

Although sophisticated political observers disparaged Dawes's fulminations, Dawes continued to make his accusations to large and enthusiastic crowds, and Republican campaign managers and pro-Coolidge newspapers throughout the nation began to emphasize the issue. In California, where La Follette at first appeared to be the strongest candidate, Coolidge's campaign manager began to emphasize the Supreme Court issue. Gus Karger reported to Taft early in September that "the Catholic element is large here and the effort is to play on their

---

[35] Taft to Calvin Coolidge, September 16, 1924, *Taft Papers*, Series 3, Reel 267.

[36] *Baltimore Sun*, September 13, 1924, p. 1.

[37] Similarly, *New Republic* declared that "every one, including even General Dawes, knows perfectly well that Senator La Follette is not a red revolutionist" (September 3, 1924, p. 2).

[38] "How Dangerous Is La Follette?" *The Nation*, September 3, 1924, p. 229.

fear that with a proposition such as LaFollette advocates . . . their constitutional rights may be placed in jeopardy." Karger reported that the "appeal to California labor on the same issue is based on their ownership of property . . . which is large because the workers, especially the railroad men, have had top notch pay and most of them own homes and even ranches."[39]

While Republican attempts to persuade voters that alteration of the Constitution would encourage revolution may have been cynical, they were bound to be effective in the highly charged political atmosphere of 1924. At a time when memories of the cataclysm of the First World War and the upheaval of the Bolshevik revolution were still fresh, it is not surprising that many voters believed that democracy in America was a fragile vessel or that Republicans easily could exploit the fears of a nation entering an uncertain new era. This insecurity had contributed to the Harding landslide in 1920 and had created a putrid political environment in which a newly revived Ku Klux Klan flourished throughout of the nation. Although many voters recognized that the times demanded reform, many also felt that an unstable era was an inopportune time for constitutional innovations that would alter the balance of power among the branches of the federal government. La Follette had unwittingly given the Republicans a potent issue that they would cleverly exploit.[40]

The Republicans' insistence upon attacking the weakest plank in the Progressive platform and using that plank as a battering ram to assail the entire Progressive program placed the Progressives in a quandary. Silence might lend credibility to Republican charges, but a defense of the plan would detract attention from what the Progressives viewed as the real issues of the campaign and would force Progressives to confront the weaknesses of the court plan. Progressives had few tactical advantages to gain from defending the Court plan, since many Progressives already supported it and the issue was not likely to win new converts to the Progressive cause. No matter how the Progressives chose to defend the plan, it was likely to alienate potential support. The very issue that helped La Follette to consolidate support among Progressives and launch his third-party candidacy now prevented him

[39] Gus Karger to Taft, September 9, 1924, *Taft Papers*, Series 3, Reel 267.

[40] Republican strategy may have been influenced by the Conservative party in Britain, which had attempted to identify the Labour party with bolshevism in the three general elections between 1918 and 1923. Conservative attempts to discredit Labour in this manner reached a new level of intensity during the campaign that preceded Labour's defeat in the October 1924 election. See William G. Ross, "The Bolshevik Bogy: An Analysis of Attempts by Liberals and Conservatives in Britain Between 1918 and 1924 to Associate Labour with Communism," undergraduate honors thesis, Stanford University, 1976.

from attracting the broader support that would have made his candidacy viable.

La Follette faced the particular danger that emphasis on the Court issue would offend ethnic voters, who were grateful to the Supreme Court for the 1923 decisions that nullified the laws prohibiting instruction in foreign languages. Continuing to seek judicial protection against other manifestations of nativism, ethnic Americans had rejoiced over a March 1924 decision in which a federal district court struck down Oregon's compulsory public education statute.[41] Throughout the 1924 campaign, the Oregon case was pending on appeal before the Supreme Court, and ethnic voters correctly anticipated that the Court would affirm the lower court's decision. The protection the courts had provided to the rights of parochial schools seemed to confirm the verity of the argument that the courts were a bulwark against majoritarian tyranny.

Although critics of the Supreme Court took frequent pains to point out that neither La Follette's proposal nor any of the pending legislation in Congress would prune the Court's power to invalidate state legislation, La Follette might reasonably have concluded that his plan might frighten or offend ethnic voters who sought to protect parochial schools. The distinction between federal legislation and state legislation probably eluded many voters. Even those who could grasp this distinction might also have recognized the danger that Congress might enact legislation that was no less intrusive. Indeed, many voters probably had fresh memories of Congress's enactment of various wartime measures restricting freedom of speech. Those measures, which were often zealously enforced against ethnic Americans who opposed America's entry into the war, demonstrated that Congress was no palladium of liberty.

The risk that the Court issue would erode La Follette's support was especially great among German and Scandinavian Lutherans, who formed two of La Follette's core constituencies. Since many Germans and Scandinavians were midwestern farmers, this constituency overlapped considerably with La Follette's agrarian constituency and was crucial to his hopes of carrying such states as Ohio, Minnesota, Iowa, Missouri, Nebraska, and the Dakotas, where early polls indicated that he had a real chance of victory. Diminution of support among these voters could even have cost him victory in his Wisconsin bailiwick. The Court issue also had the potential of cutting into the substantial support that La Follette enjoyed among Jewish, Irish, and Slavic urban

[41] *Society of the Sisters of the Holy Names of Jesus and Mary v. Pierce*, 296 F. 928 (D. Ore. 1924), *aff'd*, 268 U.S. 510 (1925).

voters, who looked to the courts for protection against discriminatory legislation.

Throughout the campaign, the Republicans made a deliberate effort to win the votes of German Americans and other ethnics by reminding them that the judiciary offered the best protection for their parochial schools. Writing to Taft on September 23, Karger observed that Coolidge's prospects in Minnesota were bleak because German Americans were for La Follette "almost to a man." Karger suggested that "there is a chance of getting some of them back, on the constitutionalism issue" by emphasizing the threat to parochial schools.[42] Taft urged the editor of the St. Louis *Post-Dispatch* to mention the invalidation of the foreign-language laws and the Oregon school law in editorials denouncing La Follette's court plan. Taft believed that this illustration would convince Lutheran and Roman Catholic voters in heavily German St. Louis "that they have some rights that they would rather not entrust to the Legislature or to Congress to violate."[43]

Meanwhile, Republican propagandists produced a spate of literature that reminded ethnic voters that the courts had helped to protect their rights.[44] Alleging that La Follette's opponents were using "subtle and pernicious" methods to spread falsehoods, especially among German ethnic voters in the northwestern states, *The Progressive* on the eve of the election disparaged the likelihood that Congress would ever enact such legislation, much less reenact it by a two-thirds vote after its invalidation by the Supreme Court.[45]

La Follette's warnings about the dangers of judicial power received

[42] Gus Karger to William Howard Taft, September 23, 1924, *Taft Papers*, Series 3, Reel 267.

[43] Taft to Caspar S. Yost, September 11, 1924, *Taft Papers*, Series 3, Reel 267.

[44] Opponents of the Court plan sometimes resorted to what a later generation would call dirty tricks. In an effort to exploit fears that that curtailment of the Supreme Court's jurisdiction would imperil parochial schools and religious freedom, an anti-La Follette pamphlet was published by unidentified opponents of La Follette under the name of "the Investigating Committee of Chicago Lutheran Pastoral Conference." Lutheran leaders in Chicago vigorously denied any responsibility for the eleven-page pamphet, which alleged that "the La Follette idea of government . . . would make our courts powerless to defend individual rights, religious liberty, and freedom of speech and the press." A copy of the pamphlet is in *La Follette Family Papers*, Series B, Box 207. The Lutheran Pastoral Conference's denial of any responsibility for the pamphlet is set forth in an undated news release published by the National Publicity Bureau of the La Follette-Wheeler campaign (ibid., Box 205).

[45] Ignoring the recent enactment of the Oregon statute and the persistence of anti-foreign language legislation after the war, the editorial dismissed such enactments as "the impulsive act of shell-shocked nerves and not a deliberate act intended to become a fundamental part of our system of laws" ("La Follette and the Parochial Schools," *The Progressive*, November 1, 1924, pp. 80–81).

some help from a 4–3 ruling of the supreme court of California, which invoked a technicality to bar La Follette's electors from the ballot.[46] The court's decision, issued in late September, was a particularly cruel blow because polls indicated that La Follette had a reasonable chance of winning California's thirteen electoral votes.[47] Although La Follette's name appeared on the Socialist line on the California ballot, the court's decision ruined any real chance for La Follette to carry California and dashed his hopes of sweeping the West.[48] LaFollette's supporters used the California Supreme Court's decision as an object lesson in their warnings about the dangers of judicial oligarchy, some of them gamely arguing that the decision had actually helped La Follette's cause by calling attention to his warnings about judicial oligarchy. A San Francisco voter declared that the justices had "done more to convince the people . . . that the courts should be curbed than La Follette could have done by arguing from now till the crack of doom."[49] Other La Follette supporters, however, conceded that the decision could have a baneful impact on his chances.[50]

Even though the California decision may have provoked greater antogonism toward the courts, La Follette recognized from the start of the 1924 campaign that the Court issue was not likely to expand his political base and could constitute a liability. Accordingly, he at first

[46] The court held that a state law that permitted nomination of state officers by petition did not extend to presidential electors, who therefore could be selected only by convention. The court's narrow reading of the statute provoked sharp dissenting opinions from each of the three dissenters, who contended that the text and legislative history of the statute compelled a broader interpretation. *Spreckels v. Graham*, 228 P. 1040–54 (Cal. 1924).

[47] "First Returns in 'The Digest's' Election Poll," pp. 7–8; "272,299 Votes in 'The Digests' Election Poll," *Literary Digest*, September 27, 1924, pp. 7–8; *The Nation*, October 1, 1924, p. 321.

[48] Although La Follette was able to run as the Socialist candidate in the forty-four states where the Socialist party appeared on the ballot, the La Follette organization recognized that many voters would be loath to vote Socialist and that the appearance of his name on the Socialist line obscured the multipartisan character of the campaign. Accordingly, La Follette's supporters undertook the arduous task of arranging to list La Follette as an Independent or a Progressive on the ballot of each state. La Follette eventually succeeded in placing slates of independent or Progressive electors on the ballots of most states (MacKay, *Progressive Movement*, pp. 179–80).

[49] John Harrowby, "La Follette and the Far West" (letter to the editor), *The Nation*, October 22, 1924, p. 445.

[50] Max Stern declared, for example, that "here we have the possibility that one California judge, a political appointee of a reactionary governor, may be the deciding instrument in the election this fall and give us four years more of Coolidge and the Grand Old Party." He observed that the decision had "emphasized once more the seriousness of allowing the courts to block the obvious will of the legislature" (Max Stern, "The California Supreme Court Does Its Bit," *The Nation*, November 5, 1924, p. 491).

attempted to ignore the issue. He also intended to minimize the Court issue because he believed that other issues were more urgent.[51] This appears to have been the consensus of his advisers. On September 13, Oswald Garrison Villard urged La Follette to distract attention from the Court issue by speaking about foreign affairs and warning against the increasing militarism of the Coolidge administration. Villard predicted, however, that Republicans would continue to emphasize the issue and that "in the last two weeks of the campaign we shall all be pictured as going around with a bomb in one hand and a tomahawk in the other."[52] Meanwhile, Taft told Justice Butler and President Coolidge in mid-September that La Follette seemed inclined to "soft pedal" the Court issue until after the election, at least in the East.[53]

La Follette did not mention the Court issue in his first major campaign address, which he delivered to a national radio audience on Labor Day.[54] His failure to mention the Court issue or a similarly controversial Progressive proposal for government ownership and operation of railroads during his thirty-five-minute speech suggests that he wished to ignore issues that might frighten or offend significant numbers of voters. He may have been particularly circumspect since his speech reached a mass audience that included many voters not favorably disposed to the Progressive cause.[55]

Even though La Follette may have resolved to ignore the Court issue, his opponents continued to emphasize it. In speeches in different parts of the nation on September 6, both Coolidge and Davis vehemently denounced the Progressive party platform's court plank, sounding themes that would echo throughout the remainder of the campaign and haunt La Follette's candidacy. Speaking in Baltimore at the dedication of a monument to Lafayette, Coolidge declared that the Court proposal was designed for "the confiscation of property and the destruction of liberty." In a tacit reference to the *Meyer* decision, Coolidge stated that the Supreme Court was the "ultimate refuge" against state legislation that deprived minorities of their constitutional rights. In warning that the plan would destroy property, Coolidge likewise averred that "the common run of people" would "see their savings

[51] "Candidates and the Courts," *New York Times*, September 8, 1924, p. 14.

[52] Oswald Garrison Villard to La Follette, September 13, 1924, *La Follette Family Papers*, Series B, Box 101.

[53] Taft to Pierce Butler, September 16, 1924, *Taft Papers*, Series 3, Reel 267; Taft to Calvin Coolidge, September 11, 1924, ibid.

[54] The text of the speech is reprinted in "La Follette Reaffirms Lincoln's Stand," *La Follette's Magazine*, September 1924, pp. 133–35.

[55] The speech was estimated to have reached several million Americans, including many who listened from receivers set up at large public meetings (Belle and Fola La Follette, *La Follette*, p. 1125).

swept away, their homes devastated and their children perish from want and hunger." Coolidge argued that Congress alone offered no bulwark against tyranny:

> If the authority now vested in the Supreme Court were transferred to the Congress, any majority, no matter what their motive, could vote away any of these most precious rights. Majorities are notoriously irresponsible. After irreparable damage had been done, the only remedy that the people would have would be the privilege of trying to defeat such a majority at the next national election.[56]

Coolidge's remarks confirmed that the Republicans intended to emphasize the Court issue. As the political correspondent for the New York *World* observed, the president "did not want to permit La Follette to escape from the Supreme Court issue if it could be forced on him." The speech also seemed to confirm that the Republicans hoped to transform the election into a contest between La Follette and Coolidge.[57] Coolidge's speech inspired journals of moderate persuasion to warn that Republican hyperbole should not obscure legitimate objections to La Follette's plan. Although *The World's Work* accused Coolidge of "simply talking nonsense" in his Baltimore speech and pointed out that parliamentary supremacy had not destroyed liberties in Great Britain and other civilized nations, it warned against the adoption of a system that would remove restraints against legislative tyranny.[58] Similarly, the *Baltimore Sun* questioned whether voters "visualized the danger he forecasts as being either imminent or quite so appalling as he pictured it."[59] Even if many voters recoiled from rhetorical excesses, the speech underscored the contrast that the Republicans sought to draw between the prudent Coolidge and the mercurial La Follette. Taft advised Coolidge that the Court issue was "so important that it is of great benefit to be stressed."[60]

Speaking in Omaha on the same day Coolidge spoke in Baltimore, Davis criticized the Progressives' Court proposal in terms that differed little from Coolidge's. Like Coolidge, Davis emphasized the importance

[56] "Coolidge Assails LaFollette Views."

[57] "Our Supreme Court—Tyrant or Protector?," *Literary Digest*, September 20, 1924, p. 12.

[58] "La Follette's 'Revolutionary' Proposal," *The World's Work*, November 1924, p. 5; "Parliamentary System for America?" ibid., pp. 5–6.

[59] *Baltimore Sun*, September 7, 1924, p. 6.

[60] Taft to Calvin Coolidge, September 11, 1924. Taft told Coolidge that he was "very glad that you dealt with the subject of the absolute necessity for the limitations of the Constitution in the maintenance of a Republican form of government and the saving of liberty to the people, and the importance of the power of the Supreme Court in enforcing those limitations."

of personal freedoms and insisted that the Supreme Court should remain the ultimate refuge of persons whose liberties had been violated. He alleged that La Follette's plan would deprive the courts of the power to review the constitutionality of any law, "no matter what right it invades, no matter if it should deny to you the exercise of your religious worship."[61] Like Coolidge, Davis unfairly suggested that La Follette's plan would abridge the Supreme Court's power to nullify state legislation.

The themes sounded by Coolidge and Davis in their speeches were repeated by a number of other prominent Republicans and Democrats.[62] The Court's critics responded swiftly and sharply. As Norman Thomas declared on September 7, "The Supreme Court has not protected individuals but property and under its decisions, it is not possible in some parts of the country legally to organize labor and legally to conduct a strike." Thomas explained, "We object to a parcel of old men reading their prejudices into the law, and . . . want some curb on that power."[63] In a reference to the Teapot Dome scandal, the northeastern director of the La Follette campaign declared that "Coolidge showed no solicitude about the Constitution when his late associates in the Administration were openly flouting it and treating their constitutional oaths as scraps of paper."[64] Meanwhile, Felix Frankfurter dismissed Coolidge's speech as the product of an ignorant mind but alleged that Davis ought to have known better.[65]

The allegations of Coolidge, Davis and other prominent public figures placed La Follette on the defensive and forced him to address an issue that he preferred to ignore. He offered his first and most painstaking defense of the Court proposal in a speech at a rally at Madison Square Garden on September 18.[66] After an extended excoriation of

[61] "Davis Announces His Farm Program, Scores the Tariff," *New York Times,* September 7, 1924, p. 1.

[62] For example, Senator Royal S. Copeland attacked Court reform in a speech before the New York State American Legion on September 6. Reminding the veterans that they had fought for physical and political freedom, Copeland declared that courts were "the cornerstones of our freedom" and "the hope of the poor" ("Copeland Defends Supreme Court," *New York Times,* September 7, 1924, p. 29).

[63] "Wheeler Pleads for Votes in Bronx," *New York Times,* September 8, 1924, p. 3.

[64] "Coolidge Speech Nonsense, Says Roe," *New York Times,* September 9, 1924, p. 6.

[65] Editorial, "The Red Terror of Judicial Reform," *New Republic,* October 1, 1924, p. 110, repr. Philip B. Kurland, ed., *Felix Frankfurter on the Supreme Court* (Cambridge, Mass.: Harvard University Press, 1970), p. 160.

[66] Fourteen thousand persons filled the Garden nearly to capacity, and several thousand more clustered outside listening through amplifiers. Although La Follette failed to fill a few high-priced seats in the boxes and the lower balcony, the political commentator Frank R. Kent reported that the crowd was "as solid and substantial as a crowd could be without being fashionable or rich. There was no touch of toughness, no trace of poverty,

what he described as the "private monopoly system," La Follette alleged that the major parties were trying to divert discussion from the "vital economic issues of the campaign" by making "foolish and preposterous assertions" that the Progressives desired "to weaken or impair" constitutional provisions concerning the federal courts. Although La Follette insisted that he intended to wage his campaign on economic issues, he grudgingly discussed the Court issue "in order that no one may have the least excuse for misunderstanding the Progressives' position." After explaining that the Progressives proposed only to submit an amendment to the people for their consideration, he discussed the cases in which the Supreme Court had invalidated the federal income tax, restricted the scope of the antitrust laws, and struck down child-labor laws. "Always these decisions of the Court are on the side of the wealthy and powerful and against the poor and weak, whom it is the policy of the lawmaking branch to assist by enlightened and humanitarian legislation."[67]

Although the crowd cheered for fifteen minutes when La Follette arrived and gave what the *New York Times* described as "vociferous approval" to his initial volleys against the courts,[68] he apparently began to bore his audience when he discussed the details of specific Supreme Court decisions. After hundreds vacated the Garden, La Follette hurried through the remainder of his speech.[69]

La Follette's speech at Madison Square Garden confirmed the popularity of the Court proposal among the Progressive faithful, but it also demonstrated that the public lacked patience for a bill of particulars against the Court or a careful discussion concerning the details of the proposed reform. Arthur Garfield Hays, La Follette's New York campaign manager, pointed out that "when he got to the end of his speech and spoke on war issues and matters of like kind, not a single person left."[70] The lesson of Madison Square Garden was not lost on the La Follette campaign. He discussed his views on court reform in only about half of his remaining speeches and never again devoted so large a

---

no hint of violence. If these were the 'forces of discontent,' they were certainly a well-fed, well-dressed, well-behaved lot, men and women" ("14,000 Pack Garden, Cheer La Follette in Attack on Court," *New York Times*, September 19, 1924, p. 1; "Ardor Makes Gotham Rally for La Follette," *Baltimore Sun*, September 20, 1924, p. 1).

[67] A transcript of La Follette's Madison Square Garden address, with transcripts of most of La Follette's other 1924 campaign speeches, is in *La Follette Family Papers*, Series B, Box 228.

[68] Belle and Fola La Follette, *La Follette*, p. 1127; "14,000 Pack Garden, Cheer La Follette."

[69] "14,000 Pack Garden."

[70] Arthur Garfield Hays to Robert M. La Follette, Jr., September 19, 1924, *La Follette Papers*, Series B, Box B-98.

portion of any speech to it. Although La Follette emphasized different issues in his various speeches, his general neglect of the Court issue after his Madison Square Garden address indicates a deliberate effort to minimize the issue. The Madison Square Garden rally marked the zenith of the Progressives' attack on the judiciary during the 1924 campaign.

La Follette's volleys against the Supreme Court during his Garden speech, widely broadcast on radio, inspired predictable expressions of outrage. The New York *Herald-Tribune* declared, "Just as there unmistakably lurk in the rear of the third party the communists and Bolsheviki . . . so there plainly stands behind this simple but momentous change a complete revolution of American rule that would open the door for . . . sudden and destructive changes."[71] Similarly, the *New York Times* alleged that La Follette failed to recognize that his proposal would allow Congress "to tear out the Bill of Rights and every guarantee of the security of the citizen."[72]

By late September, it was clear that the Republicans had no intention of abandoning the Court issue. Although Coolidge lived up to his "Silent Cal" sobriquet by remaining taciturn throughout most of the campaign, he was not completely reticent. In addition to his Baltimore speech, he also spoke in Philadelphia on September 25, the 150th anniversary of the First Continental Congress. The anniversary provided President Coolidge with a marvelous occasion for reiterating the themes he had sounded in Baltimore. Coolidge emphasized that the courts provided the most effective defense against the type of despotism against which the First Continental Congress had protested. As he had in Baltimore, Coolidge presented the courts as the defenders of both personal liberties and property rights. Once again, he placed his accent on the former. Implying that the Progressives were the heirs of George III and the brothers of Lenin, Coolidge declared, "Through the breakdown of the power of the courts lies an easy way to the confiscation of the property and the destruction of the liberty of the individual." He warned that "any kind of tyranny may follow" if judicial integrity was not maintained.[73] Meanwhile, Dawes continued to slash away at the Court plan as he toured the Midwest.[74]

The Republican strategy of insinuating that court reform would breed revolution began to vex Democratic leaders, who perceived that the Republicans were using the Bolshevist bogey to distract attention from the seamy aspects of the Republican record. Recognizing that

---

[71] New York *Herald-Tribune*, September 19, 1924, p. 14.

[72] *New York Times*, September 19, 1924, p. 22.

[73] "Text of the President's Speech," *New York Times*, September 26, 1924, p. 6.

[74] "Dawes Pipe Draws Reproof of Woman," *New York Times*, September 28, 1924, p. 2.

they could win only if La Follette siphoned electoral votes from the Republicans in the Midwest and West, the Democrats looked with trepidation at the Republican attempts to use the Court issue as a means of making inroads into Progressive strength. Accordingly, Democratic leaders began to derogate the danger of the Court plan.

Speaking in Wilmington on September 27, Davis declared that the Republicans had cynically created a specious issue to frighten the voters and draw their attention away from the real issue, honesty in government. Although Davis emphasized that he would not reduce the Supreme Court's power by "one iota," he mocked any link between the Court plan and bolshevism.[75] Davis asserted that his principal objection to La Follette's proposal was "not that it is leading us on to Moscow, but that it is trying to take us back to London" since it would substitute a British-style legislative supremacy for government under a written constitution.[76] Davis also accused the Republicans of setting up "smoke screens and men of straw" to distract attention from the real issues of the campaign.[77]

Similarly, Democratic senator Carter Glass of Virginia declared on October 26 that the Court issue was a "red herring" by which Republicans hoped "to divert attention from the shameful maladministration at Washington."[78] Gompers observed that "it has always been the practice of those who favor . . . autocratic power anywhere to attribute

[75] "La Follette Scheme a Bogy, Says Davis," *New York Times*, September 28, 1924, p. 1.

[76] Ibid. In reply, Hays protested that "the British theory under which no law can be declared unconstitutional, goes much further than Senator La Follette's proposal." Like other Progressive apologists who had pointed out that judicial review was not a feature of government in other democratic countries, Hays noted that "the British do not seem to be in danger of losing their liberties" ("Answers Davis on Court," *New York Times*, September 29, 1924, p. 2).

[77] "Big 7-Day Drive Planned by Davis to Carry New York," *New York Times*, October 22, 1924, p. 1.

[78] "Glass Challenges Hughes' Sincerity," *New York Times*, October 28, 1924, p. 4. Glass accused Republicans of hypocrisy. He argued that the Court reform proposal of Borah, who sought reelection to the Senate as a Republican and been considered by Coolidge as a potential running mate, was more drastic than La Follette's proposal. Glass also pointed out that Norris, the Republican nominee in Nebraska for reelection to the Senate, was "one of the fiercest critics of the prevailing method of deciding cases by the Supreme Court" and that other Republican senators, such as Brookhart, also favored court reform (ibid.). Although Republican leaders were probably guilty of much of the insincerity Glass attributed to them, they were not so hypocritical. Although Norris and Brookhart were nominal Republicans, they both were estranged from the administration. Although Borah may have returned to favor with the national party during the past year, Borah had virtually ignored the Court issue during that time. Indeed, Borah's temporary reconciliation with the Republican leadership rested upon his tacit agreement to eschew the advocacy of radical measures in exchange for Republican support in his bid for reelection.

dangerously radical and revolutionary tendencies to those favoring the extension or enlargement of the powers of self-government." He contended that the Court plan "does not contemplate hasty overturning of Supreme Court decisions" or the reenactment of legislation "during a temporary wave of emotion." Pointing out that "cases do not reach the Supreme Court in a day," Gompers declared that "it would be little less than a miracle if the same Congress ever got the opportunity to act for the second time upon a measure which found disfavor in the Supreme Court."[79]

These defenses of the Court plan were followed by further denunciations of it by various opponents of the Progressives. For example, the president of the American Bankers Association stated that "the Constitution has been and is now the greatest existing restraint upon an arrogant majority" and that "one of our greatest needs today is to repel the attacks now being made upon the integrity of this charter of our freedom."[80] Democratic senator Royal S. Copeland of New York told a meeting in Manhattan on October 1 that "attacks made on the courts" threatened their "purity and integrity," which protected the personal and property interests of rich and poor alike.[81]

During early October, prominent members of the bar also launched a concerted attack on the Court plan. Arthur D. Littleton told the New York State Bar Association convention that the Supreme Court's critics sought "destruction of the Constitution" by permitting the government to have unlimited powers.[82] Martin W. Littleton declared that the Court proposal would "Sovietize the American Government."[83] Speaking on behalf of Coolidge in Cincinnati, Charles Evans Hughes execrated the Court plan for permitting Congress to endanger "the rights of the States" and personal liberties. "If the proposal of the Third Party were adopted, everything you have, the security of your person and life, would be held at the mercy of Congress," Hughes warned. "And they call that progress!"[84] In St. Paul, Hughes alleged that La Follette's plan would "denature the Supreme Court,"[85] and he declared in Chicago three days later that it would "destroy our system of government."[86]

---

[79] "Gompers Defends Attacks on Courts," *New York Times*, September 29, 1924.

[80] "Bankers Denounce Demagogue as Peril," *New York Times*, October 1, 1924, p. 23.

[81] "Copeland Finds Unrest," *New York Times*, October 2, 1924, p. 3.

[82] "Littleton Assails La Follette Ideas," *New York Times*, October 4, 1924, p. 5.

[83] "Littleton Seeks to Link La Follette with Russian Reds," *New York Times*, October 23, 1924, p. 1.

[84] "Hughes Answers Critics of Party," *New York Times*, October 5, 1924, sec. 2, p. 1.

[85] "Hughes in St. Paul Scores Third Party," *New York Times*, October 26, 1924, p. 16.

[86] "Hughes in Chicago Promises Prosperity," *New York Times*, October 29, 1924, p. 8.

Many of New York's most prominent attorneys signed a statement that condemned the Court plan in similarly apocalyptic terms. "The La Follette attack upon our Constitution and the Supreme Court is but the first step toward Socialism, Bolshevism and chaos," they declared. "It would be the death knell to the stability and to the prosperity and happiness of millions of workers, honest Americans." They also warned that the Progressive proposal for election of federal judges for limited terms would make the Supreme Court "the subject of recurring political contest and destroy the independence of our judiciary."[87] Meanwhile, Attorney General Harlan Fiske Stone declared that the plan "amounts to an abolition of constitutional government."[88] While Martin Littleton identified the Court plan with Moscow, Davis traced its origins to London, and Coolidge found its provenance in both Moscow and London, Stone divined its beginnings in ancient Rome. Stone predicted that the Court plan would create in Congress "a centralized political organization not unlike that of the Roman Empire."[89]

Only a few prominent attorneys defended the Court proposal, and virtually none of them were part of the elite bar. Clarence Darrow declared, "If the security of the country rests upon the right of the Supreme Court to set aside acts of Congress it rests upon a very flimsy basis." Darrow contended that the La Follette plan was less radical than Roosevelt's proposal and argued that "there is no other great government in the world where a court is vested with the power to abrogate the laws of the legislative branch."[90]

Beset by ill health, lack of funds, and the time-consuming task of formulating campaign strategy, La Follette did not begin his first speaking tour until early October. After ignoring the Court issue in his first two speeches in Rochester and Scranton, he defended the Court plan in Detroit on October 9. Despite the firestorm of criticism of the Court proposal, La Follette's remarks were remarkably understated.

---

[87] The lawyers, including the Wall Street luminaries William C. Breed, Paul D. Cravath, James M. Gifford, Charles Evans Hughes, Jr., Franklin B. Lord, C. W. and G. W. Wickersham, William L. Ransom, Elihu Root, Jr., and Henry L. Stimson, rejected the candidacy of Davis, their fellow corporate lawyer. Having formed a campaign committee to support Coolidge, in whose Republican party most of them were already prominent, they warned against the peril of a large third-party vote. Although they acknowledged that La Follette had little chance of becoming president, they warned that the failure of Coolidge and Dawes to receive a majority in the Electoral College might result in Congress's selection of a person who would support La Follette's court plan ("Court Limitation Assailed by Bar," *New York Times*, October 7, 1924, p. 2).

[88] "La Follette Plan Called a Menace," *New York Times*, October 2, 1924, p. 4.

[89] "Stone Dissects La Follette Aims," *New York Times*, October 25, 1924, p. 8.

[90] News Release, La Follette-Wheeler National Committee, Publicity Bureau, *La Follette Family Papers*, Series B, Box 205.

Tying an attack on Republican corruption to a denunciation of the
Supreme Court's decision in *Newberry*, La Follette decried the Republican "misrepresentation" of the plan. He pointed out that the president
had no power over the amendment process and that no amendment
could be adopted without the vote of two-thirds of the members of
Congress and approval by three-quarters of the states. He also emphasized that the plan would not deprive the Supreme Court of the power
to adjudicate the constitutionality of acts of state legislatures and that it
therefore would not "imperil fundamental rights" such as those involved in the *Meyer* and *Pierce* cases.[91]

Two days later, in Chicago, La Follette again defended the Court
plan after he had ignored it in a Cincinnati speech following his Detroit
address. In addition to reiterating points that he had made in Detroit,
he explained that the Progressives merely proposed to submit a constitutional amendment at some future date and after adequate public
consideration to permit the people to determine whether they wished
to be governed by their elected representatives or by "a bare majority"
of the Supreme Court. In an argument often ignored by the plan's
defenders, he pointed out that "the proposed amendment will not
deprive the Supreme Court of any power whatever specifically conferred upon it by the Constitution of the United States."[92]

La Follette's apparent lack of zeal in defending the plan did not
reflect any lack of vivacity in the campaign. In his speeches in Detroit
and Chicago, he vigorously assailed the abuses of concentrated economic power and the corruption of the Republican administration. In
Cincinnati, he delivered an impassioned plea for peace. In Scranton,
he charged that the Republicans had raised a secret "slush fund" of
several million dollars for the purpose of intimidating citizens into
voting for Coolidge.[93]

Campaigning in an age when opinion polls were rare and unreliable,
La Follette was encouraged by the size and enthusiasm of the crowds
that received him. With no other means of gauging the effects of the
court issue, he may have interpreted the buoyancy of his receptions as
confirmation of the wisdom of his decision to avoid discussion of the
Court issue. Yet despite his evident popularity, he failed to capture the
initiative in the campaign and establish an agenda of issues that would
place his opponents on the defensive. His principal effort to embarrass
the Republicans fell flat when his allegations about a GOP slush fund

[91] La Follette speech, Detroit, October 9, 1924, *La Follette Family Papers*, Series B, Box
228.

[92] La Follette speech, Chicago, October 11, 1924, *La Follette Family Papers*, ibid.

[93] "La Follette's Slush Fund Bombshell," *Literary Digest*, October 25, 1924, p. 10;
"'Slush Fund' Charges," *The Outlook*, October 22, 1924, p. 272.

failed to ignite widespread public indignation and a special committee on campaign funding, chaired by Senator Borah, failed to uncover improprieties.[94]

The Republicans refused to drop the Court issue and did not rise to LaFollette's bait about economic oligarchy and militarism. On October 10, for example, Coolidge sent a telegram to a convention of war veterans in which he expressed his confidence that they would "resist proposals to endanger the Constitution and destroy the Supreme Court."[95] On the same day, Republican senator Irvine L. Lenroot of Wisconsin charged that the "radicals favor giving Congress the power to abolish every parochial school in the nation.[96] Similarly, Republican senator George Wharton Pepper of Pennyslvania urged a Staten Island audience to oppose La Follette's plan "unless you want to take away warning signs at cross-roads, remove emergency brakes from your motor cars and play the world series games without an umpire."[97]

Meanwhile, Dawes continue to sound his alarms. Responding to continued insistence by Democrats that the Court issue was a bogey, Dawes declared in Omaha on October 10, "If this is a man of straw, he has a pretty good punch. Don't tell me that this is not an issue. It is the whole issue. If it succeeds it means chaos. Let even there be the first intimation of success and see what it does to that confidence upon which all prosperity is based."[98]

Unable to shed what increasingly resembled a political albatross, La Follette continued alternatively to ignore and tepidly defend the plan. After avoiding the issue in speeches delivered to large attentive audiences in Kansas City, St. Louis, Des Moines, Minneapolis, and Sioux Falls during the second week of his speaking tour, he faced the issue again in Omaha on October 20. As in his earlier speeches, he seemed more anxious to assure his audiences of the difficulty of enacting a Court amendment than to persuade them of the amendment's merits. He explained again that the platform merely called for the amendment to be submitted to the people, who remained free to reject the proposal. Like other Progressives who had made the same argument to mass audiences, La Follette probably sowed more confusion than clarification among listeners, most of whom probably failed to grasp the distinction between a nonbinding referendum and the formal amendment process.

LaFollette also explained that "a constitutional amendment is not so

[94] "Looking into the Campaign 'Barrels,'" *Literary Digest*, November 1, 1924, p. 16.

[95] "Coolidge Sees Danger to the Constitution," *New York Times*, October 11, 1924, p. 4.

[96] "Lenroot Scores 'Radicals,'" *New York Times*, October 10, 1924, p. 4.

[97] "Pepper Hits La Follette," *New York Times*, October 23, 1924, p. 6.

[98] *New York Times*, October 11, 1924, p. 4.

easily passed" since it would have to run the guantlet of approval by two-thirds of the members of Congress and three-quarters of the state legislatures. In an admission that seemed to underscore the quixotic character of both the Progressives' bid for political power and the Court proposal, he conceded that only about half a dozen progressive senators favored the amendment, and he virtually acknowledged that the Progresssives were unlikely to capture two-thirds of the seats in both houses of Congress at any foreseeable time. He also pointed out again that the president had no formal role in the amendment process and that his election as president would therefore "not affect the present powers of the courts."

La Follette elicited laughter and applause by exclaiming that "if you are . . . afraid of this particular constitutional amendment and afraid of my part in its enactment, you had better elect me President, instead of leaving me in the Senate."[99] Although this remark may have amused the audience, Pepper aptly observed that this was "a strange argument from a serious contender for the Presidency. It is equivalent to a proposal to convert the White House into an isolation ward for dangerous cases."[100]

Despite these disclaimers, La Follette defended the merits of the proposal. He first recited the familiar historical litany: that an effort to confer such a power upon the Court was voted down in the Constitutional Convention; that John Marshall had argued that Congress should have the power to override any Court decision invalidating an act of Congress; that the power of judicial review was not exercised until 1803 and was not exercised again until 1857 in the notorious *Dred Scott* decision; that Jefferson, Lincoln, and Theodore Roosevelt criticized judicial review; that the Court had increasingly used its power during the twentieth century "to nullify acts of Congress which had the overwhelming support of the people"; and that the lack of judicial review in Britain had not endangered British liberties.

He also reminded his Omaha audience that "such decisions as that of the Supreme Court in the Nebraska language case would not be affected" since the proposed amendment would not alter the Court's power to invalidate the acts of state legislatures. In drawing a distinction between judicial review of acts of Congress and acts of state legislatures, La Follette advanced the rather novel idea that Congress, whose ranks included a number of eminent lawyers, was better qualified to decide constitutional issues than "the type of men who pass upon constitutional questions in the average state legislature."

---

[99] La Follette speech, Omaha, October 20, 1924, *La Follette Family Papers*, Series B, Box 228.

[100] "Pepper Hits La Follette."

La Follette also disparaged the argument that the Court was a palladium of personal liberty. Recalling his opposition to the enactment of the wartime Espionage and Sedition acts, he contended that those statutes violated the letter and spirit of the Constitution but that neither the Supreme Court nor any other federal court "came to the rescue of the liberties of the people during that period." To great applause, he went on to assert that "the Progressives contend that the people themselves are sovereign and that it is unsafe for them to entrust their liberties in the hands of judges or any other officials appointed for life and responsible to no one."[101]

Two days later, in Grand Rapids, Michigan, La Follette again defended the plan. "Don't be horrified at this proposition," he urged his audience. The plan would liberate the nation from the "bondage" of a Court that was "conducted in the interest of certain great combinations in this country."[102]

Throughout the campaign, La Follette scrupulously avoided any personal attack on any justice, including Chief Justice Taft. His refusal to assail Taft came as a surprise and perhaps a disappointment to the chief justice, who predicted with a combination of resignation and relish at the outset of the campaign that the candidate would indulge in ad hominem vituperation.[103] Although La Follette's supporters and his campaign literature also generally avoided personal attacks on the chief justice, La Follette's campaign handbook noted the irony that Taft, whom the people "refused overwhelmingly to reelect . . . after studying his acts and sympathies on public questions," now served by appointment for life as the chief justice of the Court that was the final arbiter of the constitutionality of legislation.[104] The few attempts of the La Follette campaign to criticize Taft personally[105] inspired adverse

[101] La Follette speech, Omaha.

[102] La Follette speech, Grand Rapids, October 23, 1924, *La Follette Family Papers*, Series B, Box 228.

[103] In August, for example, Taft wrote to Pierce Butler, "I suppose that La Follette will make our Court the subject of one speech and that the Chief of that Court will be a shining mark for his attack." Similarly, Taft told his brother Henry that he expected La Follette to criticize "our Court and its head" and that "we shall have to do the best we can and remain silent under it." Taft confided to Gus Karger that he expected a personal attack, which he believed might help La Follette's candidacy (Taft to Pierce Butler, August 19, 1924, *Taft Papers*, Series 3, Reel 267; Taft to Henry W. Taft, August 19, 1924, ibid.; Taft to Gus Karger, July 18, 1924, Series 3, Reel 266; Taft to Karger, July 30, 1924, ibid.).

[104] The handbook declared that "no one will contend that by vote of the people Chief Justice Taft could have been elected to this powerful office for life, but through a Presidential appointment it was possible for him to write the opinion which nullified the Child Labor law" (leaflet 4, "La Follette and the Progressives on the Courts," p. 6, *La Follette Family Papers*, Series B, Box 205).

[105] "La Follette Group Defends Court Stand," *New York Times*, September 30, 1924, p. 3.

editorial comment.[106] With only slight exaggeration, Thomas W. Shelton reminded Taft during the closing days of the campaign that the La Follette forces "never mentioned the name of Taft from beginning to end."[107]

Although Republicans continued to emphasize the Court issue, signs of a Coolidge landslide were becoming increasingly evident by mid-October.[108] Much of the shift away from La Follette occurred in the agricultural regions of the Midwest where the prices of most farm commodities increased dramatically during the summer and autumn.[109]

The Supreme Court provided an additional boon to Republican prospects on October 20, when it announced a decision that sustained the Clayton Act's requirement for jury trials in criminal contempt proceedings in cases involving labor disputes.[110] Gompers hailed the decision as "a long step ahead" and exclaimed that a "great cloak of autocratic power is shorn away. Strikers charged with breaking judge-made law . . . can no longer be put in jail at the whim of the judge who made the law." He warned, however, that "the injunction itself, as used in labor disputes, must go before the Constitution is fully and finally vindicated."[111] Saving its praise until after the election, the *New Republic* observed that the decision was "a most illuminating illustration of the enormous play of discretion open to the nine men at Washington."[112] The political significance of the decision seemed obvious to many, who believed that the Court had hoped to undermine support for the proposal to curtail the Court's jurisdiction.[113]

[106] The *Telegram-Gazette* of Worcester, Massachusetts, for example, pointed out that such criticism of Taft distorted his record since it ignored his vote in the foreign language cases and the *Minimum Wage Case* (*Telegram-Gazette*, October 2, 1924, in *Taft Papers*, Reel 267).

[107] Thomas W. Shelton to Taft, November 1, 1924, *Taft Papers*, Series 3, Reel 268.

[108] With straw ballots finally returned from every state, the *Literary Digest* reported in mid-October that La Follette led Davis in the total popular vote and outpolled him in twenty-five states, but that Coolidge was winning 56 percent of the popular vote and enjoyed a large lead in more than enough states to command an electoral college majority ("Every State Now Heard from in 'The Digest's' Big Poll," October 18, 1924, pp. 7–9).

[109] MacKay, *Progressive Movement*, pp. 205–6.

[110] *Michaelson v. United States*, 266 U.S. 42 (1924).

[111] "Labor's Magna Charta Upheld," *Literary Digest*, November 8, 1924, p. 12.

[112] Editorial, "Injunctions and Contempt of Court," *New Republic*, November 19, 1924, p. 288.

[113] The *Chicago Daily News* declared that the most significant aspect of the decision was "the circumstance that the much-criticized Supreme Court has sustained an act which abridges judicial power and enlarges to a corresponding degree the power of the legislative department." Similarly, the St. Louis *Post-Dispatch* declared that the decision "should give pause to all those who would destroy the Supreme Court's authority as one of the checks and balances of our system of government under the Constitution" ("Labor's Magna Charta Upheld").

During the final weeks of the campaign, the Republicans continued to assail the Court plan, and the Democrats continued to allege that the issue was a bogey. Ten days before the election, Coolidge delivered another shrill denunciation of the plan in a nationally broadcast radio speech contending that the plan would "destroy the States, abolish the Presidential office, close the courts and make the will of Congress absolute." He disparaged the notion that the people could expect members of Congress to be more impartial and independent than Supreme Court justices.[114]

While his opponents continued to malign the plan, La Follette spent the final days of the campaign in the East after ill health, weak finances, and a desire to make a serious bid for the electoral votes of the eastern states caused him to cut short a tour through western states that he had more hope of carrying.[115] Although he delivered a number of major speeches during the final week of the campaign, he explicitly addressed the Court issue only in a speech in Brooklyn on October 28. In contrast to his earlier strained defenses of the plan, his remarks in Brooklyn seemed relaxed and almost breezy. This may have reflected his knowledge that the election was lost, or perhaps it reflected a giddiness generated by fatigue. "Why, I suppose Morgan and the Standard Oil Company think that the Constitution sort of belongs to them," La Follette declared. "When these men talk of respect for the Constitution, they really mean respect for themselves." When he asked twice whether his listeners were "afraid to submit" the amendment to the people for their approval, they shouted back that they had no such fear. He urged "devotees of the Supreme Court, who count those nine gentlemen as infallible and quasi-divine," to recall that the Supreme Court's use of judicial review in the *Dred Scott* decision permitted the extension of slavery.[116]

La Follette did not mention the Court issue in his last major address, delivered to a large and enthusiastic audience in Cleveland on November 1. He pointed out, however, that all four of the judges of the California Supreme Court who had voted to prevent the names of Progressive electors from appearing on the California ballot were appointed and that the three judges who had dissented were elected by the people. Alleging that a California statute plainly permitted the names of independent electors to appear on the ballot, he charged that "the court usurped the functions of the legislature. . . . And these

[114] "Coolidge States Views on Issue in Last Big Speech," *New York Times*, October 24, 1924, p. 4.

[115] La Follette and La Follette, *La Follette*, p. 1139.

[116] La Follette speech, Brooklyn, October 28, 1924, *La Follette Family Papers*, Series B, Box 228.

judges . . . denied the people's fundamental right . . . by a decision of four to three. . . . One man, clothed temporarily in a judicial gown, robbed the people of their right to vote for the electors whom they had chosen."[117]

In their final radio addresses to the nation, Coolidge and Davis did not directly discuss the Court issue. The administration, however, issued a final warning through Solicitor General James M. Beck, who alleged that the "moral sublimity" of the Constitution "would be utterly shattered" by La Follette's plan since it would permit "the fleeting caprice of the majority of an idle day" to destroy "fundamental decencies of liberty." In their last major effort to counter Republican charges about the Court plan and other Progressive proposals, the La Follette headquarters issued a warning against efforts to "frighten various religious denominations into thinking that this proposal would rob them of their religious liberty."[118]

The results of the election were no surprise. Coolidge won a landslide in the electoral and the popular vote. In the Electoral College, Coolidge received 382 votes; Davis drew 136, all from the Solid South; and La Follette won only Wisconsin's 13. Coolidge received 54 percent of the popular vote; Davis, 28.8 percent; and La Follette, 17.2 percent. Despite La Follette's distant third place, his support was remarkably strong. No third-party candidate since the Civil War except Roosevelt had received a greater percentage of the popular vote. La Follette's tally of nearly 5 million votes exceeded Roosevelt's 1912 vote by almost a million. Although La Follette carried only his home state, he placed second in eleven states.[119]

Moreover, La Follette's statistics almost surely would have been even more impressive if both parties had not used questionable and perhaps illegal tactics to reduce the size of La Follette's vote.[120] As if to vindicate

---

[117] La Follette speech, Cleveland, November 1, 1924 (ibid.).

[118] "Beck Warns Voters on Constitution," *New York Times*, November 3, 1924, p. 4; "Warning against Late Half-Truths," ibid., p. 3.

[119]Those states were North Dakota (45 percent), Minnesota (41 percent), Montana (38 percent), South Dakota (37 percent), Idaho (37 percent), Nevada (36 percent), Washington (36 percent), California (33 percent), Wyoming (32 percent), Iowa (28 percent), and Oregon (25 percent). MacKay, *Progressive Movement*, p. 274.

[120] Hays estimated, for example, that election officials in New York had illegally refused to count at least 25,000 ballots because voters had placed their mark for La Follette in both the Progressive and the Socialist columns (Arthur Garfield Hays to La Follette, November 18, 1924, *La Follette Family Papers*, Series B, Box 98). The chairman of La Follette's Illinois campaign contended that "untold thousands of La Follette votes were either thrown out or counted for other candidates" in Illinois and that "crookedness ran riot" in hundreds of Chicago precincts (Charles J. MacGowan newsletter, November 15, 1924, *La Follette Family Papers*, Series B, Box 58).

La Follette's warnings against judicial perfidy and the hazards of decisions rendered by slim majorities, the Ohio Supreme Court by a 4–3
vote on the eve of the election had virtually invited ballot fraud by
refusing to permit the Progressives to deploy watchers at Ohio polls.
The court reasoned that the Progressives were not a recognized political party.[121]

Party loyalty and prosperity would probably have ensured Coolidge's victory even if the Republicans had not engaged in questionable
tactics or alleged that the plan to curtail the Supreme Court's jurisdiction threatened the Constitution. The disparity between La Follette's
strength in the polls at the start of the campaign and his less impressive
showing in the election was not necessarily attributable to public hostility toward the plan. LaFollette's apparent decline in support during the
campaign was probably more attributable to the crude polling techniques of the period, the Republicans' success at exploiting the prevalent prosperity, the superior organization and resources of the major
parties, and the natural inclination of voters to return to the major
parties at election time.

La Follette's ability to win more than one-sixth of the votes in the face
of major obstacles suggests that a remarkably large number of voters
approved of the Court plan or were not unduly opposed to it. Nevertheless, the Republicans' assiduous exploitation of the Court issue
may have lured many voters into the Coolidge camp. Although the
Court issue may not account for La Follette's failure to win the dozens
of electoral votes that he seemed to be capable of plucking at the start of
the campaign, the Court issue probably reduced his tally of popular
votes and may have cost him some electoral votes. In his 1947 study of
the 1924 election, Kenneth C. MacKay concluded that "the Supreme
Court issue, more than anything else, was responsible for the ease with
which the Republicans convinced a large segment of the American voting population of the imminent danger to the Constitution."[122] Contemporary analyses of the election agreed with this assessment. The
New Republic observed that "the natural timidity of a wealthy nation in a
poverty-stricken world was accentuated by a whipped-up panic over
the supposed danger to the Supreme Court and the Constitution."[123]
Similarly, the popular journalist Mark Sullivan contended that "La
Follette suffered greatly through dramatizing himself in opposition to
the Supreme Court." Sullivan perceived that La Follette's campaign ran
afoul of the public's profound respect for the Supreme Court:

[121] *State v. Farrell*, 111 Ohio St. 353, 145 N.E. 324 (1924).
[122] MacKay, *Progressive Movement*, p. 163.
[123] *New Republic*, November 26, 1924, p. 1.

A voter looked at a photograph of the Justices in their solemn robes; he got the impression of . . . a grave dignity approximating venerableness from even the younger ones. He saw idealism in the bright eyes of the oldest of them, Holmes; humor, geniality, almost a jovial quality in the chief, Taft; he saw sheer mental power in the broad brows of Butler and Sanford; he saw equal qualities of assurance and dependableness in Sutherland, McKenna and VanDevanter; forthright courage in the almost Andrew Jackson–like features of McReynolds; acute penetration and sympathy with progress in Brandeis.

. . . Then he turned to the campaign photographs of La Follette. . . . He saw in La Follette something of that unusualness, that aberration from the conventional, which is frequently a deterrent from confidence in the average man's mind, the pompadour hair that suggests emotional excitability—the voter turned from one photograph to the other and decided to stand by what seemed to be the picture of greater stability, in a world where the agencies of instability are already disturbingly numerous and energetic.[124]

Although Sullivan oversimplified the impact of the Court issue, the 1924 campaign and election demonstrated that public support for the maintenance of judicial power was steadfast and that proposals for radical Court reform remained as politically perilous in 1924 as they had been in 1896 and 1912. La Follette's attempts to avoid the issue during the campaign and his gingerly and often almost apologetic defenses of the plan indicate that he recognized that opposition to judicial review was not an issue that could command broad public support and was likely to alienate many voters. As in so many other episodes involving challenges to judicial power during the early twentieth century, progressives seemed to lack the courage of their convictions concerning reform, to the extent that they had any convictions.

Nonetheless, La Follette's impressive vote tally suggests that the idea of abridging judicial power did not repel millions of Americans and that the Court plan may have enjoyed much support, even though it also encountered formidable opposition. In a nation where the Supreme Court's power is regarded with almost mystical awe, one-sixth of the voters were willing to support a candidate who favored a major limitation of the Court's power of judicial review, though many of those voters may have opposed La Follette's plan or been indifferent to it. This suggests that public support for the courts was not inevitable, notwithstanding the persistence of the respect for the judiciary that is so deeply engrained in the American character.

[124] Mark Sullivan, "Looking Back on La Follette," *The World's Work*, January 1925, p. 331.

As in other recent periods when Court reform had attracted public attention, much of the success of the opposition to reform must be attributed to the vigor and skill with which the elite bar and conservative politicians defended the courts. Although the Republicans would not have dared to transform La Follette's plan into a major election issue if public support for judicial review had not been potent, their deft manipulation of public hopes and fears probably helped to reinforce the widespread belief that the courts were the ultimate guardians of personal rights and property. And, as in other periods of anti-Court agitation, popular judicial decisions handed down at critical times helped to stimulate public support for the judiciary. Even if the Court issue did not actually diminish support for La Follette, the landslide victory of a ticket that had made opposition to Court reform the premier issue of its campaign chilled all movements to curb the powers of the Supreme Court.

THIRTEEN

FINAL CONFLICTS, 1925–1937

> The camouflaged blow strikes at all our courts. It strikes at
> justice. It strikes at independent thought, action, life. I
> know things aren't as we wish. I would like to hand Mr.
> Hughes a few punches on the jaw myself. And there are
> one or two others [Supreme Court Justices] to whom I
> could spare a blow. I would like to see some of their
> decisions reversed, but that is not the point. THE COURT
> is being discredited . . . this summer I am going to be
> back on Mt. Rushmore, carving there the colossal heads of
> Washington, Jefferson and Lincoln. Don't let me feel
> that . . . they were a lot of muddling fools . . . and that
> our America deserves a Hitler—a Stalin . . . rather than a
> fair deal, equity and justice.
> *(The sculptor Gutzon Borglum, a progressive, urging Sen. George
> Norris to oppose Roosevelt's proposal to add six justices to the U.S.
> Supreme Court, February 24, 1937)*[1]

> Why do progressives and radicals in so many instances
> have to be damned fool impossibilists?
> *(Harold Ickes, expressing frustration over the failure of
> progressives to support Roosevelt's Court-packing plan,
> February 14, 1937)*[2]

THE CONTROVERSY OVER judicial review subsided for several years after the 1924 election. Criticism of the courts was muted not only by the triumph of Coolidgean conservatism but also by a lack of leadership in the anticourt movement, a renewed pragmatism among critics of the courts, and changes in the direction of the courts themselves, especially the Supreme Court. Discontent over the judiciary continued to smolder, however, and remained close to the surface of politics during the next decade until it burst forth noisily once again when the Court began to invalidate New Deal legislation.

[1] Gutzon Borglum to George Norris, February 24, 1937, *Norris Papers*, Box 117, Manuscript Division, Library of Congress.

[2] *Diary of Harold Ickes*, February 14, 1937, p. 1978, Reel 2, Manuscript Division, Library of Congress.

The movement to curb judicial power lost four of its most notable leaders during 1924 and 1925 with the deaths of Walter Clark, Robert M. La Follette, and Samuel Gompers and the retirement of Senator Robert L. Owen. Together they had spanned, symbolized, and sustained the three principal strands of opposition to judicial review—the populist, the progressive, and the trade unionist. Their political prominence had moved proposals for abrogating judicial power from the margins of politics to the center of national discourse. Each had commanded a prestige that helped to give respectability to proposals for abrogating judicial power, and they had enjoyed a high degree of political independence that gave them the freedom to speak out against alleged abuses of judicial power. No prominent judge or tireless polemicist emerged to take the place of Clark. No AFL leader could pummel the judiciary as Gompers did in his last years without fearing stigmatization as a "radical." And no progressive other than La Follette was able to muster so much support for a plan to abrogate judicial power significantly. Although Norris quietly continued to carry on his crusade to restrict or abolish the jurisdiction of the lower federal courts, no person of national stature emerged to challenge judicial power until Roosevelt announced his Court-packing plan in 1937.

The absence of new leadership reflected in part a diminution of public antagonism toward the judiciary. In particular, the increasing civil libertarianism of the Supreme Court helped to attenuate criticism of the courts. Proving that its decision in *Meyer v. Nebraska* was no anomaly but the beginning of a trend, the Supreme Court during the middle and late 1920s struck down a number of statutes that interfered with personal liberties. Although these decisions accelerated the judicial activism of which the Court's critics had so bitterly complained, few critics of judicial review were heard to complain about the Court's nullification of legislation with which those critics disagreed.

In June 1925, the Supreme Court affirmed the ruling of the court of appeals in *Pierce v. Society of Sisters*, holding that substantive due process under the Fourteenth Amendment prohibited Oregon from requiring parents to send their children to public school.[3] Although that case added little to what the Court had said in *Meyer*, it demonstrated that the Court would continue to oppose intrusions by state legislatures upon fundamental personal liberties, and it reassured countless ethnic Americans who had been alarmed by organized assaults on their parochial schools.

Some progressives, however, perceived that the use of the due process clause to invalidate socially repressive legislation would further

[3] 268 U.S. 510 (1925).

reinforce the Court's power to invalidate progressive economic legislation. Frankfurter warned that "in rejoicing over the Nebraska and Oregon cases, we must not forget that a heavy price has to be paid for these occasional services to liberalism." He pointed out that the invalidation of trade-union laws, the sanctification of the injunction in labor cases, and the veto of minimum-wage legislation were "not wiped out by the Oregon decision." Frankfurter contended that the cost of the Court's power was greater than its gains. Chauvinistic or ill-considered measures such as those enacted by Nebraska and Oregon could be repealed after hysteria subsided or liberal forces were aroused. But decisions invalidating economic legislation had far more far-reaching consequences because they were "ever so much more durable and authoritative than even the most mischievous of repealable state legislation."[4]

After *Pierce*, however, the Court began to invoke the more specific provisions of the Bill of Rights to protect personal liberties. In *Gitlow v. New York* (1925), the Court for the first time indicated that the free speech and free press clauses of the First Amendment were applicable to the states under the Fourteenth Amendment.[5] Although the immediate impact was slight because *Gitlow* upheld the constitutionality of New York's syndicalism statute and affirmed the conviction of a political radical for distributing pamphlets that were not likely to create any threat to public order, the decision laid the foundation for later decisions in which the Court invoked the First Amendment to protect freedom of speech against state infringements.

The decision also opened the way for the eventual incorporation into state law of other provisions of the Bill of Rights.[6] Two years after *Gitlow*, the Court reiterated the nexus between due process and the guarantees of the Fourteenth Amendment.[7] Not until 1931, however, did the Court finally invoke the First Amendment's free speech clause to strike down a state statute and overturn a conviction.[8] During the

[4] Editorial, "Can the Supreme Court Guarantee Toleration?" *New Republic*, June 17, 1925, pp. 85–87, repr. Philip Kurland, ed., *Felix Frankfurter on the Supreme Court: Extra-judicial Essays on the Court and the Constitution* (Cambridge, Mass.: Harvard University Press, 1970), pp. 174–78.

[5] 268 U.S. 652 (1925).

[6] Klaus H. Heberle, "From Gitlow to Near: Judicial 'Amendment' by Absent-Minded Incrementalism," *Journal of Politics* 34 (May 1972): 458–83.

[7] *Whitney v. California*, 274 U.S. 357 (1927). Despite its affirmation that the First Amendment protects freedom of speech from state infringement, the Court upheld California's syndicalism statute and the conviction of a defendant whose speech does not appear to have been calculated to create any imminent danger of a breach of the peace.

[8] *Stromberg v. California*, 283 U.S. 359 (1931). Four years earlier, in *Fiske v. Kansas*, 274

same year, the Court invoked the free press clause to nullify a Minnesota statute that provided for the suppression of any "malicious, scandalous, or defamatory" newspaper. And, in 1932, the Court held that the Sixth Amendment required a state to provide meaningful assistance of counsel to defendants charged with a capital crime.[9]

Although the Court's increasing solicitude for personal liberties may have muted hostility toward the Court and helped to erode support for curtailment of judicial review, those cases were far from enough to eliminate public antagonism to the courts. The willingness to protect individual rights was more than offset by the continuing nullification of economic legislation that failed to fall within the Court's narrow parameters of constitutionality. And the Court's abandonment of substantive due process in civil liberties decisions starting with *Gitlow* did not presage any rejection of substantive due process in economic cases.

The continuing fidelity to economic due process was manifest in case after case. In October 1925, the Court dealt yet another blow to social legislation when it invalidated Arizona's minimum wage law.[10] Although the Arizona statute was not easily distinguishable from the District of Columbia law struck down in *Adkins v. Children's Hospital*,[11] progressives had hoped that the Court would uphold the statute. While progressives admitted that the Arizona statute was badly drafted, they feared that the decision would inhibit the enactment and administration of minimum wage laws and other reform legislation throughout the nation. The *New Republic* observed that the effects of such a decision belied the common argument of the Court's defenders that the Court did not abuse its power since it struck down few laws.

In 1926, the Court struck down a Pennsylvania statute that prohibited the use of shoddy (reclaimed wool) in the manufacture of mattresses, holding that the statute bore no reasonable relationship to the protection of public health since shoddy could be effectively disinfected.[12] In another 1926 case, the Court invalidated an Oklahoma statute that required contractors to pay a minimum wage to workers on public projects.[13] In 1927, the Court nullified a New York statute that regulated the price of theater tickets resold by agencies.[14] And, in

U.S. 380 (1927), the Court had invoked the "liberty" guaranteed by the Fourteenth Amendment to reverse a criminal conviction under a syndicalism statute.

[9] *Near v. Minnesota*, 283 U.S. 697 (1931); *Powell v. Alabama*, 287 U.S. 45 (1932)..

[10] *Murphy v. Sardell*, 269 U.S. 530 (1925) (per curiam). Justice Holmes concurred solely on the ground that he believed that he was bound by the Court's decision in *Adkins*. Justice Brandeis dissented.

[11] 261 U.S. 525 (1923).

[12] *Weaver v. Palmer Brothers Co.*, 270 U.S. 402 (1926).

[13] *Connally v. General Construction Co.*, 269 U.S. 385 (1926).

[14] *Tyson v. Banton*, 273 U.S. 418 (1927).

1928, the Court nullified a New Jersey statute that regulated the fees of employment agencies.[15]

The decisions in the New York and New Jersey cases especially disappointed progressives since they reversed the trend toward expansion of the category of businesses subject to governmental regulation because they were endowed with a public interest. As Columbia economics professor Rexford G. Tugwell lamented, "Freedom of contract and the due-process clause of the Fourteenth Amendment have again been made to serve the cause of reaction."[16] The persistence of a minority bloc on the Court gave little solace to liberals. Liberals were cheered that Stone often voted in dissent with Brandeis and Holmes,[17] but they feared that the upcoming departure of the octogenarian Holmes, whose retirement was regarded as imminent during most of the 1920s, might result in the appointment of a justice who would strengthen the ranks of the conservative majority. The prospect of any realignment on the Court seemed as remote as ever.[18]

Meanwhile, the Court's decisions continued to antagonize organized labor. The decision in *Michaelson* on the eve of the 1924 election proved to be as anomalous as union leaders had feared. The unions were particularly outraged by a 1927 decision upholding an injunction against a group of stonecutters who had refused to work on limestone cut by nonunion workers. Relying on the Sherman Act's prohibition of secondary boycotts, the Court concluded that this narrow and limited strike affected interstate commerce.[19] A sharp dissent by Brandeis declared that the restraints permitted by the Court resembled involuntary servitude. According to Brandeis, "The propriety of the unions' conduct can hardly be doubted by one who believes in the organization of labor."[20] The contrast between the Court's narrow definition of commerce in the child-labor cases particularly vexed liberals and labor.[21] Although union reaction was restrained, the *American Federation-*

[15] *Ribnik v. McBride*, 277 U.S. 350 (1928).

[16] Rexford G. Tugwell, "That Living Constitution," *New Republic*, June 20, 1928, p. 121.

[17] "The Supreme Court as Legislator," *New Republic*, March 31, 1926, p. 159.

[18] Tugwell, "Living Constitution," p. 121. Tugwell observed after the decisions in the New York and New Jersey cases that the minority opinions of Stone, Brandeis, and Holmes might eventually become law but that "so long as legalists so downright as Justice Sutherland are dominant, progress is definitely blocked" (ibid.).

[19] *Bedford Cut Stone Co. v. Journeymen Stone Cutters Association of North America*, 274 U.S. 37 (1927).

[20] 274 U.S., p. 58, 65 (Brandeis dissenting).

[21] As Professor Urofsky has observed, *Bedford* demonstrated that reasonable "restrictions on trade caused by industry would be tolerated by the Court under the rule of reason; but the bench would disregard its own rule when asked to apply it to the clearly

ist warned that a "remedy for the situation created by this opinion must be found."[22]

The principal remedy advocated by the AFL continued to be legislation to restrict the power of courts to issue injunctions. Support gradually developed among many lawyers, academicians, and reformers who perceived that the industrial unrest perpetuated by "government by injunction" jeopardized economic efficiency and the legitimacy of the legal order.[23] Meanwhile, the Great Depression hastened reevaluations of labor's role in society.[24] Widespread recognition of the need to curb injunctions culminated in the enactment in 1932 of the Norris-La Guardia Anti-Injunction Act, which prohibited federal courts from issuing injunctions in any labor dispute except where unlawful acts had been threatened or committed and substantial and irreparable injury would result without an injunction. In effect, the Norris-La Guardia Act set aside the Supreme Court's narrow reading of the Clayton Act in its 1921 *Duplex Printing* decision. Although many labor leaders feared that the Court might emasculate the new law, the Court upheld it in 1938,[25] following the "Judicial Revolution" of the previous year.

Meanwhile, Norris continued to attempt to abolish the jurisdiction of the federal courts where federal jurisdiction was based solely upon diversity of citizenship between the parties. Bills introduced by Norris in 1930 and 1931 for the abolition of diversity jurisdiction were approved by the Judiciary Committee but were never acted on by the Senate.[26] These and similar measures encountered serious opposition from the ABA.[27] Among the few other court-curbing measures introduced in Congress during this period was a bill by the progressive

---

reasonable activities of a labor union." Melvin I. Urofsky, *A March of Liberty: A Constitutional History of the United States*, vol. 2 (New York: Knopf, 1988), p. 628.

[22] Editorial, "Restraining Lawful Activities," *American Federationist*, May 1927, p. 530.

[23] William E. Forbath, "The Shaping of the American Labor Movement," *Harvard Law Review* 102 (March 1989): 1227–28.

[24] As Christopher L. Tomlins has pointed out, the Depression encouraged Congress, and even some segments of the business community, to support "the proposition that collective bargaining through independent unions was, after all, a realistic model for the conduct of labor relations" (*The State and the Unions: Labor Relations, Law, and the Organized Labor Movement in America, 1880–1960* [New York: Cambridge University Press, 1985], p. 95).

[25] *Lauf v. E. G. Shinner & Co.*, 303 U.S. 323, 330 (1938).

[26] S. 4357, 71st Cong., 2d sess., 1930, Report 691; S. 939, 72nd Cong., 1st sess., 1931, Report 530.

[27] For example, *Memorandum of the American Bar Association In Opposition to the Enactment of S. 939, S. 937 and S. 3243* (1931), *Papers of George W. Norris*, Box 284. See also *Memorandum on Certain Bills Pending in Congress Limiting Jurisdiction of the Federal District Courts* (1929), *Norris Papers*, Box 278. Norris complained in 1930 that the "combined wealth of the nation" opposed the abolition of diversity jurisdiction (Norris to Norman Thomas, May 17, 1930, *Norris Papers*, Box 196).

Republican senator Smith Brookhart of Iowa to require unanimity in any Supreme Court decision striking down a federal statute[28] and a bill by Republican representative Roy O. Woodruff of Michigan to require the concurrence of seven justices in any such decision.[29]

Other critics of the courts carried on Clark's proposal for the abolition of the due process clause of the Fourteenth Amendment. Writing in 1924, Frankfurter flatly stated that the "due process clauses ought to go." Elimination of due process cases, he believed, would relieve the Court of a "contentiously political burden" and would free the Court "to meet more adequately the jurisdiction which would remain and which ought to remain." Frankfurter argued that it did not behoove progressives to "fall back upon mechanical contrivances when dealing with a process where mechanics can play but a very small part." He averred that "no nine men are wise enough and good enough to be entrusted with the power which the unlimited provisions of the due process clauses confer."[30]

Even though there was no major movement to curb the Court's powers during the late 1920s, the pent-up frustration of progressives and organized labor burst forth in 1930 when President Herbert C. Hoover nominated Charles Evans Hughes and John J. Parker to the Supreme Court. The intensity of opposition to Hughes's nomination to the chief justiceship was surprising since Hughes had developed a comparatively liberal record during his service on the Court from 1910 to 1916 and his personal integrity and intellectual acumen were widely respected. The announcement of the nomination drew almost universal public praise, with Justice Brandeis and Judge Benjamin N. Cardozo of the New York Court of Appeals joining in the acclaim.

One week later, however, when the Judiciary Committee reported the nomination favorably, Senators Norris and John J. Blaine of Wisconsin dissented. In addition to warning that Hughes's return to the bench from which he had resigned would create a dangerous precedent for the politicization of the Court, Norris objected to Hughes's record as a highly paid counsel for large corporations. Echoing his attack on Taft in 1922, Norris explained that Hughes's association with rich and powerful captains of industry had isolated him from the common people and irrevocably biased him in favor of the wealthy and big business.[31]

---

[28] S. J. Res. 162, 71st Cong., 2d sess., 1930.

[29] H. J. Res. 6762, 69th Cong., 1st sess., 1926.

[30] Editorial, "The Red Terror of Judicial Reform," *New Republic*, October 1, 1924, p. 113, repr. Philip B. Kurland, ed., *Felix Frankfurter on the Supreme Court—Extrajudicial Essays on the Court and the Constitution* (Cambridge, Mass.: Harvard University Press, 1970), pp. 166–67.

[31] 72 *Congressional Record*, 71st Cong., 2d sess., February 10, 1930, pp. 3372–73.

Norris's opposition inspired a storm of protest against the nomination by progressives who objected to Hughes's corporate connections. The nomination also encountered opposition among southern Democrats, who objected to Hughes's belief in a strong federal government.[32] Although the Senate's action on the nomination within three days of the Judiciary Committee's report prevented public opposition from galvanizing, senators received numerous protests from private citizens. A Baltimore attorney warned Borah that the nomination threatened "the rights of the people as against corporate greed."[33] Hughes's nomination may have attracted greater opposition among senators because it was the first Supreme Court nomination to be considered in open session. The willingness of so many senators to denounce the nomination on the Senate floor suggests that the lawmakers were aware of the unpopularity of many of the Court's decisions.

Hughes was confirmed by the narrowest margin of any Supreme Court nominee since Mahlon Pitney in 1912. Twenty-six senators voted against the nomination, and seven others were paired against it. Even though the fight against the nomination failed to prevent the confirmation of Hughes, progressives believed that they had won a victory since as they had demonstrated to the Court that public opposition to its corporate biases retained considerable vitality.[34] Many conservatives who favored Hughes's nomination had commended Norris's opposition to the nomination because it reminded the courts that judicial isolation from the needs and aspirations of common citizens endangered the nation's judicial institutions.[35]

Less than two months after the fight over Hughes, a controversy erupted over Hoover's nomination of Judge John Parker of the Fourth Circuit to succeed Edward Sanford.[36] The administration did not in-

[32] For example, the Boston local of the International Union of Steam and Operating Engineers wrote to Norris on February 5 to urge the defeat of the nomination because the voters had rejected Hughes at the polls in 1916 (H. M. Comerford to Norris, February 5, 1930, *Norris Papers*, Box 41).

[33] William Thomas Larkin to Borah, February 13, 1930, *Borah Papers*, Box 300, Library of Congress.

[34] Senator Johnson wrote to one of his sons that the "Hughes incident here is really significant" since "twenty-six senators stood up to be counted" despite a united press and pressure from big business. Hiram W. Johnson to Hiram W. Johnson, Jr., February 15, 1930, in Robert E. Burke, ed., *The Diary Letters of Hiram Johnson, 1917–1945*, vol. 5, *1929–1933* (New York: Garland, 1983). Johnson observed that "the opposition began with one little protest by Norris, and grew into a real contest" (ibid.).

[35] "Speech—July 1930," *Norris Papers*, Box 257.

[36] For discussions of the controversy over Parker's nomination, see Rona Hirsch Mendelsohn, "Senate Confirmation of Supreme Court Appointments: The Nomination and Rejection of John J. Parker," *Howard Law Review* 14 (1968): 105–48; Richard L. Watson, Jr., "The Defeat of Judge Parker: A Study in Pressure Groups and Politics," *Mississippi Valley Historical Review* 50 (1963): 213–24.

vite controversy, for Parker had not made a career of representing large corporations and his record on the bench was not notably conservative. Although the Parker nomination was initially greeted with widespread approval, it soon encountered opposition from the AFL and the NAACP. The AFL objected to a decision in which Parker had ruled that union efforts to organize workers against mine owners who enforced an open shop pursuant to "yellow-dog" agreements constituted a combination and conspiracy in restraint of trade.[37] Although Parker and his defenders protested that the issue was only jurisdictional and that Parker had merely followed precedent, labor leaders insisted that the decision showed that Parker personally favored "yellow-dog" contracts. The NAACP opposed Parker because he had made a speech as the 1920 Republican gubernatorial candidate in North Carolina expressing support for the exclusion of African Americans from politics and had failed to question the North Carolina Constitution's abridgement of their voting rights.

AFL and NAACP opposition encouraged progressive senators to take a closer look at Parker's record. Although the nomination became entangled with partisan politics, providing Democrats and insurgent Republicans with an opportunity to embarrass an administration made vulnerable by the increasing economic depression, opposition to the nomination also reflected a principled attempt to prevent a reinforcement of conservatism on the supreme bench and to protest the conservatism of the federal judiciary. The principal lines of opposition echoed the charges that progressives and labor leaders had been making against the Court for forty years. Norris summarized the views of the opponents of Parker's nomination:

> I believe we ought to put more humanity into the courts. . . . We ought to know that everyone who ascends to that holy bench should have in his heart and in his mind the intention of looking after the liberties of his fellow citizens . . . of discarding if necessary the old precedents of barbarous days, and construing the Constitution and the laws in the light of a modern day, a present civilization. . . . Human liberty is the issue. The preservation of our Government is the issue.[38]

An acrimonious debate over the nomination raged for several days before the Senate finally rejected the nomination by a 41–39 vote. The defeat of Parker, the first Court nominee the Senate had rejected in more than thirty years, demonstrated that anxiety about the judiciary

[37] *United Mine Workers v. Red Jacket Consolidated Coal and Coke Co.*, 18 F. 2d 839 (4th Cir. 1927). See *Hearings Before the Subcommittee of the Senate Committee on Judiciary on the Confirmation of Hon. John Johnston Parker to be an Associate Justice of the Supreme Court of the United States*, 71st Cong., 2d sess., 1930.

[38] 72 *Congressional Record*, 71st Cong., 2d sess., April 28, 1930, p. 8192.

remained intense even though public denunciations of the Court had become less frequent and demands for abridgement of judicial review and other reforms had subsided. Having recognized that radical reform was impracticable, the critics now preferred to invest their principal energies in the more viable expedient of influencing the judicial selection process.

The widespread interest in the selection process also demonstrates once again that many critics opposed the way judicial power was exercised rather than the power itself. The breadth of interest in the selection process and the scope of frustration over judicial decisions was illustrated by the widespread participation in the confirmation process by special-interest groups and private individuals. In addition to the opposition by the NAACP and the AFL, a host of other organizations and persons actively opposed the nomination.[39]

Although ACLU's founder Roger S. Baldwin contended after the defeat of Parker that few persons perceived how significantly the president's selection of justices influenced the "social life of future generations,"[40] the uproar over the nomination demonstrated that many recognized the importance of the nomination process. As Norman Thomas observed shortly after the defeat of Parker, "There are great judges who might remake our courts."[41] Parker, who faced more broadly based opposition than Brandeis in 1916, was the first nominee opposed by a wide spectrum of organizations and individuals. The ferocity of opposition to Hughes suggests that widespread opposition to Parker might have arisen even without the campaigns organized by the AFL and the NAACP, but those campaigns intensified the debate and galvanized large segments of the public. Moreover, the closeness of the vote suggests that fears of electoral reprisals from labor unions and African Americans was a decisive factor in Parker's defeat.[42] Parker's defeat clearly contributed to Hoover's decision to nominate the more moderate Owen J. Roberts to the Court in 1930 and Cardozo in 1932.

[39] For example, Senator Allen of Kansas received letters from more than two dozen organizations that opposed the nomination (*Papers of Henry J. Allen*, Series C, Box 58, Manuscript Division, Library of Congress). Senator Borah also received correspondence from a broad spectrum of liberal organizations. In addition to labor and civil rights groups, Borah heard from the Veterans' Political Organization, the Yale University chapter of the American Federation of Teachers, and the Order of Railway Conductors, (*Borah Papers*, Box 300).

[40] Roger S. Baldwin to Borah, May 13, 1930, *Borah Papers*, Box 301.

[41] Norman Thomas to George W. Norris, May 15, 1930, *Norris Papers*, Box 196.

[42] See Watson, "Defeat of Judge Parker," p. 232; William Burris, *Duty and the Law: Judge John Parker and the Constitution* (Bessemer, Ala.: Colonial Press, 1987), p. 97; Hiram Johnson to Archibald Johnson and Hiram Johnson, Jr., May 3, 1930, in Burke, *Diary Letters*, vol. 5, p. 2.

The struggle over the Parker nomination was the last major episode in the controversy over the courts before the Great Depression infused that controversy with a new urgency. Despite early signs of judicial receptivity toward anti-Depression legislation,[43] the Court's opposition to New Deal legislation finally provoked the crisis that the critics of the judiciary had so long presaged. General apprehension about the Court's receptivity toward these far-reaching and innovative measures was increased early in 1935 when the Court struck down part of the National Recovery Act[44] and invalidated a federal pension plan for railroad workers.[45]

As in earlier periods, critics proposed a plethora of remedies for reducing judicial hostility to legislation they favored. Early in 1935, Secretary of Agriculture Henry A. Wallace proposed a constitutional amendment to create a national council of four nonpartisan economic experts who would have the power to initiate proposals for amendments upon which the people would vote in national referenda.[46] Wallace's proposal was quintessentially progressive since it was designed to circumvent the normal political processes through the use of experts and direct democracy. Indeed, it was the progressive nostrum par excellence because it attempted to reconcile the tension between elite government and popular government that created contradictions in so many other progressive reforms. Meanwhile, other critics revived proposals to require the concurrence of more than a majority in decisions that invalidated federal laws.[47]

Sensitive to the Court's growing role in protecting civil liberties, however, some liberals preferred to limit judicial power only over economic legislation. For example, Charles E. Carpenter, a University of

---

[43] *Home Building and Loan Association v. Blaisdell*, 290 U.S. 398 (1934); *Nebbia v. New York*, 291 U.S. 502 (1934); *Norman v. Baltimore and Ohio Railroad Co.*, 294 U.S. 240 (1935); *Perry v. United States*, 294 U.S. 330 (1935).

[44] *Panama Refining Company v. Ryan*, 293 U.S. 388 (1935).

[45] *Railroad Retirement Board v. Alton Railroad Co.*, 295 U.S. 330 (1935).

[46] Henry A. Wallace, "America—Recluse or Trader?" *Collier's*, February 2, 1935, p. 7; "Wallace Proposes People Amend Law," *New York Times*, January 25, 1935, p. 22.

[47] In May, shortly after the Court invalidated the railroad pension statute in a 5–4 decision, Democratic representative Donald C. Dobbins of Illinois proposed a constitutional amendment to require a two-thirds vote of the Court to declare a law invalid, and Democratic representative Robert Crosser of Ohio introduced a measure to require the concurrence of at least three-fourths of the Court to invalidate an act of Congress. Meanwhile, Fiorello H. La Guardia, now mayor of New York City, disparaged conservatives who seemed "to believe that the Constitution was written for no other purpose than to guarantee exploitation of the many by the chosen few" ("For ²/₃ High Court Vote to Make Laws Invalid," *New York Times*, May 15, 1935, p. 1); see "Rail Pension Bill Revived in House," ibid., May 18, 1935, p. 23; "La Guardia Speech to Progressives," ibid., May 20, 1935, p. 2; "Mayor Is Critical of Constitution," ibid., May 20, 1935, p. 1.

Southern California law professor who favored a check on judicial review, believed that the liberties of speech, press, and religion "would fare better" if the courts retained the power to review the constitutionality of restrictions upon those liberties. Citing recent Court decisions that had imposed "wholesome restraints" on state legislation that interfered with personal liberties, Carpenter warned Norris in 1935 that the "dangerous legislative tendency" to restrict First Amendment freedoms "might become very marked and very detrimental to the progress of liberalism in the United States."[48]

Criticisms of the Court and proposals for reform sharply escalated after the Court, on "Black Monday," May 27, 1935, invalidated the National Recovery Act (NRA), nullified the Frazier-Lemke Emergency Farm Mortgage Act, and decided that the president lacked power to remove members of independent regulatory commissions.[49] These three decisions provoked a paroxysm of hostility that was reminiscent of the outrage over the Court's *Adkins* decision in 1923 and its triad of controversial decisions in 1895. Proposed reforms included a constitutional amendment to circumvent the decision; a national constitutional convention; creation of an administrative court of review to pass on both facts and law, with appeal to the Supreme Court only on questions of law; a constitutional requirement of advance advisory opinions by the Court; and removal of the Court's power of review over social and economic questions.[50] The decisions also inspired more bills to require the concurrence of more than a majority to invalidate acts of Congress,[51] although the unanimity of the three decisions probably eroded interest in such plans.

The controversy over the decisions on "Black Monday" exposed divisions in the ranks of progressives that would become critical when Roosevelt announced his Court-packing plan in 1937. These tensions were most clearly illustrated in the contrast between the reactions of Borah and Norris to the invalidation of the NRA. Borah, who had watched with growing alarm the expansion of federal powers under the New Deal, lauded the Court for "jealously guarding" the Constitution and the rights of the states. In contrast to progressives of earlier years, who had seen the Court's invalidation of legislation as an omen of "judicial oligarchy," Borah declared in a national radio address that the invalidation of the NRA was faithful to the plain language of the

---

[48] Charles E. Carpenter to Norris, June 5, 1935, *Norris Papers*, Box 118.

[49] *Schechter v. United States*, 295 U.S. 495 (1935); *Louisville Joint Stock Land Bank v. Radford*, 295 U.S. 555 (1935); *Humphrey's Executor v. United States*, 295 U.S. 602 (1935).

[50] "Plans Offered to Solve the NRA Situation Include National Constitutional Convention," *New York Times*, May 30, 1935, p. 13.

[51] S. J. Res. 149, H. J. Res. 287, H.R. 8100, H.R. 8123, 74th Cong.,1st sess., 1935.

Constitution and that the Court's failure to abide by that text would create "a complete judicial oligarchy."[52]

Meanwhile, Norris introduced legislation to prevent the Court from invalidating congressional acts without at least a two-thirds vote and to deprive lower federal courts of jurisdiction to decide cases involving constitutional questions.[53] Echoing the feelings of many other progressives who had recognized the futility of trying to enact legislation to curb the courts, Norris told a California judge that he was disappointed by the reaction to his proposal for a two-thirds rule and had concluded that "it would only be a waste of time for me to try to get it reported. It was quite evident we could not succeed in getting it passed."[54] Norris also acknowledged the impracticability of his plan to restrict the jurisdiction of the lower federal courts.[55] Similarly, Republican senator Gerald P. Nye of North Dakota pointed out that there was little hope of any amendment curtailing judicial power receiving the support of two-thirds of the members of Congress, since the administration had failed even to obtain a majority to extend the NRA.[56]

Despite the widespread outcry over the decisions, a Gallup poll in September 1935 showed that only 31 percent of those surveyed favored limitation of the Court's power to declare congressional acts unconstitutional; 53 percent opposed such a limitation, and 16 percent had no opinion.[57] These figures are particularly interesting since they represent the first scientific sampling of public opinion concerning the Court's power for the period covered by this book. The poll demonstrates the resilience of public support for judicial power, even when the Court was under widespread attack for striking down popular legislation.

Fears that the Court would continue to frustrate New Deal legislation were borne out in 1936 when the Court invalidated various recovery and reform measures, including the Agricultural Adjustment Act (AAA),[58] the Bituminous Coal Act,[59] and the Municipal Bank-

[52] "Borah Challenges 'Menders' to Risk Constitution Poll," *New York Times,* June 3, 1935, p. 1; "Senator Borah's Radio Address Supporting Court's Decision on NRA," ibid., p. 2.

[53] S. J. Res. 149, 74th Cong., 1st sess., 1935; "Norris Asks Ban on 5–4 Decisions," *New York Times,* June 18, 1935, p. 2.

[54] Norris to Francis J. Heney, September 6, 1935, *Norris Papers,* MS 3298, Box 1, State Archives, Nebraska State Historical Society, Lincoln.

[55] Norris to unidentified correspondent, March 1, 1935, MS 3298, Box 1, State Archives.

[56] "Many in Congress Oppose Roosevelt," *New York Times,* June 1, 1935, p. 6.

[57] George H. Gallup, William P. Hansen, and Fred L. Israel, eds., *The Gallup Poll, Public Opinion 1935–1971,* vol. 1 (New York: Random House, 1972), p. 2.

[58] *United States v. Butler,* 297 U.S. 1 (1936).

[59] *Carter v. Carter Coal Company,* 298 U.S. 238 (1936).

ruptcy Act.[60] The invalidation of the AAA in a 6–3 decision in January 1936 revealed the same fissures in the progressive ranks that had become apparent after the NRA decision. Although many prominent progressives deplored the decision and reiterated calls for measures to curb the courts, they could not agree upon a remedy. Republican senator Lynn J. Frazier of North Dakota demanded a statute forbidding the justices, upon penalty of impeachment, to declare acts of Congress invalid.[61] Republican senator Peter Norbeck of South Dakota introduced a bill to require the concurrence of seven justices to invalidate an act of Congress,[62] and Senator Wheeler declared that the power of the Court might need to be curtailed.[63]

Meanwhile, various other liberals continued to advocate measures to curb the courts. A Farmer-Laborite representative from Minnesota introduced legislation to increase the number of justices to eleven,[64] and a Democratic representative from Pennsylvania proposed increasing the number to fourteen.[65] Norman Thomas favored an amendment to deprive the Court of the power to adjudicate the constitutionality of economic and social welfare legislation.[66] Democratic senator James P. Pope of Idaho introduced a bill to require the concurrence of more than two-thirds of the justices to invalidate a federal statute.[67] Democratic representative Joseph P. Monaghan of Montana proposed legislation to oust any justice who voted to invalidate the Tennessee Valley Authority Act.[68] And Floyd B. Olson, the Farmer-Labor governor of Minnesota, called for ten-year terms for justices and other federal judges.[69] Leading academics also proposed restraints upon judicial power. Karl Llewellyn of the Columbia Law School favored a vote of seven justices to overrule an act of Congress,[70] and Dean Henry M. Bates of the University of Michigan Law School wanted to strip lower federal courts of the power to invalidate acts of Congress.[71]

[60] *Ashton v. Cameron County Water Improvement District*, 298 U.S. 513 (1936).

[61] "Decision Astounds Congress Members," *New York Times*, January 7, 1936, p. 13.

[62] "For High Court Vote of 7," *New York Times*, January 18, 1936, p. 9.

[63] "Wheeler for Curb on Supreme Court," *New York Times*, January 17, 1936, p. 13.

[64] "For High Court Vote of 7."

[65] H.R. 10102, 74th Cong., 2d sess., 1936.

[66] "Thomas for a Court Curb," *New York Times*, January 8, 1936, p. 14.

[67] "Offers Bill to Curb Court," *New York Times*, February 4, 1936, p. 1.

[68] "Capital Again Set for TVA Decision," *New York Times*, February 10, 1936, p. 4.

[69] "Olson Declares for Third Party," *New York Times*, March 28, 1936, p. 2.

[70] "Urge Women Back Federal Powers," *New York Times*, May 2, 1936, p. 8.

[71] "Constitution Held Ample in New Deal," *New York Times*, January 26, 1936, p. 34.

Meanwhile, Borah continued to defend the Court, attempting to make judicial independence and constitutional integrity an issue in his campaign for the Republican presidential nomination. Like so many other opponents of plans to curb judicial power, Borah emphasized that the courts protected personal liberties as well as economic liberties, and he warned that abridgement of judicial powers would lead to despotism.[72] Similarly, Henry Wallace urged patience and predicted that the Court would eventually respond to the exigencies of the times.[73]

Organized labor's ardent support of most New Deal legislation led to a revival of reform proposals by trade unionists. As in earlier times of opposition to the Court, however, unionists were unable to unite behind a specific proposal. Following the NRA decision, AFL president William Green issued a vague call for measures to restrict the power of the Court to invalidate legislation,[74] and the AFL's 1935 convention voted to authorize its executive council to study proposals to curb judicial power and to submit to Congress an amendment to protect labor legislation from adverse decisions. At the AFL's 1936 convention, there were so many proposals for circumventing judicial obstruction of legislation that the convention referred the issue to the executive committee for more study. Meanwhile, Sidney Hillman, president of the Amalgamated Clothing Workers, proposed that the NRA decision be circumvented through a constitutional amendment or packing the Court. Declaring that "the Supreme Court has reduced the workers of this country to a class of untouchables," Green predicted that the nation would "not permit itself to be starved to death, Supreme Court or no Supreme Court."[75] In January 1936, the United Mine Workers of America voted to support unspecified legislation to insulate social-welfare legislation from interference by federal courts,[76] and the

[72] "Text of Senator William E. Borah's Address to Brooklyn Republicans," *New York Times*, January 29, 1936, p. 13; "Text of Senator Borah's Address on 'The Constitution and Entangling Alliances,'" ibid., February 23, 1936, p. 32; "Text of Senator Borah's Address Opening Campaign in His Native State of Illinois," ibid., March 22, 1936, p. 40, col. 1.

[73] "Wallace Predicts Liberal Judiciary," *New York Times*, July 1, 1936, p. 17.

[74] "Labor Conference Called over NRA," *New York Times*, June 3, 1935, p. 3; "Text of Green's Address Urging Amendment to Curb Supreme Court," ibid., June 8, 1935, p. 8; "Green Would Curb Court," ibid., September 1, 1935, p. 19.

[75] *Report of the Proceedings of the Fifty-Fifth Annual Convention of the American Federation of Labor* (Washington, D.C.: Judd & Detweiler, 1935), p. 820; *Report of the Proceedings of the Fifty-Sixth Annual Convention of the American Federation of Labor* (Washington, D.C.: Judd & Detweiler, 1936), pp. 232–34, 302; 306–7; 325–26; 359–65; 695–707; "A.F. of L. Demands 30-Hour Week Law: Green Re-Elected," *New York Times*, November 28, 1936, p. 1; "Hillman for Curb on Supreme Court," *New York Times*, June 30, 1935, p. 27.

[76] "Miners Ask Curbs on Supreme Court," *New York Times*, January 30, 1936, p. 7.

Amalgamated Clothing Workers of America unanimously approved a proposal for a constitutional amendment to permit Congress to pass laws to safeguard the economic welfare of workers.[77]

Convinced that the Court would continue to obstruct the New Deal, Roosevelt began to ponder ways to mitigate judicial hostility to reform legislation. In attempting to frame a Court-curbing plan, however, Roosevelt encountered the same quandaries that had stymied earlier critics of judicial power. Roosevelt recognized that a constitutional amendment provided the surest means of curbing judicial power, but he appreciated that the amendment process would be tedious and uncertain, and that anti-Court legislation might be invalidated by the Court itself. By January 1936, Roosevelt was considering the possibility of provoking such a confrontation by proposing a law to deprive the lower federal courts of the power to rule on the constitutionality of statutes and allow the Supreme Court to render only advisory opinions about their constitutionality. Roosevelt began to welcome judicial hostility to his program, believing that judicial recalcitrance would strengthen public support for his inevitable battle with the Court.[78]

The Supreme Court was a quiet yet pervasive issue in the 1936 presidential election. Republicans repeatedly warned that if reelected, Roosevelt would somehow tamper with the Court. The Republican platform pledged to "resist all attempts to impair the authority of the Supreme Court,"[79] and opponents of Roosevelt alleged that he had hinted he would pack the Court.[80] Frank Knox, the Republican vice-presidential candidate, suggested that Roosevelt might have plans for "assaulting the Supreme Court," and Herbert Hoover asked on the eve of the election whether the president intended to "stuff the Court."[81]

Although the Democrats did not specifically advocate a measure to curb judicial power, the party's platform declared that the party would seek a constitutional amendment to clarify the power of Congress and state legislatures to enact laws to safeguard economic security if the nation's economic problems could not be solved effectively "through

[77] "Garment Workers Back Roosevelt," *New York Times*, May 30, 1936, p. 3.

[78] *Diary of Harold Ickes*, January 26, 1936, pp. 1369–70, January 29, 1936, pp. 1376–77; January 31, 1936, p. 1380, Reel 1; January 10, 1937, pp. 1895–96, Reel 2.

[79] Donald Bruce Johnson, ed., *National Party Platforms*, vol. 1, *1840–1956* (Urbana: University of Illinois Press, 1978), p. 366.

[80] "Fears for High Court," *New York Times*, October 29, 1936, p. 12; "Reed Cites Threat to Pack High Court," ibid., October 8, 1936, p. 18.

[81] "Calls Roosevelt to Bare Wage Aim," *New York Times*, October 16, 1936, p. 18; "Hoover 'Rejected' New Deal Ideas; Held They Would Shackle Liberty," ibid., October 31, 1936, p. 1; "The Text of Hoover's Denver Address Warning of New Deal 'Shackles on Liberty,'" ibid., p. 4.

legislation within the Constitution."[82] Although the Roosevelt campaign purported to respect the Constitution and the Court, there was general understanding that the impasse between the Court and the New Deal could not continue. One side would have to yield.

Accordingly, Roosevelt's landslide victory in the 1936 election encouraged proponents of judicial reform. Shortly after Congress reconvened, bills were introduced to allow Congress to reenact judicially invalidated legislation by a two-thirds vote,[83] to deprive the Court of the power to strike down a federal statute,[84] to require the Court to render only advisory opinions concerning the constitutionality of legislation,[85] and to permit the Court to invalidate legislation only with more than a majority of the justices.[86] Recognizing that lack of organization had crippled past reform efforts, critics wisely scheduled a strategy conference chaired by Norris. The conference planned to ask fifty sponsors of amendments to explain their proposals, which would be examined by the conference's committees. The conference would then decide upon a plan of action and organize a campaign in support of that plan.[87]

Before the conference could convene, President Roosevelt announced his own reform plan on February 5, 1937. Roosevelt proposed legislation to permit the president to appoint up to fifty new federal judges to supplement the services of any judge who had served for ten years and had failed to resign within six months of reaching the age of seventy. Roosevelt's plan would permit the president to appoint a maximum of six additional justices to the Supreme Court and forty-four judges to lower federal courts.

Despite the warnings of Roosevelt's opponents during the 1936 presidential election and hints by Roosevelt, Roosevelt's plan startled the nation and surprised many leading lawyers, judges, and politicians. After nearly a half century of scattered and quixotic proposals for preventing judicial obstruction of reform, a viable plan had finally emerged. Various other recent proposals for packing the Court had been lost in the cacophony of Court criticisms, but a plan sponsored by a highly popular and powerful president was certain to command attention and support that would make the myriad other Court-curbing plans proposed during the past half century seem insignificant.

[82] Johnson, *National Party Platforms*, p. 362.
[83] H. J. Res. 190, 75th Cong., 1st sess., 1937.
[84] H.R. 4279, 75th Cong., 1st sess., 1937.
[85] H. J. Res. 132, 75th Cong., 1st sess., 1937.
[86] S. 1098, S. 437, S. 1276, 75th Cong., 1st sess., 1937.
[87] "Court Critics Plan Amendment Study," *New York Times*, January 10, 1937, sec. 2, p. 3; "Norris Backs drive For Curb On Court," ibid., Jan. 14, 1937, p. 13.

Like earlier proposals, however, Roosevelt's plan failed to attract the unified support of critics. And like other reform measures, it ultimately failed because it contravened the respect for the judiciary so deeply ingrained in the American character and the Court prudently began to issue decisions that upheld popular reforms. Roosevelt's calm and frequently repeated assertion that "the people are with me"[88] underestimated the profound esteem that "the people" accord to the Supreme Court as long as its decisions do not diverge too radically from popular opinion. As an Idaho farmer wrote to Roosevelt, the Supreme Court "is a judicial body . . . and is not a plow horse for or with any one."[89]

While "the people" did not provide steadfast support for Roosevelt's plan, Gallup polls throughout the spring of 1937 indicated that the plan enjoyed considerable popularity. In six polls between mid-February and early May asking simply whether respondents favored or opposed the plan, support ranged from 46 to 48 percent; and opposition, from 52 to 54 percent. In response to a more detailed question in late February, 38 percent favored enactment of Roosevelt's plan, 23 percent favored modification, and 39 percent favored defeat.

Although the results were probably heavily influenced by the respondents' attitudes toward Roosevelt and the New Deal, they suggest that nearly half, perhaps more than half, of the general population was not averse to making institutional changes to the Court to ensure the survival of New Deal legislation. Public support for the more radical measures advocated by the progressives appear to have enjoyed less support. In a Gallup poll taken shortly after the 1936 election, 59 percent opposed limitations on the Court's power to invalidate congressional legislation, even though 59 percent also believed that the Court ought to be more liberal in reviewing New Deal legislation.[90]

Although the Roosevelt plan may have enjoyed relatively high popular support, it failed to receive assistance from critical interest groups. Like earlier plans to curb judicial power, Roosevelt's plan encountered intense opposition from the organized bar. The ABA formally opposed the measure, and an ABA poll in April 1937 demonstrated that the plan was overwhelmingly unpopular among lawyers, including those who were not ABA members.[91] Although Roosevelt had antici-

---

[88] Joseph Alsop and Turner Catledge, *The 168 Days* (New York: Da Capo Press, 1973), (repr. 1937 edition), pp. 74, 79.

[89] Earl O. Wolfe to Franklin D. Roosevelt, March 10, 1937, *Borah Papers*, Box 483.

[90] Gallup, Hansen and Israel, *Gallup Poll*, pp. 50, 51, 53, 55, 57, 58, 69.

[91] "Summary of Referendum Vote by States of Members of the Bar Upon the various proposals affecting the Courts of the United States" (Chicago: American Bar Association, April 1937).

pated opposition from the bar, he had assumed that he could count on widespread support from the traditional antagonists of judicial power, liberals and trade unionists. He believed that the Court's invalidation of the Agricultural Adjustment Act would ensure support by farmers. The president also assumed that the plan would receive the support of most of the approximately nine progressive members of the Senate, most representing farming states and critical of the judiciary.[92]

But although the AFL supported the plan,[93] the proposal encountered widespread opposition among the scattered remnants of the progressive movement. Robert M. La Follette, Jr., was the only senator who consistently and unequivocally supported the Court-packing plan. Although many of the plan's progressive opponents were Republicans, many liberal Democrats also opposed the plan. Indeed, the leader of the fight against the proposal in the Senate was Wheeler, the progressive Democrat who had vigorously supported the elder La Follette's plan when he was La Follette's running mate in 1924. Various other critics of the Court, such as Oswald Garrison Villard and Frankfurter, also opposed the plan.[94] Progressive opposition to the plan reflected both the progressive misgivings about the New Deal and the contrasts between the Roosevelt plan and the Court-curbing proposals that progressives had favored.

Although the New Deal embodied many reforms the progressives had advocated, the philosophy of the New Deal was at odds with the progressive quest for a political order that would transcend narrow interests and exalt the public good.[95] Some progressives were willing to embrace the politics of pluralism, but other progressives, as Otis L. Graham, Jr., has observed, could never reconcile themselves to a philosophy that "saw reform primarily in terms of the parceling out of material favors to clamoring groups."[96] The progressives had urged federal relief measures during the Hoover administration and welcomed federal action to combat the Depression during the early days of the New Deal, but they were troubled by Roosevelt's cooperation with big-business interests and the centralization of power in the fed-

[92] Alsop and Catledge, *168 Days*, pp. 47, 86, 94.

[93] See "Green Says Roosevelt's . . . proposal . . ." *New York Times*, February 18, 1937, p. 2.

[94] Like other progressives, Villard, who had retired from the editorship of *The Nation* in 1933, disdained Roosevelt's plan as an unprincipled expedient and favored an amendment to permit Congress to enact social and economic legislation without judicial review. Michael Wreszin, *Oswald Garrison Villard: Pacifists at War* (Bloomington: Indiana University Press, 1965), pp. 248–49.

[95] See Otis L. Graham, Jr., *An Encore for Reform: The Old Progressives and the New Deal* (New York: Oxford University Press, 1967), pp. 180–81.

[96] Ibid., p. 38.

eral government and the president.[97] A welfare state as a constant presence in the lives of all citizens was inconsistent with the progressive concept of government as a guardian of individual freedom.

The antimonopolistic legislation of the so-called Second New Deal in 1935 was more congenial to the progressive tradition, but even these reforms bothered progressives insofar as they continued the trend toward concentration of federal and executive power. As one scholar has pointed out, progressives "were willing to admit that the New Deal had been instrumental in checking some of the more obvious corporate and financial abuses, but, in the end, they believed that it had created forms of special privilege just as dangerous as those it had destroyed."[98] Progressives sought only enough state power to establish the public interest as a vital counterpart to more parochial interests, and they did not wish to end the community's primary reliance on private and voluntary action.[99]

The political composition of the New Deal, with its reliance on ethnic and urban political machines, southern conservatives, and organized labor, also tended to estrange progressives. Despite La Follette's widespread appeal to ethnic and urban voters in the 1924 election, progressivism had retained much of its rural and Protestant flavor. Although progressives heartily embraced the agricultural policies that benefited their rural constituents, they increasingly complained that the administration was attempting to perpetuate its power by catering to urban programs that drained funds from rural areas.[100] Progressives also abhorred the New Deal's relative indifference to the urban corruption against which progressives had so vigorously fought.[101] Progressives feared that the Democratic landslide in the 1936 augured the emergence of an all-powerful president and a permanent Democratic majority fed by patronage and dominated by a coalition of groups whose cultural and political norms were in many respects anathema to the progressive creed.

The Court-packing plan exacerbated progressive fears about the growth of presidential power. Unlike most of the court-reform proposals that progressives had advocated over the decades, the Roosevelt

[97] Ronald L. Feinman, *Twilight of Progressivism: The Western Republican Senators and the New Deal* (Baltimore: Johns Hopkins University Press, 1981), pp. 68–90.

[98] Ronald A. Mulder, *The Insurgent Progressives in the United States Senate and the New Deal, 1933–1939* (New York: Garland, 1979), p. 298.

[99] John Whiteclay Chambers II, *The Tyranny of Change: America in the Progressive Era* (New York: St. Martin's Press, 1980), pp. 138–39.

[100] Mulder, *Insurgent Progressives*, pp. 295–96.

[101] See Richard Hofstadter, *The Age of Reform: From Bryan to F.D.R.* (New York: 1981) p. 308.

plan enhanced the power of the executive. The president—and more particularly Roosevelt himself—was the focus of Roosevelt's plan, even though the Senate would have to confirm the president's nominees. In contrast, progressive measures enhanced congressional power. Some of those proposals, notably La Follette's plan, would have directly augmented congressional power. Other plans, such as restrictions on the Court's jurisdiction and proposals for supermajorities to invalidate legislation, would have indirectly increased congressional power to the extent that they would make it more difficult for the courts to nullify legislation.

Most progressive proposals that did not magnify congressional power, such as the judicial recall and the recall of decisions, gave additional power to the people rather than the executive. Even most of the perennial progressive proposals for limited judicial terms, which would have permitted the president to make more court appointments, did not operate retroactively and did not give the president the immediate opportunity to make judicial appointments, much less six appointments to the Supreme Court and dozens of appointments to the lower federal courts.

Several progressive senators who refused to support Roosevelt's plan emphasized their fears about the arrogation of power to the president. Nye expressed this fear, as did Republican senator Arthur Capper of Kansas, who declared that "a Supreme Court subservient to the Executive means the beginning of the end of democratic government."[102] Hiram W. Johnson suggested that Roosevelt's plan would "make the Supreme Court subservient to the Presidency,"[103] and Borah believed that the plan would effectuate "a political control of the Court" that would destroy the federal judiciary.[104] Although partisan concerns might have inspired some of these fears, liberals in the Democratic party also worried that the plan would unduly expand the president's powers. Wheeler contended, "We had better have no Supreme Court at all than to have a Supreme Court which is subservient to any one man."[105] Senatorial fears about presidential arrogance were ag-

---

[102] "Roosevelt Aides Muster to Test Court Strength; Nye Denounces Program," *New York Times*, February 22, 1937, p. 1; "Opposed to Judiciary Change," *New York Times*, February 10, 1937, p. 15; col. 1; "Borah Proposes Court Amendment," ibid., February 26, 1937, p. 4.

[103] "Compromise on High Court Sought by Some Leaders to Have 2 Justices Retire," *New York Times*, February 9, 1937, p. 1.

[104] Borah to W. W. Webb, March 16, 1937, *Borah Papers*, Box 484; Borah to Ray McKaig, March 6, 1937, ibid.

[105] "Big Court Slower, Wheeler Declares," *New York Times*, February 22, 1937, p. 4.

gravated by Roosevelt's failure to consult the senators before announcing the plan.

Progressive senators particularly resented the high-handed way Roosevelt announced his plan; they were sensitive about their loss of leadership and control of the liberal movement following the Democratic victory in 1932.[106] As William Allen White remarked to Frankfurter, discussing Roosevelt's plan, "Norris and his kind were well worth respecting. They had been in the fight when [Roosevelt] was a young man. To break their heart and drive them away from his leadership was a tragedy."[107] Like many other opponents of the plan, progressives also resented the president's disingenuous contention that the plan was needed because judges had fallen behind in their work. The president's failure to explain his obvious motives candidly hindered a full and frank discussion of the role of the judiciary in the American political system. Although many progressives would gladly have defended the need to curb judicial power, they could not bring themselves to play along with the president's charade.

Progressives joined with conservatives in warning that executive domination of the Court would endanger civil liberties. Like conservatives who had opposed the La Follette plan Wheeler had advocated so forcefully in 1924, Wheeler argued that a politicized Court could create a weapon that might extinguish the rights "of liberty, of speech, of thought, of action, and of religion; a weapon whose use is only dictated by the conscience of the wielder." Similarly, Senator Shipstead observed that what "you can do today for a good purpose . . . [s]ome one else can do for a bad purpose tomorrow."[108] And Norris feared that the precedent would "come home to plague our descendants."[109] In an echo of the 1924 presidential campaign, religious organizations, especially the Roman Catholic church, were concerned that any erosion of judicial independence would endanger religious freedom.[110] As the

[106] Mulder, *Insurgent Progressives*, pp. 206–9.

[107] William Allen White to Felix Frankfurter, October 11, 1937, *White Papers*, Box C-267, Manuscript Division, Library of Congress.

[108] Mulder, *Insurgent Progressives*, p. 206.

[109] Norris to William Green, February 26, 1937, *Norris Papers*, Box 118.

[110] Alsop and Catledge, *168 Days*, p. 73; "Episcopalian Group Opposes Court Bill," *New York Times*, February 9, 1937, p. 4. The intensity of Roman Catholic opposition to the measure was illustrated by the Jesuit publication *America*, which published a spate of editorials and articles that erosion of the power of the Court would jeopardize religious liberty. Editorial, "President Dictator?" February 20, 1937, pp. 468–69; Editorial, "Jackson vs. Marshall," February 27, 1937, p. 492; Editorial, "The Price of Freedom," March 13, 1937, p. 540; Editorial, "Trust and Liberty," March 20, 1937, p. 564; Editorial, "The Nine Old Men, March 27, 1937, p. 590; Editorial, "Free Courts" May 8, 1937, p. 109; Editorial, "The Supreme Court Bill" July 17, 1937, p. 349; Editorial, "The Court Bill,"

representative of a German-American Catholic lay organization explained, the "Supreme Court is the only factor that stands between politics and our freedom."[111]

Progressives also opposed the Court packing plan because it failed to provide an enduring institutional reform to prevent the Court from continuing to ignore the will of Congress and the people. As George Norris told AFL president Green, "It does not strike permanently at the evil we want to remedy."[112] To progressives, the plan resembled other New Deal expedients that responded to an immediate crisis but failed to address more fundamental problems. Norris pointed out that a majority of fifteen justices might eventually oppose progressive measures and that younger judges might be no more liberal than their elders. "It is not only men past 70 who see through glasses darkly," he remarked.[113] Similarly, Borah stated that if the six new justices "turned out to be ultra-conservatives, we'd be right where we are now."[114] Borah warned a constituent that "if we reach the point in this country where courts are to be packed for specific purposes, you may rest assured that the packing some of these days will take place against the common people . . . and in favor of the interests."[115] Nye argued that the greatest fallacy of the plan was its attempt to deal with "personalities rather than with basic principles."[116]

Recognizing that the controversy had created a political environment that might be uniquely receptive to the reforms they had advocated for so long, progressives attempted to interest the president and Congress in more fundamental measures. As in the past, however, progressives failed to unite behind a single proposal and advocated a bewildering array of substitutes for Roosevelt's proposal. No substitute plan attracted widespread support.

Norris was the most prolific proponent of alternative measures. On the same day Roosevelt announced his plan, Norris reiterated his support for legislation to require a two-thirds majority of the Court to

July 24, 1937, p. 373; Editorial, "No Compromise!" July 31, 1937, pp. 397–98. Opposition, however, was far from monolithic. See James J. Kenneally, "Catholicism and the Supreme Court Reorganization Proposal of 1937," *Journal of Church and State* 25 (Autumn 1983): 469–89.

[111] Charles P. Saling, on behalf of the Catholic Central Verein of New Jersey and the Catholic Women's Union, to Borah, February 9, 1937, *Borah Papers*, Box 483.

[112] Norris to William Green.

[113] "Norris Is Opposed to Expanding Court," *New York Times*, February 6, 1937, p. 11.

[114] "Cummings Starts Court Bill Drive," *New York Times*, March 11, 1937, p. 15.

[115] Borah to M. R. Hammond, March 11, 1937, *Borah Papers*, Box 483.

[116] "Roosevelt Aides Muster to Test Court Strength; Nye Denounces Program," *New York Times*, February 22, 1937, p. 1.

invalidate legislation,[117] and he later embodied this proposal in a bill.[118] He also introduced legislation to limit judicial tenure[119] and to permit a direct popular vote on constitutional amendments.[120] Norris reiterated his support for legislation to restrict the power of lower federal courts to issue injunctions and continued to urge legislation to permit Congress to override Supreme Court decisions.[121] Although Norris continued to advocate these alternative measures throughout the Court-packing fight, he did not expressly oppose Roosevelt's plan.[122]

After Roosevelt announced his plan, Borah proposed a constitutional amendment to provide that due process restraints on the states applied only to procedural issues. Borah's amendment would also have required states to observe the liberties specified in the First Amendment.[123] By ensuring that the states could enact substantive legislation to remedy social ills, Borah's proposals might have helped to prevent the further concentration of power in the federal government.

In contrast to Borah, William Allen White and liberal Democratic representative Jerry Voorhis of California proposed measures to expand congressional power. White favored an amendment that would formulate a broad definition of interstate commerce,[124] and Voorhis introduced a bill to deprive the lower federal courts of jurisdiction over cases concerning the constitutionality of federal legislation involving taxation, the general welfare, or interstate commerce.[125] As Ronald L. Feinman has pointed out, the contrast between the proposals of Borah and White demonstrated "once again how progressives could not agree amongst themselves as to the extent of federal intervention that should be allowed in social and economic affairs."[126]

[117] Alsop and Catledge, *168 Days*, pp. 94–96.

[118] S. 1890, 75th Cong., 1st sess., 1937.

[119] S. J. Res. 103, 75th Cong., 1st sess., 1937.

[120] S. J. Res. 134, 75th Cong., 1st sess., 1937.

[121] 81 *Congressional Record*, 75th Cong., 1st sess., March 12, 1937, pp. 2142–44; S. 1890, 75th Cong., 1st sess., 1937; S. J. Res. 103, 75th Cong., 1st sess., 1937; "Roosevelt Drives for Court Reform As Congress Waits," *New York Times*, February 12, 1937, p. 1; Robinson Cordial to an Amendment," *New York Times*, March 16, 1937, p. 1; "Norris for Popular Vote," *New York Times*, April 3, 1937, p. 2.

[122] Alsop and Catledge, *168 Days*, p. 195; Feinman, *Twilight of Progressivism*, pp. 124–25.

[123] S. J. Res. 92, 75th Cong., 1st sess., 1937; "Borah Asks Amendment Giving States Control of All Social Problems," *New York Times*, February 26, 1937, p. 1.

[124] William Allen White to Norris, February 22, 1937, *White Papers*, Series C, Box 269. Norris liked the idea but feared that it was impracticable (Norris to White, February 27, 1937, ibid.).

[125] H.R. 4900, 75th Cong., 1st Sess. (1937).

[126] Feinman, *Twilight of Progressivism*, p. 130.

The inability of liberals to agree on a remedy was further illustrated by the perplexing array of bills and resolutions introduced in Congress as alternatives to Roosevelt's proposal. Like Norris's bills, these measures would have limited judicial tenure,[127] permitted Congress to reenact statutes the Court had nullified,[128] and required the concurrence of more than a majority of the Court to invalidate an act of Congress.[129]

The failure of progressives to support the Court-packing measure bitterly disappointed Roosevelt and the New Dealers, confirming their suspicions that the progressives were unreliable and ineffectual.[130] Harold Ickes believed that Hiram Johnson, who had supported Theodore Roosevelt's proposal for the recall of judicial decisions, "ought not to balk at the comparatively mild reforms suggested by the President." Ickes complained in his diary that the defection of Johnson and other progressives "to the enemy" was incomprehensible.[131] *The Nation* urged progressives to support the plan since it would help the New Deal, though the editors acknowledged that the plan "does not go to the roots of our judicial oligarchy, but by reorganizing it seeks rather to perpetuate it."[132]

Although much progressive opposition was based upon misgivings about the plan's merits, the reaction of the progressives also reveals certain weaknesses in the movement that help to explain why the progressives never succeeded in generating significant support for their court-reform proposals. In addition to their failure to agree on a single plan, the progressives tended to advocate measures that would require a constitutional amendment. Although an amendment would have provided a more lasting basis for reform and would not have been vulnerable to invalidation by the Court, the amendment process was far more arduous and uncertain than simple legislation. Indeed, Roosevelt had chosen a measure that would not require an amendment because he did not believe that an amendment was likely to succeed.[133] The progressives' advocacy of measures that would necessitate an amendment illustrates again their inability to comprehend the exigencies of practical politics.

[127] H. J. Res. 496, H. J. Res. 393, 75th Cong., 1st sess., 1937.

[128] S. J. Res. 80, H. J. Res. 250, 75th Cong., 1st sess., 1937.

[129] S. J. Res. 98, H.R. 5172, H. J. Res. 303, H. J. Res. 372, H. J. Res. 496, H.R. 7154, 75th Cong., 1st sess., 1937.

[130] *Diary of Harold Ickes*, pp. 1976–78, February 14, 1937; p. 1986, February 16, 1937; p. 2007, February 27, 1937; p. 2137, May 15, 1937, Reel 2; Mulder, *Insurgent Progressives*, p. 212.

[131] *Diary of Harold Ickes*, pp. 1976, 1977–78, Reel 2.

[132] "Purging the Supreme Court," *The Nation*, February 13, 1937, p. 173.

[133] Alsop and Catledge, *168 Days*, pp. 28–29, 58.

The insistence on more durable institutional reforms lends superficial credibility to their insistence that they were opposed in principle to broad judicial power. As we have seen, however, many progressives were willing to support judicial activism when it suited their purposes. Accordingly, progressive resistance to Roosevelt's plan may have reflected only a belief that more fundamental reforms were needed to prevent the judiciary from interfering with legislation progressives favored.

The failure of so many critics of the judiciary to support the first and only reform proposal that had any serious likelihood of success suggests again that much progressive opposition to the judiciary was merely rhetorical and tactical. Although progressives were understandably wary about the concentration of additional power in the executive, their warnings about the dangers of erosion of judicial independence were somewhat hollow since the Roosevelt proposal was in many respects less radical than many of their proposals. While no progressive proposal was so nakedly political, most progressive plans would have imposed some direct curb upon judicial power. Even though many progressives explained that they sought a more fundamental reform that would impose specific institutional limitations upon the federal courts, their refusal to accept Roosevelt's proposal suggests that respect for judicial prerogatives was more profound than their rhetoric suggested.

Although the impact of progressive opposition on the ultimate defeat of Roosevelt's plan must remain problematic,[134] the proposal might have succeeded if progressive senators had vigorously supported it. If so, the failure of progressives to seize their one real opportunity to effect a major change in the political character of the federal judiciary is particularly ironic.

The measure also might have succeeded if not for the unmistakable shift in the balance of power on the Court that occurred during the height of the Court-packing controversy. On March 29, 1937, the Court upheld by a 5–4 margin a Washington minimum-wage law[135] virtually indistinguishable from a New York statute the Court had invalidated by a 5–4 vote the previous June.[136] The alignment of jus-

---

[134] The Court plan never reached a vote on the floor on the Senate, and the proposal was abandoned in July. In the only important vote on the legislation, the Senate Judiciary Committee voted 10–8 in opposition to a favorable report. Borah voted with the majority, and Norris supported the minority. No other progressives or prominent longtime critics of the federal courts were members of the committee ("Democrats Divide in Committee Poll," *New York Times*, May 19, 1937, p. 1).

[135] *West Coast Hotel Co. v. Parrish*, 300 U.S. 379 (1937).

[136] *Morehead v. New York ex. rel. Tipaldo*, 298 U.S. 587 (1936).

tices in the two decisions was the same, except for Justice Roberts who voted to uphold the law. Although Roberts always insisted that his vote could not have been influenced by the Court-packing plan because he had cast it in December, he must have been aware that Roosevelt's landslide victory in November would embolden him to propose some judicial reform.

Roberts's "switch in time that saved the nine" signaled the demise of the Court's strict scrutiny of economic legislation. In April, 1937, the Court upheld the National Labor Relations Act, Roberts and Hughes once again joining liberals Brandeis, Cardozo, and Stone in an opinion that accorded a broad scope to Congress's powers under the commerce clause.[137] In May, the Court upheld the Social Security Act, providing an expansive reading of the congressional power to tax and provide for the common welfare.[138] Meanwhile, the resignation of Justice Van Devanter gave Roosevelt an opportunity to make an appointment that would consolidate the Court's new liberal majority.

As in so many instances from 1890 to 1937, changes in the attitudes and personnel of the judiciary muted antagonism toward the courts during the Court-packing controversy of 1937.[139] This time, however, the willingness of state and federal courts to exercise restraint in their review of social and economic legislation proved permanent. The antagonism of liberals and labor to the judiciary disappeared along with judicial antagonism to legislation that liberals and labor favored. One of the most ferocious and sustained periods of hostility to the judiciary had ended.

[137] *N.L.R.B. v. Jones and Laughlin Steel Corporation,* 301 U.S. 1 (1937).

[138] *Stewart Machine Co. v. Davis,* 301 U.S. 548 (1937); *Helvering v. Davis,* 301 U.S. 619 (1937).

[139] See Gregory A. Caldeira, "Public Opinion and the Supreme Court: FDR's Court-Packing Plan," *American Political Science Review* 81 (December 1987): 1139–53.

CONCLUSION

I N HIS 1892 populist manifesto, James B. Weaver warned that the powers of the Supreme Court would "be as chaff before the gale" if the Court encountered "the storm center of public opinion, now rapidly forming."[1] Although Weaver's remarks presaged a half century of widespread public hostility to the courts, Weaver and many other critics of the judiciary underestimated the resilience of the courts. Even though the protests of populists, progressives, and trade unionists concerning judicial decisions and their many challenges to judicial power during the half century prior to 1937 were "full of sound and fury," their protests and challenges were muted, and their significance is difficult to measure.

The persistent crusade to make the courts more amenable to reform legislation "signified nothing" if we measure its success by the actual curtailment of judicial power or the elimination of judicial hostility to organized labor and legislation progressives favored. The tensions between the courts and their critics on the eve of Franklin Roosevelt's announcement of his Court-packing plan in 1937 were remarkably similar to the lines of conflict drawn during the 1890s. At both federal and state levels, the courts continued to scrutinize legislation carefully to determine whether it conformed to prevailing doctrines of due process, freedom of contract, or interstate commerce.

Although courts during the 1930s sustained the constitutionality of more statutes than they nullified, the courts of the 1890s had not been markedly less deferential to legislative bodies. Meanwhile, the powers and prerogatives of the federal judiciary remained almost entirely unimpaired. Only the Norris-La Guardia Act of 1932 had imposed any major limitation on judicial power, and the constitutionality of that statute had not yet been tested in the Supreme Court. Virtually none of the many plans for an elective judiciary, tenure limitations, or diminution or abolition of the power of judicial review had received any serious consideration by either house of Congress.

Indeed, the federal judiciary was probably stronger in 1937 than it had been in the 1880s, partly because judicial review had become more deeply ingrained in the American political culture and partly because such reforms as the Judiciary acts of 1914, 1922, and 1925 had enhanced the powers of the Supreme Court. Similarly, the judiciary's critics had failed to place significant limitations on state judges. Only a

---

[1] James B. Weaver, *A Call to Action* (Des Moines: Iowa Printing, 1892), p. 89.

half-dozen states had enacted judicial recall provisions, and the recall of judicial decisions had been judicially nullified in Colorado, the only state ever to adopt it.

Despite the agitation of its critics, the Supreme Court did not abandon the doctrine of substantive due process and other restrictive theories of legislative economic powers until a particularly powerful and aggressive president sponsored a radical measure that fundamentally threatened the Court's autonomy. And even the effect of Franklin D. Roosevelt's plan upon the Court must remain problematic since Justice Owen J. Roberts, who shifted the balance of the Court's power away from the conservatives in 1937, always denied that he was influenced by external pressures. Only Roosevelt's ability to appoint several liberal justices after the Court-packing plan failed ensured continued judicial deference to economic legislation.

This paucity of demonstrable results may help to explain why proposals to curb judicial power during the Progressive Era have received little attention. It would be a mistake, however, to assume that the intense and protracted criticism of the courts did not have subtle and profound influences. By stimulating a redefinition of public attitudes toward the judiciary, prominent critics of the courts ensured that the courts would receive widespread scrutiny from a broad segment of the population. Senator George W. Norris, for example, believed that the unsuccessful opposition to the Hughes nomination in 1930 produced "a wonderful amount of good" because it encouraged the nation "to pause and reflect" about the influence of business corporations on the judiciary.[2] Similarly, Frankfurter observed during the 1924 presidential campaign that "the contribution of Senator La Follette and the Progressive platform lies in the ventilation of this grave issue" of judicial review "rather than in the specific remedies proposed."[3]

The breadth of public dissatisfaction with judicial decisions may have influenced the courts to render decisions that did not stray too far from prevailing public sentiment regarding social and economic questions. As C. Herman Pritchett once observed, public support for judicial power has remained firm because "the Court has generally told the country what it wanted to hear, and provided a constitutional case for what the dominant interests in the nation wanted to do."[4] Although the

[2] Norris to J. M. Hammond, June 13, 1931, *Norris Papers*, Box 41, Manuscript Division, Library of Congress.

[3] Editorial, "The Red Terror of Judicial Reform," *New Republic*, October 1, 1924, p. 113, repr. Philip Kurland, ed., *Felix Frankfurter on the Supreme Court: Extrajudicial Essays on the Court and the Constitution* (Cambridge, Mass.: Harvard University Press, 1970), p. 166.

[4] C. Herman Pritchett, "Judicial Supremacy from Marshall to Burger," in M. Judd

courts throughout the period of this study remained acutely sensitive to the corporate interests that dominated much of the nation's economic and political life, they were not oblivious to the clamor for reform. Mindful that the Constitution provides a broad array of means for curbing judicial power, the courts naturally were loath to nullify so much popular legislation that public discontent with the Court would rise to a formidable level.

Although the impact of public opinion on most individual decisions must remain speculative, it is reasonable to suppose that agitation against the courts persuaded many judges to uphold progressive legislation that they might otherwise have voted to invalidate. As James Bryce aptly observed in 1891, the Supreme Court "feels the touch of public opinion. Opinion is stronger in America than anywhere else in the world, and judges are only men. To yield a little may be prudent, for the tree that cannot bend to the blast may be broken. . . . A court is sometimes so swayed consciously, more often unconsciously, because the pervasive sympathy of numbers is irresistible even by elderly lawyers."[5]

The inconsistent decisions of the federal and state courts, which within short periods of time would often invalidate one statute and uphold a like measure, suggest that popular pressure helped to influence the views of many judges. Although conservative judges refused to uphold statutes they found particularly odious, they may have been willing to take account of public opinion when the stakes were smaller, when they found the statute less offensive, or when the decision was not likely to create a significant precedent.

Progressives and labor unions recognized that their criticism could influence the courts, even if their specific remedies for reform came to naught. For example, Professor Frank J. Goodnow of Columbia observed in 1911 that "this severe, persistent, and continuous criticism" of the Court may help to explain why the Court had been "reasonably responsive to public opinion."[6] Similarly, Norris observed in 1931 that the unsuccessful struggle against the Hughes nomination "had a great influence, perhaps an unconscious influence, upon the judiciary itself."[7]

Perhaps even more influential than direct threats to judicial power

---

Harmon, ed., *Essays on the Constitution of the United States*, (Port Washington, N.Y.: Kennikat Press, 1978), p. 108.

[5] James Bryce, *The American Commonwealth*, vol. 1, 2d ed. (London: Macmillan, 1891), p. 267.

[6] Frank J. Goodnow, *Social Reform and the Constitution* (New York: Macmillan, 1911), p. 359.

[7] Norris to J. M. Hammond.

was the judiciary's growing recognition of the law's need to respond to the changing needs of society. Although judges were hardly oblivious to political and social events, the progressives' constant reminders of the need to adapt the law to the exigencies of a changing society encouraged judicial flexibility. Although progressive efforts to interject social science concepts into the legal process may have had little direct effect on many judges, these efforts helped to change judicial attitudes since they weakened the grip of legal formalism on judicial thinking and made judges more aware of the relationships between law and society.

Indeed, many judges, such as Learned Hand and Louis D. Brandeis, had been active in the reform movement before ascending the bench. Since the interests and constituencies of industrialism and progressivism often converged, it is not surprising that even many judges whose intimate connections to business corporations antagonized critics of the courts had close ties to the progressive movement. On and off the bench, for example, Charles Evans Hughes was a champion of both corporate interests and progressive aspirations. Efforts by progressives and trade unionists to educate judges about the realities of modern industrial life and to influence the judicial selection process further helped to secure judicial sympathy for reform legislation and the rights of labor. Moreover, as William E. Forbath has pointed out, "Unparalleled levels of industrial unrest combined with workers' massive, articulate defiance of judge-made law gradually persuaded the nation's political elites that the old legal order was untenable."[8]

Judicial receptivity to progressive ideals was reflected early in the century in changes in the common law and judicial validation of much of the reform legislation from 1906 to 1916. Agitation against the judiciary also contributed to the enactment of significant legislation, such as the Clayton Act of 1914. Judicial deference to reform helped to diminish criticism of the courts during the 1910s. When the opinions of the Supreme Court began to diverge from liberal opinion again during the 1920s, progressives once again began a campaign of criticism that may have mitigated judicial hostility to reform legislation and organized labor and encouraged the Court to accord a broader scope to personal freedoms. In particular, the *Meyer* and *Pierce* decisions and the decisions that incorporated freedom of speech and the press into state law seem to have been influenced by the Court's need to stimulate public support for judicial review. Arguing in 1924 that popular agitation had influenced recent judicial decisions, James M. Landis ob-

[8] William E. Forbath, "The Shaping of the American Labor Movement," *Harvard Law Review* 102 (April 1989): 1203.

served that constitutional adjudication must "give effect to the social ideals of the time and place. To ignore the formulation of these ideals, as represented in a vast popular movement, would be to attribute to the Supreme Court not judicial independence but judicial ignorance of the philosophy and end of law."[9]

In turn, judicial decisions that conformed broadly to prevailing public sentiments helped to mute antagonism to the courts among the many critics who opposed the way the judiciary exercised its power rather than the power itself. Even the more principled critics of the courts were largely propitiated by liberal decisions.

Judicial amenability to reform legislation particularly helped to blunt efforts to curb judicial power since antagonists of the courts recognized that formidable obstacles hindered such efforts. Although the vigor of the reform movement during the early part of the century may have convinced some progressives that all things were possible, few progressives could have expected to effect any significant diminution of judicial power. Despite the widespread public hostility to the judiciary that sometimes seemed to promise that judicial reform was more than a chimera, most realistic progressives recognized that earlier proposals to curb judicial power had failed and that their proposals lacked the broad public support and congressional leadership that were crucial for their success. Any significant curtailment of judicial power would have required a constitutional amendment, and progressives were keenly aware that the amendment process presented so many formidable obstacles that it was impracticable.

The conservatism of Congress, state legislatures, and the electorate that impeded any movement for constitutional amendments to override judicial decisions or curtail the power of the courts indicates that the Supreme Court's decisions did not significantly contravene the sensibilities of a substantial share of the American public. Writing in 1937, William Allen White aptly observed that "the Supreme Court, not only now with its nine old men, but always, has lagged too far but not so terribly far behind Public Opinion as manifest in Congressional majorities."[10] As we have seen, polls in 1935 and 1936 indicated that a majority of Americans opposed curtailment of judicial review even though a large majority believed that the Court should demonstrate more tolerance to New Deal legislation.

The political forces that hindered progressive attempts to curb judicial power were the same forces that thwarted earlier anticourt move-

[9] J. M. Landis, "Labor's New Day in Court," *Survey*, November 15, 1924, p. 177.

[10] William Allen White to Felix Frankfurter, October 11, 1937, *White Papers*, Series C, Box 267, Manuscript Division, Library of Congress.

ments and have defeated more recent efforts to curtail judicial power. As Jesse H. Choper has observed, "All the dominant forces of inertia— of maintenance of the status quo, of inaction due to the frequent absence of cohesive majorities and to the fragmentation of power— that are present in the national political process work to safeguard the Court, and indeed are magnified in the case of an attack on the Court's historic independence."[11] Or as Norris told Frankfurter in discussing the persistent failure of his proposals to abolish federal diversity juris- diction, legislative "victory comes only after long, strenuous effort."[12] Correctly perceiving that the nation was not yet prepared for radical judicial reform, Norris privately told a host of correspondents over the years that he neglected his various proposals for restraints on judicial power because he recognized that they were impracticable.

The impracticability of proposals for judicial reform may also help to explain why progressives failed to unite behind a single plan for judicial reform. The disunity of the progressives, however, also helped to contribute to the impracticability of reform. Even when Franklin Roosevelt finally proposed a politically viable plan, progressives not only opposed the plan but proposed such a multiplicity of alternative measures that their voices were lost in a cacophony of dissent. Harold Ickes was not altogether unfair to the progressive proponents of judi- cial reform when he observed with frustration during the Court- packing fight in 1937 that "a liberal is a man who wants what is unattain- able or who wants to reach his objective by methods that are so imprac- ticable as to be self-defeating."[13]

Although some progressives hoped that their criticisms were prepar- ing the foundations for judicial reform measures that might succeed if continued judicial conservatism brought discontent against the courts to a boiling point, they recognized that the enactment of such measures would engender new perils. Virtually all of their plans could have backfired. William E. Borah, for example, professed to oppose a fed- eral constitutional convention because he feared that "the special inter- ests would have such absolute control of it that they would write a constitution under which we couldn't live."[14]

Similarly, the proposals for an elective judiciary would not have

[11] Jesse H. Choper, *Judicial Review and the National Political Process: A Functional Recon- sideration of the Role of the Supreme Court* (Chicago: University of Chicago Press, 1980), p. 55.

[12] Norris to Felix Frankfurter, February 22, 1936, *Norris Papers*, Box 119.

[13] *Diary of Harold Ickes*, February 16, 1937, p. 1986, Reel 2, Manuscript Division, Library of Congress.

[14] William E. Borah to Frank I. Hogan, February 8, 1922, *Borah Papers*, Box 130, Manuscript Division, Library of Congress.

helped liberal causes if public sentiment turned more conservative. Indeed, the ability of conservatives to manipulate the judicial election process to their advantage in states that elected judges demonstrated the hazards of direct democracy. Similarly, curtailment of judicial review would not have helped the progressives or trade unionists if Congress had been more conservative than the Supreme Court.

The Court's willingness to broaden the scope of federally protected civil liberties during the 1920s and early 1930s enhanced the appreciation of progressives and labor leaders for the countermajoritarian role of the judiciary. Civil-liberties decisions during that period graphically demonstrated that the courts, especially the federal courts, could serve as a bulwark against legislation that may have reflected majority sentiments that progressives regarded as repressive and unjust. The emergence of the courts as tenacious guardians of personal liberties during the decades after 1937 vindicated the deference to the courts that both critics and defenders of the judiciary so persistently exhibited during the decades of controversy before 1937. However, the Court's growing reluctance since the 1970s to expand the scope of civil liberties also gives renewed resonance to progressive warnings against excessive reliance on the courts for the protection of liberties. As The Nation explained in 1924 in defending La Follette's proposal to permit Congress to override Supreme Court decisions, "Freedom for the individual and respect for minorities have no security either through Congress or the Supreme Court except in so far as there is a compelling spirit of liberty and tolerance in the community behind them."[15]

Many progressives also muted their advocacy of court-curbing measures because they recognized that a strong federal judiciary was necessary to the health of the federal system. As Thomas Reed Powell observed in the wake of the Court's invalidation of the first child-labor law, "If we wish to continue the federal system, it is idle and foolish to talk of withdrawing the power of the Supreme Court to project the lines of the Constitution which vaguely point to the boundaries between State and national authority. Some one outside of Congress and the State Legislatures must determine their respective provinces."[16] It is revealing that La Follette and many other progressives who favored limitations on the power of the Supreme Court to invalidate federal legislation did not dare to suggest that the Court should not have the power to review the constitutionality of state statutes. Progressives recognized that this power, which had so vexed Jeffersonian critics of the courts, was the

[15] Editorial, "Our Despotic Courts," The Nation, September 24, 1924, p. 300.
[16] Thomas Reed Powell, "The Child-Labor Decision," The Nation, June 22, 1918, p. 731.

linchpin of federalism and that the federal courts, despite their conservatism, were better guardians of personal liberties than the states.

Despite all of their protestations about the dangers of "judicial oligarchy," many progressives and union leaders recognized that a powerful judiciary could serve their interests. By helping to make government more orderly, stable, and rational, the judiciary helped to implement fundamental progressive goals. By offering protection against legislative and executive hostility, the judiciary also helped foster the growth of the trade union movement.

The willingness of progressives and unionists to appreciate the need for a strong judiciary was complemented by their fundamental respect for the judiciary, a respect shared by a vast segment of the American public. As William L. Ransom observed in 1912, "The people believe in their courts, they admire their judges," despite a widely shared perception "that something is wrong about a judicial system under which a few men may obstruct the will and needs of the many."[17] The Republican party's cynical but clever use of the judicial issue during the 1924 presidential campaign demonstrated that many Americans cherished the courts as bulwarks of personal liberties and property rights.

Since most progressives recognized the impracticability of radical judicial reform and many perceived a need for a strong judiciary, many of the specific remedies proposed by critics of the courts were intended to be tactical rather than practical. The tactical character of the reform proposals is suggested by the failure of the critics to make serious efforts to work for the enactment of their measures. Indeed, the most widely discussed plan, La Follette's proposal for allowing Congress to override decisions of the Supreme Court, was never even embodied in a bill.

The tactical character of the plans is also suggested by the way the proposals reflected the immediate grievances and political exigencies of the critics. Most proposals arose out of an angry reaction to adverse decisions or an attempt to rally support among progressives and trade unionists, rather than out of reasoned reflection about the proper place of the courts in American government. Although discontent with the judiciary was persistent, the intensity of this fury waxed and waned markedly in response to political conditions and individual judicial decisions. The failure of progressives to devise a constructive or realistic plan for curtailing judicial obstruction of reform legislation or to unite in support of a specific proposal was quite characteristic of the progressives, who united in opposition to conditions more readily than

[17] William L. Ransom, *Majority Rule and the Judiciary* (New York: Scribner, 1912), p. 36.

they agreed on an alternative[18] and tended to advocate naive and simplistic remedies.[19]

The tactical character of opposition to judicial power in turn may have diminished public support for the plans the progressives and trade unionists advocated. As Gary L. McDowell has pointed out, no court-curbing plan can succeed unless it is viewed as principled rather than partisan.[20] Like other criticism of the courts throughout American history, much progressive criticism represented pragmatic hostility to specific decisions rather than an principled opposition to judicial power. As one lawyer observed in 1923, opposition to judicial declarations concerning the constitutionality of legislation "grows not out of any general disagreement with the Court's right to such declarations, but arises from the manner of exercising that right."[21]

The judicial revolution of 1937 was therefore an ostensible triumph for all progressives and unionists who had protested many decisions of the courts during the past half century, since the courts after 1937 ceased to question the constitutionality of most economic legislation. It is not surprising, for example, that Walter Clark's biographer in 1944 dedicated his study of the doughty North Carolina jurist to the Supreme Court, "which now reflects the views of Walter Clark."[22]

The ghost of Clark might have winced at these words, however, for the shift in judicial attitudes after 1937 did not terminate the vigorous judicial activism about which populists, labor unions, and progressives had so bitterly complained. Judicial activism survived the judicial revolution of 1937 and continued to thrive, even if the results of decisions were usually more palatable to liberal opinion.

Although the federal courts have generally been deferential to economic legislation since 1937, the Supreme Court, particularly during Earl Warren's tenure, has often lacked deference to legislative enactments in cases concerning such noneconomic liberties as racial equality, criminal rights, abortion, free speech, voting, and separation of church and state. Indeed, the judicial activism of the Court during the post-1937 period arguably exceeded the activism of the so-called Lochner era. The shift in judicial attitudes after 1937 did not therefore

[18] Ronald L. Feinman, *Twilight of Progressivism: The Western Republican Senators and the New Deal* (Baltimore: Johns Hopkins University Press, 1981), p. 129.

[19] Otis L. Graham, Jr., *The Great Campaigns: Reform and War in America, 1900–1928,* (Englewood Cliffs, N.J.: Prentice-Hall, 1971), pp. 140–43.

[20] Gary L. McDowell, *Curbing the Courts: The Constitution and the Limits of Judicial Power* (Baton Rouge: Louisiana State University Press, 1988), p. 11.

[21] Edward D. Tittmann, *Central Law Journal,* November 5, 1923, p. 368.

[22] Aubrey Lee Brooks, *Walter Clark: Fighting Judge* (Chapel Hill: University of North Carolina Press, 1944).

constitute a victory for those critics who genuinely opposed extensive judicial power rather than merely the way that power was exercised. Proponents of states' rights—including perhaps Clark—would have been particularly disappointed by many of the Court's post-1937 decisions that expanded the power of the federal government over the states. Similarly, the Court's decisions on economic questions after 1937 did not necessarily reflect the views of those progressives who had remained suspicious of a powerful central government and opposed the transfer of power from Congress to the president during the New Deal.

The degree to which opposition to judicial power before 1937 was partisan rather than principled cannot be easily measured and tested by the reactions of progressives to the courts after 1937, since few of the most prominent progressive antagonists of the courts lived to witness much of the new era of activism after 1937. Frankfurter, the one significant critic before 1937 who remained a major figure long after the judicial revolution, continued to adhere to his philosophy of judicial restraint even after the Supreme Court began to foster many of the liberal reforms he favored. The liberal professor's warnings about the danger of judicial oligarchy were echoed in many opinions of the conservative justice.

It is unlikely, however, that many of the pre-1937 critics of the courts would have been so principled as Frankfurter, whose dedication to reform was tempered by a profound legal philosophy that most progressive politicians and social activists lacked. Many—probably most—progressives of the pre-1937 period would have been satisfied with the way the Court exercised its powers after 1937. These critics were not fundamentally opposed to judicial activism. They favored measures to curtail judicial power only because they sought to remove judicial impediments to social and economic legislation. It is ironic that the success of challenges to judicial power would have precluded many expansions of personal and political liberties for which the political and intellectual heirs of the populists and progressives fought in succeeding generations.

The sharp diminution in hostility to the courts among labor unions after 1937 suggests that labor critics of the courts, like the populists and the progressives, were motivated primarily by pragmatic considerations. Although the labor unions, unlike liberals outside the labor movement, did not generally rely upon judicial activism to help effectuate their goals after 1937, labor was not heard to complain about judicial activism that seemed to benefit the labor movement.[23]

[23] For example, the Industrial Union Department of the AFL-CIO expressed support

Unlike many antagonists of the courts before 1937, contemporary Americans are so accustomed to a powerful judiciary that modern critics of the courts have concentrated their efforts on influencing the judicial selection process rather than more radical reforms such as curtailment of judicial review or abolition of the lower federal courts. Even the most vociferous critics of judicial activism generally quail before the awesome prospect of curbing the institutional powers of the courts and resort to more practicable measures.

So many factors doomed the efforts to curtail the power of the courts between 1890 and 1937 that those efforts may seem quixotic to modern observers. Even though the role of the judiciary in the political system remains highly controversial and the courts continue to issue decisions that elicit howls of protest, the power and prestige of the courts have expanded so greatly since 1937 that the failure of radicial judicial reform before 1937 may seem to have been inevitable.

But it was not.

Although the political culture provided a tenacious foundation of deference to the judiciary and the constitutional system presented formidable obstacles to the enactment of reform measures, both of these bulwarks of judicial power might have crumbled if the courts had refused to forge decisions that accommodated the changing values of society, if the critics of the judiciary had united behind a single plan, if the elite bar had not propagandized tirelessly in support of the judiciary, and if social and economic conditions had created the necessary predicate for radical reform.

These conditions nearly converged in 1937. If Roosevelt had succeeded in uniting progressives behind a plan that altered the power rather than the personnel of the federal courts and the Supreme Court had not so abruptly shifted its course, the widespread discontent over the Court's failure to uphold popular legislation designed to respond to a catastophic economic depression would probably have ensured the enactment of a measure that would have radically altered the role of the judiciary in the political system. This is a lesson that contemporary judges can ignore only at their peril.

The ultimate failures and successes of the proponents of radical court reform between 1890 and 1937 are part of the broader history of the paradoxical frustration and vindication of the populists, trade unionists, progressives, and other liberals and radicals who sought to transform American society during the early twentieth century. Al-

---

for the Supreme Court's landmark electoral-apportionment decision in *Baker v. Carr*, 369 U.S. 186 (1962). Richard C. Cortner, *The Apportionment Cases* (Knoxville: University of Tennessee Press, 1970), p. 145.

though many of these proponents of change would be disappointed over the injustices that still plague American society and might despair over the triumph of corporate capitalism, they would surely rejoice over the reforms that have improved many of the social and economic conditions they deplored.

The transformation of judicial attitudes toward those reforms is attributable in no small measure to the persistent criticism of the courts during the half century before 1937, even though the precise impact of that criticism must remain a subject of speculation. An aroused public had sent out a series of the "loud hails" that Arthur L. Corbin believed were necessary to keep the Supreme Court "within hailing distance of civilization."[24] Although populists, progressives, and unionists failed to curtail judicial power, they provided many potent and enduring reminders that the courts cannot disregard public opinion and that judges are ultimately answerable to the people.

[24] Arthur L. Corbin, "The Law and the Judges," *Yale Review* 3 (January 1914): 242.

INDEX

Lightning Source UK Ltd.
Milton Keynes UK
UKOW06f1105081215

264331UK00001B/44/P